ROOTED GLOBALISM

FRAMING THE GLOBAL

Hilary Kahn and Deborah Piston-Hatlen, *series editors*

ROOTED GLOBALISM

Arab–Latin American Business Elites and the Politics of Global Imaginaries

Kevin Funk

INDIANA UNIVERSITY PRESS

This book is a publication of

Indiana University Press
Office of Scholarly Publishing
Herman B Wells Library 350
1320 East 10th Street
Bloomington, Indiana 47405 USA

iupress.org

© 2022 by Kevin Funk

All rights reserved
No part of this book may be reproduced or utilized in any form or by any means, electronic or mechanical, including photocopying and recording, or by any information storage and retrieval system, without permission in writing from the publisher. The paper used in this publication meets the minimum requirements of the American National Standard for Information Sciences—Permanence of Paper for Printed Library Materials, ANSI Z39.48–1992.

Manufactured in the United States of America

First printing 2022

Cataloging information is available from the Library of Congress.

ISBN 978-0-253-06253-6 (hardback)
ISBN 978-0-253-06254-3 (paperback)
ISBN 978-0-253-06255-0 (ebook)

To Maca, my greatest interlocutor
To Leo, who always inspires

CONTENTS

Acknowledgments ix

Introduction: Capitalism and Class in Global Latin America *1*

1. Progress and Lacunae in the Study of the "Global" Capitalist Class *27*

2. How Latin America Met the Arab World *76*

3. "The Tradition of Dead Generations": On the Persistence of Place-Based Longings *108*

4. Rootless Globalists? On Denationalization and Globality *144*

5. "The Flat Pluralist World of Business Class": On Constructing (and Contesting) Corporate Global Imaginaries *175*

Conclusion: The Future of Global Imaginaries: Thinking Beyond Nativism and Neoliberal Propaganda *218*

Bibliography 233

Index 257

ACKNOWLEDGMENTS

As befits an eclectic project, the ideas that coalesced into this book are multi-sited and emerged in fits and starts.

My interest in the historical and contemporary intersections between Latin America and the Arab world was originally piqued while studying in Valparaíso, Chile, where I encountered numerous manifestations of interregional exchange, ranging from seemingly omnipresent Arab restaurants and recently arrived Palestinian refugees to university students wearing *keffiyehs* and the Orthodox church where I took beginner-level Arabic classes with a Syrian-Chilean priest. Reaching further back, a childhood spent navigating schools and social spaces dominated by wealthier classmates in the ostensibly rather insular, but also very diverse, small Rust Belt city of York, Pennsylvania, sparked an enduring fascination with class, class consciousness, race, ethnicity, and inequality. It also pushed me to think beyond my immediate surroundings and instilled in me a predilection for seeing *local* dynamics—in the case of York, relating to deindustrialization as well as racialized segregation and stratification—vis-à-vis broader *global* trends and economic structures.

This book represents an attempt to grapple with and reconcile these heterogeneous concerns. In the course of conceptualizing, writing, and revising it, I benefited greatly from numerous acts of exchange with diverse interlocutors, including many I have surely forgotten to acknowledge here. As an advisor, Ido Oren was a true mensch, always willing to offer constructive and erudite feedback. His Interpretive Approaches to Political Science seminar shaped this project, along with my understanding of the social sciences, in ways I could scarcely have predicted. Aida Hozić, Dan O'Neill, and Rosana Resende were especially instrumental in pushing me to always think critically, while numerous other current and former University of Florida faculty—including Philip Williams, Leann Brown, Laura Sjoberg, Matt Jacobs, Larry Dodd, Ben Smith, Michael Bernhard, Ana Margheritis, Dietmar Schirmer, and the late Richmond Brown—contributed greatly to the sharpening of my thoughts on these and related matters. To all of them, I am thankful.

As a graduate student, I could hardly have asked to be surrounded by a more generous group of *compañer@s* and friends than Sebastián Sclofsky, Adi Mamo, Mauro Caraccioli, Vanessa Díaz, Alec Dinnin, Pilar Morales, Dan Eizenga, John Hames, Jon and Isabella Whooley, Mamadou Bodian, Lia Merivaki, Ioannis Ziogas, Diana Moreno, Chesney McOmber, Nail Tanrioven, Chonghyun Choi, Stuart Strome, *la comunidad chilena*, and many others.

Early in this project, it was with great excitement that I stumbled across a transnational body of scholarship on Latin America and the Middle East by pioneering scholars such as Silvia Ferabolli, Élodie Brun, Juan José Vagni, Cecilia Baeza, John Tofik Karam, Marta Tawil Kuri, Steven Hyland, Ken Chitwood, Guy Burton, and Ariel González Levaggi. I learned a great deal from all of them, many of whom also kindly shared source materials and contacts. The present work would also not have been possible without the dozens of (anonymous) interviewees in Brazil, Argentina, Chile, Colombia, and the United Arab Emirates who took time from their busy schedules to graciously partake in lengthy open-ended dialogues with an unknown researcher from afar. Some very kindly invited me to engage in participant observation during workday activities and office lunches, and opened doors—both literally and metaphorically—that allowed me to make connections with additional contacts. Thank you, *gracias, obrigado*, and *shukran*.

An invisible college of geographically dispersed colleagues, typically encountered at annual conferences, participated in discussions related to various aspects of the present work and offered numerous other kinds of solidarity and support. The same goes for in-person colleagues, both former and present. I am especially grateful to Isaac Kamola, Samantha Majic, Guillermina Seri, Dvora Yanow, Peregrine Schwartz-Shea, Jacqueline Braveboy-Wagner, Reed Kurtz, Nicholas Kiersey, Fernando Tormos, Jesse Crane-Seeber, Amanda Huron, A. S. Dillingham, Matthew Bagot, and Alejandro Vélez, as well as the broader Interpretive Methodologies and Methods and New Political Science communities and additional friends I have gained along the way, including Davide Prete and Giulietta Versiglia. I have been privileged to be accompanied by such obliging fellow travelers.

The team at Indiana University Press truly went above and beyond in shepherding this project from the initial stages to completion. My sincere appreciation to Jennika Baines in particular for offering invaluable guidance about how to navigate the publication process, and pushing me to sharpen, clarify, and restructure. Sophia Hebert fielded my seemingly endless questions about preparing the manuscript with patience and good humor, while Rachel Rosolina offered useful advice about cover design. Thank you, also, to Hilary Kahn and Deborah Piston-Hatlen for welcoming me into the Framing the Global series.

The anonymous reviewers grappled with my ideas on a critical but constructive basis and made numerous profoundly helpful suggestions. I am sincerely appreciative for their thoughtful engagement and am especially glad that they pushed me to make explicit and further elaborate the book's political project in the concluding chapter. Though all remaining errors, oversights, and lacunae are my own, I am confident that this is a much-improved text due to their efforts.

The extensive fieldwork that led to this book was funded through generous grants, including from the University of Florida Graduate School and Department of Political Science, as well as a Tedder Family Doctoral Fellowship in the Humanities, awarded through the Center for the Humanities and the Public Sphere. An additional Foreign Language and Area Studies grant funded language and culture study in Brazil. I was also fortunate to receive several awards related to this research, namely the Hayward R. Alker Award from the American Political Science Association's (APSA) Interpretive Methodologies and Methods Group and the Edward H. Moseley Award from the Southeastern Council of Latin American Studies, both for the best graduate student paper, as well as the Stephen Eric Bronner Dissertation Award from APSA's Caucus for a New Political Science. All of these provided timely reassurance about the trajectory of my research.

An earlier version of the second chapter, entitled "How Latin America Met the Arab World: Toward a Political Economy of Arab-Latin American Relations," originally appeared in Marta Tawil, ed., *Latin American Foreign Policies towards the Middle East: Actors, Contexts, and Trends*, Palgrave Macmillan, 2016. A revised and updated iteration is reproduced here with the permission of Palgrave Macmillan. An earlier version of the fifth chapter was published as "Between Freedom and Futility: On the Political Uses of Corporate Globalizing Discourses" in *Journal of Cultural Economy* 11, no. 6 (2018), 565–590. Scattered sections of the book also draw from "The Global South Is Dead, Long Live the Global South! The Intersectionality of Social and Geographic Hierarchies in Global Capitalism," which was published in *New Political Science* 37, no. 4 (2015), 582–603. Portions of both of the latter appear with the permission of Taylor & Francis.

Though they are probably only vaguely aware of what exactly I have been up to as I have pursued this project over the past decade, family members such as my sister, Jessica, aunts Judy and Mary, uncle Bill, *suegr@s* Alberto and Ivonne, and especially my father, Bruce, have provided a web of support, morally and otherwise, that has made this intellectual journey possible. My mother, Margaret, passed away several years before I began to conceptualize this book, and I dedicate it to her memory.

Lastly, my sincere, boundless, and heartfelt gratitude to Maca for your *cariño*, patience, love, and camaraderie, for always listening but also challenging, and for being the consummate companion for so many adventures, past, present, and future. Both personally and intellectually, *eres mi roca*. Thank you for being you. And to *nuestro Leíto*, who brings so much joy to our lives, brightens every day, and is living proof that another world is possible. This book would have been completed significantly earlier if you did not so frequently issue the command, "no trabajes, papá," but the final product would be much less meaningful, and, dare I say, of lesser quality, had I not been encouraged by your protestations to proceed with renewed vigor and focused intensity. Thank you for teaching me what matters. *Son mi todo*. To paraphrase Cerati: *si los llevo, es para que me lleven*.

ROOTED GLOBALISM

INTRODUCTION

Capitalism and Class in Global Latin America

WHILE ITS GLOBALIZING TENDENCIES HAVE LONG BEEN RECOGNIZED, it is only since the dawn of the new millennium that capitalism could reasonably be argued to have "truly encompassed the world," or at least the vast majority of it (Panitch and Gindin 2012, 1). In this context of ostensibly rapid compression of both space and time, nearly everything seems to be "going global" (Kamola 2013).

Concomitantly, state sovereignty is commonly argued to be dwindling. As political theorist Wendy Brown observes, the globalized nature of contemporary capitalist production and labor pools renders increasingly impossible the task of ascribing a nationality to either finished goods or corporations themselves, including those with hyper-patriotic credentials such as Ford. In short, as she argues, we have reached a new, hybridized normal in which "inside/outside distinctions comport ever less with the boundaries of nations and the activities of states" (Brown 2010, 82–83).

Thus, we bear witness to corporate mergers leading to the creation of behemoths such as "the first truly global beer company," Anheuser-Busch InBev, which has more than 500 brands for sale in more than 150 countries (Chappell 2015). As noted in a *BBC* report, we may need to "stop thinking of cars [as well as, presumably, many other products] in terms of nationality," given the globally integrated nature of their supply chains (Thomas 2016). For its part, the "ultra stealthy startup" Globality, which features Al Gore on its team of investors, predicts via its website that the company's efforts will help inaugurate a new and benign "global reality" in which "the process of globalization is complete" (Magee 2015). Similarly, the banking giant HSBC suggests that in the future, "even the smallest business"—down to the level of children's lemonade stands, as depicted in figure 5.10—"will be multinational."

Just as the corporation has globalized, so have understandings of social class. According to recent figures, the global super-rich—that is, the literal 1 percent—now own more wealth than the other 99 percent of the world's population *combined*. Meanwhile, the world's "62 richest billionaires" have amassed a larger collective fortune than the bottom 50 percent, equating to several billion people (Elliott 2016). The trend toward increasing stratification has only intensified, of course, in the context of the COVID-19 pandemic.

As the inequality specialist Branko Milanović observes, "We could end up with a kind of a global plutocracy, this global one per cent or even half a per cent that are very similar among themselves," even though they "belong to different nations" (quoted in *BBC News* 2016a). Hence the conclusion of Leo Panitch and Sam Gindin, in the magisterial *The Making of Global Capitalism* (2012, 21; italics added), that we have entered a new and profoundly inegalitarian global capitalist era in which "the political fault-lines . . . run *within* states [and their (globalized) class hierarchies] rather than *between* them." Crucially, they argue that the resulting milieu should not encourage defeatism. Rather, it is "pregnant with possibilities for the emergence of new movements to transcend capitalist markets and states" (21).

For those interested in lay sociological analysis concerning the protagonists behind our hyper-capitalist and increasingly unequal times, the *BBC Two* produced a program entitled "The Super-Rich and Us." Based on the accompanying website, recurring topics included private jets, yacht parties, and something called "the ultimate facial."[1] One's curiosity may also be piqued by media explorations of the strength of network ties among the "Davos Men [and Women]" who attend the exclusive annual meetings of the World Economic Forum, fittingly held in a heavily fortified ski resort in the Swiss Alps (*BBC Capital* 2016).

In this scenario of extreme, increasing, and globally interconnected concentrations of capital and power, even establishment figures such as David Rothkopf (2008)—former CEO and editor of the Foreign Policy Group, publisher of the namesake publication—have observed the rise to hegemony of a new "superclass," a "global power elite" that is remaking the world in its image. To quote from the description of the book: "Today's superclass has achieved unprecedented levels of wealth and power. They have globalized more rapidly than any other group. But do they have more in common with one another than with their own countrymen, as nationalist critics have argued? They control globalization more than anyone else. . . . Who sets the rules for a group that operates beyond national laws?"[2]

The answer, apparently, is no one. As capitalist globalization is thus causing *state* sovereignty to enter terminal decline, according to Michael Hardt and Antonio Negri (2000, xii), we are witnessing the emergence of a "new global form of sovereignty"—known as "Empire"—that knows no spatial or territorial limits and that "establishes no territorial center of power." What it *does* inaugurate, instead, is a "properly capitalist order" in which the economic sphere (that is, the logic of the market) merges with and overwhelms the political (Hardt and Negri 2000, 9, 85; see also Brown 2010, 58).

As they put it, rather chillingly: "The establishment of a global society of control that smooths over the striae of national boundaries goes hand in hand with the realization of the world market and the real subsumption of global society under capital." Accordingly, "capitalism has become a world"—specifically, an "unbounded" one in which "nothing escapes money" (Hardt and Negri 2000, 32, 35, 332, 386).

A more nuanced (yet still unsettling) argument is offered by Brown (2010, 71), who suggests that *waning* state sovereignty is flowing in two directions: to violent religious extremism and to capital. The latter, as she notes, "is both master and coin of the realm, except there is no realm, no global polity, governance, or society, and neither are there boundaries or territory that delimit capital's domain" (Brown 2010, 66). Interestingly, Brown's focus in this same text—the aptly titled *Walled States, Waning Sovereignty*—is on the contemporary spate of wall building carried out by would-be democracies in a post–Cold War order supposedly defined by a universalist, liberal-democratic zeitgeist. As a further irony, then, even the construction of ever-taller and more punishing *border walls*—that most nativist of fortifications—is currently going global.

Naturally, many capitalists would perceive the existence of a Leviathan governing structure that is able to set the rules in unfriendly ways or limit capital's domain at the global level as an existential threat to their profit-seeking potential. It is for this reason that corporate actors are salivating over (as well as seeking to construct and sell the general public on the desirability of) a future world order in which sovereign, popularly oriented state control over economic matters is but a distant memory and regulations that impede accumulation appear unfeasible. In theory if not in practice, it is a vision in which even borders themselves really are "so yesterday," per a recent poster advertisement by Emirates Airline (see fig. 5.8). Crucially, in an ostensible paradox, *walls* may continue to be a defining feature of such a desired global system, so long as their aim is to block flows of "undesirable" *people*, but not *capital* (or *capitalists*) (Brown 2010).

Predictions of such a utopian—or dystopian—and seemingly borderless, capitalist future are not entirely new. In 1972, less than a year before his death in a US-backed coup, socialist Chilean president Salvador Allende made a similar warning in a speech before the United Nations. As he declared, "Corporations are global organizations that do not depend on any state and whose activities are not controlled by, nor are they accountable to any parliament or any other institution representative of the collective interest." He went on: "In short, all the world political structure is being undermined" (quoted in Grandin 2015). Reaching further back, one also recalls Karl Marx and Friedrich Engels's (1888, 477) classic observation that the nineteenth-century bourgeoisie "compels all nations, on pain of extinction, to adopt the bourgeois mode of production," thus creating, as the story unfolds, "a world after its own image."

Yet particularly since the end of the Cold War, efforts to construct a capitalist utopia certainly seem to have intensified, and dramatically so. Providing the ideological undergirding for the fast-advancing drive to build a frictionless, capitalist world order is the familiar, if somewhat malleable, concept of *neoliberalism*. The aim, as understood by its chief protagonists—corporate leaders and their intellectual enablers—is not only the implementation of economic policies designed to force wealth to trickle up. They also seek to inspire a "cultural revolution for the free market" (Solimano 2012, 39). Their imposition of the cold, atomizing logic of individual utility maximization is in turn actively—and deliberately—undermining bonds of collective belonging and social solidarity. The rather troubling outcome, in turn, is both to obliterate "the fiber and future of democracy in any form" and to facilitate, even if unwittingly, the rise of the global far right (Brown 2015, 9; Brown 2019).

In this vein, let us consider the words of the Zapatistas, a largely indigenous autonomist movement based in southern Mexico that burst onto the international scene following its January 1, 1994, uprising against both the Mexican state and that very same day's implementation of the North American Free Trade Agreement (NAFTA). In their equally stark phrasing, "neoliberal globalization" has the effect of "destroy[ing] what exists" wherever it is implemented: "It destroys [the locals'] culture, their language, their economic system, their political system, and it also destroys the ways in which those who live in that country relate to each other. So everything that makes a country a country is left destroyed" (Zapatista 2005, 291).

According to Marx, the workers of the world were supposed to be the ones uniting to create a new society in the shell of the old. But from a contemporary perspective, (global) capitalists seem to be having a better go of it. To be sure, much of the corporate language recycled above is little more than propaganda intended to construct popular imaginaries favoring inexorable capitalist globalization rather than to accurately capture existing reality per se (a topic explored at much greater length in chap. 5). Yet there is no doubt that these have been triumphant, if crisis-filled, years for the global capitalist system and its protagonists.

Beyond (False) Dichotomies: Structure and Agency in Global Capitalism

As Margaret Thatcher so elegantly put it, "there is no alternative" to the capitalist model and its global spread. Even if we do not willingly accede to Thomas Friedman's (2005; 2012) "flat [capitalist] world," the unstoppable "electronic herd" of capitalist interests will make dissenting approaches nearly impossible—if not also unthinkable. He writes: "*No one is in charge . . . I didn't start [capitalist] globalization. I can't stop it and neither can you—except at a huge cost to your society and its prospects for growth*" (Friedman 2012, 112).

What these accounts describe is a world of all structure and no agency. It is capitalism without a working class or social movements to contest it. And in this description of a world defined in its totality by an amorphous, omnipresent, and omnipotent capitalist behemoth, it is even a capitalism without real living and breathing capitalists.

Much writing within the interdisciplinary milieu of critical global political economy, as delineated below, has responded to this era of global creative destruction by interrogating the system-level and *structural* dynamics of capitalist globalization. This focus is understandable, given that capitalism—as delineated most compellingly by Marx and Engels—is ultimately about class relations and class-specific characteristics such as the bourgeoisie's ownership of the means of production, not the personalities, individual traits, or idiosyncrasies of individual capitalists. As they write in the *Manifesto of the Communist Party*, "Capital is, therefore, not a personal, it is a social power" (Marx and Engels 1888, 485).

Yet the accompanying relative lack of sociological analysis of the very *agents* who are at the commanding heights of the global capitalist system is nevertheless problematic for both intellectual and political reasons.

Regarding the former, deciphering how capital's structural and social power is actualized in real-life human beings as they operate in real-world circumstances can only enrich our understanding of the global capitalist system as a whole. In terms of the latter, given that we inhabit a world increasingly torn asunder by massive and ever-increasing wealth disparities, power inequalities, and (racialized) class cleavages, *any* light that can be shed on the inner worlds of those at the top has the potential to serve a body politic that increasingly seeks to change that very system. As scholar-activist Susan George (2005, 8) aptly puts it, "Although wealth and power are in a better position to hide their activities and are therefore more difficult to study, any knowledge about them will be valuable to the [global justice] movement." It is thus of the utmost importance that we understand their worldviews, actions, and means of influencing all of our lives.

Bringing the intellectual and political together, Koenraad Bogaert (2018, 249) warns against the frequent anthropomorphization of neoliberalism—or, we might say, capitalism more broadly. As he observes: "Neoliberalism does not do things; people do: projects do not take shape without actors, the specific practices they deploy, the ideals they adhere to, and the rationalities that give sense to their actions" (249).

It is important that we recognize this for theoretical reasons, but it also matters for practical ones. The political danger with overlooking *agents* and *agency* in global capitalism is that this pushes us into the trap of conceptualizing global capitalism as an inexorable and amorphous "force of nature" that cannot be meaningfully challenged (Panitch and Gindin 2012). Examining the activities of real-world capitalists helps us to see that global capitalism is a structure that is reified through human activity and cognition, as well as state action (or inaction). It is, in other words, a *political project*. Accordingly, it can be subjected to contestation.

In broad terms, then, the aim of the present study is to augment our understanding of the protagonists of capitalist globalization. In particular, this work sheds light on how the members of one relatively small group of contemporary elites—that is, the Latin American figures who are responsible for the recent boom in the region's commercial relations with the Arab world—think about themselves and their roles within the global capitalist system. What this entails, most specifically, is conducting a fine-grained empirical analysis of their lifeworlds—in other words, and phenomenologically speaking, the "taken-for-granted subjective world of the individual" (Itzigsohn and Rebón 2015, 179).

The questions to be addressed are thus as follows: Do these actors form a truly *global* capitalist class that has broken free from any "national attachments or needs" (Sassen 2007, 187)? To what extent have they developed a *global* capitalist class consciousness—that is, an "identity in the global system above any local territories and polities" (Robinson 2004, 47)? At a more abstract level, how does the structure of capitalist globalization interact with and condition agency, cognition, and the ways in which this system's protagonists see the world and their place in it?

Accordingly, the aim is to understand how a particular globalizing population of capitalist elites understands its place in the world. Further, it is to determine how their sense of belonging to one or more "imagined communities"—per Benedict Anderson (2006, 6–7), peer groups whose fellow members they may never meet, but with whom they nevertheless share "a deep, horizontal comradeship"—may guide their profit-seeking activities toward some places instead of others.

At a conceptual level, these are relatively simple questions. However, addressing them doubtlessly presents numerous methodological difficulties, hence William K. Carroll's (2010, 19) astute observation that demonstrating the existence of a global capitalist class "is a far from easy task." This is especially the case, one may note, when we are concerned not with this would-be class's *material* existence (as a "class in itself," in Marx's phrasing), but its *ideational* qualities (as a "class for itself"), which leads us headfirst into the muddy waters of human consciousness.

Several extant studies do seek evidence of the extent to which a global capitalist class exists in objective terms, focusing, for example, on participation in global accumulation chains or the level of internationalization within a given corporation's directorate (Heemskerk and Takes 2016). However, markedly fewer works seriously tackle the latter issue, leaving us with a relative lack of direct evidence concerning the subjective qualities of this would-be class. This is in spite of the fact that scholars and lay thinkers alike frequently *assert* that this would-be class possesses a global consciousness and perceives its own "globality"—that is, that it is endowed with a "global sense of belonging," unlike previous generations of capitalist elites who, as the argument goes, are said to have thought primarily in "local" or "regional" terms (Rossi 2017, 164).

The story that emerges from the present attempt to address these questions has significant implications for our ability to analyze, theorize, and imagine alternatives to the global capitalist system. Further, it also has the potential to inform movements that seek to regulate the behavior of global capitalist elites and institutions as well as to contribute to efforts to forestall the recurring crises that their activities engender (Harvey 2010).

On Rooted Globalism and the Stickiness of Place-Based Imaginaries in a Globalizing World

Contemporary elites, as recounted above, have been especially forthright in asserting their own globality. Yet a diverse array of scholars also concurs with the fundamental assertion that today's leading capitalists have mentally divorced themselves from the state and are quickly congealing—or perhaps have already congealed—into a placeless, hegemonic class with a global consciousness.

This is the main thesis of the "global capitalism school," composed mainly of prominent, Marxist-inspired sociologists such as William I. Robinson and Leslie Sklair. Others, such as Carroll, also a sociologist, have advanced more nuanced but sympathetic accounts. Interestingly, little separates these notions from archconservative Samuel Huntington's (2004) characterization of the now-famous Davos Man. As he argued, such figures "have little need for national loyalty, view national boundaries as obstacles that thankfully are vanishing, and see national governments as residues from the past whose only useful function is to facilitate the elite's global operations." Even if it lacks firm empirical backing, the fundamental assertion on identity by Manuel Castells (2010b, 446), foundational theorist of the information age, seems strikingly commonsensical (and perhaps especially so in the age that produced the election of Donald Trump and the Brexit vote): "Elites are cosmopolitan, people are local."

Yet what this rather one-sided account is overlooking is the extent to which the identities of even ostensibly global actors may still be conditioned by ethnicity, race, family and ancestral ties, migration histories, nationality, geography, and so on. It also fails to account for the fact that, somewhat paradoxically, non-global axes of identity may to an extent be *reinforced* by global capitalism, as well as the reality that the *local* and *global* do not precisely exist in an either/or relationship, but along a continuum. This means that identities, for instance, typically "play out at multiple levels simultaneously" (Darian-Smith and McCarty 2017, 12). In other words, "Globals can be partial; they need not be mega-processes but can be encountered as incomplete arrangements or even fragments" (Kahn 2014, 7).

Finally, the idea that the global is entirely subsuming the local overlooks the history of what Panitch and Gindin (2012) refer to as "the making of global capitalism." This system, as they delineate, came into existence precisely because of state action, not in spite of it. This is most notable, of course, vis-à-vis the US, which led the charge in constructing a post–World War II international economic order based on the premise that global capitalism was in the country's national interest—hence their assertion that "it was the immense strength of US capitalism which made globalization possible, and what continued to make the American state distinctive was its vital role in managing and superintending capitalism on a worldwide plane" (Panitch and Gindin 2012, 1, 8).

For these and other reasons, it is thus somewhat misleading to speak of a "new *rootless* class of global billionaires" (Cuadros 2016, 211; emphasis added).

Similarly, while neoliberalism claims anti-statism as a core principle, its implementation "does not necessarily imply less government, but rather a different kind of government" (Bogaert 2018, 248)—and one with anti-democratic, and at times unequivocally authoritarian, tendencies (Brown 2015; Harvey 2007; Kiersey and Sokoloff 2019; Slobodian 2018).

This point is frequently missed. In contrast to the stated position of US provocateur and Trump whisperer Steve Bannon, the goal is not precisely the deconstruction of the administrative state. Rather, it is to deconstruct a certain kind of administrative state—that is, a state apparatus that is capable of enacting policies and enforcing regulations that promote the welfare of the general population. What is being sought instead are different state policies and regulations, namely those that favor corporate and other elite interests.

Thus, instead of advocating for a *weaker* state, the neoliberal ambition is in fact a reconfigured state: one dedicated to the promotion of capital accumulation. Insofar as maximizing profits requires social control, repressive apparatuses, and anti-worker legislation, the neoliberal state is, on these and other fronts, actually stronger. Pushing the argument further, Friedrich Hayek was only saying what many other neoliberals were thinking when he argued that to impose a capitalist order, "at times it is necessary for a country to have, for a time, some form or other of dictatorial power" (quoted in Robin 2013). The high praise he and other neoliberals expressed for the Augusto Pinochet regime is a logical extension of this sentiment. As one of the Chilean Chicago Boys put it, "A person's actual freedom can only be ensured through an authoritarian regime that exercises power by implementing equal rules for everyone" (Valdés 2008, 30; see also Slobodian 2018).

The below analysis of dozens of in-depth conversations with Latin American economic elites who are at the forefront of the region's commercial relations with the Arab world brings to the fore these important caveats concerning global identity formation and the role of the state in global capitalism.

Thus, as I argue on the one hand, the recent boom in Arab–Latin American relations is drawing both regions, and relevant actors therein, further into the network of global capitalist flows. But on the other, it is simultaneously reinforcing a sense of belonging to a Syrian, Lebanese, Palestinian, or even pan-Arab imagined community among many Latin American economic elites of Arab descent. Indeed, as the exigencies of both global capitalism and state policy increasingly drive economic elites to search for profit-seeking opportunities abroad, the Arab–Latin American commercial class finds that its "cultural capital"—that is, its *Arab-ness*, whether real or perceived—is becoming a valuable commodity (Karam 2007). In this fashion, global capitalism may incentivize elites to draw closer to their cultural backgrounds in both superficial and profound ways, rather than to abandon them.

The argument that emerges in the following pages resonates most closely with those who have adopted more ambiguous conceptualizations of the would-be making of the global capitalist class. They include globalization luminary Saskia Sassen (2011), who suggests that to the extent global identities emerge, they will still be "partly structured inside" and "dressed in the clothing of the national." Also notable is Adrian Budd's (2013, 7) reasoned contention that the case for the would-be superseding of all sub-global categories has been "over-stated" and is too "one-sided," though it is still of some use as an analytical construct for understanding important dynamics related to capitalist globalization.

My argument for the stickiness of place-based (and other) imaginaries in global capitalism also dovetails with the core assertion of the interdisciplinary scholarship on transnationalism. This literature has sought to demonstrate how simultaneous embeddedness in more than one national space, particularly among diaspora and migrant populations, is a constituent feature of our current age (Basch et al. 2003; Glick Schiller et al. 1992; Kearney 1995; Levitt 2001; Ong 1999). With notable exceptions, such as Aihwa Ong's classic work *Flexible Citizenship*, relatively few of these writings have placed class dynamics at the center of their analysis. Nonetheless, they contribute a theoretical framework that is highly relevant for understanding the extent to which the identities of ostensibly globalizing economic elites may cross borders, but without necessarily erasing them. Part of the intellectual project of this book, then, is to put the transnationalism research paradigm into dialogue with the global capitalism school.

Virtually all major theoretically inclined works on Arab Latin Americans adopt a transnational framework to analyze how these populations navigate between the cultures and identities of their ancestral Arab homelands and those of the Latin American countries that they now call home (Alsultany and Shohat 2013; Amar 2014; Karam 2007). The overall argument, to borrow from the title of an above-cited volume, is that Arab Latin Americans exist in a hybridized space that is somewhere "between the Middle East and the Americas" and that does not fully belong to either but contains elements of both. Crucially, such transnational identities cannot be defined as purely global, for they are still based on attachments to particular places—multiple places, but places nonetheless.

Rather, such thought patterns are a manifestation of what I refer to in the following pages as *rooted globalism*. I deploy this concept to refer to two fundamental dynamics. First, it captures the complicated amalgamations of different axes of identity that continue to define the interpretive frameworks of many capitalist elites, including those profiled below. Some of these indeed evince global or at least globalizing traits. Yet crucially, these coexist alongside diverse and even contradictory elements. Hence, cosmopolitan tendencies within capitalist worldviews, at least among this study's interlocutors, are still partially grounded by deep-seated roots that are less universalist. In the case of Arab–Latin American business elites, paramount in this regard are ethnic ties, ancestry, and specific ascribed Arab cultural traits.

Second, the term *rooted globalism* acknowledges that there is indeed a rising *global imaginary* among at least some capitalist elites. As revealed in the ethnographic vignettes in chapters 3 and 4, there is repeated evidence of global identity formation, even if it has not—in contrast to assertions made in less nuanced writings on this topic—washed away preceding, place-based forms of attachment. Thus, to borrow from British historian E. P. Thompson (1966), I point to a contemporary and inchoate trend toward the "making" of a global capitalist class that is increasingly aware of its own globality, if only somewhat nascently so.

The finding that elite identities may be less forthrightly global than commonly argued suggests a further point of consideration—that is, the need to determine why corporate discourses so frequently highlight the globality of economic elites and the institutions they control. Most telling in this regard is the aforementioned Emirates advertisement, which reads, in full: "Tomorrow thinks borders are so yesterday."[3]

In the last chapter, I engage in a critical analysis of the political motives behind corporate globalizing rhetoric. While these discourses suggest that globalization is bringing humanity together into a globally connected, cosmopolitan world order, such corporate advertisements also seek to convey the desirability and inevitability of a borderless economy in which they may roam unfettered.

This analysis thus elucidates how powerful actors aim to construct global (or regional-global) imaginaries for consumers by deploying aesthetically pleasing (and, at times, seemingly subversive) advertisements. Their ultimate effect is to demonstrate the would-be futility of attempts to regulate the spread of global capitalism or their own profit-seeking behavior. Accordingly, they comprise what Ong (1999, 6) refers to as "a flexible notion of citizenship and sovereignty," which is strategically deployed for the purpose of capital accumulation. To conclude, I explore how this analysis relates to important political debates concerning agency in globalization, the feasibility of state regulation of global capitalism, and, of particular salience, the construction of alternative global imaginaries and orders.

Toward a Cultural Political Economy of Globalization and a Critical Global Studies

The interdisciplinary paradigm of global studies—sometimes known, more anachronistically, as international studies—arose in the 1980s in response to the perceived rise in cross-border dynamics of myriad kinds (Kahn 2014, 2). Notably, the idea that elites the world over increasingly comprise an integrated capitalist class has frequently been identified as especially emblematic of the rising "global imaginary" that this burgeoning research area aims to interrogate (Darian-Smith and McCarty 2017, 19; Steger 2008).

Particularly since the end of the Cold War, existing academic disciplines, operating in isolation, have seemed unable to come to terms with the increasing complexity and interconnectedness of our rapidly changing and globalizing world (Darian-Smith and McCarty 2017, 1; see also

Kamola 2019). In response, there has been an ongoing coalescence of a "new synthesis"—a "global turn"—that has challenged scholars "to think globally and to develop new global theories and perspectives on issues that were previously understood as either universal, national, or local" and has shed light on how states are being reconstituted by globalizing processes (Darian-Smith and McCarty 2017, 2, 11, 70).

To be sure, there is disagreement as to what precisely defines the core of this "emerging" field of global studies vis-à-vis its disciplinary peers, such as political science, sociology, geography, or anthropology (Kahn 2014). Yet this is not inherently problematic. Indeed, it is less important to arrive at a precise definition of what global studies *is* than to engage in conversations about the global that are "messy, dynamic, passionate, and constantly open to rethinking" (Darian-Smith and McCarty 2017, 26–27). Further, and in spite of this diversity, recent stock-taking exercises concerning global studies have arrived at similar (if not identical) conclusions regarding its essential characteristics and plot generally complementary courses for its future trajectory.

In attempting to provide the "first comprehensive overview" of global studies, Manfred Steger and Amentahru Wahlrab (2016, 19–22) identify the field's four pillars: *globalization*, which serves as its "master concept"; a *transdisciplinary* approach, which is argued to be necessary for grappling with "the increasing complexity, fluidity, and connectivity of our globalizing world"; a recognition of how *space and time* are being reconfigured (and, often, compressed) by globalizing processes; and, finally, *critical thinking*, which entails both a commitment to global justice and skepticism toward positivist approaches. In sum, as globalization is said to be ushering in an "unprecedented age of interconnectivity," global studies as a field plays the important role of "foster[ing] a multireferential understanding of a social whole that is no longer exclusively normalized within a national framework" (Steger and Wahlrab 2016, 13).

However, despite the increasing consolidation of global studies as a field, as Hilary E. Kahn (2014, 2–5) argues, it still faces several obstacles. These include the challenges of transcending ingrained, disciplinary ways of thinking, the lack of an established methodological framework for studying global issues, and a tendency to rely on superficial binaries—such as the notion that the global and local are mutually exclusive, instead of mutually imbricated. In contrast to Steger and Wahlrab, Kahn (2014, 5) also points to a lack of agreement concerning whether *globalization* is truly the field's unifying theme.

What her vision for global studies entails, in short, is turning our attention toward the oft-overlooked "paradoxes, inequalities, and contradictions" that emerge at the intersections between the global and the local (Kahn 2014, 9). The aim for Kahn (2014, 6–8), then, is to pursue a grounded global studies that deploys diverse methodologies to shed light on how globalizing processes, often of a fragmentary nature, are deeply embedded in the lived experiences of, and meanings constructed by, people all around the world.

In *The Global Turn: Theories, Research Designs, and Methods for Global Studies*, Eve Darian-Smith and Philip C. McCarty (2017) attempt to address several of the problem areas that Kahn identifies by elaborating a "global transdisciplinary framework." What this entails, *inter alia*, is an effort to understand the social world from a holistic perspective that is greater than the sum of its disciplinary parts, a willingness to break down conventional categorization schemes and recognize connections across spatiotemporal and North-South boundaries, and a focus on the intertwining of the global and the local.

The authors also foreground the importance of entering into dialogue with diverse, non-Western, and non-Eurocentric perspectives, ideas, and literatures (Darian-Smith and McCarty 2017, 40–53). While intellectually pluralist in their orientation, the authors evince a predilection for critical—and especially non-Western—methodologies and approaches, including those explicitly committed to human emancipation (Darian-Smith and McCarty 2017, 34–37, 174).

In myriad ways, these diverse but complementary programmatic visions regarding global studies find expression in the present text. Facets that are particularly worth highlighting include the highly transdisciplinary nature of this work, which engages with a diverse array of academic literatures (drawn, most prominently, from sociology, anthropology, geography, and political science, and inclusive of contributions from both the North and South), as well as a concern with the ideational dimensions of capitalist globalization's socio-spatial shifts.

In regard to the latter, the aim again is not to treat the global and local as discrete categories. Rather, it is to interrogate the dialectical relationship of "unceasing tension" that exists between place-based and placeless imaginaries as they manifest themselves in the interpretive frameworks and constructed meanings of a particularly situated group of human beings (Kahn 2014, 9). Along the lines that Kahn (2014, 2) suggests, then, this study seeks to reveal how the lifeworlds of globalizing capitalist elites "are defined by and give meaning to global processes." The present effort to bridge the gap between the macro-structural and the agent-based, in turn, resonates with Carroll's (2012; emphasis added) reference to "the need for *nuance* in theorizing global capitalism."

Equally important for this work is the adoption of a critical ethos that manifests itself in numerous ways: first, through an extensive engagement with Marxist theory; second, via the development of an interpretivist approach that eschews positivism's desire for value-free scholarship and its inattentiveness toward questions surrounding reflexivity and meaning-making; and third, as a normative desire to shed light on the machinations of the wealthy and expose the ballooning inequalities that have become a constitutive feature of modern life. I return to the latter motive below as I elaborate this book's overall political project.

Yet beyond drawing heavily from the above-cited accounts that conceptualize the field of global studies, the present work also seeks to synthesize the global studies framework with another growing research paradigm that possesses much in common but whose overlap with the former has been insufficiently theorized. Specifically, I am referring to recent scholarship that self-identifies with the label of *cultural political economy* (CPE), much of which is similarly concerned with the inherently cultural nature of different kinds of border-crossing flows and global-local interactions. While direct references to CPE do not appear in any of the three aforementioned global studies texts, this is, accordingly, not for a lack of intellectual commonalities. Rather, it presumably reflects the newness of the CPE label, as well as the fact that much culturally inflected work on global political economy is conducted under other banners. Here, I aim to make explicit the numerous linkages between these intellectual projects. Indeed, the present work represents precisely a version of their synthesis—that is, a CPE *of globalization* that is informed by the move toward a *critical* global studies.

Premised on the notion that a culture-free economy could never exist—in other words, that political economy and global studies are always imbued with culture—the burgeoning (and also transdisciplinary) CPE research paradigm highlights the cultural dimensions of phenomena ranging from economic development and home ownership to financial crises. Given CPE's focus on "the ways in which culture is implicated in everyday economic practices" (Best and Paterson 2010), it resonates closely with the present, meaning-centered analysis of elite identities and corporate advertisements.

The larger purpose of a CPE approach is to move beyond the traditional dualism that has separated the study of political economy from culture. In turn, the ambition is to develop "a means of exploring the ways in which economic and organizational life is built up, or assembled from, a range of disparate, but inherently cultural, parts" (du Gay and Pryke 2002, 4, 12). This very process of "incorporating culture" into the study of political economy, as Jacqueline Best and Matthew Paterson (2010, 2) argue, will in turn surely "transform our understanding of what political economy itself *is*."

Generally, CPE focuses on "the semiotic and structural aspects of social life and, even more importantly, their articulation" (Sum and Jessop 2013, 1). Much analysis in this tradition thus focuses on how devices—again, such as advertisements (McFall 2004)—attempt to "assemble and arrange the world in specific social and material patterns" (Law and Ruppert 2013, 230). Furthermore, CPE requires a simultaneous focus on both "meaning-making" processes and the "socially embedded" nature of political, cultural, and economic practices (Sum and Jessop 2013, 1). It thus dovetails with the recent rise of interpretivism, as noted below, which also highlights the innumerable ways in which actors construct and imagine their lifeworlds (Yanow and Schwartz-Shea 2015).

As a transdisciplinary work concerned with the CPE of globalization, this book is firmly situated within the global studies paradigm. It also, in turn, advances a specific vision of this field—that is, what has been referred to as "critical global studies" (Steger and Wahlrab 2016) or "critical globalization studies" (Appelbaum and Robinson 2005).

Indeed, the present work is defined—and motivated—by an ethos of *critique*. Here, this term is not solely understood as being reducible to "critical thinking." It also evokes the spirit of critical theory—that is, it forms part of a normative political project that seeks to further the cause of human liberation (Marx 1843a). It is this ambition that Marx (1845, 145) himself boldly evokes through his deservedly famous maxim: "The philosophers have only *interpreted* the world, in various ways; the point, however, is to *change* it."

Of course, analysis for its own sake and for the betterment of the human condition are each worthy (and related) aspirations. In the present context, it is also the case that the fact that we know relatively little about the lifeworlds and interpretive frameworks of economic elites is problematic for reasons that are both intellectual *and* political (Sherman 2019). In the following pages, I pursue both sorts of agendas simultaneously.

In true reflexive fashion, this means not only acknowledging *and* embracing, as many social scientists (and political scientists in particular) are often reticent to do, the normative impetuses behind this project (Yanow and Schwartz-Shea 2015). These include a strong sense of disquiet and discontent concerning the exploding inequalities engendered by (global) capitalism, as well as a more fundamental rejection of the notion that a system can be considered "just" when working people are forced to sell their labor for the profit of others, particularly within the context of highly authoritarian employment regimes (Anderson 2017).

It also requires contemplation of this book's larger political project and how it seeks to contribute to real-world efforts for social change and justice at the global level. Invoking Catholic social teaching and liberation theology, this means cultivating within global studies what Robinson has referred to as a "preferential option for the [oppressed] majority in global society" (quoted in Steger and Wahlrab 2016, 22). Specifically, as I explore in the final chapter, this entails turning our attention to global capitalism's fissures, conceptualizing alternative global imaginaries and orders, and contemplating how the latter might be actualized—as well as, more modestly, exploring opportunities for reforming and regulating the existing global economy.

Given the enormity of the task at hand, such ruminations will only be fragmentary. Yet they are also *necessary*. This is especially the case given that mainstream social science has increasingly abdicated direct engagement with normative questions and instead gravitated toward positivist-inspired approaches that aspire to would-be scientific neutrality (Sclofsky and Funk 2018).

Relational Interviews: An Interpretive Approach

Driven by a reverence for the traditional scientific method, as understood in the context of the natural sciences, positivist research has long reigned supreme in many of the social sciences (King et al. 1994). The effects have been profound. These include the privileging of ways of knowing that are premised on and inclined toward parsimony, generalizability, the separation of facts from values, and the supposed neutrality of the researcher, who is to remain properly aloof from the social object under investigation (Jackson 2015; Smith et al. 1996).

However, in response to the hegemony of the "positivist straitjacket" (Oren 2009), there has been an increasingly notable "interpretive turn" in numerous disciplines, particularly in the past decade (Yanow and Schwartz-Shea 2015). Such is certainly the case within global studies, as demonstrated by the above engagement with cutting-edge works about the field, all of which share a critical attitude vis-à-vis at least some of positivism's features, perhaps most notably its claims to universalism and scientific detachment.

Crucially, this effervescence emerges from a robust legacy of social theorizing. Interpretivism draws inspiration most specifically from the argument—advanced by Max Weber and cited approvingly by Clifford Geertz—that "man is an animal suspended in webs of significance he himself has spun" (quoted in Yanow 2006, 6). It thus follows that studying human beings—living, breathing, sentient, and contemplative creatures—requires a fundamental concern with questions of *meaning*.

It also demands that close attention be paid to how they—as well as *we*, as researchers—utilize language and other symbolic systems to understand their (and our) own actions and construct meaning-filled worlds. In this context, it is fitting to invoke James Scott's (2007, 382) pithy summary of an argument advanced by political theorist John Dunn: "You can never create a satisfactory explanation of people's behavior without providing a phenomenological account of what they themselves think they are doing."

As I explore at length below, the fact that key existing works that focus on global imaginaries among capitalist elites tend to neglect these important methodological, ontological, and epistemological considerations produces two effects. First, it limits the amount of light they are able to shed on elite identities and worldviews. And second, it leads to the overidentification of signs of global identity formation.

The centrality of meaning-making, per an interpretivist understanding, sets the social sciences apart from their natural-science counterparts. It also makes the positivist model from the natural sciences poorly suited for analyzing certain facets of the human experience, as has long been recognized by many philosophers of social science (Taylor 1971). What is needed instead are methodologies that dovetail with Weber's view concerning the ontology of the social world (Hall 2003). Here, interpretivism offers a potpourri of possibilities, ranging from ethnography and discourse analysis to reflexive historical analysis and unstructured, ordinary-language interviews (Yanow and Schwartz-Shea 2015). Examples of research areas that readily lend themselves to such interpretivist approaches include those focusing on culture and identity, as well as those that aim to interrogate not just what *is* but what *ought* to be.

The aforementioned drive to understand how the local and global are intertwined in quotidian life and circumstances has also fed into the rise of ethnographically inspired methods. This is due, in part, to the latter's strength in allowing us "to enter the points where globals become embodied, discussed, strategized, and performed" (Kahn 2014, 8). In sum, interpretivism thus resonates clearly with the twin paradigms in which this book is situated: CPE and critical global studies.

Specifically, this study employs an interpretivist form of interviewing that is appropriate for the task, as Sassen (2007, 5) puts it, of "decipher[ing] individual imaginaries about globality." Conducting what Lee Ann Fujii (2017) referred to as "relational interviews" revolves around engaging in deep, relatively unstructured, and context-sensitive conversations with interlocutors to understand how they see the world and their place in it. As part of this reflexive and ethnographic exchange, interpersonal dynamics and the positionality of the interviewer are not extraneous details to be shorn away. Rather, they are an essential and data-rich part of the interview itself. The point, as Fujii put it, is that "interacting" instead of "interrogating" can shed much light on the lifeworlds of conversation partners.

This focus on constructed meanings and identities informs not only my methodological approach, but also the presentation of interview data, which I depict in chapters 3 and 4 in the form of ethnographically inspired vignettes. Here, I recreate key moments from our dialogues, which I contextualize through the provision of relevant sensory details. The idea is not to cherry-pick quotations in the service of an overly tidy argument or narrative, but rather to reveal the complexities of my interlocutors' worldviews, motivations, and senses of self. In the spirit of ethnographic reflection, vignettes are accompanied by my own thoughts, reactions, observations, and analysis as a reflexive researcher.

During these conversations, I asked probing, open-ended questions and paid particular attention to various forms of overt and subtle evidence. These included how interviewees use and understand keywords such as *global* and *globalization*; what they mean and whom they are including as part of their peer group when they speak of *we* and *us*; direct statements regarding and indirect allusions to their goals and motivations; references to, invocations of, and switching between national, transnational, and global symbols, ranging from soccer teams and languages to vacation destinations and family backgrounds; body language, tone of voice, and other observational cues; and even what books are sitting on the office shelf or what they post on LinkedIn and Twitter.

To elicit the clearest and most precise responses from my interlocutors, I initiated our conversations in their dominant everyday languages, Spanish and Portuguese. For ease of readability, in this work I provide only my translations of their quotations (as well as of the Spanish- and Portuguese-language texts with which I engage).

Commenting on the delicate art of translating, interpretive methodologist Frederic Schaffer (2016, 55) correctly observes that "words do not necessarily have stable or fixed sets of meaning across time and tongues." Thus, I drew heavily from my deep familiarity with Southern Cone Spanish, Brazilian Portuguese, and diverse South American cultural contexts to achieve the greatest possible level of fealty to the original utterances. On those occasions in which interviewees changed the language of conversation to, or sprinkled their speech with, English, I make note of this in the text. I also comment briefly on what these various linguistic choices reveal about their respective identities. To preserve anonymity to the greatest possible extent, pseudonyms and abstract descriptions of institutional affiliations and personal backgrounds and details are used for all interviewees.

A South-South Diaspora

The empirical referent for this study, again, is the axis of relations between Latin America and the Arab world. In particular, this study focuses on Brazil, Argentina, and Chile—the three South American countries, in order, that traditionally have had the largest amount of trade and overall economic exchange with the latter region. Brazil is by far the leader in this regard, with its annual exports to and imports from Arab countries having increased dramatically in the past two decades.

Capturing the perceived novelty and transformative nature of these relations, it was previously claimed by the Brazilian state, with some exaggeration, that they are "creat[ing] . . . a new world economic geography". This means, both literally and symbolically, that "to get from Brazil to Cairo, you won't need to pass through Washington and Paris" (quoted in Karam 2007, 174). More concretely, recent years saw the establishment of political and economic forums (such as the Summits of South

American–Arab Countries, which represented the first-ever institutionalized gathering between the regions), as well as the dramatic growth of diplomatic ties. The fact that these relations grew exponentially in the period under investigation is enticing for analytical reasons. Indeed, they provide an ideal vantage point from which to understand how cross-border economic relations are made—and, in turn, conceived of—by actors on the ground in tangible, observable circumstances.

Given the tendency in Global North academia to theorize based on Global North cases, the present focus on Arab–Latin American economic elites may seem an unusual starting place. This is precisely the point. Part of the purpose behind choosing this particular case, as discussed in chapter 2, is to subvert the commonplace and pernicious practice of exclusively utilizing Global North cases to develop theories and concepts that are then applied more broadly. At the risk of stating the obvious, the South itself may also be a source of theoretical and conceptual innovations that are of general relevance and interest.

Notably, Northern and Southern elites are all protagonists in the same general story of capitalist globalization (Chibber 2013b). It is, in fact, apparent that cross-border economic flows exhibit a growing tendency to entangle *all* of the world's capitalist elites, regardless of whether they hail from leading economic powers or the postcolonies (Dirlik 2000, 7). Accordingly, Arlene Dávila (2016, 50) concludes that, "having penetrated most Latin American industries, neoliberal capitalism has seen the rise and development of transnational capitalist classes in every sector of the economy."

To the extent that we recognize that global capitalism is a *universalizing* force but not a *homogenizing* one, we thus have every reason to expect that the lifeworlds of Northern and Southern capitalists will of course be different but also intrinsically connected (Funk 2015a). Some, such as Robinson (2014, 30–35), go so far as to assert that there should be no appreciable difference between Northern and Southern elite identities.

However, in general, much critical literature on global capitalism elides the question of North-South elite parity by focusing on the system's Global North protagonists. While this is particularly notable in regard to works such as Kees van der Pijl's (1984) *The Making of an Atlantic Ruling Class*, it is also a feature of broader-based and more contemporary writings. Carroll (2010, 54, 84), for example, acknowledges "a growing if still modest segment of global corporate capital based in the South" but justifies his own focus on Northern actors by noting that the "image of an Atlantic ruling class retained its cogency to the close of the twentieth century." Sklair (2001, 100) also recognizes that the South has its own "local wings" of the "transnational" capitalist class. However, his analysis is almost entirely centered on the "triad" areas of North America, Europe, and Japan/Southeast Asia/Australia.

This cumulative near-exclusive focus on the North serves not only to obscure the extent to which there is a growing cadre of Southern capitalist actors who operate globally; it also buttresses the long-standing and corrosive premise that Global South actors lack agency. As a corrective, recent works have usefully sought to locate a globally oriented capitalist class in a wider variety of sites, including various parts of Asia and Oceania (Sprague 2016; for a skeptical but not dismissive appraisal, see Starrs 2017), Chile (Kowalczyk 2020), and the Caribbean (Sprague 2019).

Scrutinizing the worldviews of Arab–Latin American economic elites also allows us to observe how a large and yet oft-overlooked diaspora population navigates between distinct cultural, ethnic, and economic spaces and identities. An additional factor that makes this diaspora population of special interest in the present context is the persistent association in Latin America and elsewhere of Lebanese emigrants in particular (as well as Arabs in general) with merchant capitalism, trading, and peddling (Glade 1983). In other words, at the level of popular imaginaries, Arab–Latin American economic elites are commonly understood in highly stereotypical terms as a consummate capitalist class, and one whose members have few, if any, place-based attachments.

Crude caricatures aside, it is true that there is a concentration of Arab-descendant figures at the top of the Latin American socioeconomic pyramid. Most famously, they include Carlos Slim, a Mexican business magnate of Lebanese descent who ranks among the world's richest people, and the Brazilian Joseph Safra, of Lebanese-Jewish ancestry, considered to be "the world's richest banker" before his late-2020 death (Gelles and Horch 2015). This population thus merits careful attention so that we may understand not only the intersections between national, transnational, and global identities, but also how wealth, privilege, and class dynamics operate in Latin American societies—and beyond.

The present idea, then, is not to approach the *problematique* of global identity formation by choosing a most-likely case that will provide the clearest path toward the elusive end point of generalizable knowledge. If this were the guiding criterion, it could make sense to instead proceed by analyzing capitalist elites in London, New York, and Tokyo instead of São Paulo, Santiago, and Buenos Aires. Indeed, given that many of the former are presumably better integrated into globe-spanning accumulation chains, as suggested by Carroll, one may—contrary to Robinson—reasonably expect that they should concomitantly display a more global consciousness than their Southern counterparts.

Rather, the operating logic here is to interrogate a particular social group that has received too little attention from scholars and that is well situated to allow us to further our understanding of how ethnicity and the diasporic experience intersect with place-based and placeless axes of identity. This, again, is in addition to the fact that as we live in a world of rising Southern actors (Acharya 2014), there is intrinsic value to foregrounding Global South cases. As Javier Santiso (2013, 30) comments in this regard, South-South relations have grown at a "remarkable" pace in recent years, and Arab–Latin American ties clearly exemplify "this global trend towards a more decentralized world." It is only sensible that our ways of knowing undergo a similar process of decentering (Dahi and Demir 2019).

However, a caveat is in order concerning the present focus on Arab–Latin American elites. Specifically, it is worth entertaining the objection that since I am analyzing the ideational qualities of actors who are engaged in Arab–Latin American commerce, many—but far from all—of whom are Latin Americans of Arab descent, this is hardly an auspicious place to look for global identities. That is, if the material realities of these actors appear to be defined largely by place-based relations, and their particular geographical area of economic interest is precisely the region of their ancestors, then why expect their ideational realities to transcend "place" and appear as global?

Admittedly in this regard, the present analysis does produce some perhaps obvious results. These include the case of the Lebanese-Argentine leader of a Lebanese-Argentine organization, profiled in chapter 3, who evinces strong currents of both Lebanese and Argentine nationalism and, indeed, exceptionalism. Another case, from chapter 4, is a Chilean international trade specialist who reveals no Arab ancestry and displays stronger global tendencies than his Arab–Latin American counterparts. Both examples appear to indicate that material circumstances—such as one's immigration background or the other's lack thereof—are conditioning ideational understandings in a rather direct fashion.

Yet many of the other stories that emerge reveal material-ideational relationships that are much looser, if perceptible at all. Such is the case, as discussed in chapter 4, of the Syrian-Argentine financial capitalist whose commercial focus is the countries of the Gulf, who evinces no economic interest in Syria, and who is ultimately more attracted to Asian than Arab markets. The same is true vis-à-vis the Syrian-Brazilian leader of a leading Arab-Brazilian commercial organization who displays few national or ethnic sympathies for the Arab world and whose private business dealings are mostly oriented toward the US and Europe.

In other words, it is tempting to surmise that it is because of an ethnic, cultural, regional, and/or perhaps religious identity that Arab–Latin American elites have pushed for deeper relations between the regions. Yet while there is of course a fundamental association between the material and ideational, the relationship is hardly so slavish. It must be *interrogated*, not *assumed*. In turn, it is, in theory, equally plausible that these figures have been motivated by purely profit-seeking concerns to provide their Arab cultural capital to would-be exporters or by a desire to further the interests of a global capitalist elite. Tellingly, neither of these formulations turns out to fully account for how the actors under investigation understand their economic endeavors.

Contents

I proceed, in chapter 1, by reviewing the idea of the global capitalist class, along with its intellectual history and theoretical underpinnings. I also tackle the all-important question of how we may identify such a class when we see it. Here, I construct a broader argument about the need for nuance in both theoretical and methodological terms. Chapter 2 turns to the case of interest, Latin America's linkages with the Arab world. The aims are to historicize these relations (with a focus on migration and the development of political and economic ties), bring to an English-speaking audience the relatively vast Spanish- and Portuguese-language literature that has been produced on these topics, and contextualize the reader's understanding of contemporary relations, as well as the economic protagonists that promote them.

These figures, in turn, are profiled in chapters 3 and 4, which present ethnographic-inspired vignettes based on relational interviews with selected and representative Latin American business elites. They are accompanied by an analysis of what their lifeworlds reveal about the notion of a global capitalist class for itself. The first of these chapters tells the stories of several actors with predominantly place-based (national or transnational) ties, while the second focuses on those with increasingly denationalized and/or incipiently global worldviews. Notably, more of the interviewees fit into the former categories as opposed to the latter. On the basis of this analysis, I develop a conceptual framework—rooted globalism—that captures how new, global axes of identity are slowly rising, but without painting over the place-based attachments that preceded them. The result is the generation of complicated forms of consciousness that fall somewhere in between.

Chapter 5 addresses a lingering empirical puzzle—that is, the apparent mismatch between the resilient place-based national/transnational imaginaries that predominate among interviewees and the recurring global imaginaries that are a mainstay of corporate advertisements and propaganda. Based on a discursive analysis of the advertising campaigns of three corporations that claim a global identity, this chapter argues that for elite economic actors, projecting such *globality* serves as a political-economic strategy for the further accumulation of wealth and power. Thus, such global presentations of self are not precisely the manifestation of deeply held, global mindsets. Rather, to a greater extent, they are a political performance.

Finally, the concluding chapter looks to the future of capitalist class identities and argues that we are witnessing the (slow) emergence of rooted globalism. Further, it contemplates an especially salient issue vis-à-vis today's trends toward nativism, jingoism, and wall building. Specifically, I am referring to the convoluted political conjuncture that confronts today's left as it must navigate between the "sunny globalism" and "progressive neoliberalism" of mainstream and corporate-friendly elites (Campbell 2017; Fraser 2019) and an increasingly authoritarian and strident far right that is finding electoral success in many parts of the West and beyond, in part due to the crises generated by protagonists in the former groups.

Faced with these circumstances, I argue that the left's efforts should also reflect the logic of a kind of rooted globalism by striking a careful balance between both local *and* global thinking and acting. As I suggest, global imaginaries are both politically powerful and alluring, at least for many. The larger political implication of this work, then, is to argue against the tendency toward left-wing nativism and suggest extreme caution about the impulse to retreat to the nation-state. Rather than abandon the construction of global imaginaries to corporations and neoliberal globalists, as I argue, we must push for the generation of solidarity-based, global identity constructions. Only these will allow us to overcome the "morbid symptoms" that plague the contemporary political scene (Gramsci 1971, 275–276).

Notes

1. This and other information about the show is available on the *BBC* website, accessed February 1, 2016, http://www.bbc.co.uk/programmes/b04xw4rw.

2. See the publisher's website, accessed January 5, 2022, https://us.macmillan.com/books/9780374531614/superclass.

3. See the personal website of Khatija Liaqat, accessed June 6, 2019, https://khatijaliaqat.wordpress.com/2016/05/21/taglines-of-emirates-airline/.

1

PROGRESS AND LACUNAE IN THE STUDY OF THE "GLOBAL" CAPITALIST CLASS

According to Manuel Castells's (2010b) classic framing, ours is a rising "network society" in which "spaces of flows"—including global accumulation chains—are replacing geographical spaces (such as countries) as the primary horizon that defines human identity. This is true, at least, for those who are well situated to profit from this increasing connectivity. Castells (2010a, 335) thus adds the important caveat that place-based imaginaries are still dominant for the majority of the world's population, especially those who have been excluded from enjoying capitalist globalization's "benefits." Indeed, elsewhere he cites survey data in support of the related point that as the world continues to globalize, non-elites increasingly "feel local" (Castells 2010a, xxiii).

Such assertions of (and preoccupations with) elite globality—in terms of their material realities and senses of self—have become standard fare for both thinkers on the Marxist-inspired left and the forces of the Trumpist far right. Resonating with utopian neoliberal rhetoric, they share the notion that today's capitalist elites are *stateless*, *free-floating*, and *cosmopolitan*, despite the fact, as examined later in this chapter, that there is very little evidence to support (or, conversely, to refute) the claim that they have developed a truly "global" class consciousness.

This chapter proceeds as follows in its analysis of the concept of the would-be global capitalist class: First, I explore the origins of this notion, along with its broader intellectual context. This includes diverse influences ranging from Karl Marx and Adam Smith to Samuel Huntington. I focus on the highly influential conceptualization of *global capitalists* that has emerged from the bourgeoning literature of what has been termed the *"global capitalism school,"* especially as elaborated by its most prominent theorists: the prolific, highly influential, and widely cited sociologists William I. Robinson and Leslie Sklair. Given their singularly important contributions to the development of this research paradigm and to understandings of capitalist globalization more generally, their writings merit especially careful attention.

Subsequently, I analyze the key concept of transnationalism and how it is deployed within this literature to make an original argument concerning our understanding of the political economy of globalization. Further, I interrogate the empirical basis for claims of the existence of a global capitalist class, particularly in regard to the idea that it has become a class for itself and developed a global capitalist consciousness. I also delineate and offer a critique of the different arguments within this school of thought concerning who is and is not considered a global capitalist before exploring materialist and idealist understandings of class within Marxist theory.

In so doing, I address several deficiencies in the literature of the global capitalism school, including the weak empirical basis for asserting the existence of a global capitalist class, a near-exclusive focus on objective indicators to identify it, the problematic presumption that a class's objective existence necessarily implies that it also exists subjectively, and a lack of conceptual clarity concerning the global capitalist class and what it would mean for it to have a cosmopolitan identity.

Based on these critiques and theoretical engagements, I argue for a properly nuanced approach to the study of capitalist elite identities—that is, first, one that is informed by interpretivism's sensitivity to context, meaning, and the convoluted nature of human identity; and second, one that thoughtfully interrogates the interrelationship between the subjective and objective aspects of global class formation.

I conclude by previewing my empirically based argument that the rhetoric surrounding the growth of the global capitalist class is exaggerated, particularly insofar as it fails to account for the resilience of place-based (especially, that is, national and transnational, as well as ethnic) imaginaries. Thus, as I delineate in later chapters, to the relatively limited extent that their mental frameworks are at all global, the class consciousness of these actors can be conceptualized as a form of rooted globalism. In other words, they exhibit only a nascent globalism or cosmopolitanism that is firmly embedded in a place-based framework. In this vein, my argument resonates with conceptualizations of identities as *transnational*, or simultaneously embedded in multiple places. This is quite distinct from the global capitalism school's argument—or the neoliberal fantasy—that place is ceasing to matter altogether.

As I explore here and in subsequent chapters, what is at stake politically in these conversations is that overly aggressive assertions concerning the rise to hegemony of a seemingly omnipotent global capitalist class will likely disempower those who seek to regulate the activities of capitalist elites or indeed imagine a different, alternative form of globalization. In the face of such seeming historical inevitability and teleological certainty, after all, there would appear to be little hope for contestation or resistance. For the global capitalism school, this is an unintended side effect of their theoretical musings. For neoliberalism's proponents, disciplining local polities through the constant threat by unmoored elites of cross-border capital flight is precisely the point.

Transnational and Global Capitalists: The Genesis of a Concept

In recent years, the belief that there is a global class of capitalists who do not identify with any particular country has become conventional wisdom across the ideological spectrum. It has also captured the imaginations of both lay and scholarly observers.

Motivated by an ethos of right-wing nativism that would presage our current era, Huntington's (2004) aforementioned pejorative label of "Davos Man" is perhaps the most famous and enduring formulation of this idea. As he elaborates in the appropriately titled article, "Dead Souls: The Denationalization of the American Elite"—published, also fittingly, in *The National Interest*—an army of these and other perceived "transnationalists" is actively seeking to undermine our "national identity" in favor of flat-world economics (and, as he identifies vis-à-vis the efforts of political and intellectual elites, by promoting universal values) (Huntington 2004).

These groups, he notes with ostensible populist rage, are inimical to what the "overwhelming bulk of the American people" want: "a national alternative and . . . preserving and strengthening the American identity of centuries" (Huntington 2004). To take but one of many other examples, so it is in France, where the far-right gadfly and recurring presidential candidate Marine Le Pen has sought to boost her would-be populist credentials by railing against the "globalized elites" who have sold out the country's poor, tired, and hungry (Astier 2014)—or at least those who fit her exclusivist definition of "Frenchness."

Huntington's formulation has been much quoted, particularly in the business press. In turn, Davos Man has become a stock literary figure in mainstream discussions concerning the actions and identities of the global elite.

Similar incarnations abound in centrist and center-left circles. For example, economist Lawrence Summers (2008)—the former president of Harvard University and subsequent Obama-era director of the National Economic Council—has warned that "growth in the global economy encourages the development of *stateless elites* whose allegiance is to global economic success and their own prosperity rather than the interests of the nation where they are headquartered" (emphasis added).

Positioning his thesis as an updated and globalized version of C. Wright Mills's (1956) classic text *The Power Elite*, fiercely anti-Trumpist foreign policy commentator and public thinker David Rothkopf (2008) has sounded the alarm over the existence and rise of a "superclass" of some 6,000 individuals. As he notes, members of this "global power elite" wield "vastly more power than any other group on the planet." Crucially, the result is that they are "transcend[ing]" the nation-state in their pursuit of "internationalist or supernationalist agendas" (Rothkopf 2008, xiii, 14).

Adopting an explicitly left-wing perspective, Peter Phillips's (2018, 9) *Giants: The Global Power Elite* further explores how the "activist core of the Transnational Capitalist Class," composed of some 389 individuals, together "function[s] as a nongovernmental network of similarly educated wealthy people with common interests of managing, facilitating, and protecting concentrated global wealth and insuring [*sic*] the continued growth of capital."

Scattered but recurrent news stories appear to speak to precisely this trend of global class formation. Common are depictions of the "globe-trotting" and "homeless" executive who "rarely spend[s] a week in one place" (Coomes 2015; Marston 2012). As one such figure comments: "I have a flat in London, commute to Jamaica and also spend a lot of time in the US" (Marston 2012).

Some corporate executives, such as Facebook cofounder Eduardo Saverin, have even renounced their citizenship for business reasons—in his case, apparently, to avoid US taxes (*BBC News* 2012). Similarly, a *BBC* article on Burger King's attempt to move its headquarters to Canada, where it would enjoy a lower tax rate, featured the title "Burger King abdicates US citizenship" (Zurcher 2014). Indeed, all over the world, citizenship and wealth are increasingly becoming linked. Most tellingly, many countries—including the US—now offer "investor visas," which allow the global rich to get on the "fast track to permanent residency" by making sufficiently large investments (as the *Wall Street Journal* notes, in recent years, such US visas have been "soaked up by Chinese" elites) (Jordan 2014).

Witness also the recurring proposals to create a "floating startup incubator" off the coast of California, where US law will not apply and "techies without green cards" will be able to ply their trade without encumbrance (Florida 2011). According to the vision of "libertarian software engineer" Patri Friedman—Milton's grandson—and his fellow travelers, the idea behind this "seasteading" initiative is to create a brave new world of "libertarian utopia[s]" that are "run by Silicon Valley" instead of governments (E. Robinson 2014; see also Steinberg et al. 2012). Another media report elaborates:

> Backed almost entirely by venture capitalist Peter Thiel, who cofounded PayPal, the team plans to seastead, colonize the sea beyond the reach of existing nations. Friedman's mission is to open a political vacuum into which people can experiment with startup governments that are "consumer-oriented, constantly competing for citizens," he says.
>
> "I envision tens of millions of people in an Apple or a Google country," where the high-tech giants would govern and residents would have no vote. "If people are allowed to opt in or out, you can have a successful dictatorship," the goateed Friedman says, wiggling his toes in pink Vibram slippers. (Bowles 2011)

Ours is indeed a "magical-realist" world in which Latin American and other capitalist elites increasingly take advantage of fiscal paradises (Harrington 2016), change their ships' flags (and thus nationalities) through registering them abroad (Justo 2014; van Fossen 2016), and form "untraceable" shell companies (*The Economist* 2012), all to avoid taxes and certain kinds of state regulation, as well as to inaugurate, more broadly, "a low tax, low wage, libertarian system of global capitalism" (van Fossen 2016, 359).

This is, of course, a policy agenda that is backed—and diffused to the public—by powerful interests. It is further buttressed by the proliferation of the business-friendly imaginary of a completely interconnected global capitalist economy, which has also been heavily promoted by political elites and the corporate sector. Particularly as universities have been reconstituted along neoliberal lines, these institutions have also become active agents in the dissemination of precisely this pro-capitalist, "globalist" ideology (Kamola 2019; Mittelman 2017).

In turn, and invoking both Huntington's formulation and long-standing antisemitic tropes, today's far right has made significant political hay out of tarring these and other would-be rootless globalists for their perceived lack of loyalty to their home political communities. For example, before resigning in disgrace in early 2021, Brazil's foreign minister, Ernesto Araújo, openly declared his support for Trump-style nationalism as the defining essence of "the West," an amorphous space that he hoped to help liberate—along with the rest of the world—from an "anti-human" and godless "globalism" (Caleiro and Cerioni 2018). For good measure, Araújo also implicated the empty signifier "cultural Marxism" as the driving force behind so-called globalist ideology—the latter of which he described, without irony, as an offshoot of "economic [i.e., capitalist] globalization" (Caleiro and Cerioni 2018).

Other political projects seek to create alternative global imaginaries, such as that embodied by the would-be country of Atlantium, carved out of a remote area in the Australian hinterland. As Atlantium frames its "nonterritorial" guiding ideology: "In an age where people increasingly are unified by common interests and purposes across—rather than within—traditional national boundaries, Atlantium offers an alternative to the discriminatory historic practice of assigning nationality to individuals on the basis of accidents of birth or circumstance" (quoted in Robson 2015). In other words, there would be no more place-based conception of citizenship. For his part, Yasiin Bey—the US-born rapper and actor formerly known as Mos Def—at one point attempted to leave South Africa using a "world passport" (it did not work—he was arrested for overstaying his visa) (*BBC News* 2016b).

Parallel to these lay invocations, recent decades have also borne witness to a growing and now-thriving scholarly conversation concerning the globality of economic elites. Referring to an ascendant global capitalist class, these scholars—mostly Marxist-inspired sociologists, with a smattering of political economists and contributors from other fields—have carved out a distinct research niche.

Notably, my home discipline of political science and subfield of International Relations have largely been absent from these conversations. Reasons include a congenital predilection for state-centrism, a long-standing mainstream aversion to class analysis and scholarship with a "Marxist odor" (Moore 2007, 91; Sclofsky and Funk 2018; Funk and Sclofsky 2021), the collective abandonment by many "critical" scholars of class-based analysis in favor of postmodernism, poststructuralism, postcolonialism, and cultural studies (Callinicos 1989; Chibber 2013b; Dirlik 2000, 9), and, finally, what

John Mearsheimer and Stephen Walt identify as the decline of grand theory and rise of quantitative "hypothesis testing" as the proper modus operandi (quoted in Oren 2016, 572).

Nevertheless, that the study of global capitalism and global capitalists now represents a bona fide research program is clear from its level of institutionalization and the publication record of associated scholars (Sklair 2016; Struna 2013). The Network for Critical Studies of Global Capitalism, founded in 2011, holds biennial conferences revolving around the themes of "global capitalism and transnational class formation." Many key figures also participate and hold leadership positions in the Global Studies Association and publish in its *Journal of Critical Globalisation Studies*. For example, Sklair is the president of the United Kingdom branch, while virtually all of the leading thinkers have prominent roles in its North American counterpart.

More broadly, and beyond in-house forums, there is a steady stream of books and articles within this paradigm—sometimes, again, referred to as the "global capitalism school"—flowing onto the pages of both critical and mainstream publications. Along the way, foundational works in and related to this research area have garnered significant attention and amassed substantial citation counts, as revealed by Google Scholar. As of June 2021, Kees van der Pijl's (1998) more historically oriented *Transnational Classes and International Relations* has accumulated over thirteen hundred citations, while Robinson's (2004) *A Theory of Global Capitalism: Production, Class and State in a Transnational World* possess more than eighteen hundred. Sklair's (2001) own path-breaking *The Transnational Capitalist Class* has surpassed thirty-five hundred.

While also engaging with other works, this chapter focuses primarily on the writings of the latter two theorists. Together, and by a considerable margin, they have been the most influential in popularizing this research paradigm, establishing its terms of debate, and influencing subsequent studies. They have also played an outsized role in shaping scholarly and lay understandings of global capitalism more generally. Accordingly, their intellectual output merits more sustained critical engagement and greater scrutiny than it has previously received.

Interestingly, this blooming scholarly literature makes only infrequent mention of Huntington's very similar ruminations. An exception—though only a partial one—is Robinson's *Global Capitalism and the Crisis of Humanity* (2014, 35, 215), which includes a section entitled "'Davos Man' or 'Global Capitalist Man'?," as well as an acknowledgement that his purpose has been to conduct "an ethnography of 'Davos Man.'" However, this text appears to contain no direct reference to Huntington's work or status as the originator of this concept.

This omission, both in and beyond Robinson's work, perhaps can be explained by the fact that Huntington did not develop his ideas on Davos Man in any detail or publish them in academic journals. That Huntington (2004) held notoriously noxious political views—which informed, for example, his involvement with apartheid-era South Africa (Oren 2003, 1–5)—surely did little to facilitate such cross-pollination with critical scholars. The same goes for his inclusion of "academic elites" among the aforementioned "dead souls," which echoes standard right-wing attacks on the professoriate (Huntington 2004).

Adam Smith is a further oft-unacknowledged influence. His contributions are recognized and cited accordingly by Huntington but go unmentioned in most scholarship on global class formation. As Smith argued in *An Inquiry into the Nature and Causes of the Wealth of Nations*, originally published in 1776, while "the proprietor of land is necessarily a citizen of the particular country in which his estate lies . . . the proprietor of stock is properly a citizen of the world, and is not necessarily attached to any particular country" (quoted in Huntington 2004). For him, financial capitalists are—or at least have the potential to become—the Davos Men that Huntington describes. A quote commonly attributed to Napoleon frames the issue in much starker, but still familiar, terms: "Money has no motherland; financiers are without patriotism and without decency; their sole object is gain." For his part, Smith also suggests the opposite, namely that "investors tend to have a *domestic* market bias" (Worstall 2014; emphasis added).

In terms of historical and theoretical influences on contemporary scholarship on global class formation, Marx naturally looms larger than any other thinker. As noted, unlike popular depictions of Davos Man or a superclass—which are staples of the business press and mainstream educated thought more generally—most academic studies in this area have been produced by Marxist-inspired sociologists and political economists. Yet it is important to recognize that while many of these thinkers are steeped in the Marxist tradition, they also seek to push it in a new direction.

In the *Manifesto of the Communist Party*, Marx and Friedrich Engels (1888, 476) memorably describe the bourgeoisie's role in making capitalism into a worldwide system. As they write, in characteristic imitable prose, "The need of a constantly expanding market for its products chases the bourgeoisie over the whole surface of the globe. It must nestle everywhere, settle everywhere, establish connexions [sic] everywhere." It is to their credit that over a hundred years before *globalization* became an inescapable buzzword, they had already encapsulated the core of at least the economic aspects of this fuzzy concept.

Yet what is germane to the present conversation is not their pioneering insights on global capitalism, but rather their framing of the bourgeoisie's historic, world-making role. As they observe:

> The bourgeoisie has through its exploitation of the world-market given a cosmopolitan character to production and consumption in every country.... It has drawn from under the feet of industry the national ground on which it stood. All old-established national industries have been destroyed or are daily being destroyed. They are dislodged by new industries... that no longer work up indigenous raw material, but raw material drawn from the remotest zones; industries whose products are consumed, not only at home, but in every quarter of the globe. In place of the old wants, satisfied by the productions of the country, we find new wants, requiring for their satisfaction the products of distant lands and climes. In place of the old local and national seclusion and self-sufficiency, we have intercourse in every direction, universal interdependence of nations. And as in material, so also in intellectual production. The intellectual creations of individual nations become common property. National one-sidedness and narrow-mindedness become more and more impossible, and from the numerous national and local literatures, there arises a world literature. (Marx and Engels 1888, 476–477)

What Marx and Engels describe here is precisely the globalization of capital by the bourgeoisie. While perhaps hyperbolic—the idea that there is "universal inter-dependence of nations" sounds exaggerated even today—the basic description is apt. As much of the bourgeoisie was chased around the world by the profit motive, the production and consumption of both material and cultural goods—everything from food to literature—became, to a significant and unprecedented extent, globalized.

Of course, this was not entirely new. Cross-border or -frontier exchanges have always been a part of human history, and indeed, commerce precedes the entire state system. Yet such interactions undoubtedly reached new heights with capitalism's conversion into a virtually worldwide economic system.

It is here that the contemporary literature on the global capitalist class enters the conversation and that we see both Marx's influences and emerging disjunctures between Marx and contemporary theorists. Like the latter, Marx and Engels also theorized capitalism as a system that encompassed "the whole surface of the globe." Yet from the perspective of the global capitalism school, today's capitalist system is global in a different—and more profound—respect.

Further, the global capitalist class is not precisely Marx's bourgeoisie, though it is its modern-day personification. It embodies, according to the strongest statements of this position, the dominant fraction among the capitalist class. As explored in the following section, what separates the capitalism and capitalists of Marx from those of Robinson, Sklair, and fellow travelers is precisely the concept of transnationalism, which, somewhat confusingly, invokes the rise of a *global* economy.

Transnationalism: From a World Economy to a Global Economy

As a definitive marker of the zeitgeist of the past two decades, few terms have become more stubbornly lodged in contemporary discourse—both lay and scholarly—than *globalization*. Such was the deluge, particularly in the pre-Trump era, that it became customary for works on the topic to be prefaced with apologies. Capturing the prevailing mood, one scholar introduced his own contribution by noting, "Not another book on globalization! . . . Has this hype-propelled bandwagon not already slaughtered too many trees?" (Scholte 2005).

In turn, critics have pointed to a lack of conceptual clarity in the very term *globalization*, questioned whether it represents anything new, and challenged the often-hyperbolic ideas espoused particularly, but not exclusively, in earlier works (for skeptical voices, see, *inter alia*, Hirst et al. 2009 and Rosenberg 2000).

This latter category of apparent hyperbole includes Thomas Friedman's (2005) argument that the spread of capitalism was ironing out global inequalities; Ronnie Lipschutz's (2000, 5) declaration of something approaching "the 'end' of authority, sovereignty, and national security at the conclusion of the twentieth century"; Arjun Appadurai's (1996, 21–22) contention that "the nation-state" is entering "a terminal crisis," with "diasporic public spheres" serving as "the crucibles of a postnational political order"; and futurist Parag Khanna's (2016) vision of a "new world order" that is "ruled by global corporations and megacities," peopled by "individuals for whom geographical roots are secondary to connectedness and access" and where passports based on "national identity" have been replaced with those linked to "individual credentials."

In response to the overall tenor of this literature, Justin Rosenberg (2005; 2007) went so far as to forsake use of the term *globalization* and perform a "post-mortem" on "globalization theory." On the other hand, even International Relations realists such as the late Robert Gilpin (2001, 362)—representing a school of thought that is heavily invested in the notion of a state-centric world—have acknowledged that, "at the beginning of the twenty-first century, the nation-state is clearly under serious attack from both above and below."

Key theorists within the global capitalism school have a particular interest in these debates about what defines contemporary globalization and how to situate it vis-à-vis previous ages. As they argue, globalization—understood in terms of the spread of capitalist relations—is both old and new. It is old in that capitalism, per Marx and Engel's description, for centuries has been the impetus for ever-increasing economic exchange between far-flung peoples, states, and regions. Yet it is new in that, unlike the capitalism of their day, it is now fundamentally a *transnational* system.

For example, Robinson (2008, 2, 6) elaborates his well-known "theory of global capitalism" based on the premise that we have entered a "qualitatively new stage in the history of world capitalism," representing "the near-culmination of the 500-year process of the spread of the capitalist system around the world." He points to two key features of this epoch. First, virtually everything has been (or is in the process of being) commodified, meaning that capitalist relations have significantly deepened their reach. And second, particularly after the incorporation in the early 1990s of the former Soviet Bloc and "Third World revolutionary" states such as Vietnam, the capitalist system has been "enlarged" to the extent that no significant geographical space exists outside of its confines (Robinson 2008, 6–7)—nor, as he argues, can it (Robinson 2014, 2).

From this perspective, the point is not that literally all economic relations in the world have been subjected to a capitalist logic. Rather, it is that "there is no longer anything external to the system . . . in that (1) there are no longer any countries or regions that remain outside of world capitalism or still to be incorporated through original accumulation and (2) there is no longer autonomous accumulation outside of the sphere of global capital" (Robinson 2008, 7). It is in this sense that capitalism, as the argument goes, has reached its "global moment" (Robinson 2008, 7). In sum, per Michael Hardt and Antonio Negri (2000, 8), the kind of capitalism that has emerged in recent years represents a "fundamentally new situation and a significant historical shift."

The immediate origins of this new global capitalism date back to the 1970s and the culmination of a crisis in the previous order of Keynesian (or national corporate) capitalism. This was felt in terms of a global recession, rising unemployment, stagflation, and so on (Robinson 2008, 13).

Yet a more thorough understanding requires that we go back further, as the preceding decades had also borne witness to another kind of crisis. In short, this earlier era marked an ideological crisis for the capitalist class, as increasing mobilization by the working class and popular sectors had led to the achievement of concrete improvements in their socioeconomic conditions and the constraining of capital's ability to fulfill its structurally determined end of profit seeking. As Robinson (2008, 13) notes in this regard, during the middle of the twentieth century, "organized labor, increased taxes on profits and income, state regulation, revolutions in the Third World, and the explosion of social movements and counter-hegemonic cultural practices everywhere constricted private capital's real or perceived capacity for accumulation." From the perspective of the capitalist class, these impediments could only be tolerated as long as structural constraints, and the "relative strength" of popular mobilization, prevented their undoing (Robinson 2008, 13).

The 1970s crisis in the Keynesian order provided just such an opportunity. As popularized by Naomi Klein (2008) in *The Shock Doctrine*, the logic of crises as opportunities is by now well known. The premise is clear and mirrors the political practice of the "state of exception" (Kapoor 2018). What cannot easily be achieved in normal times—such as initial neoliberal reforms in Latin America—is forced onto the agenda during (real or perceived) crises, when powerful interests are able to assert themselves in ways that previous constraints would not allow. So it was with the crisis in Keynesianism.

As Robinson (2008, 9–15) argues, during this crisis the capitalist class sought to overturn the legal, social, ideological, and cultural barriers to continued capital accumulation by "go[ing] global." Its success, in turn, "allowed capital to shake off the constraints that nation-state capitalism had placed on accumulation and to break free of the class compromises and concessions that had been imposed by working and popular classes and by national governments in the preceding epoch" (Robinson 2008, 15).

Capital, then, used this opportunity to shed its *national* character for a *transnational* one. In so doing, it has aimed to limit (though, as explored in chap. 5, not with unqualified success) the ability of its home state to impose regulations or progressive legislation (such as higher taxation to support social welfare programs). The obvious reason is that capital is now able to cross borders with relative ease and shift its operations to locales where costs are lower, workers are more pliant or easily repressed, and unfavorable regulatory frameworks are virtually nonexistent.

The policy vehicle for capitalism's global push is neoliberalism, the aim of which is to use state-based and other forms of power to suppress obstacles—whether in the form of environmental regulations, collective bargaining rights, or progressive taxation structures—that inhibit profit seeking (Slobodian 2018). In this vein, neoliberalism refers to a post-Keynesian *"political project"* to make the world safe (again) for capital accumulation and return the capitalist class to an indisputably hegemonic position through radical market reforms such as privatization, corporate-friendly regulations, and the flexibilization of labor (Harvey 2007, 19; emphasis in original).

In Robinson's (2008, 19) framing, the goal of the capitalist class in enacting neoliberal reforms is "to open up every country to its activities, to tear down all barriers to the movement of goods and capital, and to create a single unified field in which global capital can operate unhindered across all national borders." As governmental power is essential for the implementation of this agenda, it is wrong to assert that the state is now irrelevant. Instead, the state has been reconstituted as a vessel for the neoliberal agenda of promoting capitalist globalization (Robinson 2014, 10; Sklair 2017).

From a more Foucauldian perspective, the state has also come to play an increasing role in generating a neoliberal "governing rationality," the aim of which is no less than to reconstitute human beings as entrepreneurial agents and transform citizens into consumers (Brown 2015; Moulián 2014). As Thatcher once famously put it, "There is no society, only the individual"—and, more specifically, a particular kind of hyper-rational (in the vein of rational choice theory), socially detached, alienated, and isolated individual, whose chief aim in life is the pursuit of material gains (Robinson 2008, 17).

Recent scholarship has pointed to diverse sites of origin linked to neoliberalism's rise, including a globally minded Geneva School (centered around Ludwig von Mises, Friedrich Hayek, and fellow travelers) (Slobodian 2018), a Virginia School (led by US economist and public choice theorist James M. Buchanan) (MacLean 2017), and the better known Chicago School. Regarding the latter, standard accounts have long held that global neoliberal restructuring began in earnest following the coup against the democratically elected socialist president of Chile, Salvador Allende, in 1973. During much of the subsequent Augusto Pinochet dictatorship, which ruled until 1990, the country served as a petri dish for radical experimentation by the Hayek- and Milton Friedman–inspired Chicago Boy economists, who sought to create a model (and authoritarian) neoliberal state (Robinson 2008, 21; Valdés 2008). From there, of course, neoliberalism would spread not only across the region, but throughout the world. Importantly, this South-North diffusion demonstrates, according to David Harvey (2007, 9), how a "brutal experiment . . . in the periphery" can become "a model for the formulation of policies in the centre."

The argument that today's neoliberal order represents a new capitalist epoch relies on Robinson's distinction "between a *world economy* (in which nation-states are linked to each other via trade and financial flows) . . . [and] a *global economy* (in which the production process itself becomes globally integrated)" (2008, 25, 27; emphasis in original). That is, whereas the previous world economy was characterized by interactions between distinct national economies (e.g., US companies owned by US investors producing for international markets), in the current global economy, service and production chains are increasingly transnational in the sense that they bind together capitalists without regard to national boundaries. Thus, thinking in terms of global capitalist relations instead of nation-state relations requires the realization that "when copper goes from Chile to China or oil from Venezuela to China it goes to feed not 'Chinese' capitalism but global capitalism in China, to fuel transnational accumulation taking place in Chinese territory" (Robinson 2008, 200).

None of this, of course, suggests the end of intra-capitalist competition. Rather, it is argued that capitalists compete—or collaborate—based on their positions in globe-spanning accumulation chains. Largely gone are the days when capitalist competition occurs on the basis of national boundaries (though with the benefit of the hindsight offered by the Trump years, Robinson [2014, 11] perhaps spoke too soon when he observed that "inter-imperialist rivalry" and "protectionism" were merely relics of a past, state-based era).

Such a globally integrated capitalist economy is precisely the world order that neoliberal "globalists" had long predicted, posited, and sought to concretize—that is, specifically, one in which it would be impossible for, say, a Brazilian to speak of *our* soybean or automotive industry, as "political citizenship" would be fully decoupled from any notion of national "economic ownership" (Slobodian 2018, 102). By implication, this new reality represents nothing less than the end of what is commonly understood to be the modern world order, in which the conventional unit of analysis is the sovereign state.

Rothkopf (2008, 11) makes broadly the same point, noting that while elite connections across national borders used to take the form of "discrete alliances between sovereigns," what is occurring now is that "a new community has been forming, at the same time that economies are spilling across borders, global entities are proliferating, and the world is, well, flattening." Such a state of affairs also evokes the long-standing neoliberal predilection, already partially realized, for limiting state sovereignty by creating an "invisible" underlying global structural arrangement that would prevent disruptions to cross-border capital flows and property ownership (Slobodian 2018).

The distinction between a *world* and a *global* economy is important, for it delineates what is purportedly new about today's capitalist system.[1] It also helps to clarify some of the recurring conceptual murkiness in the field of global political economy. As Sklair (2001, 2) correctly observes, "For many writers the terms international, transnational, and global are used interchangeably, but this can be confusing." What distinguishes the global for Sklair (2001, 3) is that it refers to an ideal type of a perfectly globalized world—one characterized by "a borderless global economy, the complete denationalization of all corporate procedures and activities, and the eradication of nationalism." Coupled with an "economic constitution" that would protect property rights and ensure capital mobility across borders, this is precisely the utopian order that was posited by some of the Geneva School neoliberals (Slobodian 2018).

In reality, of course, both neoliberal intellectuals and capitalist elites have been forced to navigate a political context that includes at least the remnants of the preexisting territorially based system. It is thus more accurate to provide the disclaimer that "the *global* is the goal, while the *transnational*, transcending nation-states in an international system in some respects but still having to cope with them in others, is the reality" (Sklair 2001, 3; emphasis in original). Along these lines, Sklair (2001, 3) argues that it is "to the extent that private rather than national interests prevail across borders" that we may reasonably refer to the shift from a *world* to a *global* capitalist system.

To clarify, he seemingly must be referring not precisely to a shift from *national* to *private* interests—the latter have of course long been of importance—but from *national* (capitalist) to *global* (capitalist) ones (that is, from a world of national economies to one where production, service, and accumulation chains are organized globally). The argument of the global capitalism school is that this transformation has occurred or is at least in the process of occurring.

Yet despite this admirable effort to clearly distinguish between oft-conflated terms, in practice greater precision is still needed. Literature in the global capitalism school almost invariably refers to a *transnational*—instead of a *global*—capitalist class, even though what is being invoked appears closer to the latter concept as opposed to the former. Indeed, if we are referring to a class with an "identity in the global system above any local territories and polities," as Robinson (2004, 47) again puts it, then this would seem to suggest a global capitalist class, not the transnational one to which he refers. Accordingly, I favor utilization of the term *global capitalist class* here, though throughout I reproduce authors' use of *transnational* where relevant.

Unfortunately, there is also a recurring tendency in these writings to vacillate between the use of *global* and *transnational* without clearly explaining the motives for doing so. For example, in the above-cited quote, it is unclear why Robinson simultaneously refers to (and appears to equate) "global capitalism in China" and "transnational accumulation taking place in Chinese territory" or why he simultaneously argues that "subordinate classes" are also "transnationalizing" and that "capital and labor increasingly confront each other as global classes" (Robinson 2008, 29).

A further example is Sklair's (2016, 332) identification of "the [transnational capitalist class] as a global class." See also, as cited later in this chapter, Robert Cox's (1981, 147) reference to a "transnational managerial class" positioned on top of "an emerging global class structure." If, as Sklair (2013, 89) explains, "Economic transnational practices are economic practices that transcend state boundaries," then how are they different from "economic *global* practices"?

Again, common to this literature is the notion that this class's members share a positive identification with fellow elites from across the globe and an ideological commitment to capitalist globalization that goes beyond parochial concerns with profits or territorially based accumulation. Accordingly, for the sake of analytical precision we should follow Saskia Sassen's lead and refer to this would-be group as a *global* instead of *transnational* capitalist class.

Indeed, the concept of transnationalism does not typically suggest a lack of territoriality. Rather, it refers, again, to concurrent attachments to multiple places. In turn, the rather voluminous literature on transnational migrant communities does not make the claim that place is irrelevant entirely or that the global has overtaken the local, as discussed in the introduction.

Further conceptual clarity is thus needed in studies regarding global class formation. For the purposes of the present work, I thus deploy key terms related to place-based and placeless subjectivities as follows:

- *NATIONAL*: An actor who is rooted in only one place-based imaginary (e.g., a particular state or perhaps ethnic, cultural, or people group). As observed in chapter 3, interviewees who boast of their country as "the future of the world" and repeatedly use *we* to refer to their own nation likely fit in this category.
- *TRANSNATIONAL*: A place-based concept, like the previous, but one in which dual (or potentially multiple) national imaginaries coexist. Such figures are thus also in a sense national but differ from the above in that they are simultaneously embedded in two (or more) national communities. As has been said regarding transnational migrants and immigrants, "Their lives cut across national boundaries and bring two societies into a single social field" (Glick Schiller et al. 1992, 1). When a Lebanese-Argentine interviewee spontaneously delivers a monologue about the exceptionalism and superiority of both Argentina *and* Lebanon vis-à-vis their regional peers, this is a clear example of a transnational imaginary.
- *DENATIONAL*: An interpretive framework in which national/place-based attachments have been displaced and do not—or no longer—orient to any meaningful extent an actor's behavior. In other words, what sets the denational apart from the national or transnational is that it lacks national anchors. Interviewees who speak of pursuing deals and opportunities without any signs of devotion toward particular countries, ethnic groups, and so on display a denational identity—that is, one with no (or relatively few) "national attachments or needs" (Sassen 2007, 187).
- *GLOBAL*: A mental framework characterized by two components: first, a positive identification with a nonterritorial peer group (in the present context, fellow capitalist elites from across the globe); and second, an ideological commitment to globalization—understood here as the spread of the global capitalist system into the world's every nook and cranny—that goes beyond merely seeking profit.

> In other words, these are actors who see their border-crossing economic activities as advancing a global (as opposed to place-based, whether national or otherwise) capitalist agenda. Thus, interviewees who identify with a borderless imagined community and who view their economic activities as contributing to the viability, strengthening, and spread of a worldwide capitalist system belong to the global capitalist class.

For the sake of clarity, it is worth noting that a *denational* capitalist may be (but is not necessarily) a global one. As explored in chapter 4, there are indeed actors for whom place-based identities have been decentered without any apparent concomitant rise in global attachments. This is a crucial distinction. The fact that it is often overlooked in much of the literature appears to lead to an overidentification of capitalist elites as *global* when *denational* may be a more appropriate term.

As is the case with any categorization scheme, these are ideal-type, overly neat definitions that are meant to facilitate the task of generalizing from the particular. Of course, human identities, in reality, are messy, multiple, intersecting, and more reminiscent of continuums than binaries. The point of the present analysis is to embrace, rather than seek to bracket or discipline, this complexity.

An Imagined Community of Global Capitalists

If there has been an epochal shift from a world to a global capitalist economy, then so too must there be change in the overall class structure.

Direct references to a globalizing capitalist elite go as far back as the early 1970s, when economists such as Stephen Hymer began to theorize an "international capitalist class," one "whose interests lie in the world economy as a whole" (quoted in Robinson 2004, 35). This idea continued to develop with the passing of time and the further globalization of capitalism.

A decade later, Cox (1981, 147) again referred to a "transnational managerial class" that is "at the apex of an emerging global class structure." He argued in unequivocal terms: "Having its own ideology, strategy and institutions of collective action, it is both a class in itself and for itself" (Cox 1981, 147). Elsewhere, he noted that this class has a "distinctive class consciousness" (quoted in Budd 2013, 67). His fellow Gramscian political economist Stephen Gill, writing in 1990, also invoked a "developing transnational capitalist class" (quoted in Sklair 2001, 16).

The same basic notion—though not without variations—has been espoused by and gained currency among many critically minded scholars of global political economy from a variety of disciplines (in addition to those already cited, see, for example, Carroll 2010, Harris 2016, and Rupert and Solomon 2006). Though the language is different and they are less interested in the question of global class formation, a similar understanding of contemporary capitalist elites logically follows from Hardt and Negri's (2000) delineation of today's unbounded and deterritorialized global-capitalist empire.

One can also read the idea of a global capitalist class into Wendy Brown's (2010, 64–65) description of capital as an "emerging *global* sovereign." As she writes:

> Capital alone appears perpetual and absolute, increasingly unaccountable and primordial, the source of all commands, yet beyond the reach of the *nomos*. Capital produces life absent provisions of protection and ties of membership, turning populations around the world into *homo sacer*. Yet capital also links the diverse peoples and cultures of the world, supplanting other forms of association with its own. Capital creates the conditions (or their absence) for all sentient life while being fully accountable to no political sovereign. Capital mocks efforts by national and subnational communities to contour their ways of life or to direct their own fates, making such efforts appear similar to those of feudal fiefdoms at the dawn of modernity.

Naturally, such a capitalist system, operating as a "would-be global sovereign" and creating novel "forms of association" (Brown 2010, 65), must presumably be dominated by a similarly unmoored global capitalist elite. However, like Hardt and Negri, she does not pursue the point.

This line of theorizing has also spawned a relatively small number of more empirical works related to global class formation, such as Monica R. Biradavolu's (2008) *Indian Entrepreneurs in Silicon Valley: The Making of a Transnational Techno-Capitalist Class*. Additional writings have sought to analyze the extent to which one can speak of a global middle or working class (Koo 2016; Ness 2016; regarding the latter group, see also Robinson 2014, 48–51).

Almost entirely separately, a large and influential body of literature organized around the concept of transnationalism has blossomed in recent decades, focusing mostly on questions relating to culture and identity (Basch et al. 2003; Glick Schiller et al. 1992; Kearney 1995; Levitt 2001). Among the contributions of this paradigm has been to demonstrate the extent to which *methodological nationalism*—that is, the intellectual tendency to privilege the national as "the natural social and political form of the modern world"—has constrained our understanding of cross-border dynamics (Wimmer and Glick Schiller 2002, 301).

However, writings on transnationalism have generally not explicitly considered whether the political economy of globalization may be inducing economic elites to develop a corresponding identity that is truly global instead of transnational (for example, simultaneously Arab *and* Latin American). To be sure, some works in this area do helpfully interrogate how neoliberalism and capitalist globalization are producing new forms of transnational or even "flexible" identities (Karam 2007; Ong 1999). There is also a general recognition that transnationalism itself is "a product of world capitalism" (Glick Schiller et al. 1992, 8). However, despite the intellectual similarities, the transnational canon as a whole does not dwell on the question of whether the interpretive horizons of such populations are increasingly dominated by a global class consciousness.

What, then, defines this purported global capitalist class? What makes it a global class and not the national bourgeoisie of Marx's description? Let us consider the two most invoked definitions, both of which largely dovetail with Huntington's Davos Men. Though these refer to transnational capitalists, for consistency's sake, this would-be group is again in fact much closer to comprising a global capitalist class.

For Sklair (2001, 295), the essence of transnational capitalists is that "they operate across state borders to further the interests of global capital rather than of any real or imagined nation-state" (or, we might add, of their compatriot capitalists). Elsewhere, he observes that a newly ascendant transnational capitalist class has begun "to act as a global ruling class in some spheres" (Sklair 2016, 330). In turn, Robinson (2004, 47–48) argues that the transnational capitalist class can again be "distinguish[ed] . . . from national or local capitalists in that it is involved in globalized production and manages globalized circuits of accumulation, which gives it, spatially and politically, an objective class existence and identity in the global system above any local territories and polities."

To be sure, according to this school of thought, some declining number of place-based—that is, local and national—capitalists will continue to exist for some time. However, the structural imperative to "globalize or perish" will eventually force them to shed their territorial baggage and develop cross-border accumulation strategies (Robinson 2008, 29–30). Per Robinson's (2004, 48) analysis, this process has already advanced to the extent that the transnational capitalist class now represents "the new ruling class worldwide" and "is at the apex of the global economy, exercises authority over global institutions, and controls the levers of global policymaking."

At the most basic level, two characteristics thus capture the essence of these figures. First, in material terms, they are the protagonists in a globally organized capitalist system that supersedes and is rendering—or perhaps has already rendered—obsolete the demarcation of political-economic space based on state borders. Precisely this dynamic is evident, again, vis-à-vis the proliferation of globally organized production and accumulation chains, as well as globally integrated corporate ownership structures.

This is the "objective class existence" to which Robinson refers. In this sense, to return to Marx, today's "new ruling class" comprises a class in itself—that is, its members "objectively share a similar position in the economic structure of society independent of the degree to which they are aware of their collective condition or to which they consciously act on the basis of this condition" (Robinson 2004, 38).

Second, they do not identify with "any real or imagined nation-state" or feel national loyalty (Sklair 2001, 295). Instead, they share an identity based on their common global class status. In other words, they identify not with the state (or any other place-based community), but with their (global) class. On a subjective level, they perceive themselves as global capitalists (this, unlike workers, who are said to largely remain beholden to place-based imaginaries [Robinson 2004, 43]).

Per Marx, they are also then a class for itself—a class whose "members are conscious of constituting a particular group with shared interests and would be expected to act collectively in pursuit of those interests" (Robinson 2004, 38). Thus, they form an "imagined community" of global capitalists (van der Pijl 1998). While Marx did not presume that capitalism's global spread would provoke the decline of territorially defined accumulation chains and bourgeois identities, this is precisely the (novel) argument of the global capitalism school (Carroll 2010, 1).

To demonstrate the veracity of the former assertion—that global capitalists have an "objective class existence" in tangible, material terms—scholars have proposed and analyzed a number of proxies for the existence of a transnational, globalizing, or global capitalist economy. These include the increasing percentages of "imported content" in finished goods, which suggest the transnationalization of production (Rupert and Solomon 2006, 43); the extent to which the ownership and management of a given corporation is composed of individuals from a variety of nationalities (Sklair

2001); and the existence of "overlapping elite affiliations of corporate directors," which are said to create a transnational capitalist network (Carroll 2010, 7). For its part, the UN Conference on Trade and Development (UNCTAD) compiles a Transnationality Index, which measures the foreign-domestic ratios of the assets, sales, and employment of transnational corporations (TNCs) (Carroll 2010, 91). Studies in this area have tended to confirm the hypothesis of a global capitalist class.

Yet the corroborating material provided in these works falls short of justifying the rather bold aforementioned claims concerning this class's purported existence or global hegemony. Indeed, as acknowledged by Carroll (2010, 19, 37), there is universal agreement from all involved that more "direct evidence" is necessary. He is also right to note that proving that this class is real is no simple endeavor.

However, as most scholarship on this topic has been written by proponents of such ideas, these claims have not been subjected to sufficient scrutiny. Further, these existing works tend to suffer from methodological limitations and advance arguments through anecdotes instead of systematic analysis. As Carroll (2010, 2) notes, "Like Sklair's, William Robinson's prodigious writings on the ascendance of a transnational capitalist class rely primarily on aggregated statistical evidence, supplemented by citation of instances of transnational corporate mergers and quotation of corporate CEOs, rather than on sociological analysis of class organization."

One of the few outsider perspectives comes from Sassen (2007, 169), who argues that would-be global classes in fact remain "embedded, in often unexpected ways, in thick localized environments." She thus prefers to refer to these as "partially denationalized" instead of "global" classes while acknowledging that this "incipient globality" is nevertheless salient and worthy of further investigation (Sasssen 2007, 169–170).

Adrian Budd (2013, 145–146) helpfully engages with this issue at much greater length, concluding that while the evidence in favor of the transnationalization thesis "is, at least superficially, compelling," it is ultimately "a one-sided account that glosses over the capitalist world system's unevenness and contradictions" and overlooks the ongoing relevance of "state power" in the global economy (though for their part, Robinson and Sklair do again acknowledge that neoliberalism is not erasing the state, but rather reconfiguring it). Leo Panitch and Sam Gindin (2012, 11) present a similarly skeptical rejoinder to the notion that global capitalism's rise has "spawn[ed] a 'transnational capitalist class,' loosened from any state moorings." Indeed, their account demonstrates the opposite: that the state, contrary to neoliberal rhetoric, has been essential for the advent, deepening, and maintenance of global capitalism (and, we might add, for the very process of inchoate global class formation).

For his part, Harvey (2007, 35) also acknowledges the continuing relevance of states in a globalizing world, observing that "There has undoubtedly been a deepening as well as a widening of these transnational connections during the phase of neoliberal globalization.... This does not mean, however, that the leading individuals within this class do not attach themselves to specific state apparatuses for both the advantages and the protections that this affords them." Others, such as economist Ha-Joon Chang, have cast doubt on the extent to which corporate administrative structures have become globally diversified or, in turn, nurtured the formation of a global capitalist class. Questioning the idea of corporate mobility—which is central to the neoliberal utopia—he concludes that "the nationality of the firm still matters very much" (Chang 2009, 97–98). Accordingly, available evidence suggests sympathy for these more cautious (but far from dismissive) positions concerning the material existence of a global capitalist class.

What about, in turn, the central issue of concern here—that is, the ideational and subjective basis of this would-be class? Does it have a global identity, consciousness, and sense of self? This, as noted, is the second pillar of the global capitalist class—that its members form a class for itself and possess a global capitalist class consciousness.

Robinson (2004, 48) is particularly clear on this point, arguing that these actors are "class conscious" and have "become conscious of [their] transnationality," though he also dithers. In the very next paragraph, he refers to transnational capitalists as "increasingly" constituting a class in and for itself, suggesting more of a process than a fait accompli (see also Robinson 2014, 51).

Elsewhere, and more confusingly, he suggests that they are not defined by a "global perspective" at all (Robinson 2014, 26). Several pages later within the same text, however, he approvingly cites evidence in favor of capitalist elites having developed precisely such a global consciousness and largely shed their "national and other identities" and axes of belonging (Robinson 2014, 35). As he puts it: "We can identify an increasing social and cultural cohesion of the [transnational capitalist class] alongside its political identity," though this—as he notes correctly—may take "many generations" (Robinson 2014, 45).

Yet the evidence that this class exists subjectively is even weaker than the case for its objective, material existence. In fact, Sklair appears to be the only thinker in this tradition to have engaged in significant depth with this question. As a result, as Alexander Anievas (2008, 198) argues, the notion of a "globally hegemonic [capitalist] class-for-itself" is "conceptually abstract, with little concrete empirical foundation."

Pointing specifically to Robinson's work, Anievas (2008, 198) suggests that the global capitalist class framework renders us unable to countenance the extent to which capital accumulation may, in fact, follow a "territorialising logic." Accordingly, it disregards the new capitalist spatial dynamics embodied, for example, by the rise of networks of "global cities" and "transnational urban systems" (Carroll 2010, 4; Sassen 1991). There is, after all, a geographic dimension to capital's distribution, as well as an incentive, at least in certain cases, for its concentration (Harvey 2006). This is particularly evident regarding "agglomeration economies" such as Silicon Valley (O'Mara 2019). Also of relevance is the dramatic extent to which built spaces, especially within particular "superstar" cities, have been central to contemporary accumulation strategies (Atkinson 2019; Stein 2019). Further, the argument for placelessness neglects to take into account the extent to which class dynamics vary from place to place based on the particulars of local or regional accumulation processes. Accordingly, what Anievas (2008, 198) refers to as "the global reproduction of class antagonisms" may take different forms in different spaces.

It is thus reasonable to expect that, say, Latin American capitalists may not pass through precisely the same process of consciousness formation as their counterparts across the globe. Potentially relevant factors that may set them apart include their concentration in certain industries (such as food or raw materials), their domestic and international environments (including the strength [or weakness] of working-class movements in and the foreign policies of their home countries), their Global South provenance (which means that they may be affected and conditioned by various colonial and imperial legacies and present-day practices), and, perhaps, the existence of a distinct "variety of capitalism" in the region (Schneider 2013).

It may also be that race and other axes of identity and oppression—which have been almost completely overlooked in the literature on the global capitalist class—play a differentiating role in the cultivation of elite identities. Helpfully, at least one existing work examines this class's use of race to further its aims (Patterson 2013). However, there do not seem to be any existing works that interrogate issues of race, ethnicity, or national origin *within* this class. These are potentially troubling lacunae. For example, as prominent Brazilian economist and former finance minister Luiz Carlos Bresser-Pereira (2015, 12) has observed on the question of North-South differences, elites from the developing world, and particularly Latin America, differ from their counterparts in that they "suffer to varying degrees from cultural and political alienation." Especially noteworthy in this regard is a seemingly permanent angst among postcolonial elites over being accepted by their Northern peers as fully "modern" (Carvalho 2013; Mignolo 2005).

More broadly, the history and pedigree of global capitalism of course matters. We should thus not be surprised if the fact that this system was "founded on US capitalism's great economic strength and centered on the capacities of the American state," per Panitch and Gindin's (2012, 331) framing, means that it takes different forms around the globe. Simply put, capitalism in the US does not look precisely the same as capitalism in Brazil. As Vivek Chibber (2013b, 285) argues, while capitalism is a "universalizing" force, it "is not only consistent with great heterogeneity and hierarchy, but systematically generates them." Indeed, to borrow from Leon Trotsky, capitalist "development" around the world is "combined" (that is, related), but it is also "uneven" (Callinicos and Rosenberg 2008). In Chibber's (2013b, 285) framing, global capitalism is thus "perfectly compatible" with rather heterogeneous political and cultural realities. These may include, of course, elite identities.

As noted, Sassen (2007, 169) shares this skeptical reading of the class-for-itself argument, referring instead to the embeddedness of these actors in "thick localized environments." Though she acknowledges "the weakening of the exclusive objective and subjective authority of national states over people, their imaginaries, and their sense of where they belong," she also notes that would-be global classes "have a strong insertion into territorially bounded contexts—global cities and national governments" (Sassen 2007, 170, 187). This cuts against the assertion that there are "free-floating cosmopolitan classes with no national attachments or needs" (Sassen 2007, 187). Nevertheless, she argues that there is a trend in the direction of global consciousness formation and that this "incipient globality does make a difference" (Sassen 2007, 170).

Among extant studies, Sklair again takes us the furthest toward demonstrating the subjective existence of a transnational (that is, global) capitalist class. His approach is to conduct interviews with business leaders "to discover the use and meaning of the term globalization (if any) in companies' corporate vocabularies and how these relate to corporate practices" (Sklair 2001, 47). Thus, as is appropriate, he seeks to link class consciousness with material acts. Yet while he invokes and aims to provide evidence for "the material and ideological basis for transnational class formation," his account—particularly of the latter—is ultimately insufficient (Sklair 2001, 49).

Typical is the response he reports from a senior Hewlett-Packard executive, who declares the company to be "globally-minded" (Sklair 2001, 68). While Sklair takes this as unambiguous evidence in support of his hypothesis concerning the existence of a global capitalist class, it is unclear what *globally minded* means, if its use here coincides with Sklair's own understanding and presentation of its meaning, and whether the mere assertion that a corporation has a global mindset should lead us to accept his argument for this class's existence. In sum, Sklair's analysis of these interviews, while interesting, does not allow us to reach a clear conclusion about whether a global capitalist class exists in ideational terms.

Two further maladies afflict the arguments of the global capitalism school in relation to this topic. First, there is an underlying—and unstated—assumption that the material existence of a global capitalist class mechanically implies that it both exists subjectively and engages in purposive action on that basis. Along with the fact that identifying a global capitalist class consciousness presents immediate and serious methodological difficulties, this may explain the relative focus in these writings on the material instead of the subjective side of the argument, as the latter component is assumed, it seems, to hinge entirely on the former.

For example, Robinson's (2008, 31) arguments on the transnational capitalist class as "a class group with subjective consciousness of itself and its interests" and whose members "have developed a transnational class consciousness" are mostly anecdotal in nature. He cites Rothkopf, who comments, "Business leaders in Buenos Aires, Frankfurt, Hong Kong, Johannesburg, Istanbul, Los Angeles, Mexico City, Moscow, New Delhi, New York, Paris, Rome, Santiago, Seoul, Singapore, Tel Aviv, and Tokyo all read the same newspapers, wear the same suits, drive the same cars, eat the same food, fly the same airlines, stay in the same hotels, and listen to the same music" (quoted in Robinson 2008, 31). Similarly, Sklair (2001, 20–21) adds that among the lifestyle similarities within this class are a convergence in educational patterns (especially in terms of attending particular business schools), favored vacation destinations, a primary residence in exclusive gated (and segregated) communities, and a global (as opposed to local) outlook on political, economic, and cultural issues.

Yet despite their assertions, it is unclear what this all suggests about the notion of a shared global capitalist class consciousness (Gustafson 2009). It may be true that capitalist elites the world over read the same newspapers and fly the same airlines (though Robinson does not provide evidence for these claims). However, what is argued to be the *objectively* global nature of this class does not necessarily mean that its *subjective* outlook is global as opposed to national, transnational, regional, local, ethnic, a mixture of some or all of the preceding, or something else entirely.

As Benedict Anderson (2006, 51–52) argues in *Imagined Communities*, newspapers help explain the rise of nationalism and "why entities like Chile, Venezuela, and Mexico turned out to be emotionally plausible and politically viable." But not everyone who reads the same newspaper develops the same consciousness and loyalties. Again, we cannot merely assume that objective structural forces will universally condition thought in predetermined ways. Aida Hozić (2014, 237) frames the issue well, noting that the "circulation of goods alone may not be sufficient to transform political horizons as long as the institutions and interpretative frameworks through which they are filtered remain the same." Long ago, as discussed later in this chapter, Marx also (at least implicitly) recognized the difference between a class *in* itself and a class *for* itself. This link between the material and ideational existence of the would-be global capitalist class thus needs to be carefully analyzed, not presumed.

Second, there is a lack of clarity in this literature concerning the purported global consciousness of this class. As noted, for a global capitalist class to exist in ideational terms, we should expect its members to have a shared identity based around their global class status. This is to supersede feelings of national loyalty and attachments to "any real or imagined nation-state" or nationally organized class (Sklair 2001, 295).

Yet the (scant) arguments on this topic tend to conflate cosmopolitanism with profit seeking. Sklair (2001, 49), for example, asserts that "the class interest of the [transnational capitalist class] is transnational in character," and that "it is not necessarily connected with the specific sites where it does business and certainly not identical with the national interests of the states in which these sites are located." While the first part of this assertion appears more or less reasonable (with the caveat that the phrase "not necessarily" allows for the possibility of a place-based logic), the last portion in particular sets too low of a bar for the argument concerning a transnational (or global) capitalist class, as what Sklair describes does not appear to differ in a meaningful way from Marx's or even Smith's bourgeoisie. It is simply not the case that the interests of merchants and other capitalist groups were previously—or have ever been—truly "identical with the national interests" of their home states or other delimited territories. As Harvey (2007, 35) helpfully notes, "The case that the ruling class anywhere has ever confined its operations and defined its loyalties to any one nation-state has historically been much overstated."

Capitalists, after all, are interested in profits. This is their structurally determined raison d'être. It is what motivates them, again, to "nestle everywhere, settle everywhere, [and] establish connexions everywhere" (Marx and Engels 1888, 476). This does not mean that they lack other interests or motivations. It is merely the behavior that the capitalist system produces. It is for this reason that Smith again refers to "the proprietor of stock" as "properly a citizen of the world" who "is not necessarily attached to any particular country" (quoted in Huntington 2004).

But having international, transnational, or global interests based on the desire for profit does not equate to a global consciousness. Globality requires a shared global identity, not merely a shared global drive to maximize capital accumulation. If the latter is the standard for establishing the existence of a global capitalist class, then it does not take us far beyond Marx and Smith. This is a feature of *international* capital in general and says little that is new about *global* capital. If the standard is again "the extent that private rather than national interests prevail across borders," then Sklair (2001, 3) and others are really only testing whether these individuals are internationally oriented capitalists, not *global* capitalists.

As he argues elsewhere, "the [transnational capitalist class] increasingly conceptualizes its interests in terms of markets, which may or may not coincide with a specific nation-state, and the global market, which clearly does not" (Sklair 2016, 332). Yet this formulation holds true for the latter, but not the former. While identification with a global market would indeed provide some evidence for the existence of a globally minded capitalist class, generic interests in markets *do not*. This only makes them capitalists, not necessarily *global* capitalists.

Consider, for example, the telling quotation from the then chairman of Dow Chemical that Sklair (2001, 50) cites: "I have long dreamed of buying an island owned by no nation and of establishing the World Headquarters of the Dow Chemical Company on the truly neutral ground of such an island, beholden to no nation or society. If we were located on such truly neutral ground we could then really operate in the United States as US citizens, in Japan as Japanese citizens and in Brazil as Brazilians rather than being governed in prime by the laws of the United States." This is an eyebrow-raising statement, at least insofar as it demonstrates the extent to which globalizing capital seeks to tear down any and all impediments to its circulation. Indeed, it evokes the establishment of spaces in the global capitalist system—neoliberal utopias—that exist precisely to evade meaningful state regulation, ranging from tax havens and offshore banking centers to new financial hubs such as Dubai.

Yet what the fact that capital and capitalists seek "neutral" ground and do not want to be restricted tells us is that corporate leaders prioritize profit seeking above state interests. And, in turn, it suggests that they will attempt to influence state policies in accordance with their own aims. This is not new. Contrary to Sklair's suggestion, it does not necessarily establish the existence of a coherent global capitalist class that transcends state borders, seeks to advance a global capital-friendly political agenda, and has a shared and cosmopolitan consciousness.

As Sassen (2007, 169) correctly argues, these may be "global classes that are not necessarily cosmopolitan"—that is, they are driven by the "single logic" of profit rather than a genuine globalism. It is thus apparent that we must both strive for greater conceptual clarity and go much deeper to interrogate the subjective dimensions of the globality of capitalist elites.

Who Is a Global Capitalist?

Toward the former end, it is also important to delineate the boundaries of the global capitalist class. Notably, the main works in this research area often use differing criteria for who is in and who is out and generally do not provide justifications for their choices. Here, I review these different positions before ultimately arguing for an in-between definition of global capitalists.

On one end of the spectrum, Robinson (2004, 47) defines the "new transnational bourgeoisie" as encompassing "the owners of transnational capital, that is, the group that owns the leading worldwide means of production as embodied principally in the TNCs and private financial institutions." The focus on corporate and financial capital and ownership of the "means of production" represents a straightforwardly Marxist definition of capitalists.

Yet this is only one position among many. For his part, Sklair (2001, 17) divides the transnational capitalist class into four principal "fractions": corporate (comprising "TNC executives and their local affiliates"), state ("globalizing bureaucrats and politicians"), technical ("globalizing professionals"), and consumerist ("merchants and media"). These latter three groups are "supporting members" of this class (Sklair 2001, 17). As he rightfully argues, limiting one's understanding of capitalists to owners of the means of production overlooks the fact that the globalization of "money capital" also depends on political, organizational, cultural, knowledge, and other forms of capital (Sklair 2001, 17).

In other words, members of the corporate fraction "require help" from the other groups to pursue their economic agenda (Sklair 2001, 295). Further complicating efforts to focus solely on the owners of financial and industrial capital, it is also the case that while these categories are "analytically distinct," there is significant overlap among them (Sklair 2001, 17). Media moguls are particularly emblematic in this regard.

In practice, however, Sklair (2001) focuses almost entirely on the corporate fraction. This, he notes, is the "dominant group" (Sklair 2001, 17). Indeed, as he argues, "the making of a transnational capitalist class depends on the emergence of transnational corporations that are demonstrably globalizing" (Sklair 2001, 49).

A more expansive view of the transnational or global—nomenclature that again varies by author—capitalist class is also taken up by others. For example, Carroll's analysis centers on interwoven networks of corporate leaders. Yet, as he notes, "Corporate elites include not only functioning capitalists . . . but [also] their *organic intellectuals*"—which include "lawyers, consultants, academics, [and] retired politicians" (Carroll 2010, 6; emphasis in original). For Carroll, they are worthy of inclusion precisely because their efforts are essential in allowing and enabling corporations to pursue their political-economic agenda. However, like Sklair's, Carroll's (2010, 6, 17) research concerning a "transnational corporate community" is almost entirely focused on "functioning capitalists." Though acknowledging their relevance, they say little about the role of these other groups.

Adopting a similarly broad definition, Huntington's (2004) Davos Man features within its ranks "academics, international civil servants and executives in global companies, as well as successful high-technology entrepreneurs." Unlike the aforementioned authors, Huntington delves at some length into the role of these other groups—those who do not fit the traditional definition of capitalists—as would-be transnational elites.

Per Huntington (2004), what they all share is that they are "unpatriotic"—that is, they "are identifying more with the world as a whole and defining themselves as 'global citizens.'" He contrasts this "cosmopolitanism" with the "huge majorities of Americans [who] claim to be patriotic and express great pride in their country" and notes that "Americans as a whole are becoming more committed to their nation" (Huntington 2004). Whatever one makes of Huntington's argument concerning a shared lack of patriotism, it is only with great conceptual stretching that he—or today's far right—is able to lump the supposed cosmopolitanism of the left-wing (and presumably anti-capitalist) academic elite of his imagination together with that of the world's leading capitalists. Indeed, the borderless world conjured by neoliberal globalists is of course far different from the cross-border solidarity politics of working-class internationalism.

While recognizing the tendency of the global capitalism literature to focus on the existence of a class of "transnational professionals and executives," Sassen (2007, 168) also argues for taking into consideration other "global" or (at least "partly") "denationalized" classes. In particular, she refers to "the proliferation of transnational networks of government officials," many of which consist of "experts on a variety of issues critical to a global corporate economy" (Sassen 2007, 168). These include everyone from judges and immigration officials to trade and finance ministers. While not capitalists per se, she argues that they are a crucial part of the (mostly city-based) infrastructure of the global capitalist system.

We are thus far from a consensus on how to delimit the global capitalist class. The benefit of a narrow framing that revolves around ownership of the means of production is that it allows for greater conceptual coherence and a relatively clear delineation between who is and is not a transnational capitalist. Only industrial, financial, and other private property-owning capitalists count. This position is also the most faithful to Marx's view of class.

However, at least for present purposes, it is too narrow. Most importantly, it overlooks the role of the trading class as capitalist actors or the fact that commerce is a distinct sphere of capitalism that is worthy of analysis and inclusion (Hozić 2006). While merchants tend to be private actors, their activities depend fundamentally on the state and certain other private actors who also do not fit the conventional definition of capitalists. These include (public) export-promotion agencies and (private) business organizations (such as chambers of commerce), which also constitute a type of merchant class. Even though these actors are not necessarily owners of capital, they can still play an essential role in the promotion of cross-border commerce. In other words, they grease the wheels of global capitalism. Further, given that these actors are international by definition, they are a highly appropriate place to look for global capitalist identities.

To establish the importance of such a trading class, let us take the example of Brazil's economic relations with the Arab world. As discussed in the following chapter, dramatic post-millennium increases in Arab-Brazilian economic flows can in part be understood as the result of a concerted effort by both public and private merchant groups. In the former category is the state-run Brazilian Trade and Investment Promotion Agency, Apex-Brasil, which was founded in 2003. In that same year, it opened business support and distribution centers in Dubai to further its "mission and vision" of "send[ing] Brazilian companies [to] the global market."[2] The importance of Dubai in this regard is that it is seen as a "logistics hub" through which exporters can gain access to a base of around 1.5 billion consumers in and around the Persian Gulf (*WAM* 2011).

More generally, the Brazilian state—with its previous emphasis on South-South relations, particularly during the presidency of Luiz Inácio Lula da Silva (2003–2011)—was instrumental in fomenting these relations. "Businessmen are very attentive to the signals conveyed by governments," noted Celso Amorim (2011, 52), who served as Lula's foreign affairs minister and subsequently as defense minister under Dilma Rousseff. "Often leaders wave the flag and businessmen follow suit."

This dynamic suggests a more robust state role than the standard Marxist argument, which holds that "the executive of the modern State is but a committee for managing the common affairs of the whole bourgeoisie" (Marx and Engels 1888, 475). In Robinson's updated iteration, again reflecting the ambition of neoliberal globalists, the state has been refashioned to promote the interests of global capital. Yet its true role has been even more profound, as the (US) state was instrumental in the creation of global capitalism in the first place (Panitch and Gindin 2012), and like the Brazilian state, its efforts have also helped to construct globally oriented capitalists.

On the private side are actors such as the Arab-Brazilian Chamber of Commerce, which bills itself as "the quickest and safest way for [Brazilian capitalists] to find new markets and to do business with the Arab countries."[3] Among other activities, the chamber "issues 'certificates of origin' for Brazilian exports to the Middle East, plans commercial missions for Brazilian state and business elites to the Arab world, represents Brazil in Arab-sponsored international fairs, and organizes seminars that train Brazilian elites in how to do business with Arab countries" (Karam 2007, 36–37). Many of the organizations profiled in the following chapters play similar roles.

While none of these actors are capitalists in the traditional sense, they are precisely the on-the-ground enablers that make cross-border economic exchange happen. These small yet dynamic networks of public and private economic elites are thus the midwives of global capitalism, as it is through their often-hidden efforts toward fomenting global commerce that such a system is made possible in the first place. So crucial is their role that they cannot be excluded from definitions of the would-be global capitalist class.

For present purposes, then, we may arrive at a suitable definition of *transnational* (or, more appropriately, *global*) capitalists: they are global capital's ownership class but also the globalizing bureaucrats—both public and private, though Sklair (2001, 17) mostly focuses on the former instead of the latter—who make it possible for capital to travel. This definition thus includes not only the leaders of corporations and financial firms, but also the merchants, government economic officials, and private business groupings that facilitate global capitalism and promote its growth.

Marxism, Materialism, Idealism

This book analyzes how a specific population of Latin American elites views its participation in economic globalization. The aim is to interrogate the link between their objective realties—daily routines and entire lives dedicated to bringing down economic barriers, signing trade deals, building cross-border relationships, and training business leaders, all with the goals of more interregional trade, financial flows, and economic intertwining—and how they understand, process, and construct their own activities and worlds. Subsequent to delineating *what* they are doing, we must ask *why* they are doing it.

Standard Marxist accounts provide a straightforward but generally compelling framework for explaining capitalist behavior. Through the establishment of competitive markets in which there are winners and losers, capitalism operates as a form of structural power that disciplines and indeed determines human action. Capitalists are, and must necessarily be, interested in profit above all else, for this is the only way to prosper—or even survive—in a world defined by a cold economic logic. In this sense, as Marx (1843b) would have it, it is not only the worker who is alienated under capitalism; capitalists themselves are also in need of "human emancipation" through the creation of a new society that would free them from the obligation to engage in "huckstering."

For workers, too, it has long been recognized that competitive labor markets—and the looming presence of a *reserve army of the unemployed*—can incentivize certain attitudes and behaviors (such as individualistic survival strategies) while undermining others (namely labor militancy and class-based solidarity). Recurring capitalist efforts to flexibilize labor relations, which have become especially acute in the neoliberal age, must of course be understood as an attempt to produce this attitudinal shift. In turn, in an age of neoliberal precarity, structural change is driving further cultural transformation, as the general population is also increasingly reconstituted as an entrepreneurial class that must brand itself, cultivate its own "human capital," and "hustle harder" in order to thrive, or, perhaps, avoid starvation (Spence 2015).

As observed by anarchist thinker Emma Goldman (1917, 68), human nature under capitalism is "caged in a narrow space" and "whipped daily into submission" by the exigencies of the market. For her and other left-wing critics, freeing humanity from a dehumanized existence of utter servility to the profit motive thus requires transforming the structures that bring those behaviors into being in the first place. For their neoliberal counterparts, such as Mises, the fact that capital had the structural ability to curtail individual agency, drive out noncapitalist logics, and reconstitute cultures was in turn precisely the point and the reason why such a system should be promoted or imposed (Slobodian 2018, 107).

Through demanding their (and our) participation in markets and profit-seeking behavior, capitalism is thus argued to turn elites (and us) into a caged form of *homo economicus* ("economic man"). Such a caricature of the one-dimensional human beings spawned by the capitalist system (Marcuse 1964), for whom "huckstering" is their raison d'être, is introduced to us by Marx as "our friend" (Mr.) Moneybags (1867, 336, 343). As he describes vividly in *Capital*'s first volume: "As capitalist, he is only capital personified. His soul is the soul of capital. But capital has one single life impulse, the tendency to create value and surplus-value, to make its constant factor, the means of production, absorb the greatest possible amount of surplus-labour. . . . Capital is dead labour, that, vampire-like, only lives by sucking living labour, and lives the more, the more labour it sucks" (Marx 1867, 362–363). For Marx, the capitalist may be many things—"a model citizen, perhaps a member of the Society for the Prevention of Cruelty of Animals," and so on. Yet the capitalist "has no heart in its breast" (Marx 1867, 363–364). The logic of profit governs human behavior so thoroughly that "the dealer in minerals sees only the mercantile value but not the beauty and the unique nature of the mineral" (Marx 1844, 89). The desire for accumulation is "the only need" that capitalism generates (Marx 1844, 93).

Marx's account may sound hyperbolic and ideal-typical, but it contains a core truth. Extracting surplus value from labor is exactly the behavior that capitalism produces. In turn, the capitalist who eschews profit seeking for sentimentalist or other concerns will—in all probability, but perhaps not universally—be outcompeted by cold, unfeeling, and alienated economic (wo)men. It is a system that engenders Smith's (2008, 264) "vile maxim of the masters of mankind"—"all for ourselves, and nothing for other people."

Similarly, and despite their heterogeneity, capitalists of all stripes and attachments will likely find themselves advocating for the same sorts of policies—for example, privatization, cuts to social spending, and loan disbursement from the International Monetary Fund—when embedded in comparable structural contexts. After all, different varieties of neoliberalism are hegemonic among business elites essentially everywhere (Taylor 2017a).

Marx's formulation thus helpfully foregrounds the structures that condition human action. However, the plodding, subsuming juggernaut that is the capitalist system of course does not—and at least in Marxism's more sophisticated variations, is not intended to—account for the gamut of human behavior or the complexity and diversity of the entire human experience (Lukács 1972). Indeed, people—including capitalists—are multifaceted creatures with complicated identities, goals, motivations, and thoughts, which themselves are the product of social interactions and are always, to a greater or lesser extent, in flux.

To conceptualize the argument in metaphorical terms, there are sieves, filters, and lenses through which capital's awesome structural power must pass before turning into actual human behavior. The present task, then, is to shed light on them. As Panitch and Gindin (2012, 3) suggest, "The conceptual categories Marx developed to define the structural relationships and economic dynamics distinctive to capitalism can be enormously valuable, but only if they guide an understanding of the choices made, and the specific institutions created, by specific historical actors." In other words, it is axiomatic that capitalists lust for profits. Yet this structural desire is not all that defines capitalist lifeworlds. In fact, where they seek profits depends, in part, on subjective factors—including those related, potentially, to race, ethnicity, religion, and national belonging.

As the Marxist sociologist Erik Olin Wright (2015) correctly observed, consciousness can never be reduced solely to class. Likewise, capitalist behavior also varies based on temporal, spatial, circumstantial, and identity-related differences (Gilbert 2016, 260). For his part, even Marx—despite the caricatured prevailing versions of his thought—displayed a respectable sensitivity for his time to how class, race, gender, and nationalism intersect in capitalist societies (Anderson 2015).

Such intra-capitalist subjective differences may not prove to be politically salient when there are, for example, decisions to be made about reacting to legislative efforts to increase corporate taxes or when responding to a strike. In such circumstances, again, one expects to find something approaching a coherent and unanimous capitalist position, as a structural analysis of class interests would suggest. Yet insofar as the present goal is to understand capitalist behavior in its totality, there is much to be gained by capturing the diversity that exists within capitalist subjectivities.

Doing so will not upend or supplant understandings of capitalism as a material, structural force. Rather, the point is to determine how the profit motive finds expression in the daily lives of particularly situated capitalist elites—that is, to supplement a materialist understanding of global capitalism with a careful delineation of its ideational dimensions. In this regard, it is no coincidence that the principal agents behind Latin America's trade with the Arab world are of Arab descent. After all, and due to their backgrounds, these are precisely the actors who appear especially predisposed to see the Arab world as a site in which to potentially seek profits and who possess the cultural capital that facilitates their ability to serve as interregional intermediaries.

But what to make of the long-standing retort that capitalist identities are unworthy of independent analysis, as they are merely part of the epiphenomenal *superstructure* that is produced by the material *base*? Does the focus on the would-be global capitalist class as a class for itself make the present line of inquiry amount to what Marx (1846, 155) denounced as "empty talk about consciousness" that overlooks the fact that "life is not determined by consciousness, but consciousness by life"? Might we be falling into the trap of German idealism, "which descends from heaven to earth"—that is, from the ideational to the material—instead of more properly "ascend[ing] from earth to heaven" (Marx 1846, 154)? Indeed, if the ideational is entirely subservient to the material, why not instead focus on the extent to which this class exists as a class in itself?

As Marx (1846, 154) notes in *The German Ideology*: "We do not set out from what men say, imagine, conceive, not from men as narrated, thought of, imagined, conceived, to arrive at men in the flesh. We set out from real, active men, and on the basis of their real life-process we demonstrate the development of the ideological reflexes and echoes of this life-process. The phantoms formed in the human brain are also, necessarily, sublimates of their material life-process, which is empirically verifiable and bound to material premises." On the one hand, Marx (1846, 154) is correct to argue that "the production of ideas, of conceptions, of consciousness, is at first directly interwoven with the material activity and the material intercourse of men, the language of real life." Indeed, in the vignettes that follow in chapters 3 and 4, I carefully link the ideational qualities of these capitalist elites with their material realities. Yet as "directly interwoven" as they may be, he is too aggressive here in arguing that the former is merely the "direct efflux" of the latter.

In other writings, Marx helpfully adopts a more nuanced posture concerning the link between the material and ideational (Sclofsky and Funk 2018). Though often portrayed and (mis)read as a crude materialist, he in fact does not always present the relationship between them as being so automatic (Harvey 2018, 114; see also Milner 2019). This is especially evident vis-à-vis the cross-border solidarity of workers.

For example, although he and Engels (1888, 482, 500) write in the *Manifesto* that "modern subjection to capital . . . has stripped" workers "of every trace of national character," they close the same document with the exhortation, "WORKING MEN OF ALL COUNTRIES, UNITE!" They are not stating here that the workers of the world have developed a global working-class consciousness. Rather, they wish to spur it into existence with their revolutionary pamphleteering and consciousness raising. In other words, workers the world over may have been denationalized by capitalism, but they are not necessarily cognizant of this objective reality. In this formulation, there is no one-to-one relationship between existing as a class in itself and a class for itself.

Indeed, part of the critique I offer is of the notion—common to the literature on the global capitalist class and to other prevailing readings of Marx—that a seamless, one-to-one relationship exists between what appear to be global practices and a global consciousnesses. Returning to Rothkopf's example, even if business elites the world over purchase the same newspapers, suits, cars, food, airline tickets, and kinds of music, we cannot necessarily presume that they have become a global capitalist class for itself at a precisely corresponding level. The material and ideational are "directly interwoven," but the relationship is not quite so mechanical.

Yet a deeper critique is also in order. Crucially, the notion that one would expect to find free-floating and fully cosmopolitan identities among global elites can be challenged for reasons that are simultaneously historical, theoretical, and ontological. I will briefly consider them in turn.

As Panitch and Gindin forcefully argue, the US state again played a central role in the post–World War II making of global capitalism. In broad terms, they note, its "explicit long-term goal . . . was to create the material and legal conditions for the free movement of capital throughout the world" (Panitch and Gindin 2012, 10). This has entailed a deliberate, state-led effort to globalize elites, to push them to see beyond the US market, and to align their interests with the construction of a global capitalist economic order.

From this perspective, the problem with narratives concerning the existence of a detached global capitalist class, whether in ideational or material terms, is not merely that global capitalism only became possible due to state intervention (Dardot and Laval 2017, 12; Taylor 2017b). After all, from a materialist perspective, the stickiness of place-based imaginaries should in fact hardly be surprising given the historical and ongoing role of the state in global capitalism's rise and maintenance.

Further, such accounts mistakenly imply that either markets or market-based subjectivities currently, or logically could, exist independently of state action or indeed of politics (or some sort of political authority) more generally. This, as Pierre Dardot and Christian Laval (2017, 6) remind us, flies in the face of "the major lesson of Marx, Weber or Polanyi: the modern market does not operate on its own, but has always been backed by the state." Robinson (2014, 8) himself makes a similar point, recognizing that "the continued existence of the nation-state and the inter-state system appear to be a central condition for the class power of transnational capital and for the reproduction of global capitalism."

Yet if this is the case, then why expect that elite identities would not also, in turn, contain at least state-based traces? The assertion to the contrary—that today's global capitalists have completed (or are in the process of finalizing) a mental divorce from the state—thus seems to rely on one of the two following (and problematic) assumptions.

The first is an exaggerated appraisal of the extent to which capitalism has broken free from the state, which represents a misunderstanding of the state's continuing role in (global) capitalism and neoliberalism. The second involves recognizing this state-based reality of actually existing global capitalism but arguing that (globalist) subjective concerns have taken on a life of their own regardless. In other words, though global capitalists depend on state power, perhaps they have developed a cosmopolitan mindset in spite of the fact that they are not a fully formed class in itself. Yet this is far too idealist of a position. Indeed, it elides (state-dependent) capitalism's unmistakable structural and objective power, through which it conditions—but again, does not fully determine—identities, subjectivities, and class consciousness.

It would be too crude, of course, to assert a one-to-one relationship between the material and ideational, as if the reality of capitalism's statist pedigree will fully condition class consciousness in a corresponding, place-based way. But it would be similarly unsound to construct an account of global class consciousness that overlooks the state's role in establishing and maintaining global capitalism, or markets in general.

The suggestion that global capitalist elites are autonomous from the state, whether materially or ideationally, also poses a political problem. By reifying a false dichotomy in which states and markets are analytically separate instead of mutually co-constitutive, arguments for a state-averse, aloof, and entirely globally minded capitalist class risk reinforcing, however unintentionally, a dangerous myth surrounding neoliberalism in particular—that is, that its proponents "hate the state."

Thoroughly debunking this widely held notion, Quinn Slobodian (2018, 16, 22–23) explains instead that "the normative neoliberal world is not a borderless market without states but a doubled world kept safe from mass demands for social justice and redistributive equality by the guardians of the economic constitution." Indeed, much of the story of the (neoliberal) twentieth century, which he tells from the perspective of the Geneva School, consists of their search for an institutional enforcer of neoliberal rules, most prominently through the founding of the World Trade Organization (WTO).

Their goal, he writes, was not to displace states, but to "work with and through them to ensure the proper functioning of the [global capitalist] whole" (Slobodian 2018, 15; see also Dardot and Laval 2017, 301). Hence, there is simply no inherent opposition between territorially defined, national spaces and the "international space of accumulation" (Panitch and Gindin 2012, 4). Hardt and Negri (2000, 349) thus conclude, "Every morning when they wake up, capitalists and their representatives across the world, instead of reading the curses against big government in the *Wall Street Journal*, ought to get down on their knees and praise it!"

Neoliberalism's advocates may constantly proclaim "the death of distance, the obsolescence of borders, [and] the impossibility of autonomous domestic policy" (Slobodian 2018, 20). However, the actual aim has not been to liberate the market from state control, but to "encase" it through state-based regulatory schemes (Slobodian 2018, 5). And if they do seek to "depoliticize" certain issues—such as the free movement of capital across borders or the global rights of property owners—by removing them from the sphere of political decision-making, this is not an *apolitical* stance. Rather, it is a *political* project in favor of *depoliticization* (and, where applicable, *de-democratization*) (Slobodian 2018, 212–213).

In turn, economic elites—including those analyzed in chapters 3 and 4—do not typically express a universal condemnation of any kind of state intervention or policy initiative. In fact, one finds very few serious adherents of such a position outside of the world of academic economists. Rather, the tendency is to decry regulation when it inhibits (their) profit making and to more quietly push for and support it when it is to their economic benefit. Indeed, as the following analysis reveals, the private fortunes that have been built through Arab–Latin American exchange are inextricably linked to governmental decisions in foreign and commercial policy. To take a particularly dramatic example, Arab-Brazilian trade would likely be at a fraction of its current level if not for the singular efforts of Lula's presidential administrations.

Those who assert that global capitalist elites have fully liberated themselves from state-based concerns thus end up in the curious political position of echoing a neoliberal talking point, and one that is at odds with neoliberal practice. Yet we are hardly doing any favors to the reformist or anti-capitalist political left if our critiques reinforce neoliberal propaganda about the would-be impossibility of efforts to regulate capital.

If they are not omnipotent, we must also be careful with the presumption that capitalist elites are omniscient. As Slobodian (2018, 19) demonstrates, the default emotional state of Geneva School neoliberal proponents, despite their many apparent successes, "was not hubris but anxiety"—this because of the recurring and threatening appearance of legislative efforts, often (and perhaps inevitably) arising from democratic polities, to tinker with or revoke the rules that undergird the global capitalist order.

Specific to the Geneva School worldview was also the related notion that the global economy was so complex that it was ontologically unknowable (Slobodian 2018). While this is a convenient argument for those who wish to undermine regulatory efforts, it is nevertheless true that the actually existing neoliberal order that emerged was not, and could not have been, entirely planned. Instead, it was the result not only of class power, but of contingent historical processes. Its construction occurred through "battles that were initially uncertain and policies that were frequently groping" (Dardot and Laval 2017, 9).

It is true that capitalist elites tend to be quite conscious of their class status. But this does not necessarily mean that they are always aware of what is the most profitable business decision or what precise fix capitalism needs at a particular historical juncture to maintain its hegemony. As Panitch and Gindin (2012, 7) remind us, we must thus be careful not to construct frameworks in which we "exaggerate the extent to which capitalists' consciousness of their interests was always so fixed and clear."

Indeed, human cognition is too limited and convoluted to allow for such ironclad and single-minded certitude. We must thus be attuned to the myriad ways in which the interpretive horizons of economic elites may be permeated by nuances, uncertainties, biases, and forms of attachment that are not precisely or exclusively economic. And we must recognize that this does not make such figures "bad" capitalists.

In sum, attempts to grapple with class consciousness must wrestle with these complexities, especially as they relate to the state entanglements of global capitalists and the idiosyncrasies of the human mind, including for elites who are seeking to make sense of the capitalist system and their place within it, as well as the world more broadly.

The Need for Nuance and Interpretivism

Certain epistemological and methodological choices follow from the present focus on capitalist identities, worldviews, and subjectivities. As suggested in the previous section, what is needed to generate a more holistic understanding of capitalist behavior—not *if*, but *where* they choose to accumulate capital—is to go beyond viewing the profit motive in isolation by conducting a fine-grained empirical analysis that captures the extent to which this ambition is filtered through identity markers such as race, ethnicity, religion, national belonging, and globality.

Insofar as the current focus is on language and the reflexivity and positionality of actors (including the researcher), and takes as its starting point "an overarching appreciation for the centrality of meaning in human life," this study is firmly rooted in the "interpretive turn" (Yanow and Schwartz-Shea 2006, xii). The overriding critique suggested by this framework is that while mainstream social science overzealously emulates the spirit of the natural sciences (for a famous example, see King et al. 1994), the human and social realms are unique and should follow a distinct logic of inquiry.

At the moment of justifying an interpretive approach, it is justifiably commonplace to cite Clifford Geertz's aforementioned assertion, drawing from Max Weber, that "man is an animal suspended in webs of significance he himself has spun" (quoted in Yanow 2006, 6). On this basis, the former concludes that the study of the human condition entails "not an experimental science in search of law but an interpretive one in search of meaning" (quoted in Yanow 2006, 6). The present effort is oriented precisely in this direction: toward understanding the webs of significance of the would-be global capitalist class by conducting "in-depth interviews that decipher individual imaginaries about globality" (Sassen 2007, 5).

To borrow from James Scott (1985, xviii), the aim is thus to construct a "'meaning-centered' account" of global capitalism based on an interpretive analysis of the protagonists who constitute that system. This represents an attempt to gain an actor-centric, micro-level perspective on global capitalism, as opposed to the heavily structuralist approaches that have often predominated in this area (Ong 1999, 3).

As noted, Sklair (2001, 47) nods in this direction by analyzing how corporate leaders talk about globalization. However, he takes their responses at face value and does not delve into the contexts and webs of meaning in which they operate and communicate. Making analytical sense of the dynamic and complicated process through which fluctuating and intersecting identities are constructed is not a straightforward a task; accordingly, it requires a much greater appreciation for context and nuance than the natural-science model allows. This means engaging in the art of interpretation based on open-ended, fluid, and dynamic conversations—not simply asking elites about their identities (or globalization) and recording the responses. As Dvora Yanow (2006, 19) reminds us, "Meanings cannot be observed directly."

Two particular frameworks from the interpretive tradition are of particular use for interrogating (elite) identities and class consciousness. Each has to do with different aspects of "relational" interviewing (Fujii 2017).

First, such interviews are "in-depth" and "semistructured or unstructured" (Soss 2006, 135). This format frees the interviewer to explore relevant tangents, pose additional—and context-specific—questions, and probe one's interlocutor when analytically appropriate. Contrary to positivist logic, the point is to eschew "reliability-as-uniformity" in favor of "flexible, detailed exploration" (Soss 2006, 135).

A similar logic holds when analyzing data. Instead of coding keywords according to a one-size-fits-all template, the researcher is to "pursue the meanings of specific statements by locating them within a broader web of narratives, explanations, telling omissions, and nonverbal cues." This open-endedness leaves us well situated to interrogate the relationships between discrete utterances and the myriad other ways in which interlocutors make and convey meaning (Soss 2006, 128–129).

Second is Frederic Charles Schaffer's (2006, 154) conception of "ordinary language" interviews, which examine "language in use" by "provid[ing] the person with occasions to use particular words of interest in ways that reveal their various meanings." Indeed, we cannot merely *assume* shared meanings of key terms or that the interviewer and interviewee have the same meaning in mind when using them. Rather, when the interviewee says "global," the interviewer must *interpret* the meaning of that word based on contextual factors and, perhaps, by pushing for further elaboration.

Mechanically identifying (or counting) keywords in interviews is not enough. Listening for organic uses of language, along with asking respondents for their conceptualizations of terms and interpreting their responses and usages vis-à-vis their own utterances, ideas, and material acts, will yield much richer data concerning individual beliefs and cognitive processes. This effort to grapple with how a particular actor understands a given concept is precisely what Schaffer (2016, 22; italics in original) refers to as "the elucidative practice of *grounding*," which takes us beyond the "one-sidedness" of conventional, positivist approaches.

The story that emerges from a study conceived according to an interpretivist logic will doubtlessly be a complex one, as befits the human experience. Yet crucially, this does not mean that (nuanced) theoretical knowledge cannot emerge as a result.

For the notion of a global capitalist class for itself to be tenable, interviews should reveal a cosmopolitan identity that supersedes local, regional, ethnic, religious, or state-based subjective moorings. It should be an identity that does not boil down to mere profit seeking—the structurally determined hallmark of every capitalist—but suggests a sense of belonging to an imagined community of global capitalists whose interests are in the functioning, maintenance, and spread of the global capitalist system, instead of those of their state of birth or residence—not precisely Marx's bourgeoisie, but one that eschews territorial-based accumulation in favor of that which is truly global. To borrow from the Greek philosopher Diogenes of Sinope, a global capitalist should be a "citizen of the [global capitalist] world."

To preview the overall argument from the following chapters, the interviews uncovered relatively little evidence of this. At least based on the present cases, as I argue, much of the rhetoric surrounding global classes thus appears to be overblown, as the actors under investigation here think primarily (but not exclusively) in place-based terms. While there are hints of a nascent global consciousness among some interviewees, most retain an identity that is based largely on their home country (or countries). In other words, they are largely national or transnational and do not constitute a global class for itself, as they evince few signs of sharing a global identity.

This is important, for it suggests that while our world has seemingly become more global in terms of economic and other flows, and territorial categorization schemes are often argued to be increasingly obsolete (Sklair 2001), elite identities may continue to reflect, at least in part, a place- and state-based logic. Indeed, the national is far more resilient than those who see an all-encompassing and rootless capitalist globalization would allow—a motley crew that includes many neoliberal intellectuals, liberal apologists such as Thomas Friedman, and the Marxist-inspired global capitalism school (Budd 2013, 153).

In regard to the latter group, I find few reasons to disagree with Anderson's (2006, 3; emphasis in original) observation that "nationalism has proved an uncomfortable *anomaly* for Marxist theory and, precisely for that reason, has been largely elided, rather than confronted." Exploring the resilience of national imaginaries vis-à-vis Marx's insistence on the predominance of (and/or his desire to cultivate) class-based identities of course served as the inspiration for the iconic question in *Imagined Communities*: Why is there no "Tomb of the Unknown Marxist" (Anderson 2006, 10)?

However, this should not be taken to suggest that the argument for a *class for itself* of global capitalists is without merit. First, though the process of global identity formation seems to be much less advanced than is commonly asserted or believed, there still appears to be a nascent trend in this direction. In other words, while this class may be far from being *global*, it is nevertheless apparently *globalizing*. My argument validates Sassen's (2007, 164) suspicion that instead of speaking of the global capitalist class as a fait accompli, in reality what we have are "emergent" and "partially denationalized" global classes. This also largely coincides with Carroll's (2010, 233) argument that, "as a class-for-itself, the transnational capitalist class is in the making [and perhaps only slowly, we might add], but not (yet) made."

For his part, Sklair elsewhere makes a similarly tepid argument. Using language that is more qualified than usual, he notes that this class's members generally have "globalizing perspectives *as well as rather than in opposition to* localizing perspectives" (Sklair 2006, 24; emphasis added). Based on these more equivocal understandings, then, this body of literature points to an important—if exaggerated—trend (Budd 2013, 146). Accordingly, Carroll's (2012) aforementioned point concerning "the need for nuance in theorizing global capitalism" is especially well taken.

Second, instead of thinking of the global capitalist class as a current empirical reality, it is more valuable to conceive of this concept as what Weber (2004) referred to as an "ideal type"—meaning that it can serve as a useful analytical tool for conceptualizing certain globalizing processes. However, we cannot lose sight of the fact that it is ultimately a one-sided accentuation of a particular facet of reality—the complete globalization of the economy and, with it, elite identities—that is intended to clarify some features through the bracketing of others. It should not, however, be confused with reality itself.

Indeed, human consciousness is always defined by a complex mix of diverse, competing, intersecting, and intermingling ideas. The *national, transnational, denational,* and *global* thus cannot be reduced to discrete categories according to which one can mechanically plot identities. Thus, we can expect to find different levels of all such phenomena coexisting within the mind of the same individual.

To the extent we can locate a "global imaginary," as Manfred Steger (2008, 247) astutely notes, it will "erupt in fits and false starts, offering observers confusing spectacles of social fragmentation and integration that cut across old geographical hierarchies in unpredictable patterns." In other words, as it relates to the present focus, we must "see the global through the local and vice versa," as all places along the "local-global continuum" are "inseparable and continually creating and re-creating each other" as part of an "embedded" and "porous" spatial assemblage (Darian-Smith and McCarty 2017, 43–44; see also Carvalho 2013 and Zukin et al. 2015).

What we are left with is thus far from a static picture. Instead, it is a snapshot of a reality that is very much in flux and whose elements—nationalism, transnationalism, denationalization, globality, and so on—come into contact in a dialectical process that creates new amalgamations of identity. Only through an interpretivist approach can one hope to seriously grapple with such convoluted and nuanced processes of meaning making and identity formation.

To its credit, then, the global capitalism school offers key insights into what a global capitalist economy, peopled by capitalist actors on the global end of the identity spectrum, would look like. But crucially, this ideal-typical account is not an entirely accurate description of the world that we currently inhabit.

In turn, by demystifying and shedding light on the identities of a particular group of capitalist elites, this study also serves a normative purpose. Robinson (2004, 48–49) is right to criticize Thomas Friedman and others for presenting globalization as an impersonal force that is "divorced from all agency"—a self-interested story told by "global elites [who] attempt to reify global capitalism as a reality external to their own agency and interests." Instead, he highlights his own framework as a way to foreground the roles that these protagonists play in the global capitalist system. Having done so, he aims to dislodge them and push for a "democratic socialist alternative" (Robinson 2004, 178).

I agree with these critiques and Robinson's rejoinder. Yet his own arguments—which Anievas (2008, 191) fittingly refers to as the "strong globalisation thesis"—similarly "reify" global capitalism. By presenting the consolidation of the global capitalist system and ascendancy of the "transnational" capitalist class as done deals instead of emerging processes, this analysis serves to disempower the very resistance movements that he encourages and praises. After all, if confronted by a fully mobile and free-floating global capitalist class that is materially and ideationally independent from the state—but also controls the state—there would appear to be little recourse for oppositional popular movements. Robinson's hegemonic capitalist class is so global that regulation, let alone more radical alternatives, seems impossible.

In this regard, he argues that "transnational social governance" may be the "hope of humanity" (Robinson 2004, 177). One does not wish to appear myopic or fall prey to presentism, but given our collective inability (or unwillingness) to foster meaningful *national* social governance, the odds of a cross-border historic bloc rising to take on this task in the short term seem slim. Little hope seems to exist beyond waiting for the dialectic and teleology of the more deterministic forms and caricatures of Marxism to run their course. The idea of the global capitalist class thus has status quo–reinforcing ideological implications that contradict the Marxist-inspired goals of these theorists.

Notably, the theoretical construct of the global capitalist class reifies the utopian vision of neoliberal globalists like Mises and Hayek, who sought to construct precisely such a global order in which fully mobile capitalist agents were the ultimate source of sovereign power and authority. As they well recognized, arguments for the end of (popular and other forms of) sovereignty and the broader state system can be a boon for the neoliberal agenda, which posits that states should, must, and *will* cede power to the sovereign market and abdicate social-welfare responsibilities in order to be competitive in the modern global capitalist economy (Slobodian 2018).

What those who argue in favor of a fully globalized capitalist class thus tend to overlook is that it is in the material interests of at least certain capitalist elites to present themselves according to this neoliberal ideal—as a particular kind of what Aihwa Ong (1999) refers to as "flexible citizens" who are global, cosmopolitan, fully unmoored, and hence ungovernable. When capitalists boast of their global credentials, it may be—as Sklair and others would have it—evidence in favor of the arguments of the global capitalism school. Alternatively, as explored in greater depth in chapter 5, it may be a strategy to demonstrate that they and their activities simply cannot be regulated or controlled. Elsewhere, Sklair (2016, 332) appears to recognize this logic by observing that capitalist elites "seek to project images of themselves as citizens of the world as well as of their places of birth." There is thus ample reason to be particularly skeptical of the veracity of claims regarding global capitalist identities.

After all, the activities of a capitalist who is still materially and ideationally tied to—and has a "partial dependence" on (Sassen 2007, 177)—the state will be much more susceptible to popular oversight. Thus, while capitalist rhetoric—per the aforementioned political strategy—is often global, there are reasons to expect that the realities of their worldviews are much more territorial. Fortunately, the interpretivist approach that guides this project is well suited to tease out these complexities and detect where the balance truly lies.

To summarize, the interpretive horizons of the Latin American elites on whom I focus here—all of whom have significant economic linkages with the Arab world—are in fact far from being truly global. Contrary to much corporate propaganda, as well as many lay and scholarly accounts, they think primarily in place-based (national or transnational) or denational terms. Respectively, one uncovers interpretive frameworks that are primarily state- and/or ethnicity-based or that exhibit few attachments of any kind, except to profit. However, there are relatively few global signs.

Reports of the death of place-based imaginaries thus appear to be greatly exaggerated. In fact, the imagined communities of nation-states have proven to be strikingly resilient despite capitalist globalization and the slow rise of global classes.

Accordingly, Sassen (2011) is correct to note that "the national" is still "probably the most significant and encompassing condition," even though it is also true that "the imbrications of global, national, and denationalized will proliferate and begin to produce overall dynamics we have not yet seen." While we are witnessing the ascent of the global or transnational, we must recognize that these rising imaginaries are not painting on blank canvases. The human mind is not a tabula rasa, a veritable Etch A Sketch whose lines fade away with a few shakes—or, in this case, with the development of an increasingly interconnected global capitalist system. Instead, as global identities emerge, they are conditioned by the national imaginaries that predate them. Robinson (2014, 8) himself does at least acknowledge this point (if not, perhaps, the implications thereof), recognizing that the global is "nested in the national." What we observe is thus a strongly *rooted* globalism, a concept I develop in subsequent chapters.

The "capitalists of the world" have thus yet to accomplish what Marx long ago urged for the "workers of the world": to fully unite around a shared cosmopolitan consciousness. They are chased around the globe by profit-seeking impulses, but not entirely—or at least not yet—as a global class for itself. Supporting evidence is presented in subsequent chapters. First, however, we must explore the broader framework of Arab–Latin American relations, as this axis of ties forms the context in which these elites operate.

Notes

1. The idea that the current era of globalization is qualitatively unique has attracted significant criticism. Take, for example, a series of claims from the seminal text *Globalization in Question*. The authors aim to dispute the "strong globalization thesis," which "requires a new view of the international economy . . . [as] one that subsumes and subordinates national-level processes" (Hirst et al. 2009, 17). In arguing against this "ideal type" of a "globalized economy," they note that "the current international economy has only recently become as open and integrated as the regime that prevailed from 1870 to 1914"; that "capital mobility has only recently begun shifting investment and employment from the advanced to the developing countries, and here it is just a very few of the emerging economies that are benefiting"; that "the world is far from being genuinely 'global.' . . . Rather trade, investment and financial flows are concentrated in the Triad of Europe, Japan/East Asia and North America, and this dominance seems set to continue"; and that (voluntary) global migration flows have in fact decreased over time (Hirst et al. 2009, 3, 20, 31–32; Fulcher 2004).
Yet from the perspective of analyzing the global capitalism school on its own terms, these critiques miss the point. What is new about global capitalism is not necessarily the *quantity* of international trade, financial flows, or migration waves, or whether the Global South will catch up with the "Triad." Instead, the salient point is that while money and goods used to move between discrete, *national* economies, the very entities that produce and distribute them are now *transnational*. Thus, the skeptics' analytical error is that they conceptualize globalization in terms of trade volume as opposed to the (transnational) organization of production relations (Robinson 2014, 10). Likewise, whether or not migration has risen in absolute terms, the change that Robinson (2008, 203) sees is the dramatic increase in "migrant workers," which is becoming "a general category of super-exploitable labor drawn from globally dispersed labor reserves into similarly globally dispersed nodes of intensive or specialized accumulation," ranging from Buenos Aires to the southern coast of China. Finally, this line of thinking does not foresee a quick flattening out of global inequalities between states, nor does it predict that the US, Europe, or East Asia are set to lose their position of economic dominance. However, it does suggest changing our level of analysis from *states* to (global) *classes*.

2. See ApexBrasil's website, accessed September 1, 2014, http://www2.apexbrasil.com.br/en/about/who-we-are/scope-of-activities.

3. See the Arab-Brazilian Chamber of Commerce's website, accessed February 1, 2016, http://www.ccab.org.br/arabe-brasil/en/about-us.fss.

2

HOW LATIN AMERICA MET THE ARAB WORLD

As is the case with many traditional disciplines, scholarship in global studies has often privileged the Global North experience (Krishnaswamy and Hawley 2007; Richards 2014). Accordingly, it has all too frequently conceptualized the Global South as little more than a site for the exercise of Northern power—that is, a place that is acted upon, but that itself is largely incapable of independent action.[1] The idea that Southern actors have agency and may interact among themselves in meaningful ways is largely beyond the pale, according to this worldview.

This bias, in turn, explains the aforementioned call by Eve Darian-Smith and Philip McCarty (2017) for global studies to engage with non-Western methods, literatures, and ways of knowing. Such a decolonizing spirit very much informs the present study and especially this chapter, which analyzes a particular South-South axis that, at least until recently, has been mostly overlooked by Northern scholars: Latin America's relations with the Arab world.

So great has been the substantive increase in these ties that Celso Amorim could again claim (though with several touches of hyperbole) that until a slowdown in the past few years, the two regions had been creating "a new world economic geography" (quoted in Karam 2007, 174). Yet we must go back further to understand this recent rise, which is linked to what Luiz Inácio Lula da Silva referred to as a "reencounter" between two civilizations with a history of linkages (Karam 2007, 174). These include more than a century of Arab migration to Latin America, the flow of Arab petrodollars to the region in the 1970s, and the oft-ignored broader history of South-South relations through institutions such as the Non-Aligned Movement (Prashad 2007).

Here, I follow Lula's lead by recovering this history of Arab–Latin American relations. Thus, in addition to providing a general framework for comprehending current issues in Arab–Latin American relations, this chapter historicizes the more general marginalization of South-South relations. The larger aim is to participate in the decolonization of global studies and the establishment of a more inclusive field (Tickner and Blaney 2012b; Gruffydd Jones 2006).

Additionally, this chapter contributes to the growing body of literature on Arab–Latin American relations, which has mostly been produced by Southern scholars. While the sum of this scholarly production presents a useful overview of the historical trajectory and contemporary status of these relations, it is infrequently cited in Northern scholarship. Additionally, it would benefit from further development in several key areas. Here, I identify four main gaps, the latter three of which I address through this study. The aim is not to criticize individual works, but rather to highlight areas for further research.

First, too little is known about the history of these ties, particularly as it regards interstate relations. There is a long history of Third World institutions through which Latin American and Arab countries have (or had) long interacted, including the Non-Aligned Movement (NAM), the New International Economic Order (NIEO), and the Organization of the Petroleum Exporting Countries (OPEC) (Prashad 2007; 2013). Few works have seriously explored these linkages (for an exception focusing on Brazil, see Karam 2012). There is also a largely overlooked history of Third World people-to-people connections, one instance of which is highlighted in a recent analysis of Chilean exiles who settled in Algeria after the 1973 coup against Salvador Allende (Palieraki 2018). Likewise, past episodes of economic exchange, such as the aforementioned injection of petrodollars from the Arab world into Latin America in the 1970s (Howe 1974), have mostly gone unexplored. The same is true of remittance flows. There is thus a need to historicize contemporary relations.

Second, most literature on Arab–Latin American relations is state-centric and tends to neglect the question of how non-state actors have also promoted these ties (for an exception, see again Karam 2007). Specifically, there is insufficient discussion of the fundamental contributions made by private actors (particularly economic ones) and emerging networks of private and public actors in developing these relations. Here, we may point to the oft-overlooked role played by merchant capitalist groups as globalizing elites and agents that enable interregional economic exchange. Such actors include business federations (including the member organizations of the Federation of Arab–South American Chambers of Commerce, which was founded in 2018 during the Brazil–Arab Countries Economic Forum in São Paulo), state economic bureaucracies (e.g., export-promotion agencies), and facilitators of investment flows (e.g., the Gulf-focused, Buenos Aires-based financial firm profiled in chap. 4).

Third, there is a tendency to foreground what are presented as essentially "political" questions, as if the most important aspects of Arab–Latin American relations can be accurately grasped through engaging in foreign policy analysis vis-à-vis the involved states. What are often left aside, then, are more holistic approaches that can shed additional light on the economic, cultural, and other dimensions of these ties. Overall, this usual focus on country-to-country interactions again tends to come at the expense of considering the roles played by non-state actors and thus reinforces a state-centric bias. In contrast, the present work adopts a political-economy approach to account for how political and economic factors intersect to propel these relations, as well as how the relevant (both public and private) protagonists operate within larger structures, such as capitalist globalization.

Finally, extant literature on Arab–Latin American relations is overwhelmingly empirical, as opposed to theoretical, in nature. While it uncovers many interesting dynamics concerning an axis of relations that is largely unknown in the Global North, it often neglects to draw broader conclusions based on these realities or to situate them within a comparative context (for an exception, see Amar 2013). Perhaps for both better and worse, this is symptomatic of a larger issue that characterizes much Latin American knowledge production: the tendency to focus on practical instead of theoretical matters. Reasons for this predilection include both a "subservience to state cues" in some disciplines, which pushes scholars in the direction of conducting applied, policy-relevant research, and the fact that there is a strong ethos of public engagement—to resolve the region's very real social maladies—among Latin American intellectuals (Tickner 2008, 745).

Here, I do not intend to rehash the "area studies" debate (Bates 1997; Johnson 1997), nor to imply that local insights must serve some supposedly higher and more properly scientific purpose of constructing disciplinary knowledge. Rather, the argument is that Arab–Latin American relations present a fascinating case that could help reveal, for example, how capital goes global through the efforts of public-private networks, as well as how ostensibly globalizing actors navigate various axes of ethnic, class-based, and national identities. Further, engaging in theoretical work based on Global

South cases provides a useful corrective to the long-standing, hegemonic, and pernicious tendency to highlight, and exclusively theorize on the basis of, Global North histories, cases, and perspectives. It is to the place of Arab–Latin American relations (and South-South relations more broadly) in global studies, and particularly the "American social science" of International Relations (Hoffman 1977), that I now turn.

The Specter of South-South Relations

Mainstream Global North scholarship has had relatively little to say about the reality or possibility of meaningful South-South relations or Southern agency more generally. If one assumes that Global South actors "are takers, instead of makers, of international policy"—as Robert Keohane, one of the most foundational theorists of world politics in recent decades, has noted about Latin America—then, from his vantage point, there is little reason to pay significant attention to them (quoted in Carranza 2006, 814). Yet even if Keohane is literally correct, this does not justify ignoring the South. For example, in disciplines such as anthropology, more than in political science, it is of course entirely normal for scholars to lend their voices to the disenfranchised.

Crucially, this marginalization of the South is based, in part, on the perceived ontological threat that Southern agency poses to Northern domination of the global system (Krasner 1985). In other words, one reason why the South is often ignored is precisely because taking it seriously subverts the idea of Northern hegemony. What makes South-South relations dangerous from a Northern-centric perspective, in turn, is that they undermine the notion that the North always *is* and *should be* central in global politics and economics.

This sidelining of the South is unfortunate for myriad reasons. Among them is the fact that the study of South-South relations could shed light on research topics that are of perennial interest in global studies and cognate disciplines. For example, scholars concerned with the causes of war and peace (and how to prevent the former and promote the latter) should be intrigued by South America's "external-peace-and-internal-violence paradox"—that is, that despite the region's extreme internal violence, it has seen fewer major interstate wars "than any other peripheral area in the world" (Martín 2009, 143).

Thus, while famed realist theorist Kenneth Waltz (1979, 72) once opined that "it would be as ridiculous to construct a theory of international politics based on Malaysia and Costa Rica as it would be to construct an economic theory of oligopolistic competition based on the minor firms in a sector of an economy," one should more reasonably conclude the opposite: it would be ridiculous *not* to. Waltz's comment is particularly ironic given that one of the modern classics of Global North social science—James Scott's (1985) *Weapons of the Weak*—is not only based on a Malaysian case study but is also esteemed for having made a major theoretical contribution to general arguments concerning Gramscian hegemony and subaltern agency.

At the very least, the South demands our attention given that it is home to the vast majority of the world's population. Engaging with the South and Southern people's lived experiences is thus essential for any attempts at global understanding and indeed for the development of a global studies that truly lives up to its name (Darian-Smith and McCarty 2017). In turn, the persistent notion that it is exclusively *European history* that is foundational to the contemporary world order—and a sanitized version of it, which downplays the experiences and legacies of imperialism, colonialism, racism, and slavery—occludes the many *histories* of cross-border interactions that exist around the globe. Again, the field of International Relations is perhaps especially noteworthy in this regard, given that it was born as the would-be science of "colonial administration" (Long and Schmidt 2005), though anthropology and other disciplines also have their own histories as handmaidens of colonial and imperial projects (Stocking Jr. 1993).

Even if we grant that "Europe set the pattern for the organization of and interaction among nation-states that persists to the present day," per a prominent world politics textbook, it simply does not follow, as the authors argue, that "any examination of how world politics came to attain its present form must therefore begin in Europe" (Spiegel et al. 2012, 61). Rather than likening a focus on the South to studying oligopolies through the actions of minor firms, what Waltz's position in fact suggests, to take another political-economy example, is that we can somehow understand capitalism without theorizing from the perspective of the system's lower rungs.

If the South is too often invisible in Northern scholarship, then the idea of South-South relations suffers from a double marginalization: that is, if the South lacks agency, as is commonly presumed, then Southern regions are by default incapable of interacting with one another in meaningful ways. Thus, when the South does appear in mainstream scholarship, it is often as an agency-deprived site for the exercise of Northern power (Funk 2016). To be sure, Northern domination of Southern regions through economic arrangements, institutions of global governance, and even outright invasions and occupations is indeed a recurring feature of our world (Funk 2015a). However, we wander too far from a properly nuanced account of the global system if we simply ignore the realities and potential of Arab–Latin American or other axes of South-South relations (Prashad 2013).

Fortunately, there is now a relatively voluminous body of literature that focuses on—or at least makes substantive mention of—Arab–Latin American relations and how these two seemingly disparate regions came to meet one another. Yet notably, most of this scholarly production, at least until recently, has taken place in Western academia's periphery.

This is true literally, as the majority of specialists in this research area are Latin Americans who are based at Latin American universities. In fact, several of the region's universities feature academic units dedicated to the study of the Arab world and its relations with Latin America. These include the Universidad de Chile's Center for Arab Studies, the Universidade de São Paulo's Center for Arab Studies, the Rio de Janeiro–based Universidade Federal Fluminense's Center for Middle East Studies, El Colegio de México's Center for Asia and Africa Studies, and the Universidad Nacional de Costa Rica's Center for Middle East and North Africa Studies (CEMOAN). There is at least one counterpart in the Arab world: the Latin American Studies and Cultures Center at the Holy Spirit University of Kaslik in Lebanon. As a result of the resources, visibility, and community building afforded by these academic units, there is thus relatively significant institutional infrastructure in Latin America for the study of relations with the Arab world (for more on the Brazilian case, see Clemesha and Ferabolli 2020).

Other scholarly and civil society organizations—again, predominantly within Latin America—have also contributed to the production of knowledge on the intersections between the two regions. Most prominent among them are: BibliASPA (the Arab and South American Library and Research Center), located in São Paulo, which also administers its own publishing house, Edições BibliASPA; the Network for Interdisciplinary Research on the Arab World and Latin America (RIMAAL), which now appears dormant but previously functioned as a vibrant online community and resource center for Latin American and other scholars conducting research in this area; and the Center for Contemporary Middle East Studies (CEMOC) in Córdoba, Argentina.

Both CEMOAN and CEMOC publish academic journals on the Arab world and Arab–Latin American relations—respectively, *Revista Al-Kubri* and *ANMO: África del Norte y Medio Oriente*. The magazine of the Arab-Brazilian Chamber of Commerce and online *Brazil-Arab News Agency* also contribute substantially to the diffusion of news and analysis concerning biregional relations.

Accordingly, Arab–Latin American relations have ceased to be an unknown phenomenon, provided that one knows where to look. As Paul Amar (2014, 7) notes hopefully, Latin America and the Middle East are now connected through "the maturation of a new field of transregional study, the crystallization of a new generation of transdisciplinary and transnational scholarship, and the boldness of a new set of institutions and research centers."

However, due to the language of publication (for the most part, Spanish and Portuguese), prevailing notions about who is afforded the right to produce what is considered to be knowledge in the first place, and the politics of what topics are deemed by (Northern) disciplinary gatekeepers to be important, these predominantly Latin American efforts have only infrequently been cited or engaged with by Northern-based scholars. This literature is thus peripheral not just *geographically*, but also *intellectually*. As noted by Colombia-based scholar Arlene Tickner (2003, 296), who, as coeditor of Routledge's *Worlding beyond the West* series and author of numerous articles on Global South scholarship, has been instrumental in foregrounding Latin American and other outside perspectives, "The 'who' of [International Relations] studies continues to be a select number of academics hailing primarily from the countries of the core."

In sum, even though an enterprising group of mostly Latin American scholars has produced a significant body of work on Arab–Latin American relations, it has not been widely debated or cited—or, presumably, read—by their Northern counterparts. This state of affairs leads us to the question raised by Evelyn Hu-DeHart (2009): Where are Arab-descendant Latin Americans, along with other regional "immigrant" communities, in the US-dominated field of Latin American Studies?

To be sure, there are signs of improvement—such as the winter 2016 publication of an edition of the Latin American Studies Association's *Forum* newsletter focusing on the connections between the regions. Yet a larger malady continues to afflict Global North academia: the disjuncture between claims of universal inclusiveness and the reality that certain relatively privileged scholars—almost exclusively based in the North—are afforded the agency to generate "knowledge" (Kamola 2013).

To extend the analysis of dependency theory into the realm of intellectual production, just as much of Latin America remains stuck in the hamster wheel of commodity exports, so too does it struggle to break free from its imposed academic position as a recipient of ideas from abroad rather than a producer of them (Dorfman and Mattelart 1991; Mignolo 2005). It is important to recognize that the Northern academy is indeed more globally inclusive than was the case several decades prior and that protagonists within global studies—including those cited above—have been at the forefront of this salutary trend (Kristensen 2015). However, we are still nowhere near a scenario in which Latin American knowledge operates on equal epistemological footing with its North American and European counterparts.

The problem is of course less individual than structural. Naturally, it is unreasonable to ask that each scholar—Northern or otherwise—be familiar with every potential topic of interest in the vast, diverse terrain of global studies (or be capable of reading articles in Spanish and Portuguese). Yet at a collective level, the fact that language learning has increasingly been deemphasized in Northern graduate programs and so few Northern scholars study South-South relations—or at least feel compelled to incorporate them into their analyses—is highly problematic.

Unfortunately, the collective lack of attention paid to South-South issues could have real political consequences. To demonstrate, we must look no further than Latin American–Middle Eastern relations, inclusive of Iran. For the first time ever, interactions between these regions rose from obscurity to become a major topic of concern for political elites in Washington in the post–September 11 context of the "War on Terror." Central here are accusations that Latin America—and particularly the Triple Frontier area, where Brazil, Paraguay, and Argentina meet and which features a large Arab-descendant population—is a hive of activity for Middle Eastern terrorist groups, which, we are told, could use the region as a base from which to attack US interests (Karam 2020).

Indeed, in the recent past, this idea became an article of faith in the hawkish wing of the US foreign policy establishment. During a 2011 Republican Party presidential primary debate on national security and foreign policy, eventual nominee and current Senator Mitt Romney echoed the concerns of the other candidates in asserting that the would-be actions of Hezbollah and similar groups in the Triple Frontier, as well as other parts of Latin America, pose "a very significant and imminent threat to the United States" (*CNN* 2011). Addressing a question about "using the United States military," then–Texas governor and subsequent Energy Secretary Rick Perry called for "a twenty-first century Monroe Doctrine" to counter the supposed machinations of Hamas, Hezbollah, and Iran in the region (*CNN* 2011).

Not to be outdone, in response to the query "what national security issue do you worry about that nobody is asking about[?]," former Senator and *CNN* pundit Rick Santorum made the curious comment, "I've spent a lot of time and concern [*sic*] . . . [thinking] about what's going on in Central and South America. I'm very concerned about the militant socialists and the radical Islamists joining together, bonding together" (*CNN* 2011). The Trump administration apparently shared these sentiments regarding the assumed role of both Iran and Middle Eastern terrorist groups in the region. Most notable, perhaps, were the remarks of then–Secretary of State Mike Pompeo at a July 2019 counterterrorism conference in Buenos Aires, during which he focused precisely on the would-be threats posed by Iran and Hezbollah (DeYoung 2019).

To summarize, major US political figures had grown so concerned about this supposed facet of Latin American–Middle Eastern relations that they were apparently willing to countenance the (likely disastrous) use of military force. Yet neither the US government nor anyone else had, or has, provided serious evidence to support the notion that the Triple Frontier is a significant staging ground for terrorist groups (Karam 2011). Instead, concerned reporters, analysts, and politicians have constantly cited each other in a "closed loop of self-references" (Karam 2011, 263). Most notably, these culminated in unconfirmed but oft-repeated allegations that Osama bin Laden spent time in the Triple Frontier and—as incorrectly speculated by *CNN*—that a picture of the nearby Iguaçu Falls had been found in Afghanistan at an al-Qaeda training camp (Karam 2011, 263).

To be sure, the Triple Frontier has long been a haven for smuggling and unmonitored economic exchanges. It would indeed be surprising if, at the very least, there were not some individuals in the region who contribute financially and perhaps in other ways to groups such as Hezbollah and Hamas (as may have occurred with the 1992 terrorist attack on the Israeli embassy and the even more lethal 1994 bombing of the Argentine Israelite Mutual Association, both of which occurred in Buenos Aires). Yet "we" as outsiders know relatively little about what actually occurs around the Triple Frontier (for a recent exception, see Karam 2020). In turn, policy debates are being informed by wild speculation rather than honest, fact-based analysis.

Again, the issue is not precisely that there is no literature on relations between these regions. A significant number of sources exist, many of high quality. However, given that South-South relations tend to be seen as unimportant and that the scholars who engage with these topics are largely from the marginalized periphery and often write in languages other than

English, they are rarely cited, let alone read, by Northern scholars or practitioners—hence the conclusion that a spirit of "parochialism" permeates many corners of Northern academia, as reflected through the dominance of US concerns, US graduate programs, and US-based journals in their respective fields (Tickner and Blaney 2012a, 5). Bridging the academic North-South divide is thus essential for decolonizing global studies and the Northern university more broadly.

As follows, and based on extensive engagement with existing sources, I provide a relatively comprehensive analysis of historical and contemporary interactions between Latin America and the Arab world. This survey is inclusive of writings in English, Spanish, and Portuguese (and predominantly the latter two). The aim is not to delve into the intricacies of individual sources, but to provide a general overview of what is—and is not—known, isolate recurring themes, identify areas in need of further analysis, and contextualize the political-economy approach of the present work.

In very broad strokes, existing scholarship on Arab–Latin American relations can be divided into two thematic categories: immigration and diaspora, which focuses on the experiences of Arab migrants and their descendants in Latin America, as well as the cultural history produced by interactions between these populations; and foreign policy and commercial relations, which deals mainly with Latin America's current policies toward and trade with the Arab world, its posture concerning the Israeli-Palestinian conflict, and terrorism-related concerns around the Triple Frontier.

Two caveats are in order. First, this is necessarily a simplistic rendering, and second, there is overlap between the groupings (for example, the landmark volume *The Middle East and Brazil: Perspectives on the New Global South* treats both topics in fairly equal measure [Amar 2014]). Nonetheless, this categorization scheme provides a useful general sketch of the central topics of concern in this literature and an overall impression of what is (and is not) known about these relations based on existing scholarship.

Immigration and Diaspora: The Making of a Political-Economic Elite

The first—and most commonly told—story that emerges from this literature focuses on the waves of Arab immigrants who have taken residence in Latin America. Specifically, it analyzes how they and their descendants have navigated, shaped, and been shaped by Latin America's political, economic, and cultural terrains.

Arab Latin Americans form a relatively small minority group, though one of disproportionate political and economic significance. This makes it all the more surprising that Northern scholars have largely overlooked their presence, as revealed by Hu-DeHart's aforementioned rhetorical question concerning the relative absence of scholarship focusing on Arab Latin Americans and other regional minority groups within the Global North–dominated mainstream of Latin American Studies. In this sense, there is again an opportunity to explore larger theoretical issues based on the Arab–Latin American experience and to inform more general understandings of topics such as nationalism, transnationalism, globalization, and migration.

Argentina, Colombia, the Dominican Republic, Ecuador, El Salvador, Honduras, and Brazil have all had presidents of Arab ancestry, some of them on multiple occasions (including El Salvador, whose current leader, Nayib Bukele, is of Palestinian descent, and the Dominican Republic, whose present head of state, Luis Abinader, has Lebanese ancestry). Numerous members of Latin America's economic, cultural, intellectual, and athletic elites can also trace their origins back to the Arab world. Among the best known, as previously mentioned, is Carlos Slim, along with Mexican actor Salma Hayek, who is partially of Lebanese ancestry, and Colombian-born global pop star Shakira, whose paternal grandparents also hail from Lebanon.

Further examples abound. They include famed Chilean director and novelist Miguel Littín, of Palestinian and Greek heritage, whose daring secret return to Chile from exile in 1984 to capture the brutal reality of life under the Pinochet regime was immortalized in the late Gabriel García Márquez's (1986) *La aventura de Miguel Littín clandestino en Chile* (*Clandestine in Chile: The Adventures of Miguel Littín*). Another well-known figure is two-time Olympic gold medalist in tennis Nicolás Massú, also from Chile, whose father's side of the family is Palestinian and whose Jewish maternal grandparents were survivors of the Nazi Holocaust.

Arab Latin Americans also make frequent (and, at times, rather caricatured) appearances in works of popular and haute Latin American culture. Perhaps most famous are the Arab merchants of García Márquez's (1967) *Cien años de soledad* (*One Hundred Years of Solitude*) or the subject, Santiago Nasar, of his (1981) *Crónica de una muerte anunciada* (*Chronicle of a Death Foretold*). But see also famed Brazilian novelist Jorge Amado's (2008) *A Descoberta da América pelos Turcos* (*The Discovery of America by the Turks*), which narrates the romantic and economic exploits of two Arab immigrants upon their arrival in Brazil at the beginning of the twentieth century. It was during this precise time period when Arab–Latin American migratory flows reached their peak, with the majority presenting passports issued by the Ottoman Empire upon entry—hence the enduring (and not always well-meaning) tendency throughout Latin America to refer to this population and its descendants, as invoked by Amado, as *"turcos"* (Karam 2007, 10).

Turning to television, the hit early 2000s Brazilian soap opera *O Clone* (*The Clone*) featured a Muslim Moroccan-Brazilian family, while the kindly elderly shopkeeper Farid Assad from the well-known Chilean drama *Los 80* (*The '80s*), which aired from 2008 to 2014, displayed a small Palestinian flag, representing his family background, in his clothing store in downtown Santiago. Additionally, different facets of the Arab–Latin American experience have a near-constant cultural presence in the region through organizations like the Institute of Arab Culture, which opened in São Paulo in 2003, and recurring events such as the South American Festival of Arab Culture and the LatinArab Film Festival. Social institutions like the ritzy Club Palestino (Palestinian Club) in Santiago de Chile also actively organize cultural and other events.

The Latin American country with the largest Arab-descendant population is Brazil, where it is estimated, perhaps with some exaggeration, at up to ten million (though it is not uncommon for Arab-Brazilian organizations to assert even higher figures) (Karam 2007, 10). Not surprisingly, a relatively large number of sources focus on Arab Brazilians (Hilu da Rocha Pinto 2010; Karam 2007; Lesser 2013; Morrison 2005; Truzzi 2018). Most of this population is of Lebanese—and to a lesser extent, Syrian—ancestry. As is frequently noted, Brazil is said to have "more citizens of Syrian origin than Damascus, and more inhabitants of Lebanese origin than all of Lebanon" (Luxner 2005).

Other Latin American countries with particularly sizable Arab-descendant populations include Argentina (Brégain 2011; Civantos 2006; Hyland, Jr. 2011; Hyland, Jr. 2017; Pearl Balloffet 2020; Rein and Noyjovich 2018), Mexico (Alfaro-Velcamp 2007; Pastor 2017), Chile (Bascuñan-Wiley 2019; Bray 1962; Elsey 2011; Ustan 2012), Colombia (Vargas and Suaza 2007), and Honduras (Amaya Banegas 1997; González 1993; Gutiérrez Rivera 2014; Luxner 2001). For example, estimates range up to several million for the Arab-Argentine population, while there are said to be between 500,000 and one million Arab Chileans (though in both cases, again, the real figures are perhaps somewhat lower). Syrian-Lebanese ancestry predominates in most countries, including Argentina.[2] However, in countries such as Chile and Honduras, Palestinians form the largest group. Notably, outside of the Middle East, Chile is home to the world's largest Palestinian diaspora population.

Many millions of other Latin Americans also have an (often unknown) Arab background through the long Moorish presence on the Iberian Peninsula. In seeking to make the case that the Arab world and Latin America were experiencing a "reencounter," Lula himself noted that the Arab world "first came to us by way of the Iberian heritage" (quoted in Karam 2007, 174). Interestingly, as Walter Mignolo (2005, 157) comments in regard to this genealogical history, Latin America was "correlated in the nineteenth century with the inferior South of Europe, which was 'tainted' by Catholicism and the infusion of Moorish blood." The Moorish presence also explains the existence of very large numbers of Arabic loanwords in Spanish, Portuguese, and associated languages—so many, in fact, that Arabic is considered "the second most important ingredient of the Spanish lexicon" (Corriente 2008, viii).

In addition to the country-specific literature cited above, a number of works have sought to analyze Arab Latin Americans—together, in some cases, with other Latin Americans of Middle Eastern and/or Jewish ancestry—in a multicountry or regional context (Agar Corbinos and Kabchi 1997; Alsultany and Shohat 2013; Karam 2013b; Klich and Lesser 1998; Raheb 2012). As I discuss later in this chapter, common themes that arise include identity, elite formation, and Latin American Orientalism vis-à-vis the Arab Other.

Though many Arab-descendant Latin Americans now occupy a relatively privileged location within their countries' social, political, and economic hierarchies, the circumstances of the arrival of the first waves of immigrants were often less than glamorous. While the post–World War I fall of the Ottoman Empire and the continued colonial presence in the region would later send Arab emigrants to Latin America in larger numbers, the first arrived in preceding decades in a trickle, often unintentionally.

In the words of a businessman who belongs to Honduras's large Palestinian-descendant community: "Many of our fathers and grandfathers in Palestine were saving their money to go to America. . . . They bought third-class tickets, which were all they could afford. They weren't too smart geographically. The first stop was either the Caribbean or Central America. They didn't speak English, and they didn't speak Spanish. So they came without any papers, and without a penny in their pockets, and were admitted to a country that really opened its arms to them" (Luxner 2001). Similarly, according to Helmi Nasr, then director of the Universidade de São Paulo's Center for Arab Studies: "Many of these immigrants came to Brazil without really wanting to.... They had purchased steamship tickets to America, thinking they were heading for North America. After quickly recovering from the initial shock of discovering they had arrived in South America, they started to make the best of it" (*Washington Times* 2005).

Most of these immigrants belonged to Orthodox Christian families, though in recent years Islam has predominated among the much smaller numbers of arrivals (Chitwood 2021; Khan 2015; Logroño Narbona et al. 2015; Truzzi 2018). As part of their general sociocultural integration, Catholicism and, presumably, Evangelical Christianity have taken root among many of the longer-standing populations. However, relatively little is known in systematic terms about the contemporary religiosity of Arab Latin Americans, as the topic seems not to have attracted sustained scholarly attention.

In one contemporary manifestation of continuing migratory flows, several thousand Syrians have arrived in Latin America—and particularly Brazil—as refugees, fleeing the violence, chaos, and instability of their home country (Brodzinsky 2014; Lissardy 2015). Smaller groups of Palestinian refugees have also been resettled in Latin America in recent decades, mainly in Chile and Brazil (Henríquez 2008; Wellbaum 2007).

Early Arab immigrants in the region quickly established themselves as merchants. To take a particularly astonishing example, they accounted for 90 percent of "peddlers" in the 1893 São Paulo city almanac, concentrated around the city's Rua 25 de Março (March 25th Street) (Karam 2007, 25). Rio de Janeiro's Saara district would form an additional early locus of activity for Arab-Brazilian merchants (Luxner 2005). As Brazil industrialized under the protectionist policies of Getúlio Vargas during the early- to mid-twentieth century, Arab Brazilians came to play a significant role in the country's growing textile sector. Facing intense competition from Asia, they later diversified into other areas, such as real estate and imports. Subsequent generations would increasingly join the ranks of the professional class (as doctors, lawyers, politicians, and so forth) and now run some of Brazil's largest businesses (Karam 2007, 27–33; Morrison 2005, 432–434). As Brazilian sociologist Oswaldo Truzzi (2018) observes regarding the Syrian-Lebanese community in São Paulo, the intergenerational transition experienced by many can be neatly summarized as follows: "From peddlers to entrepreneurs."

Anthropologist John Tofik Karam (2007, 2) explains the contemporary status of Arab Brazilians in no uncertain terms: "Nearly a half-century after the last major waves of immigration, Middle Easterners have attained an unprecedented kind of privilege throughout Brazil. They oversee multimillion-dollar business ventures, constitute an estimated 10 percent of both the City Council in São Paulo and the federal congress in Brasília, own advertising and television enterprises, star in the top-rated soap opera *O Clone* (*The Clone*), and run some of the most envied country clubs among national elites." Similarly, a recent survey indicates that Arab Brazilians account for 10 percent of the country's business leaders, rising to 12 percent among large companies (Daniel 2020).

The history and evolution of other Arab–Latin American communities follows a broadly similar trajectory, with many early immigrants engaged in commerce and light industry and in some cases also concentrated in specific neighborhoods, such as Patronato in Santiago de Chile. In turn, subsequent generations have often branched out into positions of broader political and economic significance.

Concomitantly, Arab Latin Americans have come to occupy a distinct space within the imaginaries of their respective countries. Based in part on this story of economic and social mobility but also drawing from a longer history of ethnic biases, non-Arab Latin Americans have often associated "*turco*" ethnicity and identity with shrewdness, thriftiness, and a pathological propensity for commerce. The term "*turco*" itself is indeed at times deployed as a slur, invoking precisely the imagined stinginess and overdeveloped sense of business acumen that are also common to anti-Jewish stereotypes both in Latin America and elsewhere—hence the assessment that *turcofobia* has often permeated reactions to the presence of Arab-descendant peoples in the region (Rebolledo Hernández 1994).

In her account of the politics of soccer in modern Chile, the development of which involved the formation of sports clubs belonging to Arab Chileans and other immigrant groups, historian Brenda Elsey (2011, 156) thus notes, "Sports magazines, newspapers, and comic strips depicted Arab Chileans as parasitic. They caricatured Arab business leaders as voracious social climbers who built empires by exploiting Chilean workers and consumers."

These clubs were founded as a response to (and to counteract) discrimination, as well as to facilitate integration and "create a space for their community within popular culture" (Elsey 2011, 155). They were also an avenue for political involvement, as the Arab-Chilean community recognized that while many of its members had achieved an enviable class status, they still lacked the corresponding levels of social prestige. Indeed, and unlike other immigrant groups, such as Spaniards and Italians, Arab Chileans nevertheless continued to be seen as "permanently foreign" and were unable to fully incorporate themselves into the national imaginary of "Chilean *mestizaje* [the dominant racial mixture]" (Elsey 2011, 149–164).

In other words, Latin American Orientalism is the lens through which local majority groups have long tended to view the "exotic" Arab Other (Camayd-Freixas 2013). At times, notably, this ethnic typecasting has been stretched to also include what were seen as positive traits. Thus, for early-twentieth-century Mexican thinker and racial theorist José Vasconcelos, best known for his essentialist celebration of *mestizaje* as the foundation of a new "cosmic race," this Arab heritage was to be, in its own curious and Orientalist way, a celebrated component of the new national identity. He wrote: "Judaic striae hidden within the Castilian blood since the days of the cruel expulsion now reveal themselves, along with Arabian melancholy, as a remainder of the sickly Muslim sensuality. Who has not a little of all this, or does not wish to have all?" (Vasconcelos 1997, 22).

Unlike many other formerly colonized areas, multiethnic Latin America is a region of relatively strong national identities (and, in turn, comparatively few ethnically based social or, especially, separatist movements). Accordingly, highly diverse and relatively large immigrant groups—from the Japanese in Brazil to Jews in Argentina—have generally become recognized, if not always accepted, components of the national imaginaries of countries throughout the region (Elkin 2014; Rivas and Lee-DiStefano 2016). For example, a common saying in São Paulo holds that a typical city resident is a "Japanese who speaks Portuguese with an Italian accent while eating an esfiha," referring to a Middle Eastern flatbread that, like numerous other Arab-inspired foods, is so ubiquitous and integral to the national cuisine that its origins very often go unnoticed (Lesser 2013, 4).

The relationship between these immigrants and their descendants and the Latin American societies of which they are a part is thus a rather convoluted one. On the one hand, there is not only a sense in many parts of Latin America that theirs are immigrant societies (a framing that conveniently excludes, of course, oft-disparaged indigenous and Afro-descendant populations, as well as other marginalized groups). Further, there is a rather commonplace feeling of genuine pride in this fact, both because it speaks to their societies' would-be openness (a feeling evoked by some of the interviewees in chaps. 3 and 4) and, less sanguinely, because the valorization of lighter-skinned immigrants reinforces traditional racial, ethnic, and social hierarchies (Foote and Goebel 2014).

An advertisement for an early 1980s soap opera entitled *The Immigrants* evokes both predilections. It noted: "Portuguese, Japanese, Spanish, Italians, Arabs—Don't Miss the Most Brazilian Soap Opera on Television" (Lesser 2013, 3). Missing, quite obviously, are Brazilian society's Others.

Notably, in the Latin American context, whiteness has proved to be a much more flexible category than in the US, though common to both places is the fact that whiteness itself, however defined, has been "consistently prized" (Lesser 2013, 10). In certain places and at certain times in Latin America, whiteness has in fact been stretched to incorporate Asian, Middle Eastern, and other groups, especially—and perhaps only—when they have been seen as agents of economic development. In fact, a Brazilian politician of the 1930s concluded that Japanese immigrants and their descendants—who were commonly praised as "modern, hardworking, and docile"—were "even whiter than the Portuguese" (Lesser 2013, 15–16; see also Weinstein 2015), whose supposed indolence was often blamed for Brazil's "backwardness."

As Jeffrey Lesser (2013, 2) observes, "immigrants were often hailed as saviors because they modified and improved Brazil," racially, culturally, economically, and otherwise. This contrasts with the common view in the US that as the country is "intrinsically great," immigrants are "improved" through joining US society—not the other way around (Lesser 2013, 2). In Brazil and elsewhere, a similar dynamic again appears to be evident in the present era, as the international ties and supposed commercial proclivities of Arab-descendant and other relatively successful immigrant communities make them potentially valuable allies for globally inclined state and business elites.

However, even though their contributions to state- and nation-building projects are frequently lauded, even the grandchildren of, say, Japanese or Lebanese immigrants will often still be regarded as immigrants themselves and as belonging to the Japanese or Lebanese *colônia* or *colonia* (literally, *the colony*) (Lesser 2013, 3–4). They are, and perhaps will forever be, simply "Japanese" and "Lebanese."

This broad story applies to Arab Latin Americans in general, who have integrated themselves into national life and, in many cases, into their respective countries' white-*mestizo* elites without being able to fully shed the

Orientalist aura—that is, as a mystical (and, often, conniving) Other whose supposed cutthroat entrepreneurial mentality renders them as "pariahs" and whose sense of belonging to the larger national community is thus in doubt (Karam 2007). Hence, Karam (2007, ix), himself of Lebanese descent, recounts being told "You don't have the face of a Brazilian" and "You're *turco!*" by an exasperated Brazilian vendor who had tired of his haggling and who subsequently called him a "cheapskate."

They are also commonly portrayed as being prone to financial misconduct. Thus, the massive corruption scandal involving Paulo Maluf—the Lebanese-Brazilian former mayor of São Paulo—has often been viewed through an ethnicized lens (Karam 2007). Going back to earlier times, "Arabs were . . . assumed to use their innate business acumen for personal enrichment at the expense of the agriculturally imagined Brazilian nation," more interested in peddling their wares and accumulating wealth than contributing to the country's economic prowess, which was then—and still is, to a large extent—based on agriculture (Karam 2007, 26; see also Klein and Vidal Luna 2019). As famed Brazilian anthropologist Darcy Ribeiro (2000, 317–318) noted, in a passage worth quoting at length:

> The Arabs have been the most successful immigrants, quickly becoming integrated into Brazilian life and attaining positions in the government. They have even forgotten where they came from and their miserable life in the countries of their origin. They are blind to the fact that their success can be explained to a large degree by the casual attitude they have in addressing and working with the local society: armed with prejudices and incapable of any solidarity, detached from any loyalty and family or social obligations. All of this allows them to concentrate their entire effort on getting rich.
>
> The attitude of these immigrants is frequently one of disdain and incomprehension. Their tendency is to consider poor Brazilians responsible for their own poverty and to view the racial factor as what sinks the descendants of Indians and blacks into misery. They even state that the Catholic religion and the Portuguese language have contributed to Brazil's underdevelopment. They ignore the fact that they arrived here as a result of crises that rendered them superfluous, discarded from the workforce in their homelands, and that here they found a huge country already opened, with fixed frontiers, autonomously governing its destiny.

Of course, Arab Brazilians are deployed here as a convenient foil for Brazil's non-Arab elites. Contrary to this highly misguided construct, Brazil's ruling and governing class *in general*, regardless of national background, has demonstrated remarkably little solidarity with or loyalty toward the general population. Indeed, it has been a favorite pastime of nearly all Brazilian elites to blame the poor for their lot in life and attribute the "misery" of "Indians and blacks" to "the racial factor." To believe that Brazilian society functions otherwise is to resurrect the myth of a supposedly egalitarian and meritocratic "racial democracy," which logically could not have been corroded by the rise of Arab Brazilians, as it never existed in the first place (Twine 1997).

Whatever his motivation, Ribeiro's singling out of Arab-descendant elites thus produces two deleterious effects: first, it wrongly exonerates the traditional non-Arab elite despite its own deeply problematic views regarding the country's darker-skinned majority; and second, it reinforces an imaginary of the Arab as incapable of properly integrating. It is in this sense that Arab Brazilians, and Arab Latin Americans as a whole, have again long occupied a space in the national imaginary that evokes fundamentally similar anti-Jewish stereotypes. Specifically, all have been vilified as *cosmopolitans* (or *globalists*) based on crude characterizations that stress their would-be prioritization of getting rich over the proper, national-based concerns that are (falsely) claimed to motivate the region's traditional elites (such as the Portuguese in Brazil, the Basque in Chile, and so forth).

Yet, as Karam argues in one of the more theoretically minded works in this area, perceptions of Arab-Brazilian ethnic identity have shifted in recent years, coinciding with neoliberal economic reforms and the country's increasing insertion into the global economy. Once seen as "pariahs," (some) Arab Brazilians have become "partners" of the Brazilian state and business community, as each sought to expand its footprint in the Arab world (Karam 2007). When the Brazilian government and economic elite have searched for allies and export markets in the region, they have turned to Brazil's own Arab-descendant population to serve as intermediaries. The presumption is that they (and only they) possess the necessary cultural capital to reach economic and political agreements with other Arabs, as they are able "to negotiate and barter the way only Arabs do" (Karam 2007, 23, 41).

Thus, in recent years interested state and private-sector parties have found their way to the doorsteps of existing Arab-Brazilian economic groups that had already been promoting Arab-Brazilian relations on their own. The breadth and depth of the latter's activities would expand dramatically with the coalescence of this public-private network, which united behind the notion that Brazil and Brazilian companies *must* pay more attention to the Arab world and Arab markets. While their supposed capitalist inclinations are still the target of suspicion in other contexts, when it comes to serving the imperatives of Brazil as the "export nation," Arab Brazilians, and this particular understanding of Arab-Brazilian identity, increasingly came to be valorized, not disparaged (Karam 2007). It is in this way, again, that global capitalism may reinforce certain localized cultural practices, identities, and imaginaries, rather than obliterate them.

Whether for this or less cynical reasons, the Brazilian state has on occasion presented a more sanguine reading than Ribeiro of the history of Arab immigration to Brazil, especially in recent years. Accordingly, at the opening of the first Summit of South American and Arab Countries (ASPA, per the Spanish and Portuguese acronym), held in Brasília in 2005, Lula noted: "There are few countries that have the quantity of Arabs and Arab descendants who live in this country. . . . These people helped to build this country" (quoted in Karam 2007, 174).

Foreign Policy and Commercial Relations

In sum, many Arab Brazilian economic elites—and their associated institutions—have achieved a more favorable position in the national imaginary by offering their ethnic and cultural capital to government and corporate leaders as they seek to establish a greater presence in the Arab and Muslim worlds. As is thus apparent, private actors have been active participants in the construction of economic, political, and cultural ties between these two regions.

Most existing scholarship in this area, however, focuses on state actors in Latin America and especially on how they have engaged with the Arab world in terms of foreign policy, often relating to the Israeli-Palestinian conflict. As noted, there is also a smaller body of literature focusing on US accusations that Middle Eastern terrorist groups have a significant presence in Latin America (Costa and Schulmeister 2007; Karam 2011). In both cases, the concerns of this research are largely empirical instead of theoretical.

Scholarly interest in issues relating to Arab–Latin American interstate relations and foreign policies is mostly a recent phenomenon. This increased attention reflects moves by numerous early 2000s Latin American governments, many of which identified with the left (and were associated with the region's "pink tide"), to diversify their partners beyond the US and Europe by building new axes of South-South relations (Funk 2013).

Specifically, for some Latin American leaders, increasing overtures toward the Arab world have been motivated by a deliberate strategy of fomenting a more multipolar global order in which Northern countries are no longer the central node through which all linkages must pass—hence Celso Amorim's aforementioned comment, made during headier times, that Southern actors were well on their way toward restructuring international politics and economics so that "to get from Brazil to Cairo, you won't need to pass through Washington and Paris" (quoted in Karam 2007, 174).

One manifestation of the region's turn toward the Arab world was the aforementioned 2005 initiation of regular summits between the Arab League and the now nearly defunct Union of South American Nations (UNASUR). At the time, these comprised a landmark in the institutionalization of these relations (Ferabolli 2017), though the most recent one was held in 2015, and no further such events currently appear likely. As Amorim (2011, 50–52) commented during the boom years, these ASPA summits represented the "first time" that "these two parts of the developing world were brought together." Such was the substantive increase in these political ties that the Middle East had come to occupy "the center of [Brazil's] diplomatic radar" (Amorim 2011, 48–50). Lula himself became the first Brazilian head of state to make official visits to the Arab world, where he traveled to ten different countries, shook countless hands, and opened several embassies (Amorim 2011, 50–51).

Numerous works have contemplated this era of flourishing Arab–Latin American relations. These tend to either focus on the foreign policies of the larger, more internationally active Latin American states—especially Brazil (Amar 2014; Amorim 2011, 2015; Brun 2011; FUNAG 2001; Haffner and Holand 2012; Vasconcelos et al. 2018), Mexico (Tawil 2013), Chile (Baeza and Brun 2012), and Venezuela (Herrera Navarro 2008)—or analyze these relations from a broader or pan–Latin American perspective (Botta 2012; DeShazo and Mendelson Forman 2010; Moya Mena 2011; Saddy 2016; SELA 2012; Tawil Kuri 2016; Vélez 2015). There is broad agreement here that in the past decade, Arab–Latin American relations reached unprecedented heights in terms of breadth and scope (Moya Mena 2011), with Brazil standing head and shoulders above its neighbors by all accounts. While other countries, such as Chile, have made their own advances, they were still argued to be only in the "initial stage" of building these ties (Baeza and Brun 2012, 63).

Again, it is important to enter the caveat that the dramatic growth in Arab–Latin American relations that began in earnest a few years into the new millennium has largely subsided. Reasons include an overall slowdown in Latin American economies (which, in turn, is very much related to weakening

Chinese demand for their commodities) and the exhaustion of the region's "pink tide" or "left turn." For example, at most, Brazil's post-Lula posture has been to consolidate existing gains in its relations with the Arab world as opposed to making further advances (Brun 2017). Dilma Rousseff was notoriously less interested in international affairs than her predecessor and was distracted by a stalled economy, domestic political squabbles (which culminated in her highly dubious 2016 ousting in what has often been referred to as a parliamentary coup), and preparations for the 2014 World Cup and 2016 Olympics. Her replacement, Michel Temer, though of Lebanese descent, was also primarily preoccupied with a domestic agenda (such as a failed attempt to reduce pension benefits), as well as navigating—and surviving—a series of massive corruption scandals (Reis da Silva and Pérez 2019).

With unreconstructed Cold Warrior Jair Bolsonaro's assumption of the presidency at the beginning of 2019, the expectation was that the Arab world would fall much further down the Brazilian agenda as it instead prioritized alliances with far-right governments in the US, Europe, Israel, and beyond. It is still possible that he may even prove willing to sacrifice lucrative trade relationships in the Middle East to satisfy his Evangelical base and satiate his own desire for a Samuel Huntington-style (1993) "civilizational" struggle against Islam and other perceived adversaries. Perhaps unsurprisingly, then, he pledged during the 2018 presidential campaign to close the Palestinian embassy in Brasília and to follow the United States' lead in recognizing Jerusalem as Israel's capital and moving its embassy to the contested city.

However, he dithered on this matter soon after assuming the presidency, his anti–Third Worldism and Evangelical attachments to Israel having been tested by the strength of the Brazilian agribusiness lobby. The latter strongly backed his campaign and has demonstrated firm opposition to any political maneuvers that could jeopardize access to important export markets in the Arab and Muslim worlds. Of additional significance is that a parliamentary working group was established in the Brazilian Congress in April 2020 to further "incentivize and develop" relations with the Arab world, primarily in terms of economic exchange (Garcia Fonseca 2020). Indeed, while rational prediction making may be a fool's errand during the Bolsonaro years, the amount of trade at stake appears to have tempered his stated ambitions.

Accordingly, the Bolsonaro administration's initial move was to delay moving the embassy and instead open a trade office in Jerusalem. However, this attempt to have it both ways also proved controversial. For his part, the president of the Arab-Brazilian Chamber of Commerce noted, "As a country active in the global trade and one of the world's ten greatest economies, Brazil has to open business offices where businesses are, but this decision points to an imbalance on these relations. . . . To be balanced, the government could announce offices in the Arab countries too, including Palestine" (Rocha 2019b).

At least for now, and despite recurring political quagmires and ideological pendulum swings, there is a "new [and greatly increased] normal" in Arab-Brazilian economic relations. Tellingly, though Brazilian exports to the Arab world have decreased somewhat since the 2011 peak (that is, immediately after Lula's departure), their annual value has since stabilized at over $10 billion and is still many times higher than the baseline figure from the start of the millennium.[3] Indeed, there was a "sixfold" increase in Arab-Brazilian trade between 1989 and 2012 (Carrieri 2013).

From a broader regional perspective, commercial exchange between Latin America as a whole and the Arab world also soared after the turn of the century. South American–Arab trade more than tripled toward the end of the 2000s (*Al Jazeera* 2009; *MercoPress* 2012), with Latin America's overall annual exports to the greater Middle East and North Africa region reaching over $30 billion in the early 2010s (Daoud 2016). Additionally, the Arab world's exports to Latin America grew to approximately $20 billion in goods annually. For both sides, these figures represented a several-hundred-percent increase from baseline figures a decade prior (Saddy 2016).

Regarding the primary cases under consideration here—Argentina, Brazil, and Chile—the main Arab export markets are, in varying orders, the United Arab Emirates, Saudi Arabia, Egypt, and Algeria. The same countries—though with Morocco displacing Egypt in the case of Brazil, and Algeria for Argentina and Chile—constitute their main sources of Arab-world imports.[4]

Again, and in line with the case of Brazil, overall Arab–Latin American trade has decreased somewhat and then stagnated subsequent to Latin America's early 2010s economic deceleration and the changing foreign-policy priorities of newly elected right-wing governments. However, these figures still represent dramatic increases compared to previous periods and are highly unlikely to be wiped away entirely.

Exemplifying the broader positive trend, several years ago the Arab world became a larger export market than Western Europe for Brazilian agricultural products (dos Santos Guimarães 2012). Indeed, Latin American exports to the region are dominated by meat, grains, and sugar—thus feeding into the growth of Brazil in particular as a "global agro-food power" (Buainain et al. 2019)—while imports are concentrated in areas such as minerals and fossil fuels (*ANBA* 2021). Linking the worlds of immigration and commerce, Arab imports of South American *mate*—a caffeine-rich tea that is widely consumed throughout much of the Southern Cone—have also blossomed, having been introduced to Syria and Lebanon in particular by Arab immigrants to South America who subsequently returned to their homelands (de los Reyes 2014).

Further, there has been an increasing trade in manufactured goods, typified by the Brazilian firm Embraer, whose narrow-body E170 jet became the second most used aircraft in the Middle East (*MercoPress* 2011a). Recent years have also borne witness to the establishment of nonstop flights linking these regions. For example, the carrier Emirates launched daily flights between São Paulo and Dubai in 2007. Brazil's largest city subsequently gained service to Doha on Qatar Airways in 2010, followed by flights to Casablanca on Royal Air Maroc. Starting in 2013, Etihad Airways also offered direct service between São Paulo and Abu Dhabi, though this flight was cancelled in early 2017 due to weakening demand. Beyond São Paulo, Emirates has extended service to Santiago, as well as to Rio de Janeiro (where it is joined by Royal Air Maroc) and Buenos Aires (which has also been added to Qatar Airways' route map).

Predating the recent boom in Arab–Latin American relations, the Israeli-Palestinian conflict has long been—and continues to be—of particular interest for Latin American foreign policies (Sharif 1977). Indeed, Latin America has for decades served as a diplomatic battleground for Israeli and Palestinian influence (Glick 1959). As a Peruvian scholar observed several decades ago, "Latin America's interest in the Palestinian Question has grown considerably, up to the point of being one of the few issues invariably included in most conversations and studies about global affairs" (Abugattas 1982, 117). The trend has only intensified in recent years (Munck and Pozzi 2019). Just as generations of left-wing Latin American leaders and thinkers have openly sympathized with the Palestinian cause, inspired by a shared anticolonial and anti-imperial narrative, the Latin American right has often sided with Israeli state policy (Baeza 2012; Tawil 2016).

During the 1970s and 1980s, when much of Latin America was ruled by US-backed, right-wing military regimes, Israeli arms dealers were a frequent sight in the region (Bahbah 1986). Military-to-military ties continue to be tight, particularly between Israel and Colombia (Field 2017). In turn, Arab-descendant and Jewish populations in Latin America have frequently mobilized around and lobbied their governments about the Israeli-Palestinian conflict (Baeza 2014). The latter's twists and turns would also periodically affect the region in other ways, including through migratory links. For example, in the wake of the Six-Day War in 1967, which resulted in Israel's occupation of Gaza, the West Bank, and East Jerusalem, the Israeli government formulated and to some extent carried out a plan to encourage Palestinian emigration to South America (Karam 2013a, 756).

More recently, Latin American states—led by Lula's Brazil—became increasingly active in criticizing US ownership over diplomatic efforts to ostensibly resolve the conflict (Burton 2013; 2018). After Venezuela recognized Palestine as a state in 2009, Brazil's move to do so in December 2010 spurred nine other South American countries—all except Colombia—to do the same in the following two months. Even US-allied Colombia itself would eventually and surprisingly follow suit in August 2018, during the waning days of the center-right administration of Juan Manuel Santos. Whatever the effect on Palestine's long-standing statehood bid, the symbolic message of these declarations was clearly to assert the ability to operate independently from US influence.

Accordingly, Argentina's foreign minister at the time, Héctor Timerman, explained his country's decision as part of a foreign-policy approach to the Middle East that was free of US "hegemonic interferences" (Forero and Zacharia 2011). In leaked diplomatic cables, the US ambassador to Brazil was quoted as remarking that "Brazil does not understand Middle East affairs, it's only joining the 'anti-Israel' choir"; Brazil later rejected US calls to discuss its policies toward the region, with the foreign minister replying, "Brazil does not need US permission to conduct its foreign policy" (*MercoPress* 2011b). Accordingly, at least on this issue, Lula embodied "a growing tendency in Latin American states to break out of the ghetto of US diplomacy" (Gomez 2005). With Bolsonaro in power in Brazil, this independent streak is increasingly a distant memory, though recent left-wing or center-left victories in presidential elections in Argentina, Bolivia, Chile, Peru, and elsewhere suggest its potential return.

Thus, there have been—or at least *were*—numerous post–Cold War and post–September 11 adaptations in Latin American foreign policies in accordance with the perceived decline of US hegemony in the region. A recurring implication that emerges from this analysis by regional specialists is that, while Washington has proven incapable of serving as an "honest broker" due to its recurring favoritism toward Israel's maximalist claims, leading Latin American states—particularly pre-Bolsonaro Brazil—were better situated to play a more productive role in promoting negotiations (Ferabolli 2017). Because of this recent, pro-Palestinian posture and the aforementioned migratory ties between the regions, it should come as no surprise, as *BBC Mundo* (2014) noted, that "Latin America is a region that is well known—and loved—by the Palestinians."

Toward a Political Economy of Arab–Latin American Relations

Overall, in light of the sheer quantity of recent scholarly production on this axis of ties, one can happily observe that much has changed since the early 1980s. As one scholar then noted, while "Arab–Latin American relations have grown in the last few years to an unprecedented level ... this expansion in political and economic exchange has not received adequate attention in academic institutions or research centers and remains largely unexplored" (Saddy 1983, xi). Yet to the extent that this literature has not permeated the traditional bastions of knowledge production, this observation continues to resonate, for these relations have indeed been explored, though mostly not in the Northern-based spaces that "matter."

Leaving this critique of Northern academia aside, I now turn to more general—and theoretical—observations about Arab–Latin American relations and the motivations of various Latin American actors for reaching out to and strengthening ties with the Arab world.

According to the UNASUR Constitutive Treaty, the goal was to create a "multipolar" and "balanced" world order (Itamaraty 2008). Similarly, as argued by numerous (often sympathetic) thinkers at the time, Latin America was seeking to add to its stable of partners to lessen its traditional reliance on the North and assert itself as a "pole" in the context of a less US- and Europe-dominated global scenario (Gardini 2012; Guardiola Rivera 2011). Yet for many foreign policy analysts, one of the principal concerns has been to ascertain the extent to which either pragmatic *or* ideological concerns have been the primary factors motivating these countries to pursue relations with the Arab world and other parts of the Global South. From this perspective, the key question is whether they have they been guided by "usefulness, workability, and practicality" or "principles and doctrinaire solutions" (Gardini 2011, 17).

While framed in neutral terms, this question is itself ideological or at the very least has strong ideological undertones. This is clear from the juxtaposition of an "ideological" foreign policy that is "doctrinaire" and "characterized by relatively short-term planning and a personalized vision of international relations" with a "pragmatic" one that involves rational, "medium-term" deliberation over "practical consequences" and is more focused on broader national interests (Gardini 2011, 17).

For years it has indeed been commonplace—at least since Jorge Castañeda's (2006) classic essay on Latin America's "left turn"—to separate the region's left-leaning governments into two camps: one that is "modern, open-minded, reformist, and internationalist" and another, "born of the great tradition of Latin American populism," that is "nationalist, strident, and close-minded." According to this Manichean worldview, the former—including center-left governments, none of which remain in power, in Chile (the perennial Latin American poster state), Brazil, and Uruguay—were worthy of commendation. In contrast, the usual suspects that constitute the latter—Venezuela, Ecuador (then under Rafael Correa's leadership), and Bolivia (prior to the 2019 coup against Evo Morales)—needed to be "contain[ed]" (Castañeda 2006). And just as we can effortlessly separate Latin America's governments into *good* and *bad*, the same can be done with foreign policy. Here, Castañeda's (2006) "modern" left equates to those with a "pragmatic" approach, while the "close-minded" states engage with the outside world based on ill-conceived and myopic "ideological" strategies.

Yet the problems with this dichotomous analytical construct are multiple. At the most basic level, it is not immediately clear whether or how to draw the line between the two categories. Was Venezuela under Chávez, for example, being pragmatic or ideological—or both—in seeking to diversify its pool of allies?

More troubling is the fact that the great pragmatic-ideological bifurcation conveniently divided Latin American governments into two opposing camps: those that were more closely aligned with Washington, embraced neoliberal reforms, and did not actively seek to build political and economic relations with what the US considered to be pariah states or challenge the existing US-led regional order; and those that have found themselves on Washington's official enemies list, been at least mildly critical (rhetorically, if not in practice) of neoliberalism and neoliberal globalization, and, for better or worse, openly engaged with Washington's geopolitical adversaries (such as Iran).

Hence, the danger with such an appraisal of Latin American foreign policies is that it dovetails too comfortably with the highly ideologically charged US line—as formulated by Trump-era National Security Advisor John Bolton—that there is a "triangle of terror" in the region that is composed of the troublemaking states of Cuba, Nicaragua, and Venezuela, which in turn has "finally met its match" due to the rise of a supposedly pro-freedom coalition centered in Washington and Brasília (Borger 2018). What goes unmentioned here is that it is of course Bolsonaro's foreign policy machinations—including his nurturing of the regional and authoritarian-minded far right and stated ambition to undermine already-limited international efforts to address climate change—that are likely to prove far more damaging to Latin America's trajectory, let alone the world, than any nefarious plans concocted in Havana, Caracas, or Managua. While US president Joe Biden's administration has seemingly abandoned this rhetoric and has certainly pushed back against Bolsonaro, the first years of his presidency have yet to bring significant indications of a fundamentally different US posture toward these countries or the region as a whole.

Further, this analytical division is premised on the unstated supposition that the strategy pursued by the "good" Latin American states—which in general signals closer adherence to a neoliberal model, with fewer tariffs, trade barriers, or state regulations to soften capitalism's edges—is somehow less ideological than its more statist counterpart. Yet of course, notions such as *open markets*, *free trade*, and indeed *capitalism* as a whole are just as political as opposing ideas (Polanyi 2001). Even "pragmatic" economic relations are thus also ideological by definition.

Yet what is of more immediate concern is another intellectual assumption lurking underneath the dichotomy between a "pragmatic" and "ideological" foreign policy. This is the notion that understanding Arab–Latin American— or any other set of—relations merely requires an evaluation of the foreign policies of the involved countries. From this perspective, the study of global affairs boils down to foreign policy analysis, meaning a primary focus on the state as the unit of concern and the concomitant overlooking of the role of other actors. What this also implies is a lack of attention to the larger structural contexts, particularly the reduction of barriers to global trade and financial flows, in which these relations are embedded.

Here, we return to an aforementioned critique of many existing efforts to conceptualize Arab–Latin American relations: an excessive state-centrism. This focus is problematic for several reasons.

First, as noted, framing Arab–Latin American relations primarily in terms of state policies and interactions occludes the significant role played by other actors, including economic elites. A fuller account of these relations, as this work seeks to begin to provide, must explore how these different sets of public and private actors both work together and compete to promote their visions, goals, and interests vis-à-vis the Arab world.

The most important agents in this regard include government economic ministries and export agencies, international business organizations, and business networks, both sector-wide and those dedicated to particular country or regional relationships. The latter range from those focusing on, say, overall Arab-Brazilian, -Argentine, or -Chilean trade to others whose mandates may revolve solely around, inter alia, Lebanon, Iraq, Morocco, or Saudi Arabia. Taken together, this is precisely the web of public and private actors that enables commercial flows between the regions and is largely responsible for promoting Latin American commerce with the Arab world. In turn, protagonists from these various types of organizations are profiled in the following chapters.

Second, by mostly overlooking the role of business elites, many existing accounts downplay the centrality of economic factors for explaining and understanding Arab–Latin American relations. Yet one cannot properly contextualize these ties without understanding them as a manifestation of a global, neoliberal trend toward the free circulation of goods and capital.

In contrast, according to conventional, statist accounts, politics is naturally privileged over economics as an ontological starting point. According to this reading of Arab–Latin American relations, the interests of actors in the latter region have largely revolved around how to build new axes of South-South ties, as well as how to respond to and potentially play a role in resolving the geopolitical challenges affecting the former region, including the Israeli-Palestinian conflict, the Syrian Civil War, and the Saudi-Iranian struggle for influence. These are real issues of concern for at least a number of Latin America's more internationally active states, and there is no reason to doubt that foreign policy gurus in the region have been (or were) sincere in their desire to "break out of the ghetto of US diplomacy" or disrupt Washington's "hegemonic interferences" by pursuing more independent foreign policies.

However, this storyline fails to capture the economic interests of Latin American actors—again, both public and private—in pursuing closer ties with the Arab world or Middle East. In some cases, the aforementioned logic of multipolarity could also apply to economic relations, insofar as certain Latin American commercial elites may have sought to reduce their commercial dependency on the US and other traditional powers. Yet the question of trade relations cannot be reduced to a national or regional interest in autonomy.

Finally, parsing Latin American foreign policies without accompanying analysis of dominant economic interests and how the latter seek to influence the former smuggles in the highly problematic assumption that Latin American states are autonomous from domestic class forces. That is, by viewing Arab–Latin American relations through the prism of Latin American states, to which we attribute either a pragmatic or an ideological foreign policy, we may be overlooking the question of to what extent the state is the proper unit of analysis in the first place.

That is to say, we must be open to the likelihood that the Chilean state's interest in the Arab world, for example, originates not precisely from an autonomously generated policy decision, but rather is at least partially the product of an agenda advanced by the country's globalizing economic elite, which through various forms of structural, political, and economic power seeks to turn its provincial class interests into those of the Chilean state. Thus, focusing on foreign policy may lead us to foreground the visible (state) "superstructure" while overlooking the submerged (private) "base." The goal is not to promote a vulgar Marxist account in which states are mere empty vessels for capitalist interests. Yet it would be highly problematic to assume that the state and its foreign policy apparatus somehow operate independently from these powerful groups (van Apeldoorn and de Graaff 2016).

Accordingly, one of the present purposes is to shed light on the political economy of Arab–Latin American relations. For example, in analyzing how Argentina or the Argentine state interacts with the Arab world, we should not merely ask what kind of foreign policy or goals it is pursuing. Rather, we must go deeper and interrogate where those policies or goals come from in the first place, whose interests they serve, and how different sets of public and private elites—many but not all of whom are of Arab descent—cooperate, compete, and struggle to define the government's agenda in relation to the Arab world and to pursue their interests through both governmental and nongovernmental means. The idea is not to argue for the primacy of either political and state-based interests on one hand or economic and private ones on the other; instead, it is to capture the dynamic interplay between these forces and reveal how Latin American agents—particularly political and economic elites—operate within the global capitalist structure (and concomitant market-based exigencies) that increasingly dominate our time (Robinson 2008).

A political-economy approach is especially salient given contemporary developments in Arab–Latin American relations. First, especially during the recent boom years, there was a clear tendency for Latin American political and economic elites to feed off of each other's efforts to reach out to the Arab world. In their visits to the region, it has been customary for Latin American political leaders to travel with entourages of interested business elites. Further, the aforementioned ASPA gatherings were accompanied by parallel CEO Summits, the third of which—held in October 2012 in Lima—drew more than five hundred attendees from both regions.

There has also been a series of Latin America Mid-East Investors Forums, organized by the business intelligence outfit LatinFinance. Other, similar conventions include the Global Business Forum on Latin America, which has been staged regularly by the Dubai Chamber of Commerce and Industry since the inaugural 2016 event, and the Brazil-Arab Countries Economic Forum, last held in October 2020. Deploying the slogan "the future is now," the latter bills itself as "Latin America's Biggest, Most Relevant Online Business and Investment Platform for Arabs and Brazilians."[5]

Yet while the business community may to an extent follow government signals—per Amorim's (2011, 52) aforementioned observation that "often leaders wave the flag and businessmen follow suit"—the inverse is also true. As noted, private-sector trade groups are actively engaged in training local capital to cross borders, helping establish new axes of trade relations where the state is paying relatively little attention, and pressuring the state to adopt the very policies that allow for increased trade and financial flows between the regions.

Given this protagonist role, we should not be surprised that while political ties between Latin America and the Arab world have stagnated, and in many cases declined, in recent years with the departure of leaders such as Lula and Chávez, economic relations have proven somewhat more resilient. Given that both Latin America and the Arab world are becoming increasingly integrated into the web of global capitalist relations, this is to be expected.

To summarize, the present analysis reveals a network of public and private economic actors who are instrumental in advancing these ties. The idea is not to downplay the state's role, but rather to paint a more complete portrait by highlighting the extent to which merchant and other capitalist elites from both the private and public sectors in fact often serve as the midwives of these commercial relations. Accordingly, this work adds to current understandings of what is at stake in Arab–Latin American relations, who the key actors are, what motivates their actions, and how and why this axis of relations is significant and worthy of attention.

Through conducting dozens of in-depth interviews with the protagonists behind these economic ties, I seek answers to a series of questions with broad theoretical implications for both global political economy and global studies: To what extent is there evidence for the existence of a global capitalist class with a shared, global, and cosmopolitan class consciousness? Are the worldviews of these economic elites national, transnational, denational, global, or something else? How do such actors conceptualize their participation in the very global capitalist system that their own actions help to construct? It is to these topics that I turn in the next two chapters through telling the stories of seven representative protagonists in Arab–Latin American relations who also belong to Latin America's would-be global capitalist class.

Notes

1. *North* and *South* are contested terms whose usage often occludes more than it elucidates. I utilize them here as shorthand for regions that are characterized by disproportionately high rates of poverty and inequality, that tend to suffer from colonial legacies and ongoing imperial practices, and that have been integrated into the global economy in a subservient position (that is, based on raw-material exports). For further analysis of the North-South divide, see Kevin Funk (2015a), "The Global South Is Dead, Long Live the Global South! The Intersectionality of Social and Geographic Hierarchies in Global Capitalism." Others, such as William I. Robinson (2008) and Michael Hardt and Antonio Negri (2000), argue that the entire North-South categorization scheme has been rendered largely irrelevant by the spread of global capitalism as a universal and homogenizing force.

2. The Syrian-Lebanese amalgamation is common in the region for various reasons, including the fact that they were part of a common administrative unit—Ottoman Syria—at the time of mass emigration to Latin America (Pearl Balloffet 2020, 4–5). The term is also often used as a label of self-identification by members of this community (Karam 2007, 7).

3. See the Arab-Brazilian Chamber of Commerce's website, accessed April 19, 2017, http://www.ccab.org.br/pt/infobiz.

4. See the database of the Observatory of Economic Complexity, accessed June 3, 2021, https://oec.world.

5. See the Brazil–Arab Countries Economic Forum's website, accessed June 4, 2021, https://www.forumcamaraarabe.com.br/en/.

3

"THE TRADITION OF DEAD GENERATIONS"

On the Persistence of Place-Based Longings

THROUGH DARCY RIBEIRO'S ANALYSIS OF ARAB-BRAZILIAN ELITES, AS delineated in chapter 2, one can easily appreciate many of the ways in which understandings of race, ethnicity, and class intersect in Latin America, a region where skin color, phenotype, and socioeconomic status have been profoundly and inextricably linked since the colonial period (Mignolo 2005; Quijano 2000). To this list, of course, we must add gender, religion, and other structural categories, subject positions, and axes of identity.

The benefit of pursuing an intersectional approach to the questions at hand is that it allows us to both capture the complexity of the human experience and avoid constructing a false narrative in which, say, class and a stylized nationalism-transnationalism-denationalization-globality divide crowd out all other cognitive frameworks (Funk 2015a). Instead, an intersectional framework facilitates the analyst's ability to perceive the multiplicitous, mutually imbricated, and even contradictory nature of our interpretive horizons. Accordingly, it is especially well suited for grappling with the "rapidly changing and increasingly complex" nature of our global age (Boryczka and Disney 2015, 447). The latter, it is often argued, has undermined the tendency to divide the social world into discrete spheres by engendering border-crossing mobilities, complicated identity amalgamations, and liminal thought patterns.

To demonstrate the power of an intersectional framework, let us consider, for example, the supposed irreconcilability of economic and faith-based worldviews. Indeed, at the level of many popular stereotypes, business and religion do not mix. The latter is often viewed as being at odds with the former, given that it introduces—as the story goes—ethical reasoning and other extraneous considerations into the fundamentally amoral realm of buying and selling. As nuclear-power magnate C. Montgomery Burns from *The Simpsons* once remarked while advising children from the local junior achievers club: "Family. Religion. Friendship. These are the three demons you must slay if you wish to succeed in business. When opportunity knocks, you don't want to be driving to a maternity hospital or sitting in some phony-baloney church. Or synagogue" (Ewalt 2005). Karl Marx and Friedrich Engels (1888, 475) were similarly forthright in asserting that the bourgeoisie "has drowned the most heavenly ecstasies of religious fervour, of chivalrous enthusiasm, of philistine sentimentalism, in the icy water of egotistical calculation." And in their place, "it has substituted naked, shameless, direct, brutal exploitation."

In reality, many businesspeople—including some of the interviewees in this and the following chapter—are of course religious and religiously motivated. Further, many religious denominations and practices provide convenient spiritual justifications for the accumulation of vast personal (and institutional) fortunes. In the US, one is highly accustomed to this marriage of faith and opulence, as embodied by elegantly dressed televangelists who eschew traditional asceticism in favor of preaching wealth as a sign of God's blessing.

In the Latin American context, traditional elites have often been affiliated with exclusive sects such as the ultraconservative Catholic order Opus Dei. However, recent years have borne witness to the explosion of US-style charismatic Evangelical churches—for example, Brazil's Neo-Pentecostal Igreja Universal do Reino de Deus (Universal Church of the Kingdom of God). Appropriately for an organization that preaches prosperity gospel, the church's founder, Edir Macedo, is himself a billionaire and media mogul (Chesnut 2003; Cuadros 2016), as well as a fervent Jair Bolsonaro supporter.

While people from lower-class backgrounds were in many cases the first to convert, Evangelical congregations now draw from across the Latin American class spectrum (Levine 2012). In Brazil, they are estimated to account for over a quarter of the population and formed presumably the largest part of the BBB bloc—referring to *bullets* (that is, gun rights activists and other "law-and-order" voters), *bulls* (agribusiness and the rural landowning class more generally), and *Bibles* (Evangelicals and other right-wing Christians)—that propelled Bolsonaro into the presidency.

In sum, a new religious voting bloc has been constructed in Brazil. Crucially, it features large numbers of adherents among marginalized social groups, including *favela* residents, Afro-Brazilians, and the poor more generally. Many of them, in turn, have been incorporated politically by these Evangelical churches into the far right (Dominguez et al. 2011). In other words, a critical mass of impoverished voters both in Brazil and throughout the region are now consistently pulling the levers for candidates that espouse not only fundamentalist social views, but also a hardline neoliberal agenda of privatization, wage suppression, and anti-unionism that traditionally found few adherents beyond elite circles. This cross-class, extremist coalition is producing a radical transformation in Latin American politics, of which Bolsonaro is only the most visible manifestation.

What this example of the mutual constitution of class and religious identities demonstrates is the need to approach social class intersectionally—that is, to think in terms of "classed intersections" (Taylor 2010; see also Wallis 2015). Thus, the following discussion of capitalist worldviews is premised on the notion that while different forms of identity may indeed compete for predominance in the minds of those profiled here and in chapter 4, we cannot claim that they represent a zero-sum game (as if, for example, one's class position necessarily makes religion or ethnicity superfluous). Rather, while a strong religious or ethnic identity may supersede a class-based one, it may also mingle with it, reinforce it, combine with it, or transform it in novel ways. The present task, again, is to make sense of these complex arrangements. Specifically, I proceed by focusing on class consciousness (and its intersections), but without reifying it vis-à-vis the other interpretive frameworks evinced by my interlocutors.

This is a particularly salient point in regard to ethnic identity. Unsurprisingly, a disproportionate number of the protagonists behind Latin American trade with the Arab world are themselves of Arab descent—mostly Syrian or Lebanese in the Brazilian and Argentine cases, and Palestinian in Chile. These, in turn, are the country backgrounds of the vast majority of those who occupy leadership positions in Arab organizations throughout these countries. Overall, of those whom I profile in this and the following chapter, all but one reveal Arab ancestry.

In many of these cases, this intersection between ethnic background and economic activity reveals that Arabness can provide the subjective mooring that motivates these actors to serve as conduits for Arab–Latin American exchange. It also highlights the extent to which real or perceived Arab cultural capital is at times increasingly valorized in the context of capitalist globalization. What is thus clear is that, both in the Latin American context and beyond, attempting to separate ethnicity, race, and class is a fool's errand.

However, the other—typically, less central—protagonists I cite briefly at the end of the chapter are more mixed in terms of national and ethnic backgrounds. Further, within the realm of corporations and other economic institutions that engage with but do not focus exclusively on the Arab world, there is an overrepresentation of Arab Latin Americans, though many of the relevant actors are not of Arab descent. Building bridges between these different groups—elites of Arab and other ancestries—is in fact often recognized as an important goal by these actors. As noted in one of the vignettes in the following sections, the former leader of a now-dormant Arab-Chilean trade group, for example, has pointed to its own failure to expand its base beyond the Arab-Chilean community as one of the primary reasons that the organization did not gain more traction.

What the Arab–Latin American case offers, in sum, is a compelling vantage point from which to contemplate a particular set of intersectional identities. These revolve, most specifically, around the relationships between class status and consciousness, ethnicity, and culture, as well as the continuum between the national and the global.

Exploring Classed Intersections

In this and the subsequent chapter, I carefully analyze the classed intersections, worldviews, and actions of selected Latin American economic elites whose efforts have been fundamental in promoting the growth in this region's relations with the Arab world. Specifically, I asked interviewees both directly and indirectly about their goals and the motivations behind their activities. I also sought out subtle verbal and nonverbal cues.

Given the interpretivist philosophy and approach that undergird this study, I present these stories as ethnographic vignettes that are rich in context, sensory details, and meaning. Together, they reveal how these figures understand their globalizing activities and shed light on the complex amalgamations of diverse interpretive frameworks through which their efforts are filtered.

This ethnographic format allows me to foreground the complexities of our dialogues as well as provide my own analysis and reactions as a situated human being (and interviewer, researcher, and conversation partner) who is engaging in a fluid and dynamic exchange of words and ideas. For present purposes, in which questions of meaning are paramount, this relational style is again superior to the traditional positivist approach toward interviewing, which typically involves speaking *for* interviewees instead of allowing their own voices and lived experiences to shine through, as well as reproducing selected quotations without the surrounding context, and presenting an overly linear argument buttressed by univocal evidence from interlocutors while foregoing the complexity of the social world (Fujii 2017).

Regarding this last point, it is worthwhile to recall the methodological advice of the (former) dependency theorist and subsequent president of Brazil, Fernando Henrique Cardoso. When conducting research, as he argued, "it is necessary ... to avoid the simplistic reductionism so common among the present-day butterfly collectors who abound in the social sciences and who stroll through history ... with the blissful illusion that their findings can remove from history all its ambiguities, conjectures, and surprises." What the researcher needs instead is "patience" and to be prepared to be "astonishe[d]" by "unexpected revelations" (Cardoso 1977, 21). In the spirit of interpretivism, this project is based on a rejection of the notion that such complexity is a nuisance that must be suppressed for analytical expediency. Instead, I embrace it by seeking out "situated, intersubjective understandings that shed light on how people construct, navigate, and challenge their social worlds" (Schaffer 2016, 16).

It is crucial to note that Cardoso's is not a lambasting of theoretical knowledge. Rather, it is a call for theory that is empirically informed and disciplined by context. His own classic work, *Dependency and Development in Latin America*, which he coauthored with Chilean sociologist Enzo Faletto (1979), drew from rich case studies to intervene in debates surrounding dependency theory and is emblematic in this regard.

Each of the following chapters contains three ethnographically informed vignettes, one from each of the principal countries—Argentina, Brazil, and Chile—under consideration. The vignettes focus either on particular individuals or multiple figures within the same institution. I have chosen to portray these specific actors for two reasons. First, as noted, their backgrounds, experiences, and thought processes are representative of my interviewees in general. In turn, as my interlocutors include many prominent actors in Arab-Argentine/Brazilian/Chilean relations, they are also broadly representative of the protagonists behind these relations as a whole. Second, their stories elucidate important trends regarding the classed intersections of Latin America's would-be global capitalist class.

In this first empirical chapter, I present the stories of four individuals from three different organizations. The first is Diego Makhoul, formerly a senior administrator within Chile's international development apparatus and founding director of a private-sector Arab-Chilean trade group. He was subsequently appointed by the Chilean government to serve in a high-level diplomatic position in the Middle East. Next is Dr. Rafael Bishara, an economist by training who founded and for decades served as director of a Lebanon-focused Argentine commercial group. The final interlocutors are Kadim Al-Hassani and Aqil Qasim, both senior executives within an Iraqi-Brazilian trade association.

These vignettes reveal mental frameworks that display a strong place-based (national and/or transnational) consciousness. This subgroup, as I argue, accounts for a narrow majority among my interviewees. It is important to note that there are still hints here of denationalizing—and, to a lesser extent, globalizing—trends. Yet the class consciousness evinced by these actors is mostly filtered through an interpretive framework that is predominantly rooted within single or multiple national, cultural, and/or ethnic groups. In turn, the next chapter analyzes three sets of actors whose class consciousness is less national or transnational than denational or global.

Vignette #1: Diego Makhoul

While I was seeking to break into the seemingly esoteric world of Arab–Latin American business connections, the multi-hatted, Palestinian-Chilean Diego Makhoul—political appointee, university professor, business consultant, and charity administrator—became my lifeline.[1] As I would soon learn, the Arab-Chilean business group of which Makhoul was the founding leader had recently gone into hibernation, thus providing a retroactive explanation for my unanswered phone calls. Yet once a Google search led me to his government email account, only seven minutes separated my initial, introductory message and his amiable response, both in Spanish. He offered his personal cell phone number and an assurance that he was "delighted to support me with this topic." A few days after I stepped off the plane in Santiago, he would become the first of my several-dozen interviewees among the Latin American business elite. Two years later, during a return trip to Chile, he was also the last.

Then serving as a senior executive within the Chilean state's international development apparatus, a position to which he was appointed by the right-wing government of Sebastián Piñera, Makhoul invited me for our first encounter to his upper-floor office within the graying but stately Ministry of Foreign Affairs headquarters in downtown Santiago. So regular would my presence in the building become due to a steady stream of meetings with leaders from the Chilean state's international trade bureaucracies that I was soon on a first-name basis with the morning security guard, who began to grant me single-use access cards without the requisite inspection of my passport.

Founded during Chile's democratic transition, this organization's stated mission is to promote shared development opportunities between Chile and countries of a similar or lower level of prosperity. Accordingly, it has the dual function—or at least goal—of simultaneously promoting both national and international development. As Makhoul explains, this position has nothing to do with the Arab world, save for a few small projects with Palestine and his additional efforts to attract "Arab donors"—a term he deploys in English—to Central America.

Makhoul's other past roles have included a stint as executive director of a Santiago-based charity that seeks to harness the resources of Palestinian-descendant and other Chileans to promote health-related, educational, and recreational projects for children in Palestine and an ongoing part-time professorship in international business at an exclusive, Opus Dei–affiliated university. There, on a privileged fifty-two-hectare campus in the foothills of the world's longest mountain range, located within the posh, east-side municipality of Las Condes—the same high-powered neighborhood that is home to the city's evocatively nicknamed "Sanhattan" financial and commercial district (Boano and Vergara-Perucich 2017)—Makhoul taught a course focused on exploring investment opportunities in Latin America. Scheduled activities included instructor-led excursions to South American business hubs such as Lima and Bogotá, during which students met with political and business leaders. The stated purpose of these trips was to cultivate an appreciation for both the "opportunities" and "challenges" facing Chilean companies that operate or are seeking to expand abroad.

However, Makhoul's true pet project was—and to an extent perhaps still is—the Arab-Chilean business grouping that he helped to found in the mid to late 2000s. Its purpose was to traverse the economic gap that exists between Chile and the Arab world by facilitating an increase in trade and investment flows. Returning to the same metaphor, the organization was to become, per its self-description, the "natural bridge" linking the country to this faraway region. Specifically, it sought to help Chilean companies become "premium suppliers" of both goods and services to Arab markets, and, in turn, to develop Chile as a central node through which Arab investments to Latin America as a whole would flow.

"Regrettably," as Makhoul notes, numerous factors led him to disband the group several years after its founding, including his own assumption of public office and a perceived lack of substantive interest among Arab-Chilean business elites. Yet his belief in the viability of increased Arab–Latin American economic exchange lives on through wistful references to one day relaunching the organization as a proper chamber of commerce, as well as through the new role that he had taken on just months before our second meeting as the in-house Latin America–focused advisor with a Palestinian bank. As noted, he subsequently abandoned the latter due to his diplomatic appointment by Piñera, who returned to the presidency in 2018.

Eager to avoid a late arrival to my first meeting, I allowed well over an hour for the late-morning commute—by bus and then subway—to the city's traditional downtown core from the mixed-class, southeastern Santiago municipality of Macul. My abundance of caution afforded me a few minutes in the mid-winter cold to admire La Moneda, the same presidential palace that only four decades prior had been subjected to intense bombardment by the country's own air force. The attack formed part of a military coup that set the stage for a seventeen-year "anthology of horror" and savage repression at the hands of the Augusto Pinochet regime (1973–1990).[2]

During the short walk from the seat of government to the Ministry, I pass a monument to the deposed socialist president, Salvador Allende. Its base bears an etching from his final speech, delivered as bombs fell and fires raged: *Tengo fe en Chile y su destino* (I have faith in Chile and its destiny). Only minutes but worlds away in Makhoul's office, after crossing the Plaza de la Constitución (Constitution Square), I find myself seeking to build rapport by accepting a cup of tea and making banal conversation about crowded conditions on line 1 of the Santiago Metro, South America's longest underground rail network and one of the busiest in the hemisphere. He shrugs off my attempt to establish common ground, commenting that an unspecified number of years have passed since his last ride.

Despite Allende's hopes, perhaps no factor has done more to define Chile's economic destiny even after the "pacted" and fragmentary 1990 transition to democracy than an unwavering commitment to the free movement of goods and capital. The details of the Milton Friedman–inspired and Chicago Boy–guided authoritarian imposition of neoliberalism in the 1970s and 1980s, as well as its subsequent universalization across mainstream Chilean politics in the post-Pinochet democratic order, are indeed well known (Funk 2012; Harvey 2007; Haughney 2006; Valdés 2008). Yet what is particularly germane for present purposes is the fact that post-dictatorship, neoliberal Chile is said to have more free trade agreements than any other country *in the entire world* (*AméricaEconomía* 2013).

As Makhoul later notes approvingly, the economies represented by Chile's trade deals together make up a staggering 92 percent of global GDP (though the actual number, as cited in the following chapter, may be several percentage points lower). His subsequent declaration that "Chile has an interest in having open trade with the largest number of countries around the world" thus requires no further elaboration. In the admiring, jealous words of right-wing Argentine intellectual Mariano Grondona (2003), "Chile doesn't marry anyone. It lacks 'physical [i.e., intimate] relations' . . . its strategy is to sell wherever it can."

Makhoul's ambition boiled down to marrying Chile's promiscuous international commercial policy with an Arab world, and particularly Gulf region, that is thirsting for two kinds of partners: first, reliable suppliers of agricultural goods—thus improving "food security" in a region that depends heavily on imports to satisfy domestic consumption; and second, attractive investment destinations that can absorb the seemingly endless stream of petrodollars (along with, particularly in Dubai's case, earnings derived from tourism, services, shipping, and so on) spewing from the overflowing coffers of its sovereign wealth funds (Santiso 2013).

Chile, with its bountiful harvests of agricultural products ranging from apples, grapes, pears, almonds, and avocados to wine and farm-raised salmon, thus seems to fit the bill nicely. Also helping to open doors for Chilean exporters has been the country's global reputation, which was partially compromised during the massive social upheaval that erupted in late 2019, as an economically successful country that is "open, serious, and trustworthy"—adjectives that have been repeated ad nauseam by the country's political class (*La Nación* 2015).

In other words, as Makhoul notes at the very beginning of our conversation, he quickly realized that "there is an interesting opportunity [for Arab-Chilean exchange] that needs to be taken advantage of." Indeed, he would repeat the keywords *interesting* and *opportunities* time and again during our visits. In turn, the fact that he founded his private-sector group under the auspices of a powerful and leading organization representing the interests of Chilean industrialists marked a definite step forward in the efforts of the Chilean business class to attempt to seize them.

Makhoul's organization could certainly claim a blue-blooded pedigree. First, it was born after a series of back-and-forth exchanges with a sector-leading benchmark organization focusing on Arab-Brazilian trade. Second, its founding came on the heels of Makhoul's presence at a meeting in New York alongside Bill Clinton, Jordan's King Abdullah II, the Crown Prince of Bahrain, and a hundred CEOs from both the US and the Arab world, as well as his organization of a business forum that included such luminaries as Chile's then president, Michelle Bachelet, and Carlos Slim (Makhoul excitedly recounts that the two ate breakfast together; in response to my question, he confirms that Slim paid). In sum, the stars seemed to align for a dramatic surge in Arab-Chilean trade.

Initial signs were indeed auspicious. Adopting the model of its Arab-Brazilian mentors, who had presented then president Luiz Inácio Lula da Silva with a well-received plan to "promote trade" with the Arab world and developed a close working relationship with his administration, Makhoul's group entered into dialogue with Bachelet and the various arms of the state's international trade bureaucracy. The aim was to show that "there are opportunities" and encourage her participation, along with an "important business delegation," in the second Summit of South American and Arab Countries (ASPA), which was held in Doha in 2009. Makhoul and his collaborators placed particular emphasis on (successfully) using a government grant to obtain and diffuse information about halal certification. This effort involved working with a local mosque, conducting seminars and workshops, and helping the Chilean business community to understand "what halal is about." He quickly adds that halal certification brings access to markets beyond the Arab world, as there are also many halal consumers in Malaysia, Indonesia, China, and India (and indeed, in Europe, North America, and so on). "I'm not Muslim," he specifies. "But it's an interesting market."

Though Arab-Chilean trade, as noted, has experienced a significant increase in recent years, Makhoul continues to describe these relations as "very incipient." Several impediments presented themselves along the road to realizing his ambition of replicating the Brazilian success story. First, while Brazil "pursued a very intense policy of openness toward the Arab world," the Chilean state's commitment was never more than lukewarm, its gaze firmly directed toward more geographically immediate Asian-Pacific growth markets. "Chile isn't interested," he declares.

By way of supporting evidence, he points to a string of missed opportunities and bungled interactions—such as the two occasions on which the emir of Qatar had announced visits to Chile. Makhoul asks me rhetorically, "Do you know what Chile's response was?" With a mocking, incredulous tone, he recounts the message that the government transmitted to the Qataris: they could not receive him because it was summer, and everyone was on vacation. Instead, the emir visited Venezuela, Uruguay, Brazil, and—he reports with a special brand of consternation reserved for one of Chile's chief historical, economic, and geopolitical rivals—even *Peru*.

Thus, when he comments that "there's much to do" and, in Spanglish, that "Chile está [is] very behind," he is expressing concern not only about missed opportunities for Arab-Chilean trade, but about the fact that Chile is starting to lag vis-à-vis its peers. Prospectors from the Gulf have been circling the globe searching for investment gold, and it is much to Makhoul's dismay that the Peruvian port of Callao has received hundreds of millions of dollars in investments from DP World—a Dubai-based corporation whose portfolio of seventy-eight marine and inland terminals spans forty countries on six continents—while Chile appears as empty space on the company map.[3]

Another rhetorical question follows, this time again reflecting his tendency to sprinkle his native Spanish—the language of our dialogues—with key business terms in English: "¿Sabes cuántos investments están recibiendo esos países?" (Do you know how many investments those [aforementioned] countries are receiving?). To stop the economic bleeding, he suggests choosing diplomats—apparently, with the benefit of hindsight, like himself—who are linked to the business sector and actually understand the Arab world. As he recounts, one previous appointee "had a map of the Arab world that included Afghanistan and Pakistan, and I said no, no, no, no, no, those aren't Arab [countries]." He notes that "there's a lot of ignorance," including in elite circles, as many of his compatriots think an Arab is a "man with a turban who talks weird."

The unexpected second obstacle was precisely the Arab-Chilean composition of his Arab-Chilean business association. While its membership base essentially consisted of "businesspeople with very good names, all of Arab origin," he discovered that few of them had "a commercial link" with the region or even a particular interest in developing one. As a result, he learned an important lesson: "Obviously it doesn't matter if the businessperson is or isn't Arab, what matters is if the businessperson has a commercial interest in the region." As he later explains, contemplating my future meetings: "If you go to see an Arab businessman [in Chile] ... he's going to say a bunch of beautiful things to you, that Arabs are so good ... but"—now switching to English—"what are you really doing [to promote relations with the Arab world]?" The answer, in Spanish: "Nada."

All of the preceding translated into both difficulties with funding the group's operations and its eventual conversion into a one-man operation. By the end, he says, "*I* was the [organization]." Next time—and one imagines that there may indeed be a next time—he will try to establish a proper chamber of commerce. "I would love to," he gushes. For now, "the issue is there, like, asleep," and yet the "interesting business opportunity" remains.

At this point in our conversation, the ideas start to flow. How about a halal lamb slaughterhouse in the Chilean outpost of Punta Arenas, one of the world's southernmost cities? For reasons (geographic or otherwise) that he does not explain, that "could be a huge business." What about importing Qatari gas to curry favor so that the emir will increase investment in Chile? Plus, as he notes, someone needs to bring Islamic banking to Chile. I think that he thinks he can make it all happen.

But, he cautions in Spanglish, "necesito funding" (I need funding). As he says mockingly, he also needs for the Chilean business class—which obsesses over Orientalist images of halal certification, in which a curious figure from a mosque arrives to your farm and "plays a CD [and] ... says weird things"—to overcome its mental block against "exporting to these Muslims." Instead, the country's economic elite must come to the belated realization that the Arab world represents, once again, "an interesting business opportunity."

This is not to say that his efforts—including preparing reports for high-level officials, receiving visiting delegations of political and economic leaders, organizing business forums, participating in international trade fairs, literally taking Chilean businesspeople to Dubai, and training a new generation of trade promoters in cultural awareness and sensitivity—were for naught. Indeed, he points to certain successes, such as Chile's presence at Dubai-based Gulfood, which describes itself as "the world's largest annual food & beverage trade exhibition" and "a truly unique platform linking every aspect of the global food supply chain."[4] While the Chilean stand used to be lackluster, his protégés "took the matter seriously—really," and recently won an award for their exhibition. But there is an opportunity to do much, much more.

At this point, I wonder why he is such a stickler for cultural knowledge—what he calls "the Arab issue"—or why, beyond profit, he does any of this in the first place. What does he make of himself as a Chilean of Palestinian descent who speaks Arabic, has a local cell phone in Dubai, and is consumed by the drive to promote Arab-Chilean economic exchange? And when I comment that very little is known in the US about Arab–Latin American relations, why does he stress that this is obvious—since "my" people know essentially nothing about either region—and then begin to laugh derisively?

Further, what meaning does he attach to his observation that Latin America "is full, full, full of people of Arab-Christian descent" or that Arab Latin Americans are a prominent part of the business class in countries throughout the region? (As he observes, with a touch of exaggeration: "The big businesspeople of Central America . . . are all Arabs.") And what does he think about the fact that he is part of this diaspora and that his business dealings in the Arab world are facilitated by a cultural relationship that he describes as being "very easy" to navigate as a result of the common bond and shared values that he says were produced by the long Moorish presence in southern Spain?

Admittedly, my initial forays did not yield any epiphanic moments. Though he at times adopts the *Arab* label to categorize his own identity, when pressed he insists that it does not apply. He explains, "We're not Arabs, we're Chileans" or "Chileans of Arab origin," as "our grandparents arrived a hundred years ago." They speak Spanish, eat Chilean food, and are fully integrated into mainstream Chilean society. Their community "is not a ghetto," he remarks. When I inquire about the maintenance of the Arabic language in his family, he contrasts the "Christian" and "Levantine"—a word he deploys in English—culture of his ancestors with that of the Gulf countries where he pursues interesting opportunities. On business trips to the region, they may ask him if he is Lebanese due to his accent and dress, but he professes not to feel the connection. "It's another culture, it's another people," he declares.

I make a mild amount of progress by interrupting him mid-sentence. Do they see you as Chilean? "No, a mix," he responds casually. The fact that when he sits down for dinner at a Dubai restaurant he knows both how to order and how to eat undoubtedly unsettles the stable and discrete categorization schemes of his interlocutors. And, on three separate occasions,

Arab CEOs have pulled him aside—by the arm—after meetings involving non-Arab figures in order to ask him (since, as he recounts, they see him as "one of us") if the others are "trustworthy." But he soon returns to discussing interesting opportunities, a topic that dominates much of the rest of our encounter. Even after direct questioning about his motives, I am able to glean little beyond the fact that he is inspired by some mixture of a business recognition that "there is an opportunity" to follow Brazil's successful lead, a personal genuflection toward his "origins" and the fact that he "likes the region," and a preoccupation with Chile's economic well-being. But where does the balance lie?

On my return to Chile after two years had passed, I found myself exchanging a flurry of last-minute early-morning Twitter messages with Makhoul in response to my request for a follow-up meeting. After we made several time and venue changes in order to accommodate his cramped and ever-morphing schedule, I grabbed my messenger bag and speed-walked from my central plaza-adjacent accommodations in the coastal city of Viña del Mar, some 120 kilometers to the capital's northwest, to the nearby bus terminal. Two hours later, I emerged from a subway escalator immediately east of downtown Santiago and found myself sitting across a Starbucks table from Makhoul in the plate glass–filled business district abutting the green, urban oasis of Cerro Santa Lucía (Santa Lucía Hill).

This is his third consecutive meeting in this very café. As his legs are already shaking from two previous coffees, we refrain from joining the long line of suit-clad patrons clamoring to order. Occupying a table without consuming must be a violation of corporate policy, I muse, though I decide it is unlikely for such rules to be applied in these classier surroundings. Across the street is a branch of the Wall Street English language institute. And though we are half a dozen subway stops from Sanhattan's edge and Latin America's tallest building, clusters of clean-cut, black-suited patrons seem to people the café's every nook. Their presence evokes the same regimented, manicured, and homogenous presentation of self that seems to define business elites everywhere. Sporting frizzy, curly blond hair and a goatee and lacking a proper suit jacket, I feel both undergroomed and underdressed.

Over the steady din of the early-afternoon coffee crowd, and with a fluidity and frankness that suggest a regular gathering with an acquaintance, the conversation immediately turns to our topic of mutual interest: Chile's economic relations with the Arab world and his role in promoting them. Makhoul had not exactly been restrained during our previous encounter in his assessment of the government's missteps. However, the distance then afforded by the end of his term as a public official, provoked by the naming of a replacement after the center-left Bachelet returned to the presidency in 2014, only furthered the tendency. This would later allow him to stray as far afield as engaging in conversations concerning the reasoning behind suit purchases and family vacation destinations. Both of these, perhaps unexpectedly, proved to be fertile vantage points from which to observe national, transnational, and global imaginaries and longings.

I am quickly brought up to speed. The framework of the ASPA summits has been withering on the vine due to a lack of interest by participating countries (again, no such summits have been held since 2015). The Bachelet government, along with the country's formidable business class, was maintaining its Asia-Pacific focus. Within the state trade bureaucracy, highly praised halal expert—and fellow two-time interviewee—Ricardo Lavalle has been transferred from Santiago to Southeast Asia, leaving "nobody for halal" back in Chile, according to Makhoul. In general, the stagnant nature of Arab-Chilean trade represents "more of the same," and as of now, "there is no pressure from the private sector" to break the logjam and allow this axis of ties to surge forward. Accordingly, plans for a chamber of commerce, which still figure prominently on his crowded to-do list, remain "on standby."

Yet Makhoul had not exactly been sitting on his hands, staring ruefully out the window as unattainable "interesting opportunity" after "interesting opportunity" sped by. This familiar phrase still peppers his speech (according to a comment I scrawled in my fieldwork notebook at the halfway point of our second conversation, he had already repeated it "5+" times by this point). And he continues to discuss Arab-Chilean exchange—trade promotion, deals through which "we" (that is, Chile) can "attract investment" (the latter word again spoken in English) from the Gulf, and so on—with the unbridled optimism of a motivational speaker. But, having recently returned from Palestine, he also had a new job—and a new business card, in Arabic on one side and English on the other—with what he refers to as an "interesting agent of change between the regions."

As there appears not to be a single Arab bank in all of Latin America's twenty independent states, I initially have a hard time imagining why, out of all the former region's banks, a Palestinian one would become the first or why it would choose Chile's relatively small market as the site of its representation office. Why a Palestinian bank in Santiago instead of an Emirati one in São Paulo?

Yet the bank's president has been quoted in the local press as declaring that "it has been a dream to have a presence on the ground here in Chile." This is because, first, "when we come here and see our people having success in a beautiful country like Chile, it makes us feel nostalgia for the Palestine that we would wish to dream about, that we would wish to have." And second, it is due to the fact that "there are very big markets here so that Middle Eastern exporters and companies may do business" (Morales 2015). Accordingly, the idea is not merely to connect Chile and Palestine, but to establish this axis as a bridge via which "to strengthen business relations between Latin America and the Persian Gulf" and facilitate investment flows between the former region and the broader Middle East (*El Mercurio* 2015).

Given his previous experience with bridging, what is entirely unsurprising is that the bank appointed Makhoul as its consultant and advisor for Latin America, precisely to traverse this now-familiar terrain between nostalgia and markets.

Out of the Ministry of Foreign Affairs—to which he has since returned—and (temporarily) back into the perhaps friendlier environs of the private sector (and Starbucks), the freewheeling Makhoul is now in a contemplative, almost philosophical mood. I learn more about him that afternoon than what I have garnered from many long-term acquaintances.

Contemplating his childhood, he notes that while "kids dream about being astronauts [and] firefighters," he wanted to be like Georges Naddaf, who has dedicated his life to promoting economic relations between Brazil and the Middle East (and who is the subject of a vignette in the following chapter). Regarding his goals and ambitions, he observes that "what motivates me is not trade in and of itself, but rather the relation between the regions"—not just economic and political, but also cultural and personal. Concerning his own globality, he comments, almost worriedly, that "when borders start to get erased for you, it's not normal." It is thus with palpable unease instead of triumphalism that he notes that at a certain point, "you feel at home anywhere in the world."

Discussing the very nature of life, he muses: "What is work for?" He has friends who have struck it rich(er), but to what effect? Granted, if the gated quasi-mansion that appears on Google Maps when I type in his address—located far to the northeast of downtown, in a subway-less neighborhood that is among the city's and country's most exclusive—is any indication, his is not precisely an ascetic lifestyle, nor is he spearheading a back-to-the-land movement.

Yet there is an authentic reflexivity in his discourse. He leans in. "I love Central America," he enthuses. Family trips could be spent in Miami or Milan, Doha or Dubai, but he prefers to take his kids on three-week jaunts to rural Costa Rica, where the goal is to avoid the beach tourism of nearby Tamarindo while meeting everyday people and shopping at the everyday corner stores where they shop. "People are warmer" there, he observes. "The poorer the country, the better I feel" and the more genuine and unassuming its inhabitants. Any critiques about this implicit glorification of poverty or adherence to the ideal of the "noble savage" notwithstanding, these are curious words for a class-conscious protagonist of Chile's status-obsessed business elite.

His subsequent recollection of seeing a child sleeping on the streets of Phnom Penh, surrounded by dogs, while an unspecified international development official immediately on the other side of the fence was sporting a Rolex, is also ideological. Indeed, I would be shocked if Makhoul does not also own a nice watch. Further, part of what motivates this animated retelling is an implicit critique of the efforts of NGOs as well as his own belief that "the private [business] sector" is necessary (and superior to the government) because "it generates development." But we must not entirely dismiss the humanistic streak that both reveals itself in our conversation and propels, to some extent, his economic activities. When he says, "I believe in Palestine, I believe in [the] Middle East," a region he refers to in English, it is something more than a concocted self-justification for seeking profit.

To summarize, national—and transnational—ties loom large in Makhoul's interpretive frameworks. His economic and personal activities are filtered through a range of constructs that include both Chilean and Palestinian nationalism, a loose sense of allegiance to a larger Middle East, and even personal commitments to idealized Central American *campesinos* (rural dwellers), the global poor, and a nebulous "Southern perspective" to which he refers.

When I ask about his previous stint in the Chilean government, the bitterness over opportunities lost melts away. Perhaps foreshadowing his subsequent acceptance of a diplomatic post, he notes, "You have a good time because you're working for your country." When I make small talk about the Chilean men's national *fútbol* team's lackluster 3–3 tie with Mexico in the previous night's first-round match of the Copa América regional soccer tournament, he begins to make animated hand and arm gestures and shrieks as he recalls Chile's devastating second-round departure from the

2014 World Cup. And when I ask what he makes of the Palestine-branded credit cards that he had been promoting in Chile, he responds that even if this were not his own initiative, he would still be interested, "to feel that my children have a link" with their ancestral homeland.

After he posted a picture of one of the bank cards on Facebook, Makhoul recounts that people went *crazy*. Within the Palestinian-Chilean community, he makes the evocative observation that "the rich forgot their roots"—"but not the middle class in Patronato," Santiago's traditional Arab neighborhood. The "symbolism" of the card is important to him, as is the fact that the bank invests in and donates to relevant charitable ventures in both countries. These range from dedicating 6 percent of annual profits to community projects for Palestinians to spending millions of dollars to sponsor—and place the bank's name on the jerseys of—the Santiago-based first-division soccer team, Club Deportivo Palestino (Palestinian Sports Club), founded by Palestinian immigrants in 1920.[5]

He has not forgotten about the profitable "interesting opportunities" for Arab–Latin American trade, still finds it "curious" that there is no Arab-Chilean Chamber of Commerce, and recently developed a new idea—to link the Pacific Alliance with the Gulf Cooperation Council (GCC).[6] Further, he readily admits that his "ego" is part of what drives him to succeed in his efforts to bring Chile and the Arab world together. Though as he says that in life you must do what "makes sense to you," that he seeks to "help at the same time," and that one's actions must be "coherent with values," it becomes clear that his mission is not merely trade for the sake of trade itself or precisely to further the efforts of fellow globalizing entrepreneurial elites the world over.

On the other hand, there is, perhaps, more than a touch of irony inherent in his stated desire to further open Chile to the world. "Chile has to grow toward the outside, not toward the inside," he observes. Of course, such liberalizing moves tend to be reify the same global capitalist order whose onward march is said to be undermining those local cultures—Chilean, Palestinian, Middle Eastern, and even Central American—where he feels most at home. Yet here again we must be careful to separate the material (globalizing) nature of his activities from the (mostly, but far from exclusively, place-based) ideational constructs that undergird them.

Toward the end of our encounter, he describes a conversation with his wife over the purchase of a new suit. Should he buy Chilean or perhaps a foreign one during an upcoming trip to Miami or Buenos Aires? The anguish that goes into the decision—he does not reveal the outcome—contradicts, at least to some extent, his concluding assertion that he has a global mindset. So does the fact that while he viewed it as part of his pedagogical and capitalist mission to globalize Chilean business students by taking them to Peru and Colombia—"countries of the future," as he labels them—the motivating factor behind the mission is that this is the mentality that Chilean companies need to cultivate.

Vignette #2: Rafael Bishara

During the peak of the boom years, in the early 2010s, Argentina's annual exports to the Arab world exceeded $6 billion, representing more than a fourfold increase from a decade prior. Of this, a relatively small but not insignificant amount of mostly agricultural and other food products, valued at just over $100 million, was destined for Lebanon.[7] Since its founding in the late 1970s, on the annual anniversary of Lebanon's independence day, a Lebanon-focused Argentine trade grouping has labored to build these commercial—and also social and cultural—ties within what its website refers to as the "convoluted" and "challenging" market environment produced by economic globalization.

To that end, it performs consulting work for businesses, connects sellers and buyers, and issues certificates of origin for Argentine exports. Further, when practical—which, for reasons to be enunciated later, it has often not been—it collaborates with the Argentine government. The organization was born during and because of Lebanon's messy "civil" war (1975–1990) as a breakaway association from a now-defunct Syrian-Lebanese trade association.[8] Syria, as I am later informed, has always wanted to "swallow" Lebanon.

From its inception until the time of our interview, this Lebanon-focused group was led by Dr. Rafael Bishara,[9] an economist by training who referred to himself as the proud descendant of "the first wave of immigrants" to arrive in Argentina from Lebanon. Among the nearly several million Argentines who claim Arab descent, Lebanon and Syria are again by far the most common countries of origin.

As we chat over tea, a dark wooden mural occupying nearly the entirety of the rear wall stares back at me. It features an etching of the iconic Lebanese cedar tree, accompanied by images of Phoenician merchants and their trading ship. Lest the symbolism be lost on us, the organization's website previously noted that "the typical merchant vessel of the Phoenicians was used by these traders par excellence to crisscross all the seas of the Old World, exchanging goods, art, and culture.... The cedar—an ancient tree, almost eternal, praised time and again in the Bible—is the national symbol of glorious LEBANON." We may assume that this capitalization of the country name was not accidental. Notably, the group's then emblem also featured a cedar tree surrounded by its end product, a Phoenician trading vessel. With the organization's trade-focused title wrapped around the outside in English, Spanish, and Arabic, the evocation of the Lebanese people as preternaturally gifted merchants is clear.[10] The traditional Argentine sun—which occupies the center of the national flag—radiates outward from the ship.

The office building that hosts its offices, like much of the teeming *microcentro* (downtown) of Buenos Aires, appears tired and faded. Yet it maintains a stately, old European air. This is, after all, the self-styled Paris of the South. The area evokes the Argentina of a hundred years prior, when the country was among the top ten global economies. With the fastest growth rates of any country during the period immediately preceding World War I, according to *The Economist* (2014), Argentina "could claim to be the world's true land of opportunity." It has since gone through a "century of decline"—or, more precisely, endless cycles of booms and busts, as well as democracy and dictatorship (*The Economist* 2014).

The country's heady past is said to be reflected in the contemporary attitudes of—and stereotypes concerning—its people, none more than the reputedly, (in)famously brash inhabitants of Buenos Aires, known as *porteños* (literally, port dwellers). As the *New York Times* noted, "Argentines have long taken pride in their arrogance," one manifestation of which is the tendency to "flaunt their European ancestry and culture to their Latin American peers" (Sims 1998). Thus, as any viewer of an intraregional soccer match can attest to, "Argentines are without a doubt the most disdained group in Latin America" (Sims 1998). If nationalist sentiment should abound anywhere in Latin America, Argentina thus seems a prime candidate.

My interlocutor does not disappoint. After our initial exchange of pleasantries, I begin to answer his question about the topic of my research—only to be promptly interrupted upon my mention of Arab–Latin American relations. He interjects: Lebanon is no mere "Arab" country, nor does Argentina qualify as "Latin American." To Bishara, forcing these singular countries into such broad, plebeian regional categories is clearly a sign of sloppy thinking. As I learn, to imply equality in the relationship between Lebanon and its would-be Arab neighbors or in that between Argentina and the countries to its north (which, it bears mentioning, have larger indigenous populations) would be to "lower"—and thus demean—both of them.

As he sits behind his massive wooden desk, concluding his speech on Lebanese and Argentine exceptionalism while opening a recently arrived letter from Lebanon itself, he casually refers to "Christians like me." He and his fellow Lebanese Catholics, he later tells me, are not like other religious minorities in Argentina, as they intermarry with other groups—thus achieving a deeper sociocultural integration with the local society.

While he struggles to print me a copy of his organization's aforementioned emblem, of which he is clearly quite proud, I take advantage of a brief pause to peruse the office. Glancing at the well-ordered bookshelves that surround the exterior window, I am greeted with titles such as *Crimes against Business* and *You Can Negotiate Anything*. On cue, he erupts with a litany of accusations against the populist, statist, and ostensibly left-leaning government of then president Cristina Fernández de Kirchner, who served from 2007 to 2015: "They do everything in their power *not* to export"; "You won't find more corrupt people anywhere"; They spend everyone's precious tax money on "stupid things." For him, Argentina is a country of taxes and red tape. And so, in his presumed estimation, it will continue to be, as Kirchner assumed the vice presidency in December 2019, after her center-left ticket triumphed over her right-leaning successor, Mauricio Macri.

As I discover later, what Argentina should be doing is following the example of Chile, the perpetual neoliberal reference point. "Chile is better," he comments baldly, referring specifically to the country's "social climate." Based on this narrative of reverence for what he understands to be the uber-neoliberal "Chilean model," he even praises me—in one of our conversation's more curious moments—for having a Chilean wife. "You chose well," he quips.[11]

Indeed, the Chilean model is often invoked in fawning and hagiographic terms by Latin American elites—including members of Bolsonaro's cabinet—as being a source of inspiration for all matters economic. Yet Bishara and others tend to make no mention of Chile's rampant inequality (among the worst in Latin America, and thus, the world); the profound antidemocratic legacies left behind by the Pinochet regime (including the country's constitution, which was imposed under authoritarian rule and was overwhelmingly rejected by voters in an October 2020 plebiscite, as well as continuing impunity for perpetrators of massive human rights abuses); or recurring, mass mobilizations in opposition to the country's entire neoliberal orientation and in favor of alternatives, including free, universal, and high-quality education. Indeed, Chile's higher education system has been labeled the "most expensive" in the entire world (Loofbourow 2013).

But why work so hard to promote business in a country that, in his view—unlike the Chilean foil—has often thrown up endless obstacles to his success (and, apparently, his happiness)? Why do "everything that can be done," as he puts it, to promote trade relations between Lebanon and Argentina?

He may earn his living as a management consultant, he remarks. But what he *lives* for is his other business card—the one that reads *presidente* of his trade association. According to Bishara, there is no ambiguity in what drives his life's ambitions and why he labors without remuneration. It is "a matter of patriotism" based on "love of the land of my parents." This impulse draws on a deep reservoir of feelings and nostalgia concerning his family and ancestors, who happen to hail from Lebanon, "the most important country in the Arab world." At no other point in our conversation does he refer to Lebanon or the Lebanese people as belonging to a larger Arab collective.

The Lebanon that exists in his mind is an "outstanding country" (one of the few phrases that he utters in English). Returning to Spanish, he declares that Lebanon is "absolutely" a unique and superior place. There—and unlike in Syria, Saudi Arabia, or elsewhere among the country's supposed Arab brethren—"everyone is trilingual." As the entire population of Lebanon is not actually trilingual, of course, he cannot literally mean *everyone*. He instead apparently seeks to allude to whom he later calls *la gente bien*—a largely anachronistic term that not only refers to the affluent or well-to-do, but also evokes images of old-money aristocrats who belong to the traditional nobility and view themselves as models of moral rectitude. Tellingly, few Latin Americans beyond those who actually belong to such groups use this highly classist expression without at least a tinge of irony.

Argentina—and more specifically, the Argentine government—may have often been what he labels "an impediment" to the realization of his life's ambition to reconnect with Lebanon. Yet it is still a place that he claims as his own. "Are you patriotic?" I ask. He answers with an immediate "of course," which he repeats four times in quick succession. Throughout our conversation, he asserts a strong Argentine identity—true to stereotypes, the kind one expects to find among *porteños*. He refers to "our" Argentine flag, casually notes that Argentina has the world's best polo horses, and even boasts of the quality of the country's livestock. Pope Francis, he warmly remarks, is *our* Argentine pope and a personal friend (indeed, he offers to send me a picture of them together).

Nevertheless, one doubts that he sympathizes with the pope's condemnation of trickle-down economics as a "new tyranny" that is based on "a crude and naïve trust in the goodness of those wielding economic power" (Downie 2013). Nor is he likely to agree with his clarion call for humanity "to say 'thou shalt not' to an economy of exclusion and inequality" in which "the powerful feed upon the powerless" (Downie 2013). For Bishara, national identity apparently has the potential to (at least temporarily) trump ideological differences.

Overall, he claims a shared nationalism (and exceptionalism) between the Lebanon of his ancestors and the Argentina that he calls home. In fact, the first nationalism reinforces the latter, as evidenced by his interest in highlighting the contributions of Lebanese immigrants and their descendants to all facets of Argentine society, ranging from music to government. As he notes, the *argentinos libaneses* are in "the whole country." He sees it as his—and his people's—duty as part of this group to build relations between these two countries, so that he may "patriotically serve" both of them. In other words, he is like the local Maronite church that he frequents—as he puts it, a piece of Lebanon in Buenos Aires (he willingly recounts that the church was designed by Lebanese architects, the stones were imported from Lebanon, and even the bricklayers were Lebanese). Argentina, he notes, "is not at all easy." But it is where his cedar tree has put down its roots.

Vignette #3: Kadim Al-Hassani and Aqil Qasim

I had become convinced that the trade grouping focused on relations between Brazil and Iraq that I had found via online searches either did not exist or at best amounted to little more than a shell organization. My several initial attempts to contact its administrative staff elicited no response. Further, with an exclusive focal point on Brazil's relations with Iraq, the organization's mandate seemed too limited to warrant anything beyond the most skeletal of operations—perhaps a businessperson's hobby with a legal name, website, and little else. After all, given the seemingly hegemonic presence of larger organizations whose purview includes the entire Arab world—one of which I discuss in the next chapter—what room could there be for an outfit with a partially overlapping and much narrower scope?

The following year, after another attempt at contact, I received a prompt response from its leadership and an offer to devise a comprehensive itinerary for my visit. To my surprise, they took me under their wing for more than a week of interviews, guided visits to related organizations (including the nearby offices of a pan-Arab Brazilian trade association and the further afield and aforementioned Arab and South American Library and Research Center), shared trays of *baklava*, and buffet lunches at the Arab restaurant on the corner. Such was my level of access that I found myself sharing birthday cake with the group's dozen employees and student interns while Portuguese and Arabic office banter filtered over the cubicle walls.

The São Paulo headquarters occupies what appears to be the better part of a floor in an office tower suggestively named after a precious gemstone. Resting upon rows of dark columns, the high-rise's exterior is composed almost entirely of flat, shiny, and reflective plate glass. It is the sort of generic skyscraper that would not be out of place in any business district within a global megacity. From the nearby Arab restaurant, a quick right turn leads to an emblematic São Paulo thoroughfare and economic hub, which anchors one of Latin America's most expensive real-estate markets. Once I pass through the tower's revolving doors, a security team demands my passport and fingerprints and makes a quick phone call to verify that my presence has indeed been solicited.

In addition to its robustly staffed Brazil office—which is home to more than twice as many employees as, for example, the much older and more broadly based Arab-Argentine Chamber of Commerce—it also maintains an Iraq-based representative.

At the organization's helm were Kadim Al-Hassani and Aqil Qasim,[12] both Iraqi-born middle-aged men who have called Brazil home for over three decades—the latter having arrived in the late 1970s to avoid military service, and the former in the early 1980s because of a "woman." Each speaks native-sounding Portuguese, the language of all of our interactions.

The gregarious, chatty, and smooth-talking Al-Hassani, my primary interlocutor over the course of the visit, is a busy man, and he frequently keeps me waiting as he fields phone calls, prances from office to office, and alternates between dictating orders to and telling jokes with his staff. Along with directing this trade group, the entrepreneurial Al-Hassani was also presiding over an Islamic-focused economic association and pursuing graduate studies in business administration (appropriately, with a focus on Brazil's halal exports to the Middle East). Together, Al-Hassani and Qasim were leading an organization whose stated ambition is to export more, and a greater variety of, Brazilian goods to Iraqi consumers. And with what Al-Hassani describes as an increase from $42 million in Brazilian exports to Iraq at the time of the organization's founding in 2003 to $1.5 billion in recent years, business has been booming.

It is no coincidence that this trade group opened its doors the same year as the US invasion of Iraq. The "shock and awe" that hundreds of thousands of troops from the "coalition of the willing" visited upon the country culminated not only in the toppling of the twenty-four-year Saddam Hussein dictatorship. It also heralded the end of a strict US-led and United Nations–imposed sanctions regime that had prevented any significant growth in Brazilian-Iraqi commercial flows.

Yet economic obstacles to Brazil-Iraq ties were not exclusively external. Qasim refers to the fact that the Ba'athist regime—based on an ideological mixture of state socialism and pan-Arabism—controlled some 95 percent of Iraq's economy. Returning to Marx and Engels (1888, 476–477), it would take the Coalition Provisional Authority's Order 39, as decreed by US diplomat and then de facto ruler of Iraq Paul Bremer, to "batter down all [Iraqi] walls" and allow the bourgeoisie to "nestle," "settle," and "establish connexions" [sic] in the country. As Naomi Klein (2003) put it, "The now infamous Order 39 . . . announced that 200 Iraqi state companies would be privatised; decreed that foreign firms can retain 100% ownership of Iraqi banks, mines and factories; and allowed these firms to move 100% of their profits out of Iraq. *The Economist* declared the new rules a 'capitalist dream.'"

Currently, according to Qasim's estimates, close to 95 percent of what Iraqis consume is imported. Despite the country's "instability," he observes that Iraq "still has 32 million consumers who have to consume." In steps Brazil as "the export nation" (Karam 2007). It is a perfect match. He describes Iraq as the world's fifth largest importer of chicken. Brazil, in turn, is the world's largest exporter of chicken (Gomes 2014), as well as of halal meat (Mendes 2018). For both men, and the organization as a whole, the privatization of nearly everything in Iraq—from industry to public services—has presented a tremendous opportunity to promote Brazilian exports in the land of their birth, from food and construction materials to cars and health services.

Yet theirs are not precisely the politics of exiles waiting in the wings who attached themselves, Ahmed Chalabi–style, to an invading force with the hope and expectation of future spoils.[13] Indeed, neither speaks with any elation about the US invasion nor lets their apparent distaste for the Hussein regime color their overall opinions of the Iraq they left behind. As we sit across from each another at one end of a long conference-room table, Qasim remarks that Iraq under Hussein "was a very industrialized country" and that during the 1970s—under Hussein's Ba'athist predecessors—Iraqi citizens were more educated than Brazilians. The government, he notes approvingly, paid for the country's best students to study in the world's premier universities.

Al-Hassani's recollections are more personal but equally telling. In 2008, he returned to Baghdad—the city of his birth—for the first time in decades, accompanying a senator from the left-leaning Brazilian Workers' Party. The latter recounted that Al-Hassani grew "disappointed" during the trip, for he could no longer recognize the Baghdad of his youth, which he regarded as the most beautiful city in the world. Instead, he saw the Green Zone's concrete walls, which for him embodied the sectarian tensions and other divisions that have consumed post-invasion Iraq.

Nothing better captures his complicated emotional bond with Iraq than the famously difficult-to-translate Portuguese word and Lusophone cultural marker *saudade*, which refers literally to a yearning or longing but in more holistic terms can reflect "a melancholy nostalgia for something that perhaps has not even happened" (Garsd 2015). Further, "it often carries an assurance that this thing you feel nostalgic for will never happen again" (Garsd 2015). Accordingly, Al-Hassani may have physically returned to Iraq, but to borrow from the eponymous Thomas Wolfe novel, on a spiritual level he truly *can't go home again* to an Iraq that perhaps only partially ever was and that more certainly now no longer is.

What he and they *can* do instead, per his organization's mission, is stimulate commercial relations between the two countries they have called home and help to create more direct lines of communication between their respective business leaders. In practice, this entails everything from conducting and publicizing market research to shaking the important hands of political and economic elites from visiting delegations and making regular business trips (some seven times a year, in Qasim's case), particularly to Iraq's relatively stable north. This is precisely the sort of "detailed work" that larger but perhaps less nimble organizations that focus on the entire Arab world are reportedly unwilling and/or unable to do. And it is here, by charging interested businesses for services rendered and issuing certificates of origin for Brazilian exports, that Al-Hassani and Qasim have found their revenue-generating niche (though the organization itself is not a profit-seeking entity).

This dialectical interplay between two seemingly opposing (but ultimately intertwined) forces—the nostalgia-inducing Iraq that percolates through childhood memories and the cold, economic logic of the business world—plays itself out repeatedly during our conversations. Here, responses to my iterations of the *why* question—that is, *why* do you do what you do?—yield illustrative, if complicated, responses.

Let us take, for example, the genealogy that Qasim presents of his own involvement with this trade group. The first round of questioning reveals a compelling and coherent story: he does what he does because he is Iraqi, he wants to "help the population" and "rebuild the country," and he perceives a "need" for this kind of help. I wonder, in turn, how Qasim operationalizes and measures the success of what he claims as his altruistic endeavors; how does he know if he and the organization he helps to lead are succeeding?

He replies, succinctly, by reporting a positive "balance of trade," referring to an increase in Brazil's exports to Iraq vis-à-vis its imports. He makes no mention of previously invoked sentimental keywords like *rebuilding, reconstruction,* or *helping.* When it is Al-Hassani's turn, he responds only by citing the aforementioned increase from $42 million to $1.5 billion in annual Brazilian exports.

Whether the organization's success in promoting this astronomical growth in Brazilian trade with Iraq or creating an export surplus for Brazil actually has any salutary effects for Iraq—let alone the general population of Brazil—is beside the point. What is relevant here is the underlying assumption that it is so obvious to Al-Hassani and Qasim that their individual actions will automatically bring social benefits to their (suffering) Iraqi compatriots that they do not feel the need to present supporting evidence.

The same ideological framework rears its head to a perhaps even greater extent on the organization's website. Consider the following instance of linguistic slippage. First, it is stated that the aim is to pursue "development" by promoting stronger economic linkages between the two countries. A few lines later, we learn that the purpose behind stimulating increased trade is indeed to generate "development," but only in the context of Brazilian and Iraqi "markets" and "business[es]." Other potential beneficiaries, such as the respective countries' general populations, go unmentioned.

From here, the waters continue to muddy. Their espousal of a "[Brazilian] trade equals [Iraqi] reconstruction" ideological framework, absent the provision of an explanation of this would-be causal link, even when I ask, may appear self-serving. This is, after all, a trade group, not a beneficence society.

Yet there is still truth to the organization's claim that it has promoted various forms of social and cultural exchange between Brazil and Iraq. See, for example, its stated role in having provided aid to an Iraqi hospital or the fact that it organized the first-ever soccer match between the two countries, an international friendly held in Sweden in October 2012. Such was the symbolic importance of the latter that Itamaraty, the Brazilian Ministry of Foreign Affairs, lists the occurrence—though without referencing the results, a 6–0 Brazilian thrashing of the Iraqi side—in its "chronology of bilateral relations."[14] It is precisely on the terrain of having a *social* mission, and not just a *commercial* one, that this group professes to carve out an identity for itself that, they say, differs from that of its much larger counterpart organizations.

Though Al-Hassani later arranges and whisks me away to a cordial meeting with one such group, there is clearly a rivalry between them. He recounts that this other firm is the product of a fusion that occurred several decades ago between predecessor Iraqi and Syrian associations. Per his account, which I was not able to verify independently, the agreement was to rotate the presidency in three-year terms between leaders from the two communities. However, the Syrians (or Syrian-Brazilians), all of whom he claims hail from the western city of Homs, "never gave it up." Later, as I am being called to enter the office of a senior executive from this organization, I am told that the accompanying intern from the Iraq-focused group, who had been helping to facilitate the logistics surrounding my visit, had to wait outside.

The latter's leaders do appear genuinely interested in all types of "transfers" that may bring Brazil and Iraq together, as Qasim frames it, even when the profit motive is not involved. The fact that they seem unable to explain the link between the economic activities from which they *do* profit, and the social ones from which they *do not*, does not necessarily make them duplicitous (though it does, perhaps, suggest a certain lack of reflexivity concerning their everyday activities and place in the world); rather, it is a well-timed reminder that we must recognize that the profit motive is translated into real-world action only after passing through a series of interpretive frameworks, the sum of which may lack a degree of internal coherence to the outside observer.

That is to say, the "classed" and other intersections that define people's identities are muddy waters indeed. Perhaps we should not be surprised that Al-Hassani could salivate over the business opportunities presented by Iraq's hasty privatization scheme while simultaneously suggesting that the Brazilian government's world-famous Bolsa Família (Family Allowance) program, which established a system of conditional cash transfers to low-income households, could be a model for alleviating Iraq's social maladies. The same goes for the fact that Qasim could shift effortlessly from extolling the private sector's—that is, to a large extent, his organization's own—initiative in promoting Iraqi-Brazilian ties to declaring that it *needs*, and *gets*, the Brazilian government's help with all manner of entrepreneurial activities. These range from the staging of trade fairs, workshops, and commercial missions to organizing meetings and signing relevant accords.

Unsurprisingly, then, Al-Hassani is full of praise for Brazil's receptivity toward immigrants like himself, providing as evidence the assertion that the country "helps with business." My Argentine interviewees in particular stressed the ideological and personal conflicts that had defined their relationship with the government, except during Macri's right-wing administration. In Brazil, however, my interviewees made common cause with the left-leaning Lula and then-president Dilma Rousseff, a portrait-style photo of whom—along with one of her Iraqi counterpart—was displayed prominently in the office waiting room.

From ideology to identity, theirs is a mixed, fluid, dynamic, and hybrid world. They voice laments about Iraq's sectarian divisions and deteriorating security situation. But when I ask Al-Hassani if he is afraid to operate in this environment, he asserts that money is money for businesspeople. There are also the aforementioned invocations of reconstruction, aid for an Iraqi hospital, and building goodwill through staging a *futebol* (soccer) match, all in support of the notion that this organization, though focused on development, has a particularly social mission. But what really seems to excite Al-Hassani is when he talks about his "store," his "trade," and his role as a "farmer," as he declares that it is business that he has "in my blood."

There is also the Al-Hassani who leaves me waiting in a nearby cubicle as he lays out his prayer rug, closes the office blinds, and begins his ritual act of worship. And who, as both a Muslim and leader of an Islamic-focused trade association, is keenly aware—per an academic paper that he jointly authored—that he, and his fellow believers around the world, constitute a large and expanding global bloc of halal consumers.

How, then, do we classify their worldviews? What are the interpretive filters through which their profit motive passes? How do they navigate between the Iraqi and Brazilian flags and presidential photos that adorn the walls of the office waiting room? Searching for a more tangible heuristic, I ask for their organization's genealogy. Al-Hassani responds that it is Brazilian, though its "origin" is Iraqi. He makes a quick correction: "Some of the founders are also Brazilian." Such is the intricate latticework of intersecting—and at times competing—Iraqi and Brazilian ties that largely defines not only the group's founding, but also the worldviews of its entrepreneurial leaders. The current aim, again, is not precisely to disentangle them. Rather, the more telling point for present purposes is that it is one or another set of *place-based* (national and transnational) allegiances—and the interactions between them—that largely defines their lifeworlds and guides the trajectory of their economic activities.

Analysis and Conclusions

The preceding vignettes tell the stories of four business elites whose interpretive filters can most fittingly be labeled as *national* or *transnational* in orientation. Naturally, any act of classification obfuscates certain characteristics for the purpose of allowing the analyst to (hopefully) construct useful images of reality. Thus, we must strive to studiously avoid the worst practices of the aforementioned "butterfly collectors," for whom the complexity of the real world—and real human agents—is a scourge to be shorn away for the sake of parsimony and would-be analytical clarity rather than an ontological reality to be embraced and explained.

Indeed, there are undoubtedly less-than-national/transnational moments in the above narratives. These include the dilemmas raised by suit purchases or how to keep Chile growing "toward the outside," the perceived need to hew to the structural exigencies of capitalist globalization in Argentina, and the contradiction between professed support for state involvement in the economy or Brazilian-style social programs in Iraq and salivation over the windfalls to be reaped as a result of US-imposed privatization and austerity schemes.

However, taken as a whole, these vignettes reveal mental frameworks that are significantly more national and transnational than denational or global. As is constitutive of capitalists, theirs is, of course, profit-seeking behavior. But the point is that for them, the profit motive is mostly filtered through place-based lenses—Argentine and Lebanese, Brazilian and Iraqi, and Chilean, Palestinian, Arab, and Middle Eastern. Among these figures, relatively little evidence points to the decentering of the national imaginary and even less to its replacement with a new set of global attachments.

These processes may indeed be underway, and in fact, Makhoul's unease about his own (apparently burgeoning) global credentials provides a tentative indication of such, as does his tendency to switch to English, the lingua franca of global commerce, as his brain reaches for key business terms. Yet in the present cases, these hints are the exception rather than the rule. Tellingly in this regard, the other primarily place-based thinkers profiled above hardly uttered a word to me outside of their primary languages, Spanish and Portuguese.

Before providing further substantiation from other interviewees, let us review the evidence that has been revealed from the preceding vignettes:

- *Diego Makhoul.* An atypically reflexive thinker who is keenly aware of the global directions in which his economic activities and lifestyle are pulling him and who appears intent on resisting them. Selected posts from his busy Spanish-, English-, and Arabic-language Twitter account include the following, and rather revealing, content: condemnation of the perpetrators of the November 2015 Paris terrorist attacks for killing the innocent, as well as of the media for "kill[ing]" the Muslim faith through its biased depictions of the religion; an attached picture of an ancestor's Palestinian passport; another attached image, this time of the top of a bottle of Glenfiddich Scotch, with a large flat-screen television showing a World Cup qualifying match between Chile and Peru in the background; a reference to an ancestor's frequent observation that we are different people in each language that we speak, followed by Makhoul's suggestion that perhaps this makes him "schizophrenic"; and, on the same date, a rhetorical question suggesting that Palestinians living in the diaspora could also occupy senior positions within the Palestinian government, up to and including prime minister. The latter post also included the observation that Palestinians peacefully coexisted with their diverse neighbors until outsiders arrived and intervened, turning them into refugees in their own land. His desire to build a chamber of commerce that is filled "not with Arabs, but with Chileans who are interested in the markets," his strategic focus on Dubai as a hub from which to sell to "other places," and his angst over his identity may suggest otherwise. But for now, the many interesting opportunities that he identifies are, without

coincidence, located in a region that he holds dear. And it is precisely *because* of his affection toward the region that he has identified these opportunities in the first place. In sum, his mental frameworks are predominantly place-based: Chilean, Palestinian, Middle Eastern, Arab, and even, perhaps, Central American.
- RAFAEL BISHARA. A thoroughgoing embodiment of the national/transnational imaginary. Ideological references to the superiority of the Chilean model aside, paeans to Argentine and Lebanese exceptionalism permeate our conversation. So unadulterated is his place-based discourse vis-à-vis those of my other interviewees that one suspects that, if his type were ever commonplace, it is now an endangered species. Lacking the mores of modern political correctness, he inhabits a world where *everyone—la gente bien* (the people who matter)—talks about polo, speaks multiple languages, and similarly idealizes neoliberal Chile. Yet so utterly nationalist is his thought that the fact that Pope Francis is *Argentine* matters more to him than the would-be communist demagoguery for which he has been lambasted by other elites.
- KADIM AL-HASSANI AND AQIL QASIM. Navigators of the choppy waters that separate profit-seeking and (transnational) altruism. Both on their website and in speech, they premise their economic activities on the notion that Iraq and the Iraqi people need them and their Brazilian wares, that linking import-dependent Iraqi consumers with producers from Brazil, the export nation and budding halal superpower, will cause the tide to rise, thus lifting all boats (though they neglect to explain why or how). Nonetheless, nostalgia for the homeland looms large in their mindsets, reflected in part through a desire to build cultural linkages. That they have stumbled upon a "capitalist dream" in their native Iraq is almost beside the point, for while contradictory statements concerning neoliberal reforms in Iraq reveal a perhaps inchoate, denationalized commitment to profit, for purposes of categorization they are most similar to (a less intense version of) Bishara's transnational mindset.

Again, I have chosen to explore these figures precisely because they best illustrate the resilient nature of place-based imaginaries within capitalist globalization—that is to say, their profit motives and class-based interests are mostly filtered through national, transnational, and regional interpretations. They are, of course, chased around the globe by profit and economic incentives, but *where* precisely they choose to make money depends largely on a series of national, transnational, ethnic, and family ties.

Overall, more than half of interviewees—equating to over a dozen business elites—exhibited interpretive filters that were more national or transnational than either denational or global. In this vein, what follows are further examples of place-based longings:

- RICARDO LAVALLE (the aforementioned halal expert, now responsible for Chile's trade-promotion in Southeast Asian markets). "We are the future of the world," he casually observes, with the *we* referring to the economic rise of Chile and the Chilean people. In turn, he declares that "Chile wants to be an elite country" and does not see itself as part of the "[Global] South." Nonetheless, given Chile's position "at the vanguard" of a neoliberal, free-trade-based economic paradigm, he asserts that "we"—the Chilean people—"feel like a model in Latin America."[15]
- JULIETA FAYAD (at the time of our interview, in charge of Chile's trade relations with the Middle East and several other regions). The most gratifying part of being a civil servant is that she is "supporting the country." She recalls almost crying when a business deal was signed—not because of "self-interest" or monetary gain, but rather out of the conviction that by walking "with the hand of the private sector," she can assist small and medium-sized businesses, address Chile's (astronomical) levels of inequality, and help to develop the country's oft-neglected peripheral regions.[16]
- GUSTAVO BARI (manager of a long-standing Arab-Argentine trade association). Globalization "helps and hurts *us*," he asserts—referring to "we in Argentina" and "the Argentine nation." But Argentina's flourishing trade relations with the Arab world apparently represent more good than harm, given that—as he recounts concerning their surplus-heavy economic relationship—some 99 percent of total Arab-Argentine trade consists of the latter's exports to the former. This (im)balance is thus overwhelmingly "in favor of Argentina."[17]

Accordingly, based on the sentiments expressed in this chapter, reports of the death of place-based imaginaries among economic elites have been greatly exaggerated. To be sure, the above are all "good" capitalists who—happily in some cases, unreflexively in others—are performing their structurally determined role as profit seekers (for themselves and/or others) within a market economy. All share "the tendency to create value and surplus-value, to make its constant factor, the means of production, absorb the greatest possible amount of surplus-labor" (Marx 1867, 362). And all are "chase[d]" to different countries and regions by "the need of a constantly expanding market" (Marx and Engels 1888, 476).

Yet this crystal-clear class position only turns into real-world action once it passes through a series of interpretive filters. For the figures portrayed in the above vignettes, those lenses have a distinctly place-based tint.

It is for this reason that the title of this chapter invokes Marx's (1852, 595) observation that "the tradition of all the dead generations weighs like a nightmare on the brain of the living." This statement emphasizes the extent to which inherited structures constrain and condition human agency in the present. As he further notes: "Men make their own history, but they do not make it just as they please; they do not make it under circumstances chosen by themselves, but under circumstances directly found, given and transmitted from the past" (Marx 1852, 595).

Similarly, national and even transnational longings may appear passé in today's seemingly hyper-globalized world of free trade, cross-border interconnectivity, and time-space compression (Harvey 1990). Yet it turns out that "old" place-based interpretive frameworks, far from melting into air, continue to filter the profit-seeking activities of many ostensibly global capitalists. Such is the case with this chapter's second vignette, which frames one particular figure's raison d'être in terms of an identity dominated by notions of both Argentine and Lebanese exceptionalism. Again, this place-based worldview flies in the face of the hypothesis of a global capitalist class as a class for itself, which posits a global identity based on a shared class status and participation in particular global chains of accumulation. It is thus through these actors, and many others like them, that a place-based "tradition of dead generations" lives on.

Together, these national or transnational capitalists again form the largest group among my interviewees. Yet it may be a mistake to assume their future hegemony. As the next chapter demonstrates, there is a notable denationalizing streak in several of my interlocutors. This trend is unsurprising given the growing protagonism of Latin American actors in the global economy and finds expression in the globalizing thoughts that are percolating into the lifeworlds of Makhoul and fellow travelers—provoking torment in some and either passing imperceptibly or stirring up feelings of globalist pride in others—precisely as a result of such participation.

The next chapter seeks and analyzes evidence for a denationalized and/or global mindset among the protagonists behind Arab–Latin American economic exchange, uncovering significant signs of the former and some, but still relatively few, of the latter. As we will see, place-based imaginaries thus persist to an unexpected extent, but not without qualification.

Notes

1. In-person interviews with Diego Makhoul were conducted by the author in Santiago de Chile on June 24, 2013, and June 16, 2015. Here and in the other vignettes, unless otherwise noted, all quotes are from the interviewee(s).

2. This phrase—*antología del horror* in the original Spanish—is attributed to celebrated Argentine writer Ernesto Sábato, referring to his country's own bloody experience with authoritarian rule during the same period (de Ramón 2010, 239).

3. See the DP World website, accessed May 22, 2019, https://www.dpworld.com/what-we-do.

4. See the Gulfood website, accessed May 23, 2019, https://www.gulfood.com/why-visit.

5. Notably, the club also maintains ties to the Palestinian-Chilean population in other ways, such as through the use of uniforms with the colors of the Palestinian flag (green, red, black, and white). In a relatively recent controversy, Chilean football authorities banned the team from wearing what it deemed "anti-Israel" jerseys in which the numeral 1 had been replaced with the image of historic Palestine.

6. Established in 2011 by Chile, Colombia, Mexico, and Peru, the Pacific Alliance is a primarily economic mechanism for increasing integration between these free market–oriented member states. It also serves as a platform for their "projection to the world, with emphasis on the Asia-Pacific region." See the alliance's official website, accessed May 24, 2019, https://alianzapacifico.net/en/que-es-la-alianza/#what-is-the-pacific-alliance. Panama has also taken steps toward joining. In ideological terms, the Pacific Alliance is often seen as the foil for the more statist regional bloc Mercosur, comprising Argentina, Brazil, Paraguay, Uruguay, and Venezuela (whose membership is currently suspended due to domestic turmoil). Bolivia is in the process of being incorporated as Mercosur's sixth member. For its part, the GCC is a Persian Gulf–based regional organization focusing on political and economic coordination. Its member states—Bahrain, Kuwait, Oman, Qatar, Saudi Arabia, and the United Arab Emirates—enjoy relatively strong economies and together constitute an important market for imports and source of investments and include several major international trade hubs. (On trade negotiations between the GCC and Mercosur, see Ferabolli 2021.)

7. These figures are available at the website of the Arab-Argentine Chamber of Commerce, accessed February 1, 2016, http://ccaa.com.ar/estadisticas.html. By comparison, Argentina has been importing less than $3 million in Lebanese goods annually.

8. During its twenty-nine-year occupation of Lebanon, from 1976 to 2005, Syria "gained almost exclusive control of Lebanon's politics and economy" (Fattah 2005). It also maintained a military presence, which, at its high point, consisted of 30,000 soldiers. Lebanese reactions to the Syrian presence were mixed—from those who celebrated Syria's role as "brothers in arms in the face of the Israeli enemy" to others, such as my interviewee,

who decried Syrian involvement in Lebanon on national (as well as, perhaps, religious) grounds (Fattah 2005).

9. An in-person interview with Rafael Bishara was conducted by the author in Buenos Aires on July 28, 2014.

10. Indeed, a propensity for commerce is often held—by Lebanese and non-Lebanese alike—to be firmly implanted in the Lebanese people's DNA. This national imaginary is based in part on references to the exploits of the Phoenicians in sailing and commerce and has its contemporary equivalent in parts of the Lebanese diaspora, such as in West Africa. As the *BBC* notes, the Lebanese–West African population is estimated at anywhere from 80,000 to 250,000 and has "thrived" in "one of the most difficult and dangerous places to do business," propelled by "the Lebanese tenacity, aptitude for business and drive to succeed." Of particular relevance for present purposes is the Latin American link within the "apocryphal" story of the arrival of the Lebanese to West Africa. As legend has it, "Sometime toward the end of the 19 Century [sic], a ship-load of Lebanese immigrants was heading to Brazil, seeking profit from the booming new world. The first stop after several weeks sailing was Senegal and—the story goes—the somewhat unworldly Lebanese passengers got off believing they had arrived in South America" (Walker 2010).

11. Though subjected to an extreme market fundamentalism in many areas during the Pinochet regime (1973–1990) by the crusading revolutionary neoliberal economists referred to as the Chicago Boys (Valdés 2008), the Chilean economy continues to feature several anomalies that complicate the narrative of Chile as a neoliberal Eden on earth. These include national ownership of a significant portion of the highly lucrative copper industry and a publicly funded national healthcare plan. Despite its faults, the latter amounts to "nearly universal health coverage" (World Bank 2013).

12. An in-person interview with Kadim Al-Hassani and Aqil Qasim was conducted by the author in São Paulo on August 4, 2014.

13. A recurring figure in Iraqi politics until his 2015 death, Chalabi rose to fame (and notoriety) in the US as a darling of the neoconservative movement. Crucially, he helped to sell the 2003 invasion to both US political leaders and the general public through the provision of false intelligence concerning the Hussein regime's would-be terrorist links and weapons of mass destruction program.

14. See Itamaraty's website, accessed May 21, 2019, http://www.itamaraty.gov.br/pt-BR/ficha-pais/5251-republica-do-iraque.

15. In-person interviews with Ricardo Lavalle were conducted by the author in Santiago de Chile on July 2, 2013, and July 15, 2014.

16. An in-person interview with Julieta Fayad was conducted by the author in Santiago de Chile on July 15, 2014.

17. An in-person interview with Gustavo Bari was conducted by the author in Buenos Aires on July 24, 2014.

4

ROOTLESS GLOBALISTS?

On Denationalization and Globality

THE AIM OF THIS CHAPTER IS TO ANALYZE the claim that there exist, at least among my interviewees, economic elites whose interpretive frameworks are predominantly *denational* or *global*. At stake, again, is a crucial distinction that needs to be parsed carefully.

As noted in the previous chapter, a *national* or *transnational* capitalist is one whose profit-seeking and -generating endeavors follow a place-based logic. This means that her/his economic activities are directed toward at least one particular and delimited geographic space—such as a country or region—because the actor in question is drawn there through a personal and/or collective linkage. In turn, the terms *denational*, *denationalized*, and *denationalizing* refer to the decentering of the national imaginary, and situations in which national and other place-based subjective moorings are no longer the primary factor motivating economic activities.

What one would thus expect from a denational, denationalizing, or denationalized capitalist is profit-seeking behavior that passes through little to no filtering of a geographic, affective nature. Returning to the example suggested by Karl Marx (1867), the object for this iteration of "Mr. Moneybags" is to pursue profit across space and time with decreasing or no regard for territorial sentimentality. He or she is again "chase[d] . . . over the whole surface of the globe" in search of increasing returns, and will—or indeed "must"—"nestle everywhere, settle everywhere, [and] establish connexions [*sic*] everywhere," so long as the price is right (Marx and Engels 1888, 476).

Of course, the national, transnational, and denational capitalist are species within the same genus. All are driven by a structurally determined "need for money" and to accumulate for accumulation's sake (Marx 1844, 93). Yet whereas the national or transnational capitalist will concentrate profit-seeking endeavors within a particular space (or spaces) of personal or collective relevance, the denational capitalist has shed any such territorial logic and will instead go more or less wherever the going is good. His or her economic cartography is indeed a "flat world" (Friedman 2005).

If we imagine—for the sake of argument—that capitalist identities exist in logical and chronological order, then the final group under consideration is the global capitalist class. Continuing with the thought experiment, if Mr. Moneybags's profit motive is largely defined by a single national/place-based set of attachments, then he (or she) can be labeled a *national* capitalist. If plural, then a *transnational* capitalist. In turn, if this place-based subjective mooring were to be decentered, we would call him or her a *denational* capitalist. A *global* Mr. Moneybags represents the next leap. In this scenario, place-based imaginaries have lost much if not all of their subjective pull, and this void has been filled by global attachments—first, to a set of (likely English-speaking) global capitalist peers, and second, to a globally organized economy, hence the aforementioned imaginary of capitalist elites as "rootless globalists."

We may thus conceive of a global capitalist as a denational capitalist who has subsequently developed a new class consciousness based on belonging to an imagined community of capitalist peers the world over. Both may seek profits anywhere and everywhere. But again, only the global capitalist has an "identity in the global system" that is based on belonging to a group that exists "above any local territories and polities" (Robinson 2004, 47). Further, global capitalists are also alone in the extent to which they knowingly work in concert with peers "to further the interests of global capital rather than of any real or imagined nation-state" (or, we might again add, of their compatriot capitalists) (Sklair 2001, 295).

If an interviewee were to display profit-seeking behavior that has no territorial logic, positively identify with a global cohort of globally oriented capitalist elites (for example, through use of the word *we* to refer to such a peer group), and work jointly for the establishment of an ever-flatter capitalist world, then he or she would have the profile of an actor who belongs to a global capitalist class for itself. What sets them apart is a shared identity with other globally organized class peers. In sum, they form a stateless nation whose political project is to inaugurate a world order in which capital and capitalists may roam free (Funk 2018).

The focus of the following analysis is to search for evidence of either mentality—denational or global—among my interlocutors. Replicating the format of the last chapter, here I delve into the lifeworlds of a series of carefully chosen individuals through the presentation of ethnographically inspired vignettes. Highlighted in this chapter are Jaime Khoury, cofounder and president of a Buenos Aires–based financial firm that focuses on promoting investment flows between Latin America and the Gulf countries; Georges Naddaf, a long-serving senior executive with a São Paulo–based organization focusing on Arab-Brazilian trade and other forms of exchange; and Julio Valenzuela, an experienced negotiator and advisor within Chile's international trade bureaucracy whose portfolio includes the Middle East and Africa.

While the first two figures are most solidly in the denational camp, the last interviewee—rare among my interlocutors—displays a budding global identity. However, considering the entirety of the evidence collected from interviewees, these are minority positions. Indeed, overall, such denational and especially global moments prove to be less frequent than their national or transnational counterparts. Subsequent to the presentation of the following three vignettes, I pursue a broader analysis of their contents and return to the larger argument.

Vignette #1: Jaime Khoury

A brisk half-hour walk to the northwest of the office of the aforementioned Argentine-Lebanese trade group, as discussed in chapter 3, and overlooking the sprawling Retiro bus and train complex (presumably Argentina's busiest travel hub), lies the upmarket business district that soars upward from the city's Avenida del Libertador (Liberator Avenue). I have come to visit the offices of an English-titled organization that is dedicated to increasing economic exchange between Latin America and the Gulf countries. Here, we have traded the fading continental European architecture and steady din—"cambio, cambio" (exchange, exchange)—of the *microcentro's* (downtown's) proliferating street money changers for the glass-covered skyscrapers and well-manicured lunch-goers of the rarified, tony neighborhood of Recoleta.

These are the traditional stomping grounds of Buenos Aires's urban elite, many of whose aristocratic forebears are resting in elaborate mausoleums in the nearby Cementerio de la Recoleta (La Recoleta Cemetery). Nearby is Patio Bullrich Shopping, a mall that lures consumers with gourmet cuisine, "Argentine cultural refinement," and "an authentic experience of luxury."[1]

The office building itself is staffed by a uniformed security team, and it is only after showing my passport and informing them of my destination that I am afforded a single-use keycard that allows me to proceed to the elevators. Waiting for me in the privileged upper-floor office suite, flanked by views of the staid waters of the Río de la Plata, is cofounder and president Jaime Khoury.[2] With his gently graying hair and an expensive-looking suit, he gives every appearance of having previously worked at various global financial corporations.

As he starts explaining, Latin America and the Gulf countries—as well as the broader Middle East—had traditionally been linked mostly through European and North American institutions. Khoury helped establish a new, investment-focused firm in the late 2000s to capitalize on growing opportunities for interregional investment flows, thus "bridg[ing] the gap" (by now, a familiar metaphor) between the distant regions. He fires off several examples of increased Gulf–Latin American exchange, including the Brazilian mining giant Vale's $1 billion investment in an iron ore plant in Oman, the establishment of direct flights linking the regions, and repeated trips to Latin America by representatives of the Gulf's overflowing sovereign wealth funds.

As quickly becomes clear, Khoury's firm—to which Diego Makhoul, profiled in chapter 3, is listed as a senior advisor—is no mere neighborhood financial broker. Indeed, as the website specifies, potential members are carefully screened and must be invited to join. It goes on to note that membership offers are only extended to high-level figures from the private or public sector with both local and global reputations for business acumen and moral probity. Doors open, it is claimed, for those who pass muster. Perks include not only business opportunities, but also the possibility of discreet, informal meetings with economic, cultural, and political elites, including government officials.

As if to reinforce my preexisting impression of the elite waters in which I am swimming, our conversation is soon interrupted by a hurried phone call in which vast (at least to me) sums of money are being discussed. At this point, I dutifully comply with the request to turn off my digital recorder.

The US-educated Khoury is affable and fast-talking. Though I approach him using Spanish, he replies in fluent English, which becomes the sole language of our interactions. For business reasons, it is also the default language of his firm. He effortlessly punctuates his frank, salesman-like overview of Gulf–Latin American economic exchange with disarming references to his elite business school alma mater (for which he is the president of the Argentine alumni club), recent in-flight movies, and even my (relatively long) hair—which prompts him to jokingly suggest that I must be a member of the Democratic Party.

As becomes especially clear in a subsequent phone conversation, he shares the not-so-gentle assessment by Rafael Bishara, also profiled in chapter 3, of the then current government of Cristina Fernández de Kirchner. He refers to it as a "criminal organization" and worse. The real problem, in his view, is its handling of the economy. Taxes—which the state uses as part of a "Machiavellian" plan to "control everyone"—are too high. Companies are going bankrupt. There is no "respect" for trade agreements. Indeed, the government actively discourages imports, from his perspective, thus turning Mercosur into what he labels one of the "worst" trade blocs anywhere. With partial nationalizations of property belonging to foreign companies (as occurred with Spanish energy giant Repsol YPF in 2012), as well as drawn-out international legal battles with hedge-fund creditors, he observes that Argentina is "fighting against the world." The result is more inflation and less foreign investment.

It is no surprise, then, that he had been "waiting for this regime to end." More than a year before presidential elections that were on the horizon, he had already met with several potential opposition candidates who, if elected, would undo the damage from Kirchner's "fundamentalist" approach to the economy. As he declares, Argentina "needs change" and to get "back on its feet" as a "full member of the global economy;" if not, "we'll have another crisis"—a "tremendous recession"—and Argentina will continue "alienating" the world, joined by a cast of "inferior allies" (here, he cites Cuba, Russia, China, and Angola) while poisoning relations with the US and Europe. It is a replay, in his mind, of the 1982 Falklands/Malvinas War, which notably resulted in Argentina's humiliating surrender to Great Britain and contributed to the downfall of the country's ruling military junta (1976–1983).

In other words, Argentina should stop picking fights, whether over islands, foreign debt, or the activities of multinational corporations. Instead, it must start "to reestablish trust" with the global "financial community." Argentina needs to open itself up to the world instead of trying to force a return to the supposedly autarkic pre-globalization era, in which he notes that "every country wanted to do everything." He is thus offering not only a critique of Argentina's maladies, but a solution: foreign investment and global markets. These of course can be accessed—for a price—by people like him. "The private sector will lead," he proclaims. "People like us. Not the government."

According to his analysis, the state appears to have two roles. The first is to help businesses succeed. Here, he cites the example of US-based Boeing—which, as he notes, "wouldn't survive" without unspecified forms of government assistance. The second is to get out of the way. He illustrates this with a folksy simile: "The economy is like a wedding cake . . . the more you touch the cake, the worse the wedding." While the purported causal mechanism by which low cake consumption correlates with an enjoyable celebration of marriage vows is unclear, what he claims to want is more certain: the state should keep its hands off the economy.

Yet there is an obvious contradiction between calling for government support of large corporations and simultaneously espousing laissez-faire principles. Indeed, the European Union has spent many years pursuing the US government through the World Trade Organization (WTO)—with some amount of success—for allegedly providing Boeing with billions of dollars in "improper subsidies" and, more recently, "illegal tax breaks" (Drew and Clark 2012; Miles 2014). Yet given my concern about the potential derailing of our conversation, I decide not to press for clarification.

His role in Gulf–Latin American exchange is just one of Khoury's several hats. In fact, this firm resides within the offices a larger investment corporation, of which he is also a cofounder and managing partner. The latter claims a "competitive advantage" in the financial-services marketplace due to its long trajectory, privileged access to profitable investment deals, and broad network of contacts nearly all over the world, including in the Middle East. In turn, among Khoury's additional projects, according to news reports, is a hedge fund focused on investing in Argentine financial instruments. For this, he plans to raise well over $100 million from "wealthy families" in the Middle East, Europe, and Latin America.

Yet it is still not clear to me what makes him tick. I ask: Might these efforts help to return Argentina to its glory days of a century prior? I question whether such investments can be wielded to repair the country's infrastructure, which he argues has been "completely destroyed" by the current administration. There is an unnatural pause before he responds. When he does, it sounds as though he is reciting one of the business-first platitudes that pepper his organization's website. I learn little beyond the fact that both the Gulf and Latin America are economically dynamic, opportunity-laden regions that naturally complement one another.

Soon, he is back on his home turf, where life revolves around "making deals," with the goal of "creating links in a chain" of Gulf–Latin American economic relations. In no time, he has again mounted his favorite hobby-horse, declaring to me that the Argentine government "does everything it can to destroy the productivity of companies."

I try once more, but with a reconsidered approach and a more direct question: Why the deal-by-deal drive to build Latin America's relations with the Gulf, as opposed to Europe, China, the US, or anywhere else?

His own past starts to emerge. Khoury was born abroad to a Syrian-Argentine family. Despite the fact that he is quick to point out that his Syrian ancestry "may not mean anything" and that he does not speak Arabic, it clearly *does* mean something to him. "I always felt that I was Middle Eastern in many ways," he reflects. Having attended a school in which everyone else was "European," as he puts it, he liked being "different." He recalls, "I thought it was cool to be Arab."

Later in life, he had the chance to travel to the region and "meet high-profile people," whom he describes as "intelligent, global players." Since there was already "enough going on" in terms of economic relations between Argentina and the US, he saw an "opportunity" in the Gulf, as he was the "first Latin American there." He is "not interested" in Syria, the country of his ancestors, because of civil strife and a lack of business opportunities and contacts. But it is precisely because of his Syrian ancestry that he has been able to become a conduit for exchange between Latin America and the Gulf, as he is recognized throughout the region as "Middle Eastern" and is seen to possess the requisite cultural capital.

But he is also Argentine. And when he says that "*we're* large food exporters" or "*we* consume," he is referring to his Argentine compatriots. He then tells the story of a trip to Egypt, where he was invited by an unnamed individual he refers to as the "richest man" in Kuwait. Soaking in the sights, sounds, and brutal repression of the 2011 revolution from its epicenter in Cairo's Tahrir Square, he manages to emerge unscathed. How? Because "nobody messes with an Argentine." As I ponder what this means, he throws in obligatory references to footballing legends Lionel Messi and Diego Maradona for good measure.

The Gulf countries serve two (strategic) functions in Khoury's world. First, they are a "tremendous source of capital," and he is unwavering in his conviction that a significant portion of those funds should be invested in Latin America—naturally, under his tutelage. Second, he tells me to look at a map. As he observes, the Gulf countries are located "in the center" of the world, about "halfway to China." Per the website, there is thus a historic opportunity for Latin American capital to establish a foothold in the Gulf that will subsequently allow it to spread to other parts of the broader Middle East and beyond. After all, Gulf markets pale in comparison with the Asian behemoths that lay further afield, where billions of consumers beckon—a pot further sweetened by access to abundant and cheap labor, open tracts of land, and low-tax regimes. His firm may be a "bridge" between Latin America and the Gulf, but the Gulf itself is also a bridge between his firm and China, India, and other rising economies.

Thus, while his own familial past and personal interest have led him to the Gulf, the Arab world in general appears largely epiphenomenal vis-à-vis his larger ambition of making deals wherever opportunities exist. If he had been "smart"—and he quickly indicates that he is not—he notes that he would have been the one to create the BRICS grouping, referring to the then-booming, "developing world" economies of Brazil, Russia, India, China, and South Africa. This, he notes, would have earned him a privileged position as a mediator of exchange between the key "emerging markets" of our time. In this alternative storyline, both Latin America and the Arab world lose their starring roles.

Vignette #2: Georges Naddaf

As a diminutive elderly man with a receding white hairline, forward-curved posture, and aloof facial expression, Georges Naddaf[3] does not immediately evoke the image of a young boy's superhero. And yet Makhoul relayed to me that when he was himself coming of age, he forewent the tried-and-true childhood fantasies of becoming an astronaut or firefighter. Instead, he fixed his sights on a then senior executive within a leading organization dedicated to Arab-Brazilian trade as his North Star.

As Makhoul explains with characteristic excitement, Brazil had been exporting approximately $10 billion worth of goods annually to the Arab world. Since Naddaf's enterprise was earning a 0.1 percent commission for providing certificates of origin, there has been a steady flow of funds as of late into its revenue stream. He explains: "0.1 percent in commission is $10 million in income for [them]. That is business"—and precisely the model he yearns to replicate one day in Chile.

On second thought, as far as Arab–Latin American business leaders go, Naddaf—and the organization that he was then leading—are not such bad role models for the budding international trader. Indeed, as noted on this institution's website, it claims the better part of a century's legacy of promoting cultural, economic, social, and other forms of development in, and various forms of connectivity between, Brazil and the Arab world.

Unlike the relative penury of Makhoul's essentially one-man and now-dormant group, this well-resourced commercial organization has offices in both Brazil and Dubai. At its São Paulo headquarters, it employs a robust staff of close to a hundred, spread over several sprawling floors of one of the countless generic, slightly drab high-rises that fill the horizon for as far as the eye can see in both directions along one of the city's most emblematic and business-friendly thoroughfares. Downstairs is the office of the honorary consulate of an Arab country with which Brazil enjoys relatively little trade. It is headed by one of Naddaf's colleagues, a fellow interviewee who is of Lebanese descent and claims no ancestral ties to the state he represents.

Business-minded media consumers may avail themselves of Naddaf's organization's bilingual magazine (printed in Portuguese and Arabic), online news agency (Portuguese and English), and digital TV channel (also available in Portuguese and English). The latter features well over a thousand videos, which are spread out over categories ranging from "economics and foreign trade," "business opportunities," and "cases of success" to food, music, and the Arabic language.

Its office also features a well-stocked if somewhat disheveled on-site library whose several rows of bookshelves include writings on Arab, Latin American, and Arab–Latin American politics, economics, and culture, as well as travel guides, dictionaries, and country-specific file holders. With cover images of former president Luiz Inácio Lula da Silva's face staring back at me from a stack of Arabic-language texts and flanked by copies of its *Relatório de atividades* (*Activities Report*), I am reminded of the website's claim that this trade group provides the fastest and most secure pathway for Brazilian and other entrepreneurs who seek to access Arab markets.

Both Naddaf's and his institution's activities exude power, influence, and success. To push the Brazilian government to modify its foreign-policy approach in ways that would favor increased Arab-Brazilian exchange, the group had presented Lula with a report on opportunities for increased trade that could be realized if his administration were to follow the specified steps. It did, and the result was as predicted: dramatic growth. To draw the attention of Arab business leaders to the economic opportunities that were waiting to be seized in the Brazilian promised land, as recounted to me by the organization's market intelligence manager, they brought representatives from ten Arab companies, all expenses paid, to witness Brazil's successful title run during the 2013 FIFA Confederations Cup.

To teach Brazilian business elites the proper tactics for negotiating with Arab clients and partners, they also offer training sessions in cultural capital and awareness. Indeed, Naddaf offers me one such tip for free: to do business in the Arab world, "the presence of an authority figure" is fundamental. This sentiment goes part of the way toward explaining the organization's emphasis on cultivating a relationship with Lula and the Brazilian state in general.

In turn, an "exclusive" workshop previously promoted on its website promised guidance—for members only—"so that your company can initiate or expand its business in these markets." After Naddaf uses "humor," per the promotional page, to make his pedagogical point that business negotiation requires being patient, resilient, and determined, attendees at this landmark São Paulo business hotel, located adjacent to the city's traditional economic hub, were to be treated to a networking breakfast. For companies seeking to diversify their stable of partners, the group's offices also play host to "matchmaking sessions" between Brazilian exporters and Arab importers.

To push for Latin America as a region to "have more dealings with the Arab world," Naddaf was to become the leader of a fledgling pan–South American association of Arab-focused trade organizations, which at the time was still in the planning stages and subsequently formally opened several years later. Its aim is not only to promote collaboration among existing groups, but to foment the founding of additional ones in countries such as Uruguay, Peru, and Chile.

As Naddaf recounts in Portuguese at the beginning of our conversation, his organization's focus during its decades-long trajectory has been on cajoling "governments and businesspeople" to put the Arab world on their respective radars. To that end, over its life span it has organized an estimated 400 delegations and participated in approximately 170 trade fairs, both of which make for impressive annual rates.

Notably, for reasons specified in chapter 2, the election of Jair Bolsonaro appears to have complicated these substantial efforts at state outreach. Of course, the group is unlikely to be bothered by the administration's pro-corporate posture (especially as it regards its favoring of agribusiness). However, the same cannot be said for its open embrace of Israel, and in particular the far-right government of Benjamin Netanyahu, who as prime minister (from 1996 to 1999 and again from 2009 to 2021) sought to further crush the cause of Palestinian independence—hence the recent headline "Brazil's Nods to Israel May Displease Arab Consumer" (Rocha 2019a). Again, however, the hesitance by some in Bolsonaro's administration to jeopardize access to large export markets in the Arab and Muslim worlds has delayed plans, at least for now, to follow the US in moving the Brazilian embassy from Tel Aviv to Jerusalem. In fact, during 2019, and coinciding with Bolsonaro's first year in office, the Arab world as a whole jumped from the fifth position to become the third largest importer of Brazilian goods, behind only China and the US (*ANBA* 2020).

Having joined the front office in the early 1980s, Naddaf was near or at this organization's helm for literally half of its existence. Notably, these have been its most productive—and successful—years. His appears to have been a lifetime of holding closed-door business meetings with political and economic elites, showing Brazilian capitalists how to navigate Arab markets, and then literally organizing their way there (including inviting them to accompany Lula on official visits). He and this trade group have also doggedly pushed for the Brazilian state to expand its economic linkages with the Arab world through policy measures that include tax cuts, the pursuit of free trade agreements and investment deals, the deployment of more and larger trade delegations, and the promotion and creation of joint ventures.

It is for all of the preceding that, the very day after his aforementioned hotel workshop, he was honored for his contributions to the Arab-Brazilian community by a sponsoring organization of Arab ambassadors during an invitation-only dinner celebration in the capital, Brasília. Beyond overall increases in trade and financial flows—along with many apparent matchmaking successes—institutional advances in Arab-Brazilian economic relations during the boom years include the signing of free trade agreements with Egypt (2010) and Palestine (2011) (Baldissarelli 2014), the latter of which is still pending final approval. Notably, Brazil is the sixth largest source of Egyptian imports (immediately following the US) and eighth largest in the case of Palestine (true to form, Brazilian imports of both Egyptian and Palestinian goods are relatively insignificant).[4]

This is the last and climactic interview of my second round of fieldwork in South America's financial capitals, and I have reason to suspect that my conversation with Naddaf will be a relatively smooth ride. With a lifetime of experiences in his briefcase, he must have much to share—his own ethnographic vignettes about sending Brazilian businesses to the Arab world and bringing Arab businesses to Brazil, frontline tales of capitalist intrigue, folksy anecdotes about deals that have either succeeded or gone sour, and behind-the-scenes disclosures about lobbying the government for fewer and lower taxes, more free trade agreements, and increased attention to be paid to the Arab world.

I am thus expecting his comments to be punctuated throughout by revealing, Makhoul-esque reflections in which he provides a compelling and coherent account, from the privileged perch of a childhood superhero who is now looking down from the apex of a mountain that he has climbed for decades, of *why* he has spent so long seeking to broaden the horizons of Brazil's business class that he is, at the time of our conversation, about to be honored for this very dedication.

Our conversation does not quite match these (perhaps unfair) expectations. Throughout, I receive mostly one-word responses that reflect a taciturn disposition (or at least state of mind at the time) and lack of deep engagement with my questions. There are no epiphanies, no moments in which I feel that he is losing himself in our conversation, and no grand revelations about who or what led him to be sitting across from me in a central executive office within his organization's expansive headquarters.

Is his life's work motivated by the fact that he is of Syrian descent? No, he says, and in fact his own company—about which he shares no other information—exports much more to the US and Europe.

Is he merely seeking the most lucrative trading relationships regardless of region and cultural attachments? He responds that it is not about money, since his trade group "is nonprofit."

Why is any of this important? I interrupt his soliloquy about investments from the Arab world to sharpen my question. Why is any of this important *for Brazil*? Similar to what occurred when I posed such queries to the protagonists behind Brazilian-Iraqi trade, as recounted in chapter 3, I earn a spirited and number-laden lecture about how "exports are growing." I want depth but am being met with platitudes spoken with a gravelly yet soporific inflection.

Likewise, when I inquire about his and his organization's goals for the future, I learn only of its ambition to again double trade within the next six years and—in a mixture of Spanish and Portuguese that he attributes to time spent elsewhere in Latin America—that he is soon planning to retire.

Does he feel that his life's work has been a success? "Yes, of course." We move on to the next topic. As far as loquaciousness is concerned, he is certainly unlike the other figures profiled here and in chapter 3. In a sense, he offers very little beyond my interview from the previous year with the trade group's market intelligence manager. I start to wonder whether my dogged email and in-person efforts to reach the top of the organization's hierarchy—culminating in a virtual tongue-lashing by one of Naddaf's coworkers for bothering too many of his colleagues with my messages—were in the end worth so many valuable fieldwork hours.

It is of course entirely possible, as appears to be the case, that Naddaf is simply terse by nature. He may also have merely been in an especially quiet mood during—or perhaps because of—my visit. Certainly, the many years he has spent in the leadership of a prominent organization, in the public eye, and sustaining sensitive dialogues with political elites could have engendered within him a reticence to engaging in a frank exchange of ideas, especially with an unfamiliar and foreign interviewer. However, as revealed in the rest of this vignette, there are sufficient hints—betrayed by both his words and deeds—to reach at least partial conclusions concerning his would-be globality.

Subsequent to our conversation, after having reviewed, processed, and analyzed field notes, recordings, and personal recollections from and about many interviews, I am finally struck by a revelation. In the wake of months of international travel, dozens of interviews, and careful refinement of my subtly probing questions, confidence-building techniques, and presentation of self, I arrive at the conclusion that Naddaf disorients me because I *assume* that he has a real and deeper essence that he is unwilling or unable to share.

Quick and somewhat superficial readings of Marx suggest that an award-winning international trade specialist who has dedicated his adult life to the deepening of capitalist relations both at home in Brazil and abroad would have naturally developed a corresponding self-awareness.

After all, to return to a quote from *The German Ideology*, consciousness is determined "by life," and "the phantoms formed in the human brain are also, necessarily, sublimates of their material life-process, which is empirically verifiable and bound to material premises" (Marx 1846, 154–155).

What is initially confusing about Naddaf, then, is the seemingly insignificant extent to which his capitalist, globalizing circumstances appear to have ascended from earth (his material surroundings) to heaven (his thought processes concerning his lived reality). He is a capitalist, to be sure, and displays a class-based worldview. However, the depth of his reflexivity concerning his long-standing material conditions seems nearly imperceptible to the naked eye of the observer.

Here, it is useful for analytical purposes to speculate: What if Naddaf is more of an *unthinking* than a *thinking* capitalist? What if Naddaf wakes up, grabs his figurative lunch pail from the refrigerator, and goes to work just like "normal," non-rich people? What if he is so absorbed in his daily capitalist grind—as is often the case with most of us—that he muddles through without subjecting his own work, goals, and activities to meaningful scrutiny? What if he is the proverbial dog that did not bark, neglecting to engage in Makhoul-esque analysis of his own positionality not entirely because he is a shy and guarded public figure, but at least in part because he is not thinking such reflexive thoughts in the first place?

It is indeed the case that not all capitalists are supermen and superwomen of reflexivity. Nor do they necessarily have fully formed worldviews, ideologies, or identities that completely match their material circumstances. This is presumably true not only of capitalists, but of most (if not all) of us in general.

Based in part on this particular conversation, I believe such is the case of Georges Naddaf, the childhood superhero. As I wrote at the conclusion of my field notes, "It's really all [about] economics w/ him." It goes on: "He's not very reflective on his role." And, to summarize: "I don't know why he cares."

Yet hindsight indicates I was wrong in my initial assessment of Naddaf as an especially tough nut to crack, for it turns out that his abrupt responses still speak volumes. When he denies the relevance of his Syrian heritage, he appears to mean it, hence the non-Arab focus of his own profit-seeking endeavors. When nearly the entirety of his discourse centers on investments, exports, and the recitation of trade figures, he does not seem to be concealing deeply held Brazilian, Syrian, or pan-Arab attachments. Indeed, he makes no mention of any such interpretive frameworks, confounding my initial expectations for the recipient of a major award related to his belonging, and contributions, to the Arab-Brazilian community.

During our conversation, when he begins to discuss capitalist globalization, he describes it in terms similar to William Robinson (2008), who likens "global capitalism" to insertion into global production and service chains. Yet here, Naddaf says nothing about any actual global affiliations of his own. What could explain this omission?

The most likely reason is that he neither has nor feels global attachments in the first place (though he may indeed *desire* them). Why, after all, would he neglect to mention them if they truly defined him? Conclusions of this sort are necessarily speculative, as is the case with all inferences derived from interviews, whether of the positivist or interpretivist variety. Yet there are sound reasons to take Naddaf seriously vis-à-vis the words he does or does not utter during our open-ended conversation. After all, the choice to speak—or remain silent—about such a topic is itself an important data point, as it reveals what he deems worthy of verbalizing in the first place.

What he is loudly and clearly focusing on, instead, is what we can infer probably matters most to him: trade for trade's sake and taking the actions (holding export seminars, drafting government briefs) and pushing for the policies (trade agreements, lower taxes, pro-business state intervention in the economy) that will, he believes, help to bring it about. Again, these ends are accomplished through, among other means, applying precisely the sort of Arab-Brazilian know-how that he and the organization he represents are uniquely well positioned to offer.

Indeed, as John Tofik Karam (2007) argues concerning contemporary, neoliberal Brazil, the Syrian-Lebanese ethnicity of many Arab-descendant business elites has recently coalesced into a more general form of pan-Arab cultural capital. One key reason for this transformation relates to the demands of the Brazilian state and private sector for the requisite knowledge that will allow for increased exports to the overall Arab world (as opposed to specific countries such as Syria and Lebanon, which are the ancestral homes of most Arab Brazilians but constitute relatively insignificant export or import markets for Brazil).

Naddaf is virtually a paragon in this regard; whatever may be the personal import of his Syrian heritage, he declares that it is unrelated to his business activities. But the invocation of that same ethnic background has allowed him to rise through the ranks of this *Arab*-Brazilian group, as well as to become a sought-after authority on "how to negotiate with Arabs."

Thus, he is an Arab-Brazilian man engaged in Arab-Brazilian trade, but in a sense this appears to be an epiphenomenal link. In turn, his actions and words suggest that his true desire is to follow the money. His organization's website may refer to its decades-long promotion of cultural, social, and economic "development." But he speaks only of the latter, with no reference to the lofty ambition to unite Brazilians and Arabs on planes beyond the economic. Such is the lifeworld of this capitalist antihero and the formidable organization that he was then leading.

Despite occasional hints of all three, our conversation indicates that Naddaf's goals are thus neither national, transnational, nor global to any significant degree. Rather, it is apparent that they revolve around a denationalized quest for capitalist exchange. He may have been a reluctant interlocutor, but a careful analysis of how his limited words intersect with his actions reveals a fairly clear overall story concerning his worldviews and ambitions.

Vignette #3: Julio Valenzuela

A medical doctor by training, Julio Valenzuela[5] has a background that is somewhat unusual for a protagonist in the world of global capitalist exchange. Yet as noted in an online profile, he possesses "vast experience" in negotiating trade deals. This includes over twenty years within the Chilean state's international trade bureaucracy, during which he has participated in talks leading to, and helped to manage, over a dozen trade agreements (including with both the US and EU, as well as the Comprehensive and Progressive Agreement for Trans-Pacific Partnership, which encompasses major Asian and Pacific Rim economies). For much of the past decade, Valenzuela's portfolio has also encompassed Africa and the Middle East, with which he has actively sought to cultivate deeper economic relations.

In terms of disposition, Valenzuela was Naddaf's antithesis: loquacious, gregarious, and eager to explore his sentimental state while speaking into the digital recorder of a stranger. Such was the earnestness of his engagement that at the end of our second conversation, he made the unusual move of thanking *me* for my time and for giving him the chance to take a step back and reflect on his day-to-day activities. In addition to commenting that he enjoyed "the opportunity to get out of the daily routine" through this probing interview, he further—and even more surprisingly—observed that normally, and unfortunately, "nobody criticizes them," referring to Chile's international trade protagonists specifically and globalizing economic elites more broadly.

Also making Valenzuela an intriguing interlocutor is the claim, drawn from an online profile, that his worldview is defined by a "permanent global vision" regarding the promotion of cross-border trade. Further, he stands out from many of my interviewees in that he reveals no Arab ancestry—the potential significance of which I explore through this vignette.

The state agency through which he is employed was created by the Augusto Pinochet dictatorship in the late 1970s, at the same time that it continued to exile, torture, and disappear dissident and other inconvenient bodies. Simultaneous to his office's birth, the regime also implemented a controversial labor law that codified the neutering of the country's badly repressed union movement (Kremerman 2013).

From the beginning, the agency's legal mandate has been to implement the executive branch's international economic agenda. Through the post-dictatorship period, this commercial policy has displayed a remarkable and perhaps disquieting continuity with that of the military regime, reflecting the fact that an unwavering commitment to *free trade* and *open markets* has been stamped into the DNA of Chilean parties from across the mainstream political spectrum. There is, of course, an enormous contradiction between the Chilean political class's singularity of voice on important economic matters and the fact that Chilean society has long been plagued by deep social, economic, racial, and ideological divisions. Naturally, this marginalization of dissenting voices calls into question the vibrancy of Chile's supposedly consolidated and enviable democracy. This incongruence was made especially evident in late 2019 by the eruption of mass protests, which have targeted the country's neoliberal orientation and the sclerotic, unresponsive nature of its political institutions, as well as by the 2021 election of former student protest leader Gabriel Boric to the presidency.

What is acknowledged across the political spectrum is that the results of this neoliberal consensus have been extraordinarily profound. As cited in chapter 3, Chile has perhaps more free-trade agreements than any country in the entire world—twenty-eight in total, per the government's official count, encompassing an impressive sixty-four foreign markets. Together, they are said to represent 63 percent of the world's population, 86 percent of the global economy (as measured by GDP), and 95 percent of Chile's foreign trade. Thus, if the Chilean state and its economic arms have been married to anyone or anything, it is definitively a neoliberal, export-led "free-market" ideal.

Valenzuela's role in putting this ambition into practice as a doctor-cum-negotiator of major international trade deals may seem low-key or even inconsequential. Yet he is precisely the type of merchant capitalist actor whose behind-the-scenes efforts—launched from deep within the Ministry of Foreign Affairs building in downtown Santiago—are essential for the functioning and propagation of the global capitalist system.

Speaking in Spanish, he divides his work duties into three parts: "a lot of negotiation," "management," and interacting with relevant embassies. With noticeable contentedness, he comments that the Michelle Bachelet administration was "closer to the Arab world" than Piñera, her right-wing predecessor (who also would become her successor). In particular, he cites a "political rapprochement" with the region based on Chile's large and influential Palestinian-descendant population, increased interest on Chile's behalf in pursuing free-trade agreements with Middle Eastern countries, and a more activist foreign policy vis-à-vis Israeli human rights abuses against the Palestinians.

Valenzuela attributes the latter to the Bachelet government's critical posture toward Chile's authoritarian past. Indeed, Bachelet's own father, an air force general who was loyal to the Salvador Allende government, died in military custody after months of torture at the hands of the Pinochet regime, and Bachelet herself was subsequently detained, tortured, and exiled. Notably, during the same fieldwork trip, while I was descending the stairs that lead to the ministry's lobby, I was met with a seemingly impromptu, standing press conference held by several legislators to denounce Israel's bombardment of the Gaza Strip.

Yet ultimately, of course, I am much less concerned with *what* Valenzuela does than with *why* he does it. Fortunately, he was more than happy to oblige, even as I posed for his consideration unconventional questions about place-based imaginaries and his own globalizing role.

Indeed, the dialectical interplay between the two seemingly opposing forces that are of interest here—that is, national/transnational longings and global consciousness—became clearer through my exchanges with Valenzuela than was the case with perhaps any other interviewee. As I jotted down in my post-interview notes, he "switches back [and] forth between [the] national and global," is "navigating [the] global [and] local," and "denies [any] contradiction" between them. The present task, then, is to explore where the balance lies.

There is a recurring nationalist tick in Valenzuela's speech that surfaces in two forms: first, vis-à-vis the now-familiar *we-means-the-homeland* framework that is delineated in the previous chapter, and second, through even balder pronouncements of Chilean interests and/or exceptionalism. Thus, in regard to the former, Valenzuela refers to "a new rapprochement that *we* [Chileans] are trying to make" with the Arab world. As he comments similarly near the beginning of our first encounter, "*We* want to be an agro power" (in both cases, emphasis added). Again, by *we*, he means *Chile*, and by *agro*, he is alluding to the budding halal industry, "a gold mine" that the country is sitting on top of, even if its agricultural producers have only started to take notice.

Evincing a seemingly left-of-center ideology that is also at odds with my other interviewees, he notes, "We're going to continue in underdevelopment without quality education." This observation clearly invokes the sustained, mass student movement that for years has mobilized against Chile's political class for its collective failure to improve overall standards and address chasmic inequalities within the country's ailing public educational system. "It's condemning us," he declares solemnly, as if to a premature death.

Time and again, he repeats *nos* (us), *nosotros* (we), *este país* (this country)—Chileans, the Chilean people, Chile, and its *selección* (national soccer team). Valenzuela laments—apropos of Robert Keohane's aforementioned observation that Latin American countries "are takers, instead of makers, of international policy" (quoted in Carranza 2006, 814)—that for now "Chile is a taker of regulation." And, in turn, he looks forward to a future world in which Chile "puts a developed country in check" in regard to a matter of international political or economic import. As he extols Chile's virtues as "a serious [and] stable country" that has peace, is safe, and suffers from "fewer social problems" than its neighbors, I cannot help but recall its national anthem, which compares the countryside to a "happy copy of Eden" and twice promises "future splendor" for the country.

Our second conversation proved to be more revealing, perhaps because on this occasion we were not joined by any of his work colleagues. Soon after our initial exchange of pleasantries, we found ourselves deeply immersed in a discussion about globalization and what it means both for him and for the Chilean state that contracts his labor to promote international trade. While he had previously defined our globalized world as one in which "ideas travel quickly," citing the examples of world-spanning protest movements and the global repercussions of Middle Eastern conflicts, he now foregrounds the same economic angle of the globalization of ideas and mindsets that motivates my research and presence in his office.

Chile may be geographically isolated "at the end of the world," but through what he refers to as its aforementioned and expansive "network" of free-trade agreements, he remarks that it is beginning to sketch the contours of a globally integrated (capitalist) economy.

What about Valenzuela the medical doctor and merchant capitalist? Does he consider himself a global actor? "Yes, without a doubt." Through his international trade-promotion activities, he has constructed a "network of contacts throughout the world." As he observes, they see each other three times a year at international meetings, much more often than he crosses paths with fellow public-sector employees in Chile who happen to work in the relatively nearby Ministry of Health. Based on his (material) global meeting schedule and global assemblage of merchant capitalist peers, he claims to have developed a(n) (ideational) global consciousness to boot. Yet he acknowledges that this kind of globalizing dynamic that he experiences is an uneven process, for not all similarly placed trade officials either in Chile or around the world participate in the same sorts of globe-spanning *networks* (the latter being a rather telling preferred word of his that evokes writings on globalization by Manuel Castells [2010b] and others).

This globalizing process is also lumpy in a further sense that he does not explicitly mention during either of our conversations. Though Valenzuela asserts that "there is no conflict" between the national and global, at the level of his own mindset there is at least a hint of tension that merits careful analysis in the following paragraphs. Indeed, it is precisely by exploring these seemingly contradictory yet in reality intertwining axes of identity that we may start to establish where precisely his own sympathies lie, as well as address the much larger question of how place-based and global allegiances rise, fall, and interact among capitalist elites.

Valenzuela may initially refer to *his* people as the Chilean nation and to being motivated as a college student by the desire to "work for [and] lift up the country." But as his material circumstances changed upon joining Chile's international trade bureaucracy, his goal morphed into something far greater. "I wanted to feed the world," he declares.

He immediately clarifies that his concern with "food security" also translates into wanting to feed the world in his own country and ensure that

Chile's poor—whose current lack of educational opportunities also concern him—have reliable access to a healthy food supply. Here and throughout our conversation, it is thus clear that he does not subscribe to a facile local/global binary. Rather, he consistently and deliberately asserts the peaceful coexistence of *both* identity axes in his own mindset.

Valenzuela is paid by the Chilean state, as he notes, to promote "Chilean products," improve Chile's "national image," and "defend Chile" in international forums, and he seems to perform these tasks with great passion and aplomb. Yet when he subsequently reflects that his labor is directed toward benefitting "everyone," it is apparent that he means not only his country, but the world. Just as he describes Chile's international political and economic relations as being composed of interlocking networks, stretching from regional to global, so are Valenzuela's identity frameworks stacked on top of one another like layers on a cake. That is to say, they are simultaneously identifiable as distinct and yet are also coherent parts of the same mass.

He closes by asserting that in today's globalizing world, in which he is an important (at least for Chile) if somewhat unconventional protagonist, "everything is connected" and "everything that [we] do has a global repercussion." As he speaks, I cannot help but think that the same is true of Valenzuela and his identity. His nearly two decades of participation in international trade negotiations have clearly internationalized his own worldview and led to his incorporation into global networks. These, in turn, have elevated his interpretive framework beyond the Chilean national container that used to filter, more or less exclusively, his reality.

Valenzuela's distinctive background vis-à-vis my other interviewees is of course of analytical relevance. He is one of the few who do not claim Arab ancestry and is seemingly the only one to have completed doctoral studies or voice even remotely left-of-center politics. Crucially, his quasi-cosmopolitanism appears to bear some relation to these material conditions. Indeed, one detects in him a globalizing ethos that has a basis in his status as an apparent non-Arab who strives to promote Chilean trade with the Arab world (and beyond), who engages with a global community of colleagues, who subscribes to the universal ethics of the medical profession in which he was trained, and who espouses a solidarity-based belief system.

Not everyone in Valenzuela's demographic profile or who navigates similar structural circumstances will think the same. Yet in his case, there is a clear correlation between material conditions and mental frameworks.

It would be too much to speculate that, these initial advances aside, he is moving in the direction of an unadulterated global identity. Rather, at least for the time being, he is perfectly content to allow the local and global to coexist within himself. Similarly, and perhaps like many on the center left, he holds a dual status as a promoter of global capitalist relations and critic of the inequalities that capitalism generates.

Valenzuela's story thus highlights two key dynamics: First, he is an outlier among my interviewees in terms of his background, the relatively high level of globality evinced during our conversations, and his elaboration of a belief system that is atypical for a protagonist of capitalist globalization. Thus, among my interlocutors, Valenzuela appears as a sui generis figure, as opposed to one who necessarily represents the emerging prototype of a new breed of global capitalists—though it is entirely possible that others will begin to develop similar interpretive frameworks as time passes. Second, and more generally, identities and worldviews are convoluted phenomena that reflect complex cognitive processes as they unfold within living, breathing, and reflexive human agents.

Analysis and Conclusions

Again, chapter 3 demonstrated how heavily the "tradition of dead generations" weighs on the brains of many of today's living capitalists through corresponding place-based attachments—to nations, states, cultures, and homelands of various kinds. Among them, national and transnational concerns proved to be paramount.

In this chapter, we witness a distinct, if not entirely contradictory, trend. Here, there is a noticeable supersession of national and/or ethnic concerns in favor of either a (partially) denationalized quest for profit or a (partially) globalized set of identifications and attachments. Indeed, I have chosen to portray these three individuals in the preceding pages precisely because of the extent to which their interpretive frameworks differ from those depicted in the previous chapter.

In sum, these figures display significant *denationalizing* (Khoury, Naddaf) or *globalizing* (Valenzuela) trends. To be sure, the usual caveats apply here as well. First, it is not that national or ethnic ties are irrelevant in these cases. Even among Khoury and Naddaf, they are still part of the general background of cultural capital that has led them to the particular—and profitable—niche of Arab-Latin American relations. Also, decidedly *un*global moments continue to make appearances, particularly in the form of Khoury's slow-to-come but nevertheless meaningful references to his family background, as well as Valenzuela's tried-and-true Chilean nationalist tendencies.

Such place-based manifestations are not entirely dissimilar to those uncovered in chapter 3. Yet what is important for categorization purposes is that here they turn out to be the exception rather than the rule. Notably, conceptualizing these different interpretive horizons in terms of *less* and *more*, rather than *either* and *or*, takes us back to this work's ontological starting point: identities are not binaries but rather take the form of continuums and intersecting pieces of latticework.

The second caveat is that there is again great diversity among this chapter's interviewees. For example, one appreciates a particularly noticeable gap separating Khoury and Naddaf's profit-first mindsets from Valenzuela's budding sense of global solidarity. However, they are nonetheless united by a crucial trait: in one or another form, the place-based interpretive filter has been decentered to a significant extent.

To briefly recapitulate their stories:

- JAIME KHOURY. The closest among my interviewees to Marx's (1867, 362–363) Mr. Moneybags, whose "life impulse" is profit, whose "soul is the soul of capital," and who is chased around the globe by the desire—the *need*—"to create value and surplus-value." Sentimental longings for particular homelands or compatriots surface occasionally vis-à-vis his "cool" immigrant past and the sort of uninhibited nationalist tendencies that are so often attributed to Argentines in general and residents of Buenos Aires in particular. Yet ultimately what has led him to the Arab world is not a Makhoul-, Bishara-, Kadim Al-Hassani-, or Aqil Qasim-style quest to reconnect with the hallowed lands of ancestors and coethnics, nor a deep-seated desire to promote Argentina's economic development or address what he identifies as the country's many maladies. Rather, it is a denationalized quest for profit and the fact that it is in the Arab world that he is able to turn his cultural capital—his Syrian family background and ascribed corresponding ability to harness business opportunities in the larger Arab world—into capital itself, at least, that is, until Asian or other markets prove more attractive or accessible. According to his supremely class-conscious worldview, the imagined community that appears as the most salient is in fact the private sector and, more specifically, financial capitalists. Those are the human beings he labels as "people like *us*" (emphasis added).

Though inchoate, there are indications that he understands that this imagined community exists beyond Argentina's borders.
- GEORGES NADDAF. From childhood superhero to capitalist on apparent autopilot. In terms of reflexivity, he is no less than Makhoul's opposite. As it turns out, the motives driving the actions of this award-winning and seasoned interviewee—an especially important protagonist behind Brazil's remarkable sixfold increase in trade with the Arab world—were not buried deep below the interpretive surface. Rather, one seems to see what one gets with Naddaf: a straightforward, largely denationalized capitalist desire to change Brazilian foreign policy, internationalize Brazil's economic elites through exclusive workshops, spread his organization's institutional model throughout the region, and pursue a business-friendly agenda of lower corporate taxes and more free-trade agreements. At the level of demeanors, his sobriety is the polar opposite of Khoury's free-flowing assertiveness and gregariousness. Yet if a mutual conversation were to turn to the use of cultural capital in support of a largely denationalized quest for profits, the two would have much to discuss.
- JULIO VALENZUELA. A refreshingly reflective and obliging interlocutor who is a perhaps unlikely negotiator for a country that has pursued international trade deals with dogged and unmatched enthusiasm. He embodies both the local *and* the global, as well as how the latter may arise alongside of—and not precisely to replace—the former. Indeed, he is nearly equally at home among an atypical, class-inclusive rendering of the Chilean people and a global epistemic network of trade contacts. Valenzuela wants to simultaneously feed the world and ensure that Chileans of all socioeconomic statuses have access to quality education. Indeed, as he puts it, "everything is connected" in his world and interpretive frameworks.

Notably, in two of these three cases (with Valenzuela unsurprisingly proving to be the exception), the prism of linguistics is helpful for shedding light on and making sense of their mindsets. Speaking a particular language is a choice made by interviewees. This decision, of course, reflects their material conditions (e.g., their educational experiences and family backgrounds, the frequency with which they travel, and the extent to which they participate in a global business community for which English, instead of their native languages, is the lingua franca). But it may also, in turn, reveal important fragments of their identities (McCrum 2011).

For Valenzuela, his exclusive use of Spanish reflects the fact that he is based in Chile and as a public servant does less jet-setting than many of his fellow interviewees. He is certainly proficient in English, given that he obtained a graduate degree from a US-based institution. Yet in our conversations, despite knowing about who I am and where I am from, he chose not to speak it. In Naddaf's case, Spanish appears alongside his native Portuguese due to the considerable amount of time he spent living elsewhere in Latin America. However, this linguistic choice, or habit, also seemingly evokes the fact that he has dedicated considerable energy toward bringing Brazil's Spanish-speaking neighbors together to create a pan-regional trade federation focusing on the Arab world, which—as noted previously—has since come to fruition.

Khoury's decision to respond to my (fluent) Spanish with (fluent) English hints at his belonging to an imagined community of business colleagues, both from his alma mater and beyond, that is decidedly global. It also suggests that he regards *me*—his US interlocutor—as a linguistic peer, with whom he feels comfortable sharing at-times controversial ideas and opinions. Finally, and returning to the previous chapter, Makhoul's recurring recourse to English when engaging in business speak evinces the inchoate global identity that simultaneously motivates and unsettles him.

Of course, many factors beyond the above influence language use. Further, for some interviewees—most notably, Valenzuela—the spoken language does not directly correlate with a corresponding mindset in the way we may expect. Yet, for many of these elites, language choices do hew closely to place-based (their native and/or dominant languages) or placeless (English) class identities. Accordingly, they comprise an important data point for deciphering national, transnational, denational, and global interpretive frameworks.

The above cases thus provide some validation of the hypothesis concerning the existence of a global capitalist class. One uncovers partial evidence here for the existence of a capitalist elite that features an "identity in the global system above any local territories and polities" (Robinson 2004, 47) or at least for whom national and transnational imaginaries have been decentered to a significant degree. Among these interviewees, *place* either lacks the ability to determine much of the direction of current or planned capitalist flows (Khoury, Naddaf) or exists as only one part of a larger, mixed, and intertwined local-global framework (Valenzuela). Particularly in regard to the former type, they are not alone, as demonstrated by the following brief examples from two other interviewees:

- *Julieta Fayad* (also cited in the previous chapter; again, at the time of our interview, in charge of Chile's trade relations with the Middle East and several other regions). Responding to my inquiry about her global credentials, she comments, with noticeable surprise, that she "had never thought about it that way [before]." Yet she is quick to note that the experiences of promoting international trade, traversing the globe, and finding her bearings when arriving in foreign airports have caused her to realize that we live in an era of "total worldwide connectivity" and to develop a corresponding "mental opening." In turn, it has become her life's work to transmit that mentality "to the private sector." Putting these comments into dialogue with those reported in chapter 3, her case evokes the potential simultaneity of place-based and placeless identity markers.[6]

- *Luz Catrani* (then director of international and technical relations for a private-sector association of Argentine exporters). Displays precisely the denational streak that one would expect from a merchant capitalist without a particular national or regional focus, along with a Khoury-esque—though less incendiary—appraisal of then-president Kirchner. Her organization's objective is to export "wherever," she observes, including—but of course not limited to—the Arab world. "We're immersed" in globalization, she declares. Invoking Thomas Friedman, Catrani comments that "globalization isn't 'choosable' [that is, it is not a choice]." Rather, it is the "motor" of our time "for the whole world." In this predetermined context, her role is to export whenever, however, and to whomever.[7]

Denational and to a lesser extent global capitalists—that is, respectively, those for whom the place-based imaginary has largely been decentered and those with a positive set of global attachments—are thus a real phenomenon. In the above vignettes, one does indeed encounter several utterances that evoke, to return to this chapter's title, a kind of rootless globalism.

Further, as I speculate, there appears to be a nascent trend among capitalist elite identities away from nationalism or transnationalism and toward both denationalization and globalization. Thus, arguments in favor of the existence of a global capitalist class are not without merit and bear consideration as we contemplate the contours of our present, and especially future, world.

However, it is clear that here these are still minority positions, with only a handful of interlocutors beyond those profiled in the preceding pages fitting most comfortably into the denational category. Further, among the entire universe of interviewees, Valenzuela is the only one whose interpretive framework can be said to be global to a significant degree (and notably, in his case, class-based affinities resonate much less strongly than they do among his peers).

In sum, place-based filters for profit-seeking activity continue to resonate to an extent that calls into question many common scholarly and lay understandings of global processes, ranging from the arguments of the global capitalism school to proponents of the "strong globalization" thesis (Hirst et al. 2009, 17). Accordingly, at least in terms of the present case, a global capitalist class for itself has yet to supersede its place-based counterparts. Instead, as Adrian Budd (2013, 171) concludes more broadly, "The contradictory interpenetration of the national and global that has characterized its entire history continues to shape the capitalist world system." One thus witnesses more continuity than change, though there are also instances of the latter.

Toward a Rooted Understanding of Globalism

By way of conclusion, I now turn to the task of drawing from the above empirical analysis to elaborate a conceptual framework that aids our collective understanding of ongoing and seemingly likely future changes in capitalist identities. Specifically, I argue that the term *rooted globalism* encapsulates the contradictory, halting, and nascent trend toward the denationalization and subsequent globalization of capitalist elite identities. Yet crucially, it also accounts for the fact that these processes are unfolding within the shells of national and transnational imaginaries that continue to resonate—hence, again, the likening of would-be global identities to palimpsests. In sum, rooted globalism is a nuanced concept that sheds light on how the global and local interact and intersect in diverse geographical contexts.

This effort at concept formation again inverts (and subverts) the longstanding practice of building theory almost exclusively on the basis of Global North realities (Aydinli and Biltekin 2018). Thus, the broader aim here is to explore how the study of the would-be global identities of Latin American capitalist elites can potentially further our understanding of this same phenomenon the world over and, in turn, contribute to theoretical debates in global studies and related fields. The idea is not to blindly export these Latin American–based findings around the globe; rather, it is to engage in a nuanced, context-sensitive theory-building exercise.

To summarize the empirical findings, place-based (national and transnational) imaginaries are the dominant interpretive filters among this group of Latin American business elites. However, there are also important ideational forces—denational and, to a lesser extent, global—pushing in contradictory, or at least differing, directions. As I have suggested, identities are complicated and intersectional. It is unsurprising, then, that seemingly opposing interpretive horizons often exist simultaneously within the same individual. To invoke the logic of continuums, at the end of the day we may all have at least a little bit of everything.

Within this lumpy framework, we seem to be witnessing signs of a *trend* toward the denationalization of identities and even more speculatively their potential subsequent globalization. Corroborating evidence appears in the form of witnessing how globalizing material circumstances are transforming the mental frameworks of actors (and thinkers) as diverse as Makhoul and Valenzuela, albeit in distinct ways.

Here, one is reminded of Saskia Sassen's (2007; 2011) ponderings concerning the convoluted rise of global classes. Specifically, she points to the continuing embeddedness of global elites in specific places as well as the simultaneous persistence of place-based imaginaries and rise of placeless ones. Global class formation, as she argues, is an incipient process (and an important one to analyze), but it is far from complete. Accordingly, we would be wiser to refer to such elites as "partially denationalized" instead of "global" (Sassen 2007, 169–170).

The current study provides supporting empirical evidence for her nuanced conceptualizations of identity-transformation processes and her overall argument about where the balance lies. The local and global are both real, can and do coexist, and are seemingly undergoing transformation. It is thus important that we pay attention to how these processes may unfold.

However, we cannot lose sight of the stickiness of place-based imaginaries. Thus, this study also validates the (nuanced) core assertions of the literature on transnationalism, which recognizes "the internationalization of capital and the transnationalization of populations" but also that "nation-states and nationalism persist and must be the topic of further analysis" (Glick Schiller et al. 1992, 15).

Here, I argue that the concept of rooted globalism provides a useful framework for aiding our efforts to identify what we see—and, potentially of even greater importance, perhaps *will* see in the future—when we stare out at the vast expanse of capitalist identities.[8] It is relevant to speak of *globalism* because of the above-mentioned hints that this is the direction in which elite (and perhaps other) identities are headed. Indeed, the denationalization of place-based capitalist worldviews, as observed in some of the preceding cases, logically seems to be a precondition. There is no ironclad *telos* or implied suggestion that such a denationalization process is guaranteed to eventually occur, nor that if (not when) it does, it will inevitably lead to the development of globalism. Rather, I offer these arguments in the spirit of empirically informed conjectures concerning the path and paths that future capitalist elite identities appear likely to take.

And yet it is also relevant to specify that it is *rooted*, because, as and if they develop, globalist tendencies will grow within a milieu dominated by the national and/or transnational. As is the case with a set of watercolors, one coat of paint cannot be applied on top of another of a different color without combining to create an entirely new fusion that contains elements of each. Thus, if or as globalism rises, it will not produce a fundamentally and ahistorically new global identity, but rather a new-old one in which the local and global cohabit within the same mental space, in spite of any ontological tensions that may exist between them. In this regard, identities are again akin to palimpsests (Carvalho 2013).

Most specifically, then, rooted globalism refers to an identity formation in which, to significant and observable extents, place-based filters have to an appreciable degree been denationalized and global attachments and longings are developing or have developed. Crucially, however, local, national, transnational, ethnic and/or other such axes continue to resonate, thus producing complicated, convoluted, and braided new-old identity amalgamations. Though these characteristics may appear contradictory, such is the convoluted nature of intersectional human identities (and, in turn, class consciousness).

Valenzuela emerges as the closest to a real-life personification of this category. Through his story, we are able to witness how the desire to "work for, [and] raise/build/lift up the country" transformed into the ambition to "feed the world," accompanied by a "permanent global vision" relating to international trade and the development of a "network of contacts throughout the world." Simultaneously, he continues to speak in terms of *us, we, this country*, and *la selección* to mean Chileans, Chile, and its national soccer team. As we have seen, Valenzuela is a figure who "switches back [and] forth between [the] national and global," is "navigating [the] global [and] local," and in general asserts that "there is no conflict" between them. Returning to Sassen (2007, 169–170; 2011), it is in these ways that capitalist elites may don nationalist garb while simultaneously displaying an "incipient globality," thus producing novel identity "imbrications" that represent a mixture of the local, national, denationalized, global, and so on.

Notably, per this account, Valenzuela does not precisely qualify as a member of the global capitalist class for itself of the global capitalism school's description, for whom identity is to transcend "any local territories and polities" (Robinson 2004, 47). However, such a formulation does retain value as an ideal type. Indeed, the very act of presenting an exaggerated vision of a flat world peopled by global actors with fully global mindsets can aid our efforts to engage in analytical exercises concerning potential future trajectories of the world system that surrounds us. However, this particular analytical construct of a global capitalist class for itself does not reflect the empirical realities revealed in the present study.

Taking Valenzuela as rooted globalism's exemplar, my argument is instead that, at least for the foreseeable future, global identities can be expected to exist *alongside* their place-based counterparts, not *above* them. Thus, this framework incorporates, but also moves beyond, the place-based logic of transnationalism, which suggests simultaneous embeddedness in multiple spaces as a first-order principle. What *rooted globalism* refers to is a similar simultaneity of embeddedness, but one that also coexists with interpretive horizons, even if extremely nascent, in which place ceases to matter entirely. Such is the mindset that prevails among both the elites who are the focus of this study, as well as presumably—to varying extents—their peers elsewhere.

This chapter thus brings to a close the present empirical engagement with the question of the extent to which we can speak of and identify a global capitalist class for itself among a particular population of Latin American business elites and, perhaps by extension, in the world more broadly. Going forward, there is much room for additional works of both the methodologically sophisticated and regionally diverse varieties that seek to add to our collective understanding of this important but mostly neglected topic.

However, this conclusion—a skeptical but not dismissive response to the ideational half of the global capitalist class hypothesis—raises additional questions. Specifically, it is necessary to reconcile the above argument with the fact that elites frequently declare that they possess a global identity. The following chapter thus tackles this seeming paradox: If the present study provides grounds for concluding that global capitalist identities are much less real (and much more rooted) than commonly thought, then why are they so commonly asserted? Why are we bombarded—through advertising and otherwise—with tales of their existence? As I explore in the next chapter, squaring this circle requires that we analyze the material benefits that may accrue to capitalist elites through their assertions of global identities.

Notes

1. See Patio Bullrich's website, accessed January 14, 2022, http://www.shoppingbullrich.com.ar/about.php.

2. An in-person interview with Jaime Khoury was conducted by the author in Buenos Aires on July 12, 2013; an additional phone interview was conducted on July 31, 2014. Here and in the other vignettes, unless otherwise noted, all quotes are from the interviewee(s).

3. An in-person interview with Georges Naddaf was conducted by the author in São Paulo on August 12, 2014.

4. See the database of the Observatory of Economic Complexity, accessed June 1, 2019, https://oec.world.

5. In-person interviews with Julio Valenzuela were conducted by the author in Santiago de Chile on July 3, 2013, and July 14, 2014.

6. An in-person interview with Julieta Fayad was conducted by the author in Santiago de Chile on July 15, 2014.

7. An in-person interview with Luz Catrani was conducted by the author in Buenos Aires on July 21, 2014.

8. This term, which does not appear to have enjoyed significant previous use, bears a surface resemblance to the idea of *rooted cosmopolitanism*. The latter has become a serious topic of conversation in the field of liberal political theory. It refers to the attempt to reconcile global, universal ethics with local ties and attachments without giving up on either. See, for example, Kwame Anthony Appiah's (2005) blockbuster *The Ethics of Identity* (for a brief review focusing on rooted cosmopolitanism, see Freedman 2005), as well as Will Kymlicka and Kathryn Walker's (2013) *Rooted Cosmopolitanism: Canada and the World*. For another instance of this term's use, see Sidney Tarrow's *The New Transnational Activism* (2005, 29). He writes (emphasis in original): "Transnational activists are a subgroup of rooted cosmopolitans, whom I define as *people and groups who are rooted in specific national contexts, but who engage in contentious political activities that involve them in transnational networks of contacts and conflicts.*" Similarly, Margaret E. Keck and Kathryn Sikkink (1998) made significant waves in various disciplines with their earlier analysis of "transnational advocacy networks."

Insofar as *rooted cosmopolitanism* also wrestles with the intermingling of the local, global, transnational, cosmopolitan, and universal, it bears at least a surface resemblance to my use of *rooted globalism* (see, for example, Erkmen 2015). What I add to this broader area of inquiry, aside from the focus on the identities and class consciousness of capitalist elites, is a specific empirical hypothesis, as articulated above, relating to the apparent evolution of these identities and an ontological argument about how *new* interpretive frameworks tend to arise only gradually and within the shells of the old.

5

"THE FLAT PLURALIST WORLD OF BUSINESS CLASS"

On Constructing (and Contesting) Corporate Global Imaginaries

THE PREVIOUS TWO CHAPTERS DELVED INTO THE IDEATIONAL qualities of the Latin American capitalist elites—merchant, financial, and otherwise—who are most responsible for the marked growth in this region's commercial relations with the Arab world. The principal finding, as noted, is that while denational and occasionally global interpretive frameworks do manifest themselves, national and transnational imaginaries continue to filter the profit-seeking activities of the majority of interviewees to a significant extent. While I do not wish to imply that the present case is representative of all others, this observed stickiness of place-based attachments nevertheless provides some justification for a skeptical, but not dismissive, response to arguments for the existence of a global capitalist class for itself.

In turn, the present chapter begins by tying up a theoretical loose end that arises out of this conclusion: If the "strong globalization" thesis is overdrawn (Hirst et al. 2009, 17), at least as it concerns elite identities, then why is the general public so often bombarded with media and visual references to global capitalist entities that seemingly have, as Saskia Sassen (2007, 187) again puts it, "no national attachments or needs"? What explains the apparent contradiction between the present argument and the prevalence of corporate advertisements declaring that global elites and firms have cut the national umbilical cord? What are we to make of the recurring assertion that ours is a *flat* world in which place no longer matters?

The aim of this chapter is not to interrogate the veracity of these corporate discourses or determine just how global these actors really are in either material or ideational terms (though again, the previous chapters produced revealing results about the second of these issues in particular). It is, rather, to interrogate the frequency of and motives behind the circulation of these corporate global imaginaries.

Thus, the ambition here is to discover *why* and *how* capitalist elites again "project images of themselves as citizens of the world as well as of their places of birth" (Sklair 2016, 332), even while their own interpretive horizons may revolve more strongly around the latter than the former. Specifically, I explore these advertisements' effects on audiences, interrogate the political calculations behind these representations, and discuss efforts to contest these globalist narratives.

The Political Uses of "Banal Cosmopolitanism" in Corporate Globalizing Discourses

From nearly ubiquitous television and magazine advertisements to posters competing for passengers' attention in jet bridges all over the globe, consumers are continuously subjected to messages affirming the inception of a "flat," borderless, and fully globalized world (Friedman 2005). Such discourses suggest that time-space compression is inexorably bringing humanity together into a globally connected, cosmopolitan world order.

As the below Emirates Airline advertisements put it: "Tomorrow never stops exploring" (with an image featuring what appears to be a middle-aged white tourist joyfully listening to music from an adjacent Asian teenager's handheld device) (fig. 5.1); "Tomorrow brings us all closer" (fig. 5.2); "The world is your playground" (this ad also boasts of "A multilingual cabin crew from over 100 nations") (fig. 5.3) or, alternatively, "The world on your doorstep" (fig. 5.4); "Beijing. Once Forbidden. Now daily" (fig. 5.5); and, finally, "7 billion people. One bridge that connects us all" (fig. 5.6.).

Such assertions motivate the following questions: What understanding of globality do corporations attempt to sell through such advertisements, how do they sell it, and what effect does this have on audiences? What is the corporate interest in promoting an ethos of "banal cosmopolitanism" among consumers "in which everyday nationalism is circumvented and undermined and we experience ourselves integrated into global processes and phenomena" (Beck 2002, 28)—though in some cases, as observed later in

Figure 5.1 Advertisement from Emirates Airline's "Hello Tomorrow" series depicting intercultural exchange in an unknown location. (Source: Khatija Liaqat, https://khatijaliaqat.wordpress.com/2016/05/21/taglines-of-emirates-airline/.)

this chapter, with a regional or local twist?[1] In turn, how can these recurring assertions of a global identity be reconciled with the above argument that place-based imaginaries are far more resilient than is commonly portrayed? More broadly, what does addressing these questions reveal about the importance of analyzing visual and other discourses relating to the cultural political economy (CPE) of globalization?

These corporate messages focus on globalization's humanistic side, as they highlight cross-cultural exchange, limitless travel, and our belonging to a universal community. They also tap into capitalism's "emotional logic," which enchants audiences with promises of choice, endless consumption, and economic mobility (Konings 2015).

Figure 5.2 Additional advertisement from Emirates' "Hello Tomorrow" series, this one featuring a montage of iconic buildings, structures, and sites from around the globe. (Source: Khatija Liaqat, https://khatijaliaqat.wordpress.com/2016/05/21/taglines-of-emirates-airline/.)

Further, their assertion of a multiculturally inclusive and globally integrated, borderless world order possesses a potentially subversive edge, as these discourses (ostensibly) challenge existing material and epistemological hierarchies by claiming to open an uneven global playing field to those often excluded from participation (Chandra 2013; Mignolo and Escobar 2013)—that is, those who hail from what Vijay Prashad (2007) labels the "darker nations": Global Southerners, immigrants, asylum seekers, hijab wearers, and others whose stubborn existence "interrupts the flat earth, borderless world, and smooth space conceits of globalists, highlighting asymmetry and inequality amidst intensifying global interdependency" (Sparke 2007, 117; see also Smith 2005).

Perhaps it is in part for these aspirational reasons that, according to a survey on global citizenship, respondents from "emerging" economies were significantly more likely than their counterparts in the industrialized world to identify "as global rather than national citizens" (Grimley 2016). Notably, however, whatever radical critique may be implied by these cosmopolitan,

Figure 5.3 Emirates advertisement depicting the joy of travel. The fine print includes the aforementioned observation that the airline features a "multilingual cabin crew from over 100 nations." (Source: Khatija Liaqat, https://khatijaliaqat.wordpress.com/2016/05/21/taglines-of-emirates-airline/.)

corporate messages is blunted by the fact that what is being sought is of course in no way anti-capitalist or anti-systemic in nature; rather, it is a tepidly reformist call for greater inclusion in existing (and still exclusionary) power structures.

Most importantly, this chapter argues that beneath the humanistic, cosmopolitan, and visually alluring imaginary of these and similar advertisements—complete with pithy, memorable slogans written over lush, seductive backgrounds—lurks a self-interested, ideological mission. This is, of course, the corporate raison d'être: to seek profit. Specifically, transnational corporations seek to convey to consuming classes

The world on your doorstep.
From 1st September fly daily from Newcastle to China.

Figure 5.4 Emirates advertisement celebrating the launch of direct flights between the North East English city of Newcastle and Dubai, thus allowing for one-stop connections to airports in China and around the world. (Source: Khatija Liaqat, https://khatijaliaqat.wordpress.com/2016/05/21/taglines-of-emirates-airline/.)

around the world (and those who aspire to join them) the desirability and inevitability of a borderless economy that cannot be regulated and in which they may roam unfettered.

Specifically, I argue here that capitalist elites are naturally driven to flaunt and even exaggerate their global credentials as part of a "self-conscious propaganda campaign" because doing so is in their material self-interest (Beder 2005, 116). In short, adopting and promoting their own "flexible citizenship" are "strategies to accumulate capital and power" (Ong 1999, 6). This is the case because Sassen's (2007, 187) aforementioned "free-floating cosmopolitan classes with no national attachments or needs" would be significantly harder to regulate than their nationally oriented and rooted counterparts. Indeed, existing regulatory regimes, which are primarily centered on *national* laws and means of enforcement, are ill-equipped to constrain truly *global* actors (Rodrik 2012).

Further, these global discourses feed into the public image—also beneficial for elites—that we live in the real-world equivalent of an ideal-type

Figure 5.5 Emirates advertisement invoking Beijing's rise as a cosmopolitan and global city. (Source: Khatija Liaqat, https://khatijaliaqat.wordpress.com/2016/05/21/taglines-of-emirates-airline/.)

capitalist fantasyland. In this corporate utopia, meaningful regulation of global capitalism's inevitable spread appears unthinkable and impossible and thus is not worth attempting. This vision, as noted, resonates with both the Marxist-inspired analysis of the global capitalism school as well as the political project of neoliberal "globalists" (Slobodian 2018). Naturally, in turn, even social movements with a keen interest in fighting for alternative, politically progressive forms of globalization are more likely to feel disempowered than energized by the implicit message that capitalist elites or corporate globalization cannot be tamed by the state or the general will.

Yet here, an important caveat is in order. The fact that capital does often seem to operate without borders due to the insufficiency of both national and global regulatory frameworks does not automatically imply that these

Figure 5.6 Text-based Emirates "Hello Tomorrow" advertisement. (Source: Khatija Liaqat, https://khatijaliaqat.wordpress.com/2016/05/21/taglines-of-emirates-airline/.)

advertisements are literally correct in asserting the *impossibility*—as opposed to the potential *difficulty*—of regulation (Harrington 2016). As suggested in this chapter's concluding section, we must turn our sights toward the obstacles that make regulation seem so implausible in the first place. These include state capture by powerful interests and a lack of both political will and counter-imaginaries that challenge the cultural-ideological hegemony of corporate globalization (Juris 2008).

There is thus no contradiction between the seemingly opposing empirical realities presented by the previous chapters' findings and the frequent circulation of corporate global discourses. For while the present analysis demonstrates that elite identities appear to be less global than is commonly thought, it is also true these same elites stand to gain materially from global presentations of self. The logic, again, is straightforward: in a world in which capitalist elites are materially and ideationally global but most forms of meaningful governance are in fact national, these actors would be able to sidestep such place-based regulatory mechanisms with relative ease.

Thus, while seemingly global capitalist elites may not in fact form a highly developed global capitalist class for itself, as I argue, many such figures and entities find it advantageous to present themselves as global to various audiences. For them, *globality* is both an aspiration and a political project, advanced through advertising campaigns and other means. The aim is to demonstrate the futility of efforts to regulate both their activities and the broader global capitalist system of which they are a part and from which they profit.

That these messages are conveyed through catchy slogans written over attractive background images only increases their appeal. As explored in greater depth later in this chapter, this speaks to a larger truth about pop culture and its political relevance: we engage with it, in part, because we often find it pleasurable (Grayson et al. 2009).

These aesthetically pleasing advertisements thus attempt to perform two simultaneous tasks. On the one hand, they evoke a globe-spanning imagined community that appears politically liberal if not subversive in composition; on the other, they advance a political project that does not necessarily reflect a genuine expression of a deeply felt global identity, but instead seeks to further the interests of capitalist elites. That is, such advertisements are selling teleological global capitalism and corporate globalization as the "end of history" (Fukuyama 1992) to audiences, who are meant to accept, embrace, and perhaps even participate in this fait accompli.

Accordingly, this chapter delineates how these polyvalent advertisements operate at multiple levels to convey related but distinct messages about the global. In turn, it responds to the above discrepancy vis-à-vis previous chapters by explaining why these messages differ from the less-than-global interpretive horizons identified among most of the aforementioned interviewees.

In short, while inclusive, cosmopolitan, people-first globalization is the superficial idea meant to attract audiences upon first glance, the deeper meaning that is transmitted more subtly is that capitalism's global march is unstoppable. In this way, as analyzed later in this chapter, these advertisements seek to disarm target audiences—and undermine their agency—by playing to their humanistic impulses in order to sell them on a global-capitalist ideal that is under increasing fire from numerous quarters (Stiglitz 2017).

Yet while such campaigns appear to be successful to a meaningful extent, their effects can only be partial, rather than totalizing. Of course, audiences may understand and respond to them in either unintended or even oppositional ways.

In turn, the political project of this book is precisely to buttress the latter tendency. In other words, and based on the preceding analysis and empirical findings, the aim is to promote skeptical readings of commonly advanced arguments for elite globality (and associated claims of total capital mobility, the inability of state or international mechanisms to regulate capital, and so on) and to suggest the need for alternative, people-first global imaginaries. I return to this latter point in the book's concluding chapter by highlighting the dangers of left-populist responses to corporate globalization that reinforce the same nativist tendencies that have fed into the current rise of the far right.

A Cultural Political Economy of Globalization: Corporate Imaginaries and the Formation of Global Subjects

To illustrate the delicate balancing act pursued by capitalist elites as they navigate between promoting (border-crossing) *freedom* and (regulatory) *futility*, I investigate three emblematic cases of transnational corporations that promulgate aesthetically and rhetorically appealing advertisements with a global twist: the above-cited Emirates Airline, which promotes itself using such slogans as "Tomorrow thinks borders are so yesterday"; HSBC, whose advertising tells us that "There's a new world emerging" and urges us to "Be part of it"; and the Brazilian bank Itaú, which developed the "I Am a Global Latin American" campaign. By interrogating their public discourses, this chapter demonstrates how (and why) powerful actors attempt to construct global (or regional-global) imaginaries in the minds of consumers.

In this regard, what makes corporate advertisements a particularly compelling site of inquiry is both the extent to which they are regularly consumed by mass and elite audiences around the world and the role they play, as pop-culture artifacts, in shaping received wisdom. In turn, as I argue, this critical analysis of corporate globalizing discourses bears directly on important political debates concerning agency in globalization, the feasibility of state regulation of global capitalism, and the construction of alternative global imaginaries and orders.

The point of this chapter, then, is to illuminate the material incentives that motivate advertisers to celebrate their (and their customers') would-be globality and, more importantly, to demonstrate how they construct global (capitalist) imaginaries among and for audiences. Additionally, this chapter adds to our understanding of what Manuel Castells (2010b, 442) refers to as "the space of flows" around which the contemporary world order is structured. Such flows include not only capital, information, and organizational interaction, but also "images, sounds, and symbols." As he suggests, these are "the expression of processes" that are "*dominating* our economic, political, and symbolic life" (emphasis in original).

The circulation of corporate advertisements involves an especially important (cultural) flow, as it aids in the production of a particular kind of global imaginary whose diffusion furthers the rule and hegemony of global capital. This idea of a fully globalized capitalist system—one dominated by a fully globalized bourgeoisie—resonates widely despite the reality that, as argued in previous chapters, today's elites do not appear to be as global as diverse thinkers conventionally argue (and are certainly less global than these advertisements suggest). Indeed, in this and myriad other ways, place still matters in the global economy (Smith 2005).

Advertisements, like other forms of "low data," are particularly salient in the construction of global and other "common sense" imaginaries and cultural understandings among audiences (Weldes 2015, 230; see also Caso and Hamilton 2015; McFall 2004; Nexon and Neumann 2006; Shepherd 2013). Jutta Weldes (2015, 234) frames the issue well, noting, "If we are asking why this neoliberal discourse makes sense—what renders this vision of globalization seemingly self-evident—we need to look at the broader cultural resources, the cultural image bank, that provide the tropes and narratives out of which it is constructed." In other words, and more broadly, "popular culture helps to create and sustain the conditions for contemporary world politics" (Weldes 2015, 231; see also Kiersey and Neumann 2013).

It does so by reaching mass audiences around the world—not just elites or consolidated middle classes, but also "middling groups" (in societies from both the Global North and South) with growing acquisitive power, or at least aspirations for such (Dávila 2016, 38). Certain popular culture artifacts, such as those analyzed here, seek to incorporate all of them symbolically "as participants in global consumer culture and modernity" (Dávila 2016, 10). It is thus necessary that we engage with advertisements as objects of analysis precisely because they are key terrain for struggles over meaning and meaning making and the concepts at the core of this text.

Accordingly, this chapter explores the intersections between culture and political economy. What a CPE framework offers, again, is a more powerful lens that not only reveals what Emirates, HSBC, and Itaú do in terms of making investments, facilitating financial flows, and lobbying governments. Crucially, it also elucidates the myriad ways in which these and other economic practices are always culturally embedded and reveals how they, in turn, can "reconstitute" cultures (Best and Paterson 2010, 3).

This chapter furthers our understanding of how such processes unfold in relation to the CPE of globalization (Best and Paterson 2010; Harvey 1990; Weldes 2015) and, specifically, global identities. In particular, it analyzes how corporate actors seek to globalize cultural milieus and interpretive horizons through the circulation of material-culture artifacts such as advertisements and to what effect.

Corporate Case Studies

This section proffers case studies of three corporations' globalizing discourses, focusing on especially emblematic and evocatively global advertisements from their respective campaigns. To uncover how they seek to make meanings for audiences, I conduct a discursive analysis of their words, images, and representations as they relate to the global (Neumann 2008). By "taking [corporate] language seriously" and analyzing its role in (global) meaning making, this chapter thus continues with the interpretivist approach pursued throughout this text (Yanow and Schwartz-Shea 2015, xiv).

Here, I pay particular attention to nuances, subtleties, and contextual clues that shed light on how these advertisements, as meaning-imbued cultural artifacts, attempt to construct global imaginaries that simultaneously appeal to and allure audiences, on the one hand, and promote (inevitable) capitalist globalization and the idea of a global capitalist class for itself, on the other. Together, these examples elucidate how corporate actors communicate through language and imagery to construct the would-be reality of a borderless capitalist fantasyland among global consumers.

Specifically, this section interrogates Emirates Airline's bountiful production of evocatively cosmopolitan, lush, and visually enticing posters, which invoke connectivity, cultural exchange, and our ostensibly shrinking world; the banking giant HSBC's more workmanlike advertisements, staples in global jet bridges, many of which stress capitalist globalization's inexorable spread; and the Brazilian megabank Itaú's "I Am a Global Latin American" campaign. The latter deploys regional cultural icons to convince potential Latin American customers that it is the bank through which they can *go global*, as well as to show potential extra-regional partners that Itaú is a natural bridge that will allow their foreign capital to further globalize Latin America's economic relations.

These advertising campaigns are of particular interest for two reasons. First, as the specific advertisements chosen for analysis demonstrate, these corporations have invested especially heavily in the cultivation of global images. One would expect no less from institutions whose lifeblood is global connectivity and whose very activities—that is, facilitating commercial, financial, and travel flows—provide critical infrastructure that makes contemporary capitalist globalization possible in the first place. In turn, their global advertising campaigns have put them on the radar of numerous scholars of globalization and media observers, as cited below.

Second, as evidenced by an abundance of online commentary, their advertisements have elicited significant attention from audiences, who have expressed recurring interest in their aesthetic qualities and overall campaigns. While most advertising efforts seem to pass largely unnoticed, internet commentators have written a relatively large body of (generally fawning) blog posts and compiled numerous image repositories related to these three cases.

Regarding Emirates, a Google search for the slogan "Tomorrow thinks borders are so yesterday" returns over two hundred results, the vast majority of which seem to be user-generated social media content. In turn, nearly twenty-five thousand results appear about Emirates' broader "Hello Tomorrow" campaign, along with approximately fifty citations in academic sources (as revealed via Google Scholar).

As the latter slogan's creator notes, "When writing the phrase Hello Tomorrow, I wanted to give people less to worry about and more to feel optimistic about. We are curators of culture and looking for what's the unmet need, what's emotional and pleasurable and beneficial to travelers"—hence his rather bold reference to "the now famous Hello Tomorrow *Cultural Movement* strategy and marketing campaign" (Goodson 2016; emphasis added). Another member of the creative team behind the campaign comments that

"'Hello Tomorrow' is an open-arms greeting to our new borderless world, and positions Emirates as the first real global airline, inspiring interconnectedness and open-mindedness among *every class* of traveler."[2]

As for HSBC, marketing-focused media observe that the financial institution "has staked its claim as the go-to bank for the consumer in transit." Indeed, "These days it's rare to cross an airport terminal or air bridge and not see an HSBC ad" (Levy 2010). Accordingly, one online forum participant poses the question "Why Does Every Jetway Have HSBC Ads?" Of the sixty-two posted responses, one notes, "Excellent question! I never thought about it, but now that you mention it, it is true! Almost feels like [HSBC] ads only ever appear on jetways, but almost everywhere in the world. Like they had the monopoly for advertising on jetways."[3]

Media and scholarly references to HSBC's campaigns also abound, a small selection of which is cited later in this chapter. As a further demonstration of its (apparently successful) attempts to allure audiences, a 2015 HSBC project "turned the 194-metre sky bridge at [London's] Gatwick Airport into a sound installation mimicking China's Yangtze River as part of a conservation campaign with the [World Wildlife Fund]."[4]

The final case is that of Itaú. In the words of a business consultant, referring to having encountered one of the "Global Latin American" advertisements in *The Economist*: "Every once in awhile [*sic*] you come across some magazine advertising that makes you actually stop and look." Another online commentator labels the campaign "a brilliant translation of what Latin American professionals are doing outside the region" and invites readers to "send [her] a short bio explaining why you are Global Latin American."[5]

In sum, these cases demonstrate how corporations in different sectors—aviation and finance—and with heterogeneous but overlapping consumer audiences (such as air travelers, magazine readers, and English-language internet users) pursue related strategies to construct similar global imaginaries (Steger 2008, 181, 247). These very industries, as suggested above, are not only essential to capitalist globalization itself; they are also central to how both scholars and lay audiences imagine capitalist globalization and "increased mobility" (Steger 2008, 11, 182, 247).

It is worth noting here that the diffusion of such globalizing discourses is not entirely new. Take, for example, a 1987 advertisement from Alcatel, then a French telecommunications firm (now part of Nokia). It shows a series of shrinking globes, accompanied by the assertion that "THIS IS THE YEAR THE WORLD GOT SMALLER" (cited in Harvey 1990, 242).

However, in recent years, the circulation of such discourses has indeed become more common.

There has been considerable recent discussion in global studies–related fields concerning diverse methods for studying visual materials (Bleiker 2009, 2015; Callahan 2020; Campbell 2007; Rose 2001, 2014; Shim 2014). Given the present focus on imaginaries constructed through advertisements, this chapter's interpretivist approach is again sensitive to the stated and unstated meanings evoked by corporations and advertising agencies through images and text. Specifically, drawing from Weldes (2015, 231), I understand corporate discourses as "capital in the ubiquitous battle over meaning." It is through them, as I argue, that ideologically charged and self-interested global imaginaries become "common sense" by "constitut[ing] the world as we know it" (Weldes 2015, 230). However, this does not mean, again, that place-based interpretive horizons have gone extinct, even among self-avowedly global elites.

This analysis takes as its starting point that, at least in the present cases, these forms of "visual imagery" and cultural products reflect the class structures in which they are embedded and in which they were produced (Rose 2001, 20). As David Harvey (1990, 287) further suggests in *The Condition of Postmodernity*, "Advertising and media images . . . have come to play a very much more integrative role in cultural practices and now assume a much greater importance in the growth dynamics of capitalism." In the decades that have followed the publication of the cited text, this tendency has surely become even more salient.

On the other hand, Harvey (1990, 287) is also rightly critical of the assertion that "capitalism is now predominantly concerned with the production of signs, images, and sign systems rather than with commodities themselves." Indeed, an increasing recognition of the former cannot lead us to overlook the still-essential nature of the latter.

The present point, then, is not necessarily to suggest that we have entered a profoundly new cultural age—an "economy of signs and space" in which people have an increasingly strong sense of "*aesthetic* reflexivity" (Lash and Urry 1994, 4–5; emphasis in original). Rather, it is, at a more basic level, to highlight the extent to which the economy always has been and will be inherently cultural. In other words, "it's the economy *and* culture, stupid!" (Cooper and McFall 2017, 1; emphasis in original).

Thus, and perhaps now more than ever, there can be no "political economy" that is completely analytically separate from a "*cultural* political economy" or an "aesthetic" one (Belfrage and Gammon 2017). This means that there is an acute need to analyze the intersections between ideational and material processes, as has been the aim throughout this book. Specifically, what this conclusion implies about the task at hand in this chapter is as follows: to understand contemporary capitalism and assertions of capitalist globality, we must analyze how global discourses intermingle with and indeed reconstitute cultures to promote corporate self-interest.

The following pages analyze polyvalent, globally inflected meanings as powerful corporations seek to convey them, with a significant degree of success, to media consumers. While recipients may of course develop unintended or oppositional understandings of and responses to (fractured) corporate discourses, this section focuses primarily on the agency of corporate actors. In this regard, Jon Bohland (2013, 102) correctly stresses the importance of "reveal[ing] what the ideal reading of texts is as intended by their authors, even if we concede that the audience does not always receive them." This "ideal reading," as noted, is multifaceted and operates at distinct levels as it attempts to seduce audiences. The concluding section, in turn, considers audience agency and the possibility—and necessity—of constructing more inclusive global counter-imaginaries.

The following subsections address each individual case.

Emirates Airline: "Tomorrow Thinks Borders Are So Yesterday"

Less than forty years after its founding, the Dubai-based and state-owned Emirates Airline has joined the ranks of the world's largest carriers by flying "the fanciest product on the biggest planes on the longest routes" (Campbell 2017). Its meteoric rise has paralleled—and contributed to—that of Dubai, which in a few short decades rose from obscurity as a dusty port city and emirate to become a powerhouse of global capitalism and connectivity, a "neutral ground on which to play, work, and cut deals"; additionally, it has "a top-notch airline to bring the world to its door" (Campbell 2017; see also Kanna 2011 and Khalili 2020).

As I peruse Emirates' website, I am greeted by former *Friends* actor Jennifer Aniston. The commercial for which she was paid a reported $5 million depicts her moral outrage upon discovering that not all airlines match Emirates' amenities, which include showers and a cocktail bar. It is little wonder, then, that a cover (see fig. 5.7) of *Bloomberg Businessweek*—a source

Figure 5.7 *Bloomberg Businessweek* magazine cover, January 9–15, 2017. (Source: *Bloomberg Businessweek*, https://www.bloomberg.com/magazine/businessweek/17_03.)

not prone to Marxist hyperbole—referred to Emirates as "the airline of the global ruling class" (Campbell 2017).

Emirates is also a prolific producer of magazine and poster advertisements, a particularly telling example of which features the "Tomorrow thinks borders are so yesterday" slogan. It forms part of the aforementioned and ongoing "Hello Tomorrow" print, digital, and television international advertising campaign. This was launched in 2012 to mark the airline's "evolution from a travel brand to a global lifestyle brand."[6]

The background image, reproduced in figure 5.8, displays child or adolescent skateboarders—including a hijab-wearing girl—gliding down a mostly barren street. It evokes a sense of gender equality and, perhaps

192 | *Rooted Globalism*

Figure 5.8 Emirates "Hello Tomorrow" advertisement. (Source: Khatija Liaqat, https://khatijaliaqat.wordpress.com/2016/05/21/taglines-of-emirates-airline/unknown/.)

more subversively (and politically charged) from a Global North perspective, depicts the full participation of visibly practicing Muslims in a cultural activity (skateboarding) that is constitutive of a middle-class, white, and suburban version of Americana. It is the Springfield of *Simpsons* lore, but with desert-like surroundings and olive-skinned bodies from what Samuel Huntington (1993)—and many fellow travelers—malign as the "West's" great "Other," the Islamic *civilization*.

What explains this forthright statement of borderless creed? Why does Emirates pay to disseminate this message of what *Bloomberg Businessweek* refers to as "sunny globalism" (Campbell 2017)? Moreover, how does this idea resonate with audiences?

Emirates, like all airlines, navigates a world order in which national documents—passports and visas—of course determine who can enter a given country or take one of its flights (though notably, some of the Trump administration's various executive orders on travel, immigration, and refugee policy—including the "Muslim ban"—provide a reminder that ostensibly democratic governments may also declare states of exception and deny entry even to those with valid, state-issued travel and residency documents [Kapoor 2018]). A borderless world in which "everybody travels" (Lisle 2006) is thus an appealing utopia for a business that profits from increasing global connectivity.

The centrality of the temporal signifier *tomorrow* to this particular advertisement and overall campaign suggests an inevitable trend in this direction. This is hardly a surprising message. As Harvey (1990, 232) puts it, under capitalism, "The incentive to create the world market, to reduce spatial barriers, and to annihilate space through time is omni-present." Here, transportation infrastructure spaces, such as airports, emerge as especially important sites.

Though Emirates—with its massive Dubai hub—is a particularly evangelistic espouser of this ambition, it is shared broadly within the industry. Take the statement by the International Air Transport Association CEO, French businessman Alexandre de Juniac, whose organization represents some 265 airlines. During the chaos that followed the first of the aforementioned executive orders, he argued at the US Chamber of Commerce's Aviation Summit that "we are deeply concerned with recent developments that point to a future of restricted borders and protectionism" (Jansen 2017).

Emirates seeks to concretize this ideal of a borderless world through aggressive campaigning for the neoliberalization and would-be deregulation of global commercial air travel. Specifically, what Emirates desires, according to its website, is "true international competition and open skies."[7] Perhaps ironically, Emirates and other Middle Eastern airlines have also repeatedly been accused of benefiting from "massive government subsidies." Such was the charge levied on the homepage of the Partnership for Open and Fair Skies, which represents the interests of several major US airlines and unions.[8]

Indeed, the *Bloomberg Businessweek* cover cheekily refers to two of Emirates' competitive advantages, which are of course the direct outcome of state policy (and, in the former case, repression): "No unions" and "no shareholders." As revealed by Jaime Khoury's comments, from chapter 4, such (self-interested) state entanglements are commonly advocated for, often surreptitiously, by those who profess an unyielding commitment to neoliberal or laissez-faire principles. The idea of a *free* and *flat* global capitalist world order thus appears to be less of an objective reality or a universal principle to which the capitalist class subscribes than a political project advanced by certain elite interests in particular contexts—that is, when, and only when, it is to their material benefit to do so.

Tellingly, the phrase *open skies* is also the name of Emirates' in-flight magazine. As noted by company president Tim Clark, "We are a product of the multilateralism, the liberalization of trade." He asserts that despite Brexit, the world is not "going back to the '30s" and the global-capitalist order "will prevail"—inevitably so, it seems—though he adds, "Maybe I'm just being a little bit naive, overoptimistic" (Campbell 2017). The airline's global spirit also filters down to hiring practices, with the Emirates website emphasizing that "our employee diversity of over 160 nationalities is our unique strength as a global organization."[9]

The immediate aim, as stated in their advertisements' fine print, is to encourage customers to "Fly Emirates to 6 Continents." But the larger political project is to tear down state-based obstacles to the circulation of (certain) people, goods, capital, and indeed airlines (while also, as noted, relying on state assistance and perhaps repression when advantageous to do so). This would buttress fast-growing Emirates' efforts, as noted on its website, to cement Dubai's status as a—or the—global "aviation hub."[10] Notably, this would represent the supplanting of traditionally dominant Western nodes such as New York, Paris, London, Frankfurt, and Amsterdam.

Emirates' international advertising campaign is directed not only at the "global ruling class"—first-class passengers who enjoy, as described on the Emirates website, private suites, a "shower spa," "the world's first moisturizing sleepwear for the skies," and "exclusive... amenity kits" designed by a "luxury Italian brand" (featuring "fine leather" for men and "sophisticated satin" for women)[11]—but also at (English-speaking) "middling groups" from both the North and South who sit in the back of the plane. Indeed, some of Emirates' double-decker jets feature economy-only class configurations (Campbell 2017).

In this vein of increasing connectivity for paying customers, Dubai International Airport "has been designed as a massive machine to facilitate [passenger] movements, a polished-stone fulcrum between Dar es Salaam and Guangzhou, Dallas and Dhaka" (Campbell 2017). It handles more international traffic than any other airport, much of it, as suggested, connecting faraway South-South and North-South city pairs. Gone are the days when North–North traffic, connected through Northern hubs, dominated global aviation.

In turn, an additional airport, still under construction but already partially open, aims to dramatically enhance Dubai's status as node of all aviation nodes. With a planned capacity for more than 160 million annual passengers, "its ambitions are consonant with its name: Dubai World Central" (Campbell 2017). This would easily surpass the passenger count for the busiest airport pre-COVID 19—Hartsfield-Jackson Atlanta International. It is in this rhetorical (and self-interested) sense that, to borrow from another Emirates ad, "Dubai re-imagines the world"—both for itself and its passengers.

HSBC: Promoting (Capitalist) Globalization at an Airport near You

Second is the case of HSBC, born in the great entrepôt of Hong Kong and currently based in London. Now one of the world's largest financial institutions, HSBC notes online that it "was established in 1865 to finance trade between Europe and Asia." A baldly phrased heading, also from the website, declares, "We are different." What sets HSBC apart, it observes, is that from the beginning, "we brought together different countries and cultures, as we still do today."[12] Largely missing from this official history is direct acknowledgement that HSBC—originally incorporated as The Hongkong and Shanghai Banking Corporation—was founded as a "colonial bank" under British rule before transforming itself into an "imperial bank" that "spread itself all over the regions under British influence" (Bonin 2016, 178).

Its website further notes, "Our aim is to be acknowledged as the world's leading international bank." Accordingly, HSBC maintains "an international network of around 6,100 offices in 72 countries and territories" with shareholders from 131 "countries and territories."[13] Having previously declared itself through a global marketing campaign "the world's local bank," HSBC subsequently reduced retail operations due to financial pressures and decided to focus instead on "global banking and markets and commercial banking" (Farrell 2011).

The website asserts that in recent years, dating at least as far back as the "world's local bank" days, HBSC has sought to "bring [its] global network to life and demonstrate the power of international connections" by placing poster advertisements in jet bridges the world over. The altruistically framed purpose of this "global brand campaign" is "to encourage people"—English-speaking travelers—"to think about where they are going in life and, by doing so, demonstrate our support to help them along their way."[14] According to the trade publication *Adweek*, HSBC "pioneered jet bridge advertising," and after placing its first such advertisement at London

Heathrow Airport in 2001, it has spread the campaigns to dozens of airports worldwide (Bachman 2010). At one point, HSBC controlled every jet bridge in Tokyo's Narita International Airport (Levy 2010).

Typical are ads with trivia-style yet politically suggestive observations. They include: "Only 4% of US films are made by women, compared to 25% in Iran"; "Five times more people are learning English in China, than there are people in England"; and "Holland makes more exporting soy sauce than Japan."[15] These are followed by clarion calls for weary travelers to "find" or "see" the world's potential (for further examples, see Best and Paterson 2010). Such provocative references to Iran, Iranian women, and China in particular represent a nod to the rise of the postcolonial Other.

Some of the slogans evince clearer normative assumptions about the evolving world order, with prodding implications about how audiences can join the (profitable) action. Evoking Arab–Latin American and other growing axes of relations, they read: "In the future, South–South trade will be norm not novelty" (accompanied by the message "There's a new world emerging"); "In the future, new trade routes will reshape the world economy" (accompanied by the more imploring message "There's a new world emerging. Be part of it."); "In the future, even the smallest business will be multinational" (as mentioned in the introductory chapter, and featuring the same accompanying message); and, as shown in figure 5.9, "In the future, there will be no markets left waiting to emerge" (accompanying message: "HSBC's international network can help you discover new markets wherever they emerge next").[16] One can easily imagine Khoury in particular uttering any of the above slogans.

In other words, according to this utopian vision—which resonates with the analysis of some in the global capitalism school—corporate globalization is creating a flat world by erasing traditional North-South distinctions. Notably, there are recurring references here to an emerging and future global reality that *will* culminate when *all* businesses, markets, and geographical spaces have been fully integrated into the global capitalist system. Thus, we are to understand that its spread is inevitable and cannot be impeded or regulated. In turn, again, even the neighborhood lemonade stand—as pictured, with prices in three different currencies (see fig. 5.10)—*will* also have globalized accordingly.

The ostensibly democratic and egalitarian message is that *everyone*, including would-be capitalists with no capital to their names, can, should, and will participate. This includes passengers who are willing to pause and

Figure 5.9 HSBC advertisement featuring a globally oriented set of Matryoshka dolls. (Source: Foresight in Hindsight, http://www.foresightinhindsight.com/article/show/3043.)

Figure 5.10 HSBC advertisement. Lemonade prices are listed in US dollars, euros, and Hong Kong dollars. (Source: Mustard Post studio, http://mustardpost.com/hsbc-airport-ads/.)

reflect on HSBC's aphoristic slogans, through which they may imbibe precisely the heightened global awareness that will be necessary to stay ahead of the business curve in *tomorrow*'s evolving and increasingly borderless capitalist landscape.

Indeed, business opportunities know no boundaries, whether geographical, political, racial, socioeconomic, or otherwise. It is also the case that—as another advertisement puts it—"Over 138 million people work outside their country of birth." Accordingly, given that you, as a viewer, are on your way to and/or from a flight at a global aviation hub, nor should your own profit-seeking activities know any limitations. Again, in an increasingly nativist Western world, such observations—especially about the mobility of workers—take on a subversive quality when juxtaposed with prevailing trends of xenophobia and parochialism.

For many audiences, and perhaps particularly those from traditionally excluded postcolonial societies, this is indeed an appealing message. After all, there is a big capitalist world out there, and passengers who adopt a proper global mindset and break free from what are implicitly portrayed as antiquated place-based concerns and imagined communities will be well situated to reap substantial material rewards. In this regard, audiences are being called on to see the world through the interpretive horizons of the would-be global capitalist class for itself.

However, thriving in that world requires navigating the "confusion" and "frustration" that may accompany cross-cultural engagement (Fitch 2015, 31). Conveniently, and as portrayed in another commercial, HSBC provides, for a price, the solution for the would-be global entrepreneur, as it "will be there to help guide us through such foreign places" (Fitch 2015, 31)—hence the slogan "At HSBC we never underestimate the importance of local knowledge."

As Jacqueline Best and Matthew Paterson (2010, 4) observe regarding HSBC's advertising campaigns, "The cultural character of contemporary political economy is decidedly global, both in that there are a set of shared meanings across the globe which enable similar marketing strategies to operate everywhere (even while those strategies highlight cultural difference as a particular marketing ploy) and that specific management cultures become globalized through the strategies of a firm like HSBC." Thus, evoking the world's cultural heterogeneity is a moneymaking strategy for a bank that commodifies and sells cross-cultural expertise. Purchasing this product, we are told, will allow us to overcome these barriers to additional capital accumulation. Accordingly, as Veronika Koller (2007, 129) further argues, "HSBC seems to have recognised the *zeitgeist* in times of glocalisation"—the simultaneous valuation of the universal and particular—"by metaphorically constructing itself both as a sophisticated cosmopolitan and as a friendly next-door neighbour."

Here, one is reminded of a tension embedded in Diego Makhoul's mentality, as revealed in chapter 3—that is, a concurrent rhetorical valorization of the local and global, even though the universalizing tendencies of the latter are often argued to undermine the vitality and diversity of the former (Chibber 2013b). Somewhat ironically, then, this very process of cultural homogenization is thus advanced by the very same HSBC advertisements that ostensibly celebrate local particularities.

The recent rise of the exclusivist, jingoist, and highly reactionary global far right has, if anything, made HSBC's brand of "progressive neoliberalism" even more palatable for consumers (Fraser 2019; Funk 2020). Especially notable was the UK-focused "Together We Thrive" advertising campaign, the first commercial for which—titled, rather forthrightly, "Global Citizen"—began airing in December 2017. Though the company denied that it was taking sides in the Brexit debate, a headline from the business press captured the assumed intent: "HSBC shares internationalist vision for Brexit Britain with 'Global Citizen' campaign" (Brownsell 2018). Tellingly, the campaign was reportedly designed to overcome the perception that the bank was only interested in a particular kind of global citizen—that is, "the international elite or the wealthy" (Rogers and Fleming 2019).

It is perhaps no coincidence that the self-described "HSBC UK Global Citizen TV ad" was narrated by British actor Richard Ayoade, who himself evokes Britain's global, cosmopolitan, and multicultural milieu, as he was born to a Norwegian mother and Nigerian father. He begins the minute-long advertisement—a print version of which is reproduced in figure 5.11—by recounting the highly globalized nature of everyday Britons' quotidian actions, from consuming Costa Rican coffee and driving Japanese cars to cheering on Brazilians, Argentines, and Chileans in the Premier League, struggling to assemble Swedish flat-pack furniture, and "watch[ing] American movies on Korean tablets." He concludes with the following dramatic observation: "We live on a wonderful little lump of land in the middle of the sea. But we are not an island. We are part of something far, far bigger." While Ayoade speaks, he inserts the UK piece into a world map puzzle.[17]

As if it were not already clear that capitalist globalization was being invoked, other figures associated with the campaign noted, "We believe that

WE ARE NOT AN ISLAND. WE ARE A COLOMBIAN COFFEE DRINKING, AMERICAN MOVIE WATCHING, SWEDISH FLAT-PACK ASSEMBLING, KOREAN TABLET TAPPING, BELGIAN STRIKER SUPPORTING, DUTCH BEER CHEERS-ING, TIKKA MASALA EATING, WONDERFUL LITTLE LUMP OF LAND IN THE MIDDLE OF THE SEA. WE ARE PART OF SOMETHING FAR, FAR BIGGER.

HSBC UK   Together we thrive

Figure 5.11 "We Are Not an Island" early 2019 HSBC advertisement, released in the midst of Brexit negotiations. Created by J. Walter Thompson. (Source: *The Drum*, https://www.thedrum.com/news/2019/01/03/hsbc-continues-its-together-we-thrive-pledge-with-we-are-not-island-campaign.)

the people, communities and businesses in the UK thrive most when connected and open," as well as that "many of the things that make us quintessentially British are the things that make us inescapably international" (Watson 2019). The latter speaker, who is the creative director at the London office of HSBC's ad agency, continued by making transparent the extent to which this particular construction of global citizenship is linked to a broader discourse about global capitalism: "And who better to point that out than the bank that's been connecting the world through trade for over 152 years" (Watson 2019).

Itaú: Cultivating Global Latin Americans

Also discursively navigating between the local, regional, and global is the São Paulo–based Itaú, which declares itself via its branding as a "Global Latin American bank."[18] While its operations date back to 1924, its current incarnation—Itaú Unibanco Holding—is the product of a 2008 merger. This "gave rise to one of the most important conglomerates in the Southern Hemisphere," according to its website's "Who We Are" section, and "created a corporation with a market capitalization that ranks it among [the world's] largest financial institutions."

Itaú's operations encompass nearly two dozen countries and territories, ranging from South America, the US, and Western Europe to China, the Bahamas, and the United Arab Emirates. With thousands of branches within Brazil, it is, the website claims, "the leading choice for Latin American Corporate & Investment banking" (here, "Latin American" is highlighted in orange, the official company color). Therein, Itaú also calls itself "a Brazilian bank with global reach" that "goes wherever the clients are."

Itaú's Portuguese-language digital presence further evinces a predilection for corporate clichés, including: "We are the bank that invests the most in people"; "We want everyone at [Itaú] to be able to think and act like an owner"; and "The secret of life is not in the minutes that pass, it's in the moments that remain." For a time, this latter assertion, accompanied by an image of a smiling, smartphone-wielding middle-aged woman snuggling with her black Labrador, occupied nearly the entire homepage. The link transported me to the bank's now-defunct "Moments that Count" domain, where visitors were invited to view two ninety-second inspirational videos in which mostly white, upper-middle-class interlocutors extolled the virtues of family time and living in the present.

A more profound message emerges from Itaú's well-known English-language "I Am a Global Latin American" international advertising campaign, which was launched in 2011 to great fanfare but no longer appears to be active (Robertson 2015, 13; Hellinger 2015, 480). The responsible advertising agency is a "Brazil-based premium global brand" named Africa that claims to have "no boundaries." Its website notes that it intended for this series of full-page magazine spreads (placed in publications such as *The Economist*) and online videos to promote "international awareness" of Itaú by inviting "well-known personalities to present the bank that is Brazilian, but also Latin American and global."[19]

The campaign featured Latin American cultural and sporting elites from rarified realms including polo, modeling, ballet, and wine tasting—as well as, per figures 5.12 and 5.13, the visual arts (respectively, the actor Alice Braga and photographer Vik Muniz, both Brazilian). These personalities all appear to be light skinned, thus conjuring for foreigners (and local English-speaking elites) an unrepresentative white version of Brazilian society. Such racial exclusions reflect the long-standing propensity, in Brazil and elsewhere, "to associate whiteness with economic development and progress" (Legg 2015, 220).

In these advertisements, orange text is maintained for the bold heading "I AM A . . . LATIN AMERICAN," with "GLOBAL" inserted in white. The same slogan also appeared on Itaú-branded notebooks. Audiences can thus

202 | *Rooted Globalism*

Figure 5.12 Advertisement from Itaú's "Global Latin American" campaign featuring Brazilian actor Alice Braga. (Source: Africa, a Brazil-based "global brand," https://africaagency.files.wordpress.com/2011/12/aft_12959 -092_internacional_alice_braga_rv_trip_195x275.jpg.)

perceive that Latin Americanness is able to both stand alone as a regional identity and exist within a broader global (capitalist) framework. Accordingly, Itaú's interpretive horizons are performed as simultaneously globally interconnected *and* regional. Further, when expressed in written form, they are in English, the international business language, not the Portuguese (or Spanish) that a locally (or regionally) rooted consciousness would suggest. As also witnessed vis-à-vis HSBC (and the case of Makhoul), this local-global balancing act is itself reflective of the tension between cultural homogeneity and heterogeneity that defines globalizing processes (Appadurai 1990, 295).

Figure 5.13 Advertisement from Itaú's "Global Latin American" campaign featuring Brazilian artist Vik Muniz. (Source: Africa, https://africaagency.files.wordpress.com/2011/12/afd_12959-092-itau_vick_muniz_r_trip_2_19-5x27.jpg.)

In his accompanying remarks, Muniz notes, "My goal is to create art that's as fascinating as Latin America, my continent." He continues: "I'm a global Latin American. And Itaú is the global Latin American bank" (see fig. 5.13). Other advertisements in the series note the following: "I play the leading role in my own life. And that's the kind of growing recognition Latin America is experiencing on the global stage"; "My continent is already changing the whole world"; and "Just like my continent, I've struggled hard to earn my place in the world and to become an agent of change."[20] Throughout this campaign, there is thus a recurring motif in which privileged individuals serve as metonymic stand-ins for the rhetorical construction of a then dynamic and rising Brazil and Latin American region (Needell 2015).

Itaú's message is perhaps less straightforward than Emirates' borderless utopia or HSBC's not-so-subtle implication that we summon our entrepreneurial spirit and join the emerging and profitable flat-world global capitalist reality. That the Latin American regional context is built into Itaú's campaign suggests that place still matters in globalization, but perhaps only in the sense that not all places have traditionally experienced the same degree of integration into the global capitalist system.

If the above-cited cultural elites wish to celebrate that they have broken out from the postcolonial periphery to make waves in the core, then so too is Itaú asserting its pride of place as not merely *a*, but *the* "global Latin American bank." As the story goes, Latin America may be a late entrant to capitalist modernity. But the region's elites, capitalist and otherwise, can compete with anyone's. Latin Americans, too, can take pictures that appear in Parisian art galleries, act in films that captivate audiences from Miami to Milan, build new axes of economic relations with the Arab world, and operate a vast international banking network that greases the wheels of global commerce, exchange, and financial flows.

As the Itaú advertisement in figure 5.14 frames the issue (in Portuguese): "The world powers changed. Itaú changes with them." A smiley face emoticon is included for good measure. Next to this text stand three smiling young boys, whose respective phenotypes and the larger context surrounding "emerging powers" (and the BRICS grouping) suggest they represent Brazil, China, and India. Naturally, the Brazilian—who is noticeably less white than Itaú's standard actors and models—is holding the soccer ball. Capitalist globalization, we are to understand, is not a game to be played (or won) exclusively by the North.

How, then, to understand this assertion of me-too-ness?

Itaú's message can be read as nationalist/regionalist, political-economic pride in Brazil, Latin America, and the Global South, with the implication being that formerly colonized peoples from Washington's "backyard" can pull themselves up by their bootstraps and become *makers* instead of *takers* in the global economy (Funk 2015b). Such triumphalist sentiments again shine through in many of the above-cited accounts of the recent rise of Arab–Latin American relations and in the words of numerous interviewees (including, most notably, Julio Valenzuela, who is profiled in chapter 4). They have also been a recurring feature of much analysis of Latin American

Figure 5.14 "World powers" advertisement from Itaú. (Source: Prêmio Renato Castelo Branco, http://prcb.espm.br/2011/o-mundo-muda.)

foreign policy and South-South relations more broadly, particularly in the heady, growth-filled (and seemingly now-distant) years of (at least supposedly) progressive governance in the 2000s and early 2010s, often described as the "pink tide" or "left turn" (Gardini 2012; Guardiola Rivera 2011; Murshed et al. 2013).

This is, again, a mildly subversive message. However, it does not seek to subvert the global political-economic order itself, nor does it highlight capitalism's contradictions or exclusions. What it does, instead, is critique the notion that only Northerners can be capitalism's winners (Funk 2013).

More mundanely, Itaú suggests that Latin America is part of a global (capitalist) story and that the path for Latin Americans to participate in global capitalism—or for extra-regional actors to engage economically with Latin America—goes through them. If Latin America is your point of departure or destination, then Itaú is your bank.

Yet beyond Itaú's narrow business concerns, the larger narrative is familiar: there is an objectively globalizing capitalist world that is inevitably compressing both time and space. This is hinted at through references to South-South relations and is also evident based on the fact that even a traditionally peripheral region like Latin America could become, at least temporarily, a success story and an evangelist for global capitalism.

Moreover, it is a world in which you can be an "agent of change," to borrow Makhoul's phrase, *no matter your provenance*, whether it be in the core or periphery, First or Third World, or Global North or South. Globalization is for *you*. It is a true universal to which all may aspire, including if your aim is to create a "new world economic geography" linking Latin America to the Arab world and other far-flung regions (Karam 2007, 174).

The world has thus changed indeed, and we are being called on to celebrate Latin America's growing protagonism within it. Yet what we are toasting, per Itaú's vision, is less the rise of a long-suffering region; rather, it is the consolidation of a seemingly totalizing global capitalist model and, crucially, the efforts of a globally oriented and globally minded capitalist elite, in Latin America and beyond, that is said to be inexorably remaking the world—from North to South—in its image.

Summary and Analysis

This chapter deconstructs recurring global imaginaries in corporate advertisements and analyzes the ways in which such discourses function as key sites in the production of common-sense understandings. In so doing, it draws from and contributes to the burgeoning field of CPE, which is premised on the notion that political-economic practices are always embedded in, and constitutive of, cultural milieus. Through analyzing how Emirates, HSBC, and Itaú assert their—and current and prospective customers'—global credentials in diverse ways, the present aim is to explain the prevalence and prominence of assertions of global identities and a global capitalist class consciousness. Specifically, I seek to reconcile the diffusion of global discourses with the above finding concerning the resilience of place-based imaginaries.

On the surface, these advertisements construct global subjects by deploying discourses that suggest that humanity is crossing national, racial, religious, cultural, geographic, and gender boundaries to create a new and more fully integrated global society. These "sunny" global imaginaries evoke harmonious cross-cultural contact, cosmopolitan consumption patterns (in food, music, film, and so on), and a mentality seemingly inspired by *Condé Nast Traveler*'s slogan, "At home in the world" (notably, the magazine declares itself "the global citizen's bible and muse").

They also bring to mind a progressive political project defined by adherence to and advocacy for universal human rights and values. In other words, these discourses are reminiscent of the great Roman playwright Terence's the pithy observation, "I am human, I think nothing human alien to me" (Appiah 2016). Of course, this contrasts with contemporary ethnonationalist surges in the US, Europe, and elsewhere.

After all, for (global) capitalism to persuade, it requires an accompanying—and appropriately sanguine—narrative (García Canclini 2014, 42). Indeed, the success of such advertisements is in part due to their ability to tap into existing (pleasing) mental frameworks among (some) audiences. They also succeed as pop-culture artifacts that captivate viewers through suggestive (and at times subversive) sloganeering and seductive visual displays that undermine traditional North-South dichotomies. Here, one is naturally reminded of the aforementioned notion that what flows between Brazil and the Arab world no longer needs to pass through central nodes in Washington and Paris (Karam 2007, 174).

It is thus unsurprising that Emirates, HSBC, Itaú, and other corporations would invest in the diffusion of global or regional-global presentations of self—and of customers, current or potential—for reasons independent of any sort of real, felt globality (Funk 2015a). Instead, what accounts for the propagation of global imaginaries is the corporate quest for profit and ideological hegemony. Indeed, as Ong (1999, 6; emphasis added) notes, "In their quest to accumulate capital and social prestige in the global arena, subjects *emphasize*, and are regulated by, practices favoring flexibility, mobility, and repositioning in relation to markets, governments, and cultural regimes."

In other words, global elites deploy such advertisements to challenge regulatory efforts (and the body politic) to "catch them if they can" through conjuring "spaces where the production of profit can evade or minimize contestation" (Appel 2012, 698). They also seek to make it known that we live in an inevitably globalizing and "frictionless" world in which they *cannot* be caught or contained (Appel 2012, 706). Thus, the imagined corporate globalization of their conjuring is a capitalist paradise in which capitalist elites have no material or ideational attachments to the state (that is, they exist as a global capitalist class in itself and for itself), inexorable globalizing dynamics are rendering borders meaningless (at least for some), and the regulation of flows of goods, services, and capital is unthinkable and impossible.

According to this imaginary, regulation of capital is thus "futile" (Chang 2009, 97), just as Khoury would want it. As Dani Rodrik observes, business elites (and some economists) have for years advanced a "hyperglobalization agenda" that asserts corporate rights over states' abilities to promote social welfare (quoted in Pearlstein 2011). One way in which this business-friendly agenda—a deep-seated aversion to particular kinds of regulation—is pursued is through corporate advertising that stresses the global credentials of their own institutions and capitalist elites more generally, along with the inexorability of capitalism's global spread (Beder 2005).

As demonstrated through the above case studies, these advertisements thus play a multilayered game by foregrounding an accessible *text* celebrating the freedom of humanistic globalization at eye level, accompanied by a subtler *subtext* relating to corporate freedom and the notion of regulatory futility. Accordingly, the intent is for the audience's interpretive focus to be channeled in the former direction, while the latter message is to be absorbed implicitly.

An article that comments on the difficulties inherent in conducting surveys on global identity formation frames this duality of meaning well: "One problem with polling attitudes on identity is that 'global citizenship' is a difficult concept to define and the poll left it open to those taking part to interpret. For some, it might be about the projection of economic clout across the world. To others, it might mean an altruistic impulse to tackle the world's problems in a spirit of togetherness—whether that is climate change or inequality in the developing world" (Grimley 2016). Following a similar logic, corporations are thus able to craft Janus-faced advertising messages, as reviewed above, that simultaneously appeal to viewers' cosmopolitan sense of global solidarity *and* construct for them the image of a flat, entirely integrated, and ungovernable global capitalist economy.

Here, several caveats are in order. First, the extent to which viewers properly internalize the intended, polyvalent messages is necessarily a subject for future research. However, the fact that these campaigns have enjoyed such popularity—and that hyper-globalist imaginaries in general have proven so alluring (Tsing 2000)—certainly suggests a degree of success. This is despite the fact, as I argue, that there are also openings through which audiences can develop more variegated (and critical) readings of capitalist globalization (even though the latter are precisely what these advertisements seek to forestall).

Second, fully elaborating the link between private interests and public images would require insider knowledge and evidence of a kind that does not appear to be available. One must also not lose sight of the fact that devices such as advertisements may have *effects* that go beyond, or even contradict, their intended *aims*. Further, it may be the case that, at least for some of the originators of these advertisements, the creation of "sunny" globalist campaigns is not an entirely conscious process. This would be unsurprising, given that global capitalist elites, as demonstrated in the above chapters, do not always display the robust levels of reflexivity that one may expect from actors who are situated thusly.

We must also not overlook other motives behind the promulgation of cosmopolitan discourses, such as the fact that universal connectivity, freedom to travel, and participation in border-crossing economic exchanges again represent a desirable imaginary for (many) would-be consumers. This is a particularly appealing message not just for Huntington's (2004) US-based "dead souls," but for numerous others, including Global Southerners (Meena 2016). Indeed, many of the latter encounter either literal or bureaucratic walls (such as increasingly stringent visa or asylum requirements) when attempting to cross borders and continue to have their humanity and agency questioned (and outright denied) by outsiders (Dabashi 2015).

However, it is important to note that the fact that such advertisements may give (some) audiences what they want does not contradict the following realities.

First, as argued above, there is a happy coincidence between the global messages that (some) consumers desire and the material, profit-seeking interests of these advertisements' creators. This makes for smart advertising—that is, these advertisements not only play off of audiences' existing understandings and frames of reference (as opposed to evoking imaginaries with which audiences are unfamiliar and to which they are unlikely to respond); they also do so in a way that benefits the corporate bottom line. Profit seeking, after all, is the structurally determined "spirit" of the capitalist system (Weber 2011).

The temporal element of these advertisements—most notably, Emirates' use of *tomorrow*—is particularly instructive in this regard, as it leverages the deeply "seductive" nature of "global futurist" narratives (Tsing 2000, 334). This is an especially palatable message for progressive and postcolonial audiences who dream of a better future, as opposed to the traditional conservative insistence on preserving the status quo and established hierarchies (Robin 2017) or on literally rolling back the clock (e.g., to "Make America Great *Again*").

Second, and more importantly, these campaigns not only respond to, but also actively *construct* ideas, identities, and interests among audiences. Anna Tsing (2000, 330) captures this duplexity well, observing that globalization both "draws our enthusiasm" and "helps us imagine interconnection, travel, and sudden transformation" (and indeed, the former because of the latter). Emirates, HSBC, Itaú, and others have thus astutely perceived the extent to which many audiences already find "charisma" in "the global" (Tsing 2000, 328). Yet their campaigns also heighten this existing interest.

This point raises the question of what to make of these arguments following the rise of Global Trumpism. If, as suggested by Mark Blyth (2016) shortly after Trump was elected in 2016, "The era of neoliberalism is over" and "The era of neonationalism has just begun," have we entered a new world order—since reinforced by the COVID-19 pandemic—of protectionism, beggar-thy-neighbor policies, and public shaming of outsourcing transnational corporations by heads of state via Twitter? If so, what does this mean for the circulation of global imaginaries?

Recent phenomena such as the Brexit vote and Trump's ascendance do speak, in part, to a resurgent economic nationalism and the increasingly frequent espousal of state-first mercantilist sentiments. However, as predicted by John Weeks (2016) and others, the end result in the US and elsewhere has largely been more of the pre-Trump same—that is, "a strengthening of the neoliberal vision of a world economy dominated by corporate capital."

Thus, and especially in the US, the public was bombarded during the Trump years with a mishmash of nationalist-populist economic rhetoric (and haranguing Tweets) about saving or bringing back domestic manufacturing jobs, primarily through the lowering of the corporate tax rate and suppression of wages and unions. This was accompanied by the implementation of overall policies designed to cement plutocratic rule at home and facilitate the profit-seeking activities of "our" corporations abroad (Fraser 2019).

In sum, as noted by Daniel Bessner and Matthew Sparke (2017), "Trump's agenda aims to realize the foremost goals of neoliberalism: privatization, deregulation, tax-cutting, anti-unionism, and the strict enforcement of property rights." What we have been left with as a result is "a neoliberal president in populist clothing"—or, as Wendy Brown (2018; 2019) puts it, a "Frankenstein monster" variety of neoliberalism that is increasingly authoritarian, jingoistic, populist, and infused with the values of right-wing Evangelical Christianity.

Some level of shielding from the exigencies of the global market, in the form of both state protectionism at home (the "populist clothing" that Trump has promised) and state promotion of certain economic sectors abroad, is of course a violation of the supposedly sacrosanct free-market ideals to which corporations and economic elites routinely pay homage. We should not be surprised, then, that there are numerous cases around the world of successful state-owned enterprises—such as Singapore Airlines—that deliberately "underplay their connection with the state" (Chang 2009, 112).

Yet such market distortions could certainly be good for the bottom line, as Khoury, Boeing, and capitalists everywhere recognize. For them, this combination of state protection on the domestic front and state support for seeking profits abroad within a corporate-friendly, open global playing field is a true utopian vision, far preferable to the *creative destruction* of the much-vaunted free market. Thus, there is a constant drive not precisely for *de*regulation in the economic sphere, but *re*regulation—that is, a regulatory regime that further facilitates capital accumulation (Dardot and Laval 2017; Slobodian 2018).

Indeed, both in theory and practice, *states* and *markets* have again proven to be mutually co-constitutive instead of inherently oppositional forces, as Karl Polanyi (2001) long ago recognized. In other words, and in contrast to neoliberal rhetoric, what capital seeks is not precisely a total lack of regulation, but rather regulation in its own favor. Examples of the latter include criminalizing "undesirable populations," enacting legislation aimed at privatization and undermining unions, and the signing of free-trade agreements with strong provisions for cross-national investor and corporate rights (Stanford 2011, 333; for specific examples relating to the investor-state dispute settlement system, see Moore and Pérez-Rocha 2019). Such pacts, for example, typically allow for national treatment of capital across borders (that is, global [capitalist] citizenship).

In the same vein, see also the aforementioned rising popularity in the West of "investor visa" policies, which essentially auction off residency rights to the highest bidders. This has occurred at the same time that many of these governments have taken draconian steps to deter entry by lower-class migrants.

It is salient to highlight that for some publics, "America First" and "Brexit" may be more appropriate marketing devices than the global or regional-global imaginaries evoked by Emirates, HSBC, and Itaú. Indeed, the current political climate in the US and elsewhere is of course incentivizing, at least to some extent, a renewed corporate advertising focus on national roots and embeddedness (though presumably without entirely shedding the message that when it comes to regulation or global governance, economic elites are the dog wagging the tail of state action, and not the other way around). Should this current ethno-nationalist wave continue to rise, one may expect even global corporations to increasingly perform a national identity and to grow warier of flaunting their own (real or imagined) globality.

However, seemingly more prominent as of late, at least in the US, has been the corporate diffusion—and co-option—of messages that are ostensibly friendly to marginalized populations the world over. Included among these discourses, naturally, is the alluring global imaginary. This is not, of course, an entirely new phenomenon. Yet the conditions for it to increase are certainly in place in our politically charged times.

Now, it is commonly perceived by corporate actors that the key to influencing the spending habits of the young, diverse, and connected millennial generation in the US entails couching efforts to peddle their wares in socially progressive understandings of equality, multiculturalism, and cosmopolitanism. As Alex Holder (2017) comments in *The Guardian*, "They used to say sex sells; now, evidently, it's activism." She continues: "In reaction to Trump's [January 2017] immigration ban, Starbucks CEO wrote an open letter to staff committing to hiring 10,000 refugees and Airbnb's Brian Chesky tweeted that it was providing free accommodation to anyone not allowed in the US. Even Uber, presumably in a bid to outdo Lyft, created a $3m fund to help drivers affected by the 'wrong and unjust' ban. Companies are now attempting to outdo each other with major acts of generosity, but there's a catch; they'll do good as long as they can make sure their customers know about it."

Indeed, Trump's restrictive immigration policies drew a particularly significant amount of ire from US corporations (Molloy 2017). We can welcome these corporate responses while simultaneously retaining a critical posture toward the self-interested impulses that often underlay, or at least incentivize, them.

It is thus of note, per a recent US marketing survey, that slightly over half of Democrats (but only less than a quarter of Republicans) prefer corporate advertising that focuses on "what unites us around the world," as opposed to messages centered around "what companies are doing to celebrate and honour what unites as Americans" (Bond 2017). Given the strong correlations in the US between party affiliation and age, race, ethnicity, and religion, these figures also suggest that cosmopolitan sentiments resonate much more deeply with the younger and more diverse publics toward which marketers often direct their messages.

The idea of a global capitalist class for itself thus appears to be less of an empirical reality, as discussed in chapters 3 and 4, than a rhetorical strategy in favor of both profit-seeking and capitalist hegemony (Ho 2005). For their part, the above advertisements function as a rhetorical form of "heavy artillery" with which to "batter down all walls"—regulatory, ideational, and otherwise—that prevent further capital accumulation (Marx and Engels 1888, 477). Ironically, then, many Marxist-inspired writings on global class formation, despite their theoretical or empirical value, may again produce the political effect of encouraging defeatism insofar as they conjure up the rise of a seemingly omnipotent and omniscient borderless elite.

In this context, to borrow from Paul Krugman, corporate globalism—the utopian vision of a borderless and flat capitalist world, for elites if not others—is an idea that spreads precisely because it is "in the interest of powerful groups" (quoted in Chomsky 1996). Yet, as explored in this chapter's concluding section, the present analysis and deconstruction of these seemingly hegemonic corporate discourses also bring to the fore "fissures" that allow for the contemplation of regulatory efforts and alternative global imaginaries (Ho 2005).

Conclusions: Between Sunny Globalism and Alternative Futures

This chapter's analysis of the underlying importance of pop-culture representations in constructing global-capitalist imaginaries and interrogation of how corporate globalizing discourses function as devices vis-à-vis particular audiences lead to broader issues of great importance—that is, the present work's real-world implications. These are especially worthy of careful delineation given that the interpretive approach adopted here demands self-reflection about the author's ideological leanings and the book's overall political project.

Of particular interest is where this analysis leaves us regarding contemporary (and recurring) debates relating to agency in globalization. These, in turn, bring to the fore questions surrounding the ability of popular forces to end state capture by economic elites (W. Robinson 2014), the power of national governments to regulate global capitalism (Chang 2009), and the imagining and construction of alternative globalizations (Evans 2008; Steger 2008).

As I argue, the borderless imaginary exists more in corporate advertisements than in the material world. The latter, after all, is defined by passport controls at airports, wall building and the militarization of borders

(Brown 2010), and *national* governments that function as both lenders and spenders of last resort during (global) economic crises and pandemics. As I emphasize here, at least the stronger among the world's states can also choose to circumscribe the activities of even heavily globalized corporations such as Facebook. That is to say, regulatory efforts to limit the rule of capital are possible (Rodrik 2012), even if they are of course currently somewhat limited in practice by structural forces and the relative weakness of popular movements.

Also possible is another global order entirely. Indeed, we do not actually live in a placeless, Thomas Friedman–inspired world of inexorable capitalist globalization, nor one in which all can participate and prosper. As the eminent geographer Neil Smith (2005, 894) put it in his polemic against "the flat pluralist world of business class":

> It would indeed be nice if the world were flat and non-hierarchical. Many of us have long been struggling for just such a result, and it is a vision we can easily identify with. But it is precisely the self-serving trick of neo-liberalism to assume that such a flat world is already here, hierarchy is gone, equality rules. The world may be flat for those who can afford a business class ticket to fly around it, gazing down on a seemingly flat surface, while for those gazing up at passing airplanes in Sub-Saharan Africa or the Indian countryside, the opportunity represented by London or Bombay or New York is an impossible climb to a destination visible only as mediated television or movie fantasy, if even that. For those in Bombay's shanties, or for that matter in New York's Harlem or London's East End, the price of the same business class ticket to see the world as flat is just as prohibitive.

It follows that if our world is not actually flat, then contrary to Margaret Thatcher's (in)famous assertion, there *are* alternatives, whether for better or worse. At issue is the extent to which there is sufficient political will and mobilization to pursue them. Future possibilities range from the noxious global Trumpist mix of xenophobia and white identity politics to the inclusive forms of people-first globalization that have been espoused by prominent political leaders such as Bernie Sanders and Alexandria Ocasio-Cortez. Perhaps most notable in this latter regard is the call for a global "Green New Deal" (Aronoff et al. 2019). They also include Karl Marx and Friedrich Engel's (1888, 490) radical ambition to make "despotic inroads on the rights of property, and on the conditions of bourgeois production" (though it is worth noting here that in the *Manifesto*, they argue not only for abolishing private property, but also for progressive taxation and other reform-oriented regulatory measures).

Indeed, outside of utopian neoliberal rhetoric or anarcho-capitalist fantasies, *states* and *markets* are always mutually imbricated forces, as has been suggested throughout this book. Naturally, actors in the latter sphere have proven quite successful in limiting the policy options available to those operating in the former in myriad ways, including by subverting the democratic process (MacLean 2017). Yet the fact remains that wielding the power of the state remains perhaps the most viable option for those seeking to curtail capital's globalizing and totalizing ambitions.

Considering how to engage in meaningful forms of global governance of the capitalist system and imagining other possible worlds are thus imperatives for our time. They are also fully within the public's collective power to contemplate (Acharya 2016). To be sure, these are doubtlessly *difficult* tasks, but not the *near-impossible* ones that would confront us if borders had truly become "so yesterday" and sovereignty had devolved completely to capital (Brown 2010; Hardt and Negri 2000). Whatever its utopian desires, a would-be global capitalist class that still has "national attachments" and "needs" (Sassen 2007, 187) and that must navigate a world order in which state-based authority structures matter will be easier to regulate or even potentially unseat.

Contrary, then, to still-prominent discourses of inevitability, teleology, and the "end of history," the global capitalist discursive utopia of a fully borderless economy, dominated by a global capitalist class in itself and for itself, has only been partially realized in practice. It is not a fait accompli. Rather, it is an ideological project advanced through corporate advertisements and other means.

Contrary to these deterministic messages, global capitalism—and particularly its neoliberal variety—are not naturally occurring systems. Instead, they have "political origins" (Schwartz 2014, 519). Accordingly, by critically analyzing such efforts to sell these ideas to audiences through advertising and by attempting to conceptualize and construct counter-imaginaries, we may come to the ultimate realization that these seemingly timeless structures can also be "politically reversed" (Schwartz 2014, 519; see also Polanyi 2001).

That is to say, the body of global capitalism is much more "open, porous, seeping, and dripping"—and thus vulnerable to variegated responses and audience agency—than its corporate promoters seek to portray (Maurer 2000, 672). The same is true regarding the rhetoric of much of the literature on global class formation. As Karen Ho (2005, 68, 83, 86) observes, beyond the veneer of "totalizing" and "triumphalist discourses of global capitalism," there are opportunities to expose it as "partial, incomplete, high-pressured, and ephemeral."

In fact, there are numerous prominent examples of audiences constructing counter discourses in response to corporate advertisements, many of whom engage in "culture-jamming" activism that aims to subvert corporate messages through "playfully appropriating commercial rhetoric" for oppositional purposes (Harold 2004). They include *Adbusters* magazine (and its spoof ads), the "laughtivist" efforts of the "Yes Men"—who seek to satirize the machinations of "corporate evildoers" and others by "infiltrat[ing] conferences, produc[ing] fake newspapers, and do[ing] various other weirdness"—and Banksy's subversive graffiti art (Branscome 2011).[21]

By revealing the resilient nature of place-based imaginaries and complicated identity amalgamations that predominate among a particular population of globalizing capitalist elites, my hope is not, precisely, to elaborate in the present work what form an alternative system might take, nor how to arrive there. Rather, the aim is to disrupt conventional narratives surrounding the state's role in global capitalism and the globality of elites.

The effect of such discourses, wittingly or not, is to forestall the conceptualization of noncapitalist (or even reformist) realities; this book, instead, seeks to inspire the opening of doors to new possibilities—that is, to take seriously what Mark Rupert and M. Scott Solomon (2006) refer to as "the politics of alternative futures."

Along with delineating and exploring the broader implications of this study's overall findings, the concluding chapter considers how to proceed politically while navigating the convoluted spatial dynamics that seem to define our time. At issue is how to navigate between two unpalatable and seemingly equally hegemonic forces: a globalized *politics of placelessness* that promotes the rule of border-crossing capital and capitalists over local sovereignty, popular or otherwise, and a localized *politics of place* that offers a toxic brew of nativism, nationalism, and right-wing populism as a would-be response and solution.

Notes

1. This term is derived from Michael Billig's well-known concept of "banal nationalism." This refers to the firmly entrenched "ideological habits which enable the established nations of the West to be reproduced" (Billig 1995, 6).

2. See the Behance-hosted gallery of the presumptive designer, accessed April 10, 2018, https://www.behance.net/gallery/11980197/EMIRATES-hello-tomorrow. Emphasis added.

3. See OpenNav, accessed April 11, 2018, http://opennav.com/forum/airchive/5097248.

4. See "HSBC 'A Living River' by J. Walter Thompson," November 11, 2015, accessed April 11, 2018, https://www.campaignlive.co.uk/article/hsbc-a-living-river-j-walter-thompson/1372279.

5. See, respectively, Enlightened Conflict, accessed April 4, 2018, http://brucemctague.com/tag/i-am-a-global-latin-american, and the personal website of Giuseppina Russo, accessed April 4, 2018, https://giuseppinarusso.wordpress.com/2011/02/19/%E2%80%9Ci-am-a-global-latin-american%E2%80%9D/.

6. See World Airline News, accessed January 28, 2018, https://worldairlinenews.com/2012/04/09/emirates-launches-its-hello-tomorrow-ad-campaign/.

7. See Emirates' website, accessed January 14, 2022, https://www.emirates.com/us/english/about-us/our-communities/.

8. See the Partnership's website, accessed January 31, 2017, http://www.openandfairskies.com/.

9. See the "Cultural Diversity" section of Emirates' website, accessed January 17, 2016, http://www.emiratesgroupcareers.com/english/about/cultural_diversity.aspx.

10. See the "Emirates Story" section on the Emirates website, accessed January 17, 2016, http://www.emirates.com/english/about/the_emirates_story.aspx.

11. See the "Emirates Experience," "First Class," accessed March 17, 2017, https://www.emirates.com/us/english/experience/cabin-features/first-class/.

12. See the "Company History" and "Diversity and Inclusion" sections of the HSBC website, accessed January 17, 2016, http://www.hsbc.com/about-hsbc/company-history and http://www.hsbc.com/citizenship/diversity-and-inclusion.

13. See the "About" and "Our Purpose" sections of the HSBC website, accessed January 17, 2016, http://www.hsbc.com/about-hsbc and http://www.hsbc.com/about-hsbc/our-purpose?WT.ac=HGHQ_Ah_h1.2_On.

14. See the "Advertising" section of the HSBC website, accessed January 17, 2016, http://www.hsbc.com/about-hsbc/advertising.

15. See these and other cited slogans at Rev.com, accessed January 17, 2016, http://blog.rev.com/articles/culture/hsbc-airport-ads-share-remarkable-insight-to-our-world/.

16. The advertisements were available for viewing on the website of the Mustard Post studio, accessed June 11, 2019, http://mustardpost.com/hsbc-airport-ads/.

17. See "HSBC UK Global Citizen TV Ad," YouTube, December 3, 2018, accessed October 17, 2019, https://youtu.be/KJ3uwPHUV9w.

18. See Itaú's website, accessed January 17, 2016, http://www.itau.com/.

19. See Africa's website, accessed June 12, 2019, https://africaagency.wordpress.com/tag/global/.

20. Ibid.

21. See, respectively, the *Adbusters* website, accessed January 29, 2018, http://www.adbusters.org/spoofads/; and the Yes Men, accessed January 29, 2018, http://theyesmen.org/index.php/about/.

CONCLUSION

The Future of Global Imaginaries: Thinking Beyond Nativism and Neoliberal Propaganda

OURS IS AN ERA DEFINED NOT ONLY BY ballooning and Gilded Age levels of inequality (Hickel 2018; Piketty 2017), but also by a relative lack of in-depth, sociological effort to understand the lifeworlds of capitalism's "winners" (or its facilitators and enablers). As three prominent mainstream specialists in democratic politics noted, "It is striking how little political scientists actually know about the political attitudes and behavior of wealthy citizens" (quoted in Stevens 2015, 725). The same could be said about their beliefs and actions in general.

Notably, this oversight is not limited to either political science or US academia. Accordingly, the Brazilian sociologist Antonio David Cattani comments (perhaps, or at least hopefully, with a tinge of exaggeration) that nearly 99 percent of research in the social sciences focuses on the poor, working, and middle classes. In turn, relatively few study those whose control of media outlets, wielding of corporate power, and well-funded political interventions allow them to play an outsized role in shaping the social structures in which we all live (Costas 2014).

This class-based disparity in knowledge production is certainly common in Global North universities, where critically minded social scientists seem naturally drawn, and not without good reason, to studying normatively appealing social movements and groups, often in the Global South. In turn, within Latin American Studies—where many scholars rightly sympathize with the region and lament its subservient position in larger and oppressive political-economic structures—there is often a tendency to overlook the extent to which certain actors in the region in fact participate in the maintenance of those very same structures (North and Clark 2018). As is the case in the literature on global capitalism, many of us are simply used to thinking of economic elites as a phenomenon of the North.

This preferred focus on subaltern actors is such that it has even inspired its own well-known joke. As one scholar begins a review essay about the *favelas* of Rio de Janeiro: "You've probably heard the one about Eskimo demography: how many Eskimos in the typical igloo? Five—a mother, father, two kids, and an anthropologist. The same joke might be made about Rio de Janeiro's favelas, but it would vastly undercount the anthropologists, to say nothing of the sociologists, political scientists, and assorted external agents of nongovernmental organizations" (McCann 2006, 149). Notably, Cattani suggests that these epistemological trends hold true even in extremely inegalitarian societies such as his native Brazil (Costas 2014). In addition to the understandable desire to highlight and draw attention to how the weak fight back against the onslaught of the powerful, disciplinary norms also surely play a role in producing this imbalance. Postmodern and particularly postcolonial approaches, with their frequent focus on subaltern agency, have largely displaced Marxist-inspired analysis as *the* standard-bearer for "radical" critique in the social sciences. Concurrently, there has been a decrease in the analytical focus on class and thus on capitalist elites (Chibber 2013a).

Through analyzing the thought processes, identities, and cultural contexts of many of the key agents behind Latin America's economic relations with the Arab world, this study thus responds to the call for greater attention to be paid to the sociology of elites. Simply put, we need more scholarship focusing on the world as seen from corporate boardrooms, executive offices, and centers of state power. Such studies are of tremendous normative appeal; namely, they hold the possibility of subjecting these actors and their activities to greater public scrutiny.

Specifically in this vein, the present effort contributes to our understanding of the interpretive frameworks of a particular population of border-crossing business elites. While various studies attempt to measure the extent to which globalization as an objective, material economic phenomenon is spreading around the planet (Figge and Martens 2014), we know much less about the ideational qualities of this system's protagonists. Though the present focus is on Arab–Latin American relations, the arguments that emerge are also intended to shed light on larger dynamics and trends the world over.

In short, this study reasserts the importance of the state in global capitalism. As Latha Varadarajan (2014, 377) notes, "While the expansion of capitalism on a global scale is real, so is persistence of the territorial nation-state system." As it regards capitalist class consciousness, the present analysis indicates that—at least in the Arab–Latin American case—the pull of the latter is stronger than that of the former.

In other words, place-*based* motivating imaginaries continue to reverberate more frequently than their place*less* counterparts among the capitalist elites analyzed in this study. The same is presumably true, to greater or lesser extents based on the particularities of each case, among many other populations of capitalist elites around the world. The argument for the existence of a fully formed imagined community of global capitalists retains analytical utility as an ideal type and as a representation of a class that has yet to coalesce but perhaps one day will. However, it is not a fully accurate description of living and breathing capitalist elites as they exist today.

Notably, this finding contradicts (or at least adds nuance to) many lay and scholarly accounts, as well as much conventional wisdom surrounding the topic of global elite formation. It also provides a useful reminder about the palimpsest-like nature of cognitive frameworks. Again, new axes of identity do not paint on tabulae rasae, but rather on already colored slates. In the process, they may create what are indeed *novel* identity formations, but within the context of the *old*—hence the term *rooted* globalism.

As Karl Marx would likely have suggested, we may return to the (reasonable) objection that, at least in an immediate sense, what these actors are doing (the material) is of much greater relevance than why they think they are doing it (the ideational). I do not wish to dispute this contention. Nevertheless, it is also true that there are real, political consequences at stake vis-à-vis the *problematique* of global class consciousness. Two are particularly worthy of mentioning here.

First, if place-based imaginaries are in fact quite resilient, then there are stronger grounds for considering how to engage in more meaningful forms of both domestic and global governance. Logically, a class that has some level of "national attachments" and "needs" will be easier to regulate (Sassen 2007, 187). Bringing such efforts to fruition will be no simple task, but nor are they necessarily, and in all places and at all times, doomed to failure.

Second, focusing on the lifeworlds of individual economic elites helps to expose the fragmentary and partial nature of capitalist hegemony. To be clear, nothing in the above analysis is meant to detract from the importance of structuralist or materialist analysis. However, it is important to recognize that overly structural accounts of economic globalization can feed into deterministic and teleological understandings of capitalism as a timeless and immutable system. Ironically, as we have seen, these in fact resonate with the messages that are also diffused through much neoliberal theory and corporate advertising.

In turn, integrating actor-centered and ideational accounts into a broader, structural understanding of the capitalist system provides a pathway for countering the arguments of those who see the current power and economic inequalities that have risen alongside global capitalism as fait accompli. Such is the present aim. By recognizing this fact, publics may thus feel increasingly empowered to conceptualize, posit, and fight for alternative globalizations (Fisher and Ponniah 2019).

Additionally, this analysis reveals that corporate discourses promoting globality, along with *tomorrow*'s borderless utopia, amount to a political performance by capitalist entities to promote their own material, profit-seeking interests. Indeed, declarations of a new, borderless world order in which transnational corporations may roam unfettered, unhindered by our present patchwork of mostly national regulations, is a capitalist utopia. Behind the sunny globalist rhetoric, the image transmitted through the aforementioned advertisements is that of a flat, ungoverned, and seemingly ungovernable milieu. Within this constructed reality, profit-seeking behavior, the structurally determined lifeblood of any capitalist, can find its highest and most lucrative expression.

As noted, the advertisements deployed by certain capitalist entities and elites—as well as corporate advertising firms—evince a clear recognition of the material benefits that may accrue to the global 1 percent if or when it increasingly sheds its territorial baggage. The concretization of a global capitalist class is thus a haunting specter, and serious efforts—from combative social movements to new forms of global governance—would be needed to confront it.

Accordingly, embedded within this study, just like any other, is a series of critiques, normative assumptions, and political aspirations. First, this work is motivated by the desire to contribute to the decolonization of global studies by better integrating Global South case studies into theoretical understandings of our evolving global political-economic order. Second, it is premised on the notion that we have much to learn by closely observing the agents who labor within and whose actions help to create global capitalism's seemingly faceless, anonymous structures. Karen Ho's (2009) *Liquidated: An Ethnography of Wall Street* is exemplary in this regard. As noted, focusing too much on structure as opposed to agency can reinforce the (undesirable) status quo by strengthening the presentist bias and making change seem impossible.

Further, in terms of methodology, it is clear that standard, positivist approaches, at least in isolation, are often inadequate for addressing questions that involve meaning and identity. This is perhaps especially true for studies about class, a notoriously complex phenomenon to observe and analyze (Emerson et al. 1995, 138). Here, interpretivism proves its analytical utility. Approaches in this tradition are defined by a spirit of context sensitivity, promote an ethnographic sensibility, and are premised on a more fluid (and thus more realistic) view of human thought and action. The argument is not that all areas of inquiry lend themselves naturally to an interpretive approach (Funk 2019). Rather, for consistency's sake, methodological choices should match our research questions and ontologies (Hall 2003).

Perhaps most importantly, this study highlights the inherently political nature of the global economy. There is no capitalist marketplace, global or otherwise, without the enforcement of a particular set of rules, by some kind of enforcer, whose actions are also political by definition. To correct neoliberal rhetoric, at issue is not *whether* to regulate, but rather *whose* interests should be served by regulation (Slobodian 2018). The key question, in turn, is how popular forces can amass sufficient will and power to overcome the very real structural impediments that confront any movement that seeks a regulatory order that is based on the public good as opposed to endless accumulation by elites.

As the present analysis demonstrates, global imaginaries are also inherently political. Further, they are politically and strategically necessary, as I argue below. The continuing globalization of capital of course presents innumerable challenges to the exercise of popular sovereignty, as well as to democracy itself (Kuttner 2018). Yet the implicit message behind the sunny globalist rhetoric of corporate advertising campaigns—that state-based regulatory and governance structures no longer have any capacity to regulate capital—is a self-serving illusion.

For example, witness, as of mid-2019, the deep bipartisan skepticism in the US vis-à-vis Facebook's proposed launch of Libra, a global digital currency to be managed by corporations instead of central banks. As a *Wired* headline put it, "*Everyone* Wants Facebook's Libra to Be Regulated" (Barber 2019; emphasis added). What needs to be determined is not *if* initiatives such as Libra should be regulated, but again, *how* and in the interest of *whom* (as well as, more fundamentally, whether it should be allowed to exist in the first place). For its part, even Facebook, in rhetoric if not in practice, has been forced by state and public opprobrium to acknowledge that it must "fully address regulatory concerns" and that it "recognize[s] the authority of financial regulators and support[s] their oversight of this project" (quoted in Paul 2019).

More problematically, see also the Trump administration's (partly successful) advancement of a policy agenda—including cracking down on the approval of H1-B visas for "highly skilled" workers and openly pursuing a trade war against China—that directly conflicted with the core interests of certain major corporate players. Aggrieved parties included, respectively, Silicon Valley and US agribusiness. My point, of course, is not to defend Donald Trump's particular intrusions into the vaunted free market. Rather, it is to make the more general argument that the US state, for example, retains a significant amount of capacity to act in ways that contradict the desires of capital and capitalists—including by choosing to tax them (Young 2018).

Given the real-world relevance of the topics at hand, this book concludes by considering an all-important political matter that is of much interest from the perspective of a self-avowedly critical global studies—that is, the complicated politics of opposition to the neoliberal and corporate global imaginaries that I have analyzed in this text, as well as consideration of how popular forces might seek to create space for alternatives while also confronting a surging global far right. As I argue in this context, it is of the utmost importance that the left maintain its traditional internationalist tendencies and refuse to fall into nativist traps.

Corporate and Other Global Imaginaries

To the extent that state and popular sovereignty are in fact "waning," it is largely due to the "militant globalism" of neoliberalism's proponents, the resulting global spread of a "neoliberal rationality," and the consequences thereof (Brown 2019; Slobodian 2018). As Wendy Brown (2019, 8) forcefully argues, in today's world, "nothing is untouched by a neoliberal mode of reason and valuation." She further remarks without hyperbole that "neoliberalism's attack on democracy has everywhere inflected law, political culture, and political subjectivity" (Brown 2019, 8; see also Dardot and Laval 2017). Meanwhile, inequality surges, jobs are outsourced, unions are crushed, austerity is implemented, schools are privatized, and social programs are decimated, usually at the hands of an increasingly discredited, self-styled centrist (and, often, cosmopolitan) elite.

Naturally, such a dire state of affairs is producing numerous, contradictory, and diverse forms of political blowback. Most prominent, of course, is the rise of an intolerant, jingoistic, retrograde, demagogic, and illiberal global far right. Summarizing this contemporary trend, Brown (2019, 1) notes, "Every election brings a new shock: neo-Nazis in the German parliament, neofascists in the Italian one, Brexit ushered in by tabloid-fueled xenophobia, the rise of white nationalism in Scandinavia, authoritarian regimes taking shape in Turkey and Eastern Europe, and of course, Trumpism."

Regarding the countries that are the focus of this book, Jair Bolsonaro's assumption of the Brazilian presidency in 2019 provided another obvious and particularly jarring example of right-wing extremism's rising electoral fortunes. But see also the more traditional and supposedly "moderate" right's increasing reliance on xenophobic rhetoric and draconian legislation to mobilize voters in both Sebastián Piñera's Chile and, before his late-2019 defeat, in Mauricio Macri's Argentina. Notably, in the former, though José Antonio Kast fell short of succeeding Piñera and winning the presidency, the authoritarian-nostalgic culture warrior and unabashed defender of elite privilege earned more than 44 percent of the vote in the second-round election in December 2021, gaining support along the way from many mainstream, and allegedly pro-democratic, "center-right" factions.

Bearing witness to the reactionary political formations that have emerged out of the "crisis of hegemony" facing the neoliberal establishment (W. Robinson 2014), one is naturally reminded of Antonio Gramsci's (1971, 275–276) oft-cited observation that "the crisis consists precisely in the fact that the old is dying and the new cannot be born; in this interregnum a great variety of morbid symptoms appear" (see also Fraser 2019).

The current maelstrom evokes Karl Polanyi's (2001, 245–246, 265) old but also prescient argument that "the fascist solution" emerged as a response to a hegemonic liberalism that had "degenerate[d] into a mere advocacy of free enterprise" and proved immune to reform. In such circumstances, and perhaps previous even to the appearance of a "fascist movement proper," one observes a variety of "morbid symptoms," indeed (Polanyi 2001, 246). These include "the spread of irrationalistic philosophies, racialist aesthetics, anticapitalistic demagogy, heterodox currency views, criticism of the party system, [and] widespread disparagement of the 'regime,' or whatever was the name given to the existing democratic setup" (Polanyi 2001, 246). Also included, it seems, are pandemic denialism and the propagation of anti-mask and -vaccination sentiment (Callison and Slobodian 2021).

Not unlike their predecessors, today's reactionary forces demonize a common and familiar set of targets, including the political left, immigrants, and racial and other minorities. Particularly in the West, they have fully embraced a firmly xenophobic agenda and an ethos of "white identity politics" (Jardina 2019).

Yet, with a bit of variation according to national context, they also place some understanding of the global within their rhetorical crosshairs. As noted in the introduction, France's Marine Le Pen, for example, has gone so far as to equate globalization with "another kind of totalitarianism, the ideology of free business with no boundaries" (quoted in Chak 2015). Trump, wittingly or not, seemed to evoke antisemitic tropes by railing against a "globalist" elite that is insufficiently committed to the US national project. Hungary's Viktor Orbán is even more explicit, attributing to the financier and philanthropist George Soros the elaboration of a global conspiracy to "flood" his country with Muslim and other migrants.

We must enter an important caveat here. Of course, today's self-styled, right-wing populists are not, in general, actually opposed to *globalism*, per se. Indeed, Trump, for example, is far more of a *globalist* by virtue of his far-flung real-estate empire than those to whom he typically attaches the label. Indeed, his business model—such as it is—depends on neoliberal property regimes that allow for foreign participation in local ventures, as well as a neoliberal financial infrastructure that facilitates global capital flows. In turn, the self-declared "antiglobalist" formation spearheaded by Steve Bannon—dubbed, rather ominously, "The Movement"—is precisely an internationalist, if floundering, effort at cross-border, far-right solidarity.

More profoundly, the political work done by these neoliberal "Frankenstein monsters" is to graft a series of racialized, masculinist, religious, and cultural grievances onto a popular malaise with capitalism's dislocating effects and the infrastructure, rules, and organizations that sustain actually existing global politics and economics (Brown 2018; 2019). Completing the circle, the resulting political energy is subsequently channeled into a broader effort to reinforce social and other hierarchies, as well as the very same neoliberal, capitalist order out of whose discontents this "movement" draws much of its energy (Brown 2019; Fraser 2019; Robin 2017).

With this sleight of hand, today's ascendant right is able to resignify *antiglobalism* as opposition to the free circulation of (certain) people, cultures, and ideas, if not precisely capital itself (though this, too, occasionally serves as a useful rhetorical punching bag for Le Pen and others). The political ideal that emerges is of a future world order composed of "walled" neoliberal states with only thin commitments—at best—to universal, democratic, or liberal values (Brown 2010; Harrington 2019).

Our current conjuncture—a veritable "age of authoritarian neoliberalism"—presents profound challenges with few easy solutions in sight (Kiersey and Sokoloff 2019). Indeed, the machinations of the global Trumpist far right, even after the protagonist's fall 2020 electoral defeat, appear poised to cast a long shadow over political trajectories in most of (but not only) the West for some time to come. In this context, at stake is no less than the survival of the entire edifice of liberal democracy—a highly problematic and contradictory space, to be sure, but one worth defending against the contemporary onslaught.

This work closes by considering what to make of its central concern—global imaginaries and their uses—in light of this rather convoluted political scenario. The dominant right-wing position, as delineated above, is as noxious as it is clear. Also transparent—and problematic—is the establishment's reaction. Sensing that the center will not hold, today's mainstream technocrats commonly argue that the only way to stop bleeding support to right-wing populists is to move toward the latter's policy platform by, for example, further restricting immigration and criminalizing migrants.

This explains Hillary Clinton's "moderate" position that "for people who then keep coming, you turn them back, unless they qualify for asylum" (quoted in Wintour 2018). See also the tendency of establishment Trump critics to rush to the defense of flawed institutions that represent the "old order," such as the North Atlantic Treaty Organization (NATO) and the World Trade Organization (WTO) (Haass 2017). On offer from these quarters, then, is what Nancy Fraser (2019, 11) aptly refers to as a "progressive neoliberalism" (and, perhaps, militarism) that has increasingly seen fit to don the cloak of "feminism, antiracism, multiculturalism, environmentalism, and LGBTQ+ rights" (or at least their more establishment-friendly varieties) and that now perceives the opportunity to rebrand itself (that is, to become even less progressive) by latching onto far-right grievances. Needless to say, this hardly presents a palatable alternative, nor one that appears likely to succeed politically.

Where does the left go from here? In a hopeful sign, in the US and elsewhere, there is increasing popular skepticism toward neoliberal arrangements that privilege the power and free circulation of capital, a tendency that has only been reinforced by the COVID-19 pandemic (Tooze 2021). As a result, there is an increasing appetite for alternatives to a world order defined not just by Trumpism, but also by the machinations of globalizing elites.

Notably, on some parts of the left—perhaps particularly in Europe—there is a retreat from globalism in its many and ideologically diverse forms. Most prominent in this regard is a critique of current migration levels, as well as of the concepts of *open borders* and *freedom of movement.*

In a widely cited (and profoundly controversial) article, "The Left Case against Open Borders," Angela Nagle (2018) argues against what she regards as current left-wing orthodoxy. Noting that "open borders and mass immigration are a victory for the bosses," she invokes big business' long history of undermining labor rights and solidarity through hiring—and in some cases trafficking—a lower-cost, nonunionized, and more easily exploitable immigrant workforce.

Dismissing the potential for a left-wing global imaginary or alternative, she notes, "Perhaps the ultra-wealthy can afford to live in the borderless world they aggressively advocate for, but most people need—and want—a coherent, sovereign political body to defend their rights as citizens." The alternative, Nagle observes, is to keep feeding the fire that is fueling the far right. In such arguments, she is joined by fellow travelers such as Slavoj Žižek and German sociologist Wolfgang Streeck, who in turn is affiliated with the new and migrant-skeptic political formation, Aufstehen (alternatively translated as Get, Stand, or Rise Up), which was founded in 2018.

Leaving aside a discussion of the humanitarian, ethical, or economic dimensions of these fraught conversations, I will only address their political aspects, particularly as they relate to global imaginaries. At least some capitalist "fractions" do benefit from a relatively permissive migration regime (though instead of open borders, the ideal from their perspective may more closely resemble a mixed approach—that is, one that allows many migrants to enter but also disciplines and renders them a super-exploited class upon their arrival through repressive enforcement mechanisms and by denying them political and workers' rights [Brown 2010]). Naturally, it is also true that a "left case" (if not an unequivocal one) can be made against certain open-border arrangements, such as that embodied by the EU, which facilitates—and requires—the free movement not only of people, but of capital, services, and goods (Lapavitsas 2019). At least in the latter three regards, the EU thus embodies a fundamentally neoliberal logic in that it can restrict democracy by tying the hands of member states that wish to enact different regulatory policies, even though it also serves as a space that allows for relatively progressive agendas to be advanced in regard to climate policy and other areas.

Summarizing the discontent with globalist rhetoric and echoing the above analysis of corporate advertising campaigns, critics correctly recognize that the imaginary of global citizenship often functions in practice as little more than "neoliberal propaganda" (Chapman et al. 2018). Focusing on its deployment in higher-education contexts such as many global studies programs, as Debra D. Chapman, Tania Ruiz-Chapman, and Peter Eglin (2018, 148) correctly note, "What [this framing of global citizenship] does *not* do . . . is educate young people about their actual place in the neoliberal world order of accumulation by dispossession, managed, supervised and protected by imperialist Northern states, above all the United States. It thus serves as propaganda for that very order." In this way, global citizenship—and, we might say, the global imaginary more broadly—becomes "a concept steeped in Northern privilege implicating and implicated in neo-colonial relationships with the global South" (see also Chapman et al. 2020).

Within this world order, as constructed by Emirates, HSBC, Itaú, and others, ideal global citizens such as corporations and business elites are able to pass through immigration checkpoints as if they amounted to "nets" rather than "walls" (Eggert 2015). In contrast, others tend to meet rather different fates when attempting to traverse "violent borders" (Jones 2016).

In spite of these valid critiques, this book closes with a plea: the left must be careful not to retreat into nationalism, parochialism, and ostensibly popular anti-migrant politics or to cede the construction of global imaginaries to corporations. Global citizenship may currently function as neoliberal propaganda, but political mobilization could turn this contested concept into something very different. After all, it is not an idea that corporate elites "own" (Chapman et al. 2018, 145). We can thus oppose corporate global imaginaries without abandoning the struggle for a different kind of cosmopolitan vision. And, as I wish to suggest, alternative global imaginaries *are* worth fighting for (Hardt and Negri 2000).

Part of the logic here is strategic (leaving aside, again, ethical and other relevant concerns). First, it seems a tragic mistake to believe that the left can beat the right at nationalist or nativist politics. Instead, efforts to grovel in those directions appear predisposed to both sap the vitality of the left (by alienating natural allies and diluting commitments to universal values) and play into the right's hands by waging political battles on the latter's turf.

Second, it is important to recognize the political limitations of appeals to nation-based imaginaries. The deployment of such rhetorical constructs is completely understandable (and even laudable) in certain circumstances, such as anticolonial and anti-imperial struggles (though even in such cases, Frantz Fanon's *The Wretched of the Earth* [2005] reminds us that today's national liberators may turn into tomorrow's oppressors, a prescient observation that appears to have been largely borne out by subsequent events and postcolonial trajectories). However, in general, nation-based appeals all too easily lend political cover to troubling exercises of state power.

This precise dynamic is on display in War on Terror–era Britain, as revealed by Nisha Kapoor (2018). The mobilizing slogan of "British justice for British citizens," deployed as part of an understandable strategic gambit by local activists to combat the extradition to the US of Muslim "terror" suspects, produced a noxious side effect. Specifically, this invocation of place-based pride ended up lionizing a British justice system that is also riddled with biases, exclusions, and racialized logics. In other words, it buttressed the idea of a "sovereign" Britain's right to carry out its own miscarriages of justice. Further, of course, any sort of paean to a national imagined community will by default exclude some Other, who is rhetorically constructed as an outsider undeserving of political rights.

Accordingly, *nativism of the left* may resonate among some as a viable short-term political strategy. But this is hardly the raw material with which to build a solidarity-based politics. To invoke Michel Foucault, national pride is not precisely always *bad*, but it is surely always *dangerous* (Rouse 2005, 115). If the left chooses to fan nationalist flames, it will almost certainly get burned—as well as find itself straying from core principles relating to universal and global emancipation.

In response to the diffusion of corporate global imaginaries, on the one hand, and the electoral temptation to invoke the national, on the other, I argue for the fundamental importance of keeping alive an alternative internationalist tradition: a left-wing, people-first global imaginary—not an abandonment of the national terrain, but rather a rooted globalism of the left that both thinks and acts globally and locally.

One may reasonably counter that a popular global consciousness, political movement, or body politic is not within the realm of current possibility. But what is the alternative? What is to be gained by ceding the global to the progressive neoliberal rhetoric of corporate advertising?

As former Greek finance minister and perennial rabble-rouser Yanis Varoufakis (2018) puts it in regard to political strategy, "While globalised financial capital can no longer be allowed to tear our societies into shreds, we must explain that no country is an island. Just like climate change demands of us both local and international action, so too does the fight against poverty, private debt and rogue bankers." Faced with these and other similarly vexing, border-crossing issues, seeking succor in the arms of the national thus appears unviable in moral, political, and strategic terms.

Crucially, a sense of global community is part of the left's DNA. Marx and Friedrich Engels (1888, 482) do note in the *Manifesto* that, for strategic reasons, "the struggle of the proletariat with the bourgeoisie is at first a national struggle." Yet they later add the caveat that the working class is certainly not a "national" community "in the bourgeois sense of the word" (Marx and Engels 1888, 488).

Indeed, their understanding of class struggle is fundamentally based on building cross-border solidarity among workers. One could point to the iconic end-of-document slogan, "Working men of all countries, unite!" (Marx and Engels 1888, 500). Yet perhaps even more forthrightly, they note earlier that "the working men have no country," that we thus "cannot take from them what they have not got," and that in this earlier period of capitalist globalization, "national differences and antagonisms between peoples are daily more and more vanishing" (Marx and Engels 1888, 488).

Notably in this regard, it is rather misleading to argue, as Nagle (2018) does on the basis of selective quotations, that Marx's posture on immigration "would get him banished from the modern Left." Contrary to Nagle, his position was not, in fact, that the observed lack of solidarity evinced by "native" English workers toward their Irish immigrant counterparts represented an inherent feature of human society, nor that it should be taken as justification for nativist, nation-based, or closed-border policies. Rather, he saw this lack of cross-community solidarity as a political problem that *should*, *must*, and *could* be solved (Anderson 2010, 145; see also Sclofsky and Funk 2018).

Constructing global imaginaries is thus too important and politically salient of a task to be relegated to corporations. Yet movements of the left do, it seems, have something to learn from the advertisements of Emirates, HSBC, Itaú, and others. Global imaginaries are alluring to many, especially in younger and more diverse communities, and, in part for that reason, they are politically powerful.

Global imaginaries and forms of consciousness thus hold the potential not only to socialize audiences into neoliberal ideals or facilitate the profit-seeking activities of Arab–Latin American or other business elites. If constructed differently, they can also help heterogeneous publics develop broader and more global understandings of their individual and local situations and struggles—in other words, to empower them to see themselves as part of something bigger, which is a prerequisite for precisely the kind of politics that is needed to defeat the far-right "Nationalist International" (Varoufakis 2018) or indeed to overcome global capitalism itself (Hardt and Negri 2000). The question we are left with, then, is not *whether* to imagine the global or imagine citizenship or popular sovereignty in global terms, but *how*.

Through delineating the corporate-friendly uses and abuses of the rhetorical construct of "universal global citizenship," Chapman, Ruiz-Chapman, and Eglin (2018, 159) render the rather bleak verdict that a truly egalitarian incarnation of this paradigm "is an impossibility until there is a complete dismantling of the neoliberal world order." I agree with their analysis but see fit to interpret their conclusion about this particular global imaginary in a less politically disempowering light, for it is at least the case that we are left with a concrete idea about how to organize ourselves politically, since the nature of the task that faces us—system change—is quite clear.

In contemplating how to construct the sorts of global imaginaries that will meet the daunting challenges posed by our current political conjuncture, we can perhaps do no better than return to another of Gramsci's (1971, 175) well-known adages, this one concerning the productive synergy that can emerge when "pessimism of the [intellect]" is combined with "optimism of the will."

BIBLIOGRAPHY

Abugattas, Juan. 1982. "The Perception of the Palestinian Question in Latin America." *Journal of Palestine Studies* 11, no. 3: 117–128.
Acharya, Amitav. 2014. *The End of American World Order*. Malden, MA: Polity.
———, ed. 2016. *Why Govern? Rethinking Demand and Progress in Global Governance*. Cambridge, UK: Cambridge University Press.
Agar Corbinos, Lorenzo, and Raymundo Kabchi, eds. 1997. *El mundo árabe y América Latina*. Madrid: Ediciones UNESCO.
Alfaro-Velcamp, Theresa. 2007. *So Far from Allah, So Close to Mexico: Middle Eastern Immigrants in Modern Mexico*. Austin: University of Texas Press.
Al Jazeera. 2009. "Arab-Latin American Ties Hailed." March 31, 2009. Accessed May 31, 2014. http://english.aljazeera.net/news/middleeast/2009/03/2009331131144938569.html.
Alsultany, Evelyn, and Ella Shohat, eds. 2013. *Between the Middle East and the Americas: The Cultural Politics of Diaspora*. Ann Arbor: University of Michigan Press.
Amado, Jorge. 2008. *A Descoberta da América pelos Turcos*. São Paulo: Companhia das Letras.
Amar, Paul. 2013. *The Security Archipelago: Human-Security States, Sexuality Politics, and the End of Neoliberalism*. Durham, NC: Duke University Press.
———, ed. 2014. *The Middle East and Brazil: Perspectives on the New Global South*. Bloomington: Indiana University Press.
Amaya Banegas, Jorge Alberto. 1997. *Los árabes y palestinos en Honduras, 1900–1950*. Tegucigalpa: Editorial Guaymuras.
AméricaEconomía. 2013. "Chile es el país con más acuerdos comerciales en el mundo." October 26, 2013. Accessed February 1, 2016. http://www.americaeconomia.com/node/103784.
Amorim, Celso. 2011. "Brazil and the Middle East: Reflections on Lula's South-South Cooperation." *Cairo Review of Global Affairs* 1, no. 2: 48–63.
———. 2015. *Teerã, Ramalá e Doha: Memórias da Política Externa Ativa e Altiva*. São Paulo: Benvirá.
ANBA (*Agência de Notícias Brasil-Árabe*). 2020. "Árabes se tornam 3º maior destino da exportação brasileira." January 29, 2020. Accessed February 18, 2020. https://anba.com.br/arabes-se-tornam-3o-maior-destino-da-exportacao-brasileira/.
ANBA (*Brazil-Arab News Agency*). 2021. "UAE–Latin America Relations Subject of Roundtable." June 2, 2021. Accessed June 4, 2021. https://anba.com.br/en/uae-latin-america-relations-subject-of-roundtable/.
Anderson, Benedict. 2006. *Imagined Communities: Reflections on the Origin and Spread of Nationalism*. New York: Verso.
Anderson, Elizabeth. 2017. *Private Government: How Employers Rule Our Lives*. Princeton, NJ: Princeton University Press.
Anderson, Kevin B. 2010. *Marx at the Margins: On Nationalism, Ethnicity, and Non-Western Societies*. Chicago: University of Chicago Press.

———. 2015. "Karl Marx and Intersectionality." *Logos: A Journal of Modern Society & Culture* 14, no. 1. Accessed February 7, 2016. http://logosjournal.com/2015/anderson-marx/.

Anievas, Alexander. 2008. "Theories of a Global State: A Critique." *Historical Materialism* 16, no. 2: 190–206.

Appadurai, Arjun. 1990. "Disjuncture and Difference in the Global Cultural Economy." *Theory, Culture & Society* 7, no. 2–3: 295–310.

———. 1996. *Modernity at Large: Cultural Dimensions of Globalization*. Minneapolis: University of Minnesota Press.

Appel, Hannah. 2012. "Offshore Work: Oil, Modularity, and the How of Capitalism in Equatorial Guinea." *American Ethnologist* 39, no. 4: 692–709.

Appelbaum, Richard P., and William I. Robinson, eds. 2005. *Critical Globalization Studies*. New York: Routledge.

Appiah, Kwame Anthony. 2005. *The Ethics of Identity*. Princeton, NJ: Princeton University Press.

———. 2016. "There Is No Such Thing as Western Civilization." *The Guardian*, November 9, 2016. Accessed March 7, 2017. https://www.theguardian.com/world/2016/nov/09/western-civilisation-appiah-reith-lecture.

Aronoff, Kate, Alyssa Battistoni, Daniel Aldana Cohen, and Thea Riofrancos. 2019. *A Planet to Win: Why We Need a Green New Deal*. Brooklyn: Verso.

Astier, Henri. 2014. "French National Front's Black and Arab Supporters." *BBC News*. May 17, 2014. Accessed January 29, 2016. http://www.bbc.com/news/world-europe-27446261.

Atkinson, Rowland. 2019. "Necrotecture: Lifeless Dwellings and London's Super-Rich." *International Journal of Urban and Regional Research* 43, no. 1: 2–13.

Aydinli, Ersel, and Gonca Biltekin, eds. 2018. *Widening the World of International Relations: Homegrown Theorizing*. New York: Routledge.

Bachman, Katy. 2010. "HSBC Campaign Arrives at L.A. Airport." *Adweek*. January 20, 2010. Accessed January 28, 2018. http://www.adweek.com/brand-marketing/hsbc-campaign-arrives-la-airport-106961/.

Baeza, Cecilia. 2012. "América Latina y la cuestión palestina (1947–2012)." *Araucaria: Revista Iberoamericana de Filosofía, Política y Humanidades* 14, no. 28: 111–131.

———. 2014. "Palestinians in Latin America." *Journal of Palestine Studies* XLIII, no. 2: 59–72.

Baeza, Cecilia, and Elodie Brun. 2012. "La diplomacia chilena hacia los países árabes: entre posicionamiento estratégico y oportunismo comercial." *Estudios Internacionales* (Santiago de Chile) 171: 61–85.

Bahbah, Bishara. 1986. *Israel and Latin America: The Military Connection*. New York: St. Martin's Press.

Baldissarelli, Adriana. 2014. "Abertura para novos negócios com 11 países da Liga Árabe." *Notícias do Dia* (Florianópolis, Brazil). April 29, 2014. Accessed February 1, 2016. http://ndonline.com.br/florianopolis/colunas/panorama/162834-dupla-tributacao-afasta-negocios-de-sc-com-arabes.html.

Barber, Gregory. 2019. "Everyone Wants Facebook's Libra to Be Regulated. But How?" *Wired*. July 18, 2019. Accessed July 19, 2019. https://www.wired.com/story/everyone-wants-facebooks-libra-regulated-but-how/.

Basch, Linda, Nina Glick Schiller, and Cristina Szanton Blanc. 2003. *Nations Unbound: Transnational Projects, Postcolonial Predicaments and Deterritorialized Nation-States*. New York: Routledge.

Bascuñan-Wiley, Nicholas. 2019. "*Sumud* and Food: Remembering Palestine Through Cuisine in Chile." *Mashriq & Mahjar: Journal of Middle East and North African Migration Studies* 6, no. 2.

Bates, Robert H. 1997. "Area Studies and the Discipline: A Useful Controversy?" *PS: Political Science and Politics* 30, no. 2: 166–169.
BBC Capital. 2016. "These Are the Surprising Connections between the Davos Elite." January 19, 2016. Accessed February 1, 2016. http://www.bbc.com/capital/story/20160115-who-are-the-most-connected-at-davos-2016.
BBC Mundo. 2014. "En fotos: los grafitis del muro de la discordia en Medio Oriente." May 20, 2014. Accessed February 1, 2016. http://www.bbc.com/mundo/video_fotos/2014/05/140515_galeria_muro_grafitis_cisjordania_ch.shtml.
BBC News. 2012. "Facebook's Eduardo Saverin Quits US Ahead of Flotation." May 14, 2012. Accessed February 1, 2016. http://www.bbc.com/news/technology-18057926.
———. 2016a. "How Much Inequality Is Too Much?" January 8, 2016. Accessed February 1, 2016. http://www.bbc.com/news/business-34987474.
———. 2016b. "Rapper Mos Def Ordered to Leave South Africa in Passport Row." January 15, 2016. Accessed February 1, 2016. http://www.bbc.com/news/world-africa-35330365.
Beck, Ulrich. 2002. "The Cosmopolitan Society and Its Enemies." *Theory, Culture & Society* 19, no. 1–2: 17–44.
Beder, Sharon. 2005. "Corporate Propaganda and Global Capitalism—Selling Free Enterprise?" In *Global Politics in the Information Age*, edited by Mark J. Lacy and Peter Wilkin, 116–130. Manchester, UK: Manchester University Press.
Belfrage, Claes, and Earl Gammon. 2017. "Aesthetic International Political Economy." *Millennium: Journal of International Studies* 45, no. 2: 223–232.
Bessner, Daniel, and Matthew Sparke. 2017. "Don't Let His Trade Policy Fool You: Trump Is a Neoliberal." *Washington Post*, March 22, 2017. Accessed March 29, 2017. https://www.washingtonpost.com/posteverything/wp/2017/03/22/dont-let-his-trade-policy-fool-you-trump-is-a-neoliberal/?utm_term=.984d3696cce5.
Best, Jacqueline, and Matthew Paterson, eds. 2010. *Cultural Political Economy*. New York: Routledge.
Billig, Michael. 1995. *Banal Nationalism*. London: Sage.
Biradavolu, Monica R. 2008. *Indian Entrepreneurs in Silicon Valley: The Making of a Transnational Techno-Capitalist Class*. Amherst, NY: Cambria Press.
Bleiker, Roland. 2009. *Aesthetics and World Politics*. New York: Palgrave Macmillan.
———. 2015. "Pluralist Methods for Visual Global Politics." *Millennium: Journal of International Studies* 43, no. 3: 872–890.
Blyth, Mark. 2016. "Global Trumpism: Why Trump's Victory Was 30 Years in the Making and Why It Won't Stop Here." *Foreign Affairs*, November 15, 2016. Accessed January 24, 2017. https://www.foreignaffairs.com/articles/2016-11-15/global-trumpism.
Boano, Camillo, and Francisco Vergara-Perucich, eds. 2017. *Neoliberalism and Urban Development in Latin America: The Case of Santiago*. New York: Routledge.
Bogaert, Koenraad. 2018. *Globalized Authoritarianism: Megaprojects, Slums, and Class Relations in Urban Morocco*. Minneapolis: University of Minnesota Press.
Bohland, Jon D. 2013. "'And They Have a Plan': Critical Reflections on *Battlestar Galactica* and the Hyperreal Genocide." In *Battlestar Galactica and International Relations*, edited by Nicholas J. Kiersey and Iver B. Neumann, 98–118. New York: Routledge.
Bond, Shannon. 2017. "Super Bowl Ad Lands Budweiser in US Immigration Debate." *Financial Times*. January 31, 2017. Accessed June 29, 2019. https://www.ft.com/content/ffc860a6-e800-11e6-893c-082c54a7f539.
Bonin, Hubert. 2016. "Concluding Remarks: Colonial Banking, Imperial Banking, Overseas Banking, Imperialist Banking: Convergences, Osmoses and Differentiation." In

Colonial and Imperial Banking History, edited by Hubert Bonin and Nuno Valério, 174–182. New York: Routledge.
Borger, Julian. 2018. "Bolton Praises Bolsonaro while Declaring 'Troika of Tyranny' in Latin America." *The Guardian*. November 1, 2018. Accessed January 12, 2022. https://www.theguardian.com/us-news/2018/nov/01/trump-admin-bolsonaro-praise-john-bolton-troika-tyranny-latin-america.
Boryczka, Jocelyn M., and Jennifer Leigh Disney. 2015. "Intersectionality for the Global Age." *New Political Science* 37, no. 4: 447–457.
Botta, Paulo. 2012. "Las nuevas relaciones entre Latinoamérica y Oriente Medio." *Araucaria: Revista Iberoamericana de Filosofía, Política y Humanidades* (Seville) 28: 71–72.
Bowles, Nellie. 2011. "Patri Friedman Makes Waves with 'Seasteading' Plan." *SFGate*. June 1, 2011. Accessed January 29, 2016. http://www.sfgate.com/news/article/Patri-Friedman-makes-waves-with-seasteading-plan-2369999.php.
Branscome, Eva. 2011. "The True Counterfeits of Banksy: Radical Walls of Complicity and Subversion." *Architectural Design* 81, no. 5: 114–121.
Bray, Donald W. 1962. "The Political Emergence of Arab-Chileans, 1952–1958." *Journal of Inter-American Studies* 4, no. 4: 557–562.
Brégain, Gildas. 2011. "L'influence de la tutelle mandataire française sur l'identification des élites syriennes et libanaises devant la société argentine (1900–1946)." *Revue Européenne des Migrations Internationales* 27, no. 3: 177–199.
Bresser-Pereira, Luiz Carlos. 2015. "State-Society Cycles and Political Pacts in a National-Dependent Society: Brazil." *Latin American Research Review* 50, no. 2: 3–22.
Brodzinsky, Sibylla. 2014. "¡Bienvenido, Habibi!" *Foreign Policy*. September 16, 2014. Accessed January 29, 2016. http://foreignpolicy.com/2014/09/16/bienvenido-habibi/.
Brown, Wendy. 2010. *Walled States, Waning Sovereignty*. Brooklyn: Zone Books.
———. 2015. *Undoing the Demos: Neoliberalism's Stealth Revolution*. New York: Zone Books.
———. 2018. "Neoliberalism's Frankenstein: Authoritarian Freedom in Twenty-First Century 'Democracies.'" *Critical Times: Interventions in Global Critical Theory* 1, no. 1: 60–79.
———. 2019. *In the Ruins of Neoliberalism: The Rise of Antidemocratic Politics in the West*. New York: Columbia University Press.
Brownsell, Alex. 2018. "HSBC Shares Internationalist Vision for Brexit Britain with 'Global Citizen' Campaign." *Campaign*. January 2, 2018. Accessed October 17, 2019. https://www.campaignlive.co.uk/article/hsbc-shares-internationalist-vision-brexit-britain-global-citizen-campaign/1453460.
Brun, Élodie. 2011. "Brazil into the Mediterranean: Strategic Outbreak on Socio-historical Background." *Revista Conjuntura Austral* (Porto Alegre) 2, no. 5: 26–44.
———. 2017. "Brazilian Links with the Middle East Since the Impeachment." *Mundorama—Revista de Divulgação Científica em Relações Internacionais*. April 8, 2017. Accessed April 18, 2017. https://www.mundorama.net/?p=23466.
Buainain, Antônio Márcio, Rodrigo Lanna, and Zander Navarro, eds. 2019. *Agricultural Development in Brazil: The Rise of a Global Agro-Food Power*. New York: Routledge.
Budd, Adrian. 2013. *Class, States and International Relations*. New York: Routledge.
Burton, Guy. 2013. "Emerging Powers and the Israeli-Palestinian Conflict: The Case of Brazil and Venezuela." Issam Fares Institute for Public Policy and International Affairs (American University of Beirut) working paper: 1–21.
———. 2018. *Rising Powers and the Arab–Israeli Conflict since 1947*. Lanham, MD: Lexington Books.

Caleiro, João Pedro, and Clara Cerioni. 2018. "Bolsonaro anuncia diplomata Ernesto Araújo para Relações Exteriores." *Exame* (São Paulo). November 14, 2018. Accessed January 5, 2019. https://exame.abril.com.br/brasil/diplomata-ernesto-araujo-e-anunciado-ministro-de-relacoes-exteriores/.

Callahan, William A. 2020. *Sensible Politics: Visualizing International Relations*. New York: Oxford University Press.

Callinicos, Alex. 1989. *Against Postmodernism: A Marxist Critique*. Cambridge, UK: Polity.

Callinicos, Alex, and Justin Rosenberg. 2008. "Uneven and Combined Development: The Social-Relational Substratum of 'the International'? An Exchange of Letters." *Cambridge Review of International Affairs* 21, no. 1: 77–112.

Callison, William, and Quinn Slobodian. 2021. "Coronapolitics from the Reichstag to the Capitol." *Boston Review*. January 12, 2021. Accessed January 15, 2022. https://bostonreview.net/articles/quinn-slobodian-toxic-politics-coronakspeticism/.

Camayd-Freixas, Erik, ed. 2013. *Orientalism and Identity in Latin America: Fashioning Self and Other from the (Post)Colonial Margin*. Tucson: University of Arizona Press.

Campbell, David. 2007. "Geopolitics and Visuality: Sighting the Darfur Conflict." *Political Geography* 26, no. 4: 357–382.

Campbell, Matthew. 2017. "Is Emirates Airline Running Out of Sky?" *Bloomberg Businessweek*. January 4, 2017. Accessed March 13, 2017. https://www.bloomberg.com/news/features/2017-01-05/is-emirates-airline-running-out-of-sky.

Cardoso, Fernando Henrique. 1977. "The Consumption of Dependency Theory in the United States." *Latin American Research Review* 12, no. 3: 7–24.

Cardoso, Fernando Henrique, and Enzo Faletto. 1979. *Dependency and Development in Latin America*. Berkeley: University of California Press.

Carranza, Mario E. 2006. "Clinging Together: Mercosur's Ambitious External Agenda, Its Internal Crisis, and the Future of Regional Economic Integration in South America." *Review of International Political Economy* 13, no. 5: 802–829.

Carrieri, Marcos. 2013. "Further Space for Growth." *Brazil-Arab News Agency*. March 25, 2013. Accessed January 30, 2016. http://www2.anba.com.br/noticia/20002528/special-reports/further-space-for-growth/.

Carroll, William K. 2010. *The Making of a Transnational Capitalist Class: Corporate Power in the 21st Century*. New York: Zed Books.

———. 2012. "Global, Transnational, Regional, National: The Need for Nuance in Theorizing Global Capitalism." *Critical Sociology* 38, no. 3: 365–371.

Carvalho, Bruno. 2013. *Porous City: A Cultural History of Rio de Janeiro*. Liverpool, UK: Liverpool University Press.

Caso, Federica, and Caitlin Hamilton. 2015. *Popular Culture and World Politics: Theories, Methods, Pedagogies*. Bristol, UK: E-International Relations.

Castañeda, Jorge G. 2006. "Latin America's Left Turn." *Foreign Affairs* (May/June). Accessed October 31, 2014. http://www.foreignaffairs.com/articles/61702/jorge-g-castaneda/latin-americas-left-turn.

Castells, Manuel. 2010a. *The Power of Identity*. 2nd ed. Malden, MA: Wiley-Blackwell.

———. 2010b. *The Rise of the Network Society*. 2nd ed. Malden, MA: Wiley-Blackwell.

Chak, Avinash. 2015. "Trump v Le Pen: In Their Own Words." *BBC News*. December 12, 2015. Accessed January 29, 2016. http://www.bbc.com/news/magazine-35075439.

Chandra, Uday. 2013. "The Case for a Postcolonial Approach to the Study of Politics." *New Political Science*. 35, no. 3: 479–491.

Chang, Ha-Joon. 2009. *Bad Samaritans: The Myth of Free Trade and the Secret History of Capitalism*. New York: Bloomsbury.
Chapman, Debra, Tania Ruiz-Chapman, and Peter Eglin. 2018. "Global Citizenship as Neoliberal Propaganda: A Political-Economic and Postcolonial Critique." *Alternate Routes: A Journal of Critical Social Research* 29, no. 1: 142–166.
———, eds. 2020. *The Global Citizenship Nexus: Critical Studies*. New York: Routledge.
Chappell, Bill. 2015. "Anheuser-Busch InBev and SABMiller Agree On Merger Terms." *NPR*. November 11, 2015. Accessed January 29, 2016. http://www.npr.org/sections/thetwo-way/2015/11/11/455597514/anheuser-busch-inbev-and-sabmiller-agree-on-merger-terms.
Chesnut, R. Andrew. 2003. *Competitive Spirits: Latin America's New Religious Economy*. New York: Oxford University Press.
Chibber, Vivek. 2013a. "How Does the Subaltern Speak?" *Jacobin* (April). Accessed March 3, 2014. https://www.jacobinmag.com/2013/04/how-does-the-subaltern-speak/.
———. 2013b. *Postcolonial Theory and the Specter of Capital*. Brooklyn: Verso.
Chitwood, Ken. 2021. *The Muslims of Latin America and the Caribbean*. Boulder, CO: Lynne Rienner.
Chomsky, Noam. 1996. "Old Wine in New Bottles: A Bitter Taste." *Electronic Journal of Radical Organization Theory* (June). Accessed January 15, 2022. https://chomsky.info/199606__/.
Civantos, Christina. 2006. *Between Argentines and Arabs: Argentine Orientalism, Arab Immigrants, and the Writing of Identity*. Albany: State University of New York Press.
Clemesha, Arlene, and Silvia Ferabolli. 2020. "Studying the Middle East from Brazil: Reflections on a Different Worldview." *Estudos internacionais* (Belo Horizonte) 8, no. 4: 97–109.
CNN. 2011. "Full Transcript of CNN National Security Debate." November 22, 2011. Accessed May 27, 2014. http://transcripts.cnn.com/TRANSCRIPTS/1111/22/se.06.html.
Coomes, Phil. 2015. "Instagram: The 'Homeless' Chief Executive." *BBC News*. January 22, 2015. Accessed January 29, 2016. http://www.bbc.com/news/in-pictures-30912897.
Cooper, Melinda, and Liz McFall. 2017. "Ten Years After: It's the Economy and Culture, Stupid!" *Journal of Cultural Economy* 10, no. 1: 1–7.
Corriente, Federico. 2008. *Dictionary of Arabic and Allied Loanwords: Spanish, Portuguese, Catalan, Galician and Kindred Dialects*. Leiden, The Netherlands: Brill.
Costa, Thomaz G., and Gastón H. Schulmeister. 2007. "The Puzzle of the Iguazu Tri-Border Area: Many Questions and Few Answers Regarding Organised Crime and Terrorism Links." *Global Crime* 8, no. 1: 26–39.
Costas, Ruth. 2014. "Fortuna de super-ricos é 'incontrolável', diz pesquisador." *BBC Brasil*. November 10, 2014. Accessed February 1, 2016. https://www.bbc.com/portuguese/noticias/2014/11/141104_superricos_ru.
Cox, Robert W. 1981. "Social Forces, States and World Orders: Beyond International Relations Theory." *Millennium: Journal of International Studies* 10, no. 2: 126–155.
Cuadros, Alex. 2016. *Brazillionaires: Wealth, Power, Decadence, and Hope in an American Country*. New York: Spiegel & Grau.
Dabashi, Hamid. 2015. *Can Non-Europeans Think?* London: Zed Books.
Dahi, Omar Sami, and Firat Demir. 2019. *South-South Trade and Finance in the Twenty-First Century: Rise of the South or a Second Great Divergence*. New York: Anthem.

Daniel, Isaura. 2020. "Lideranças empresariais: 10% são árabes e descendentes." *ANBA (Agência de Notícias Brasil-Árabe)*. July 22, 2020. Accessed June 4, 2021. https://anba.com.br/liderancas-empresariais-10-sao-arabes-e-descendentes/.

Daoud, Arezki. 2016. "Energy Cooperation with Latin America: An Arab Perspective." In *The Arab World and Latin America: Economic and Political Relations in the Twenty-First Century*, edited by Fehmy Saddy, 207–223. London: I. B. Tauris.

Dardot, Pierre, and Christian Laval. 2017. *The New Way of the World: On Neoliberal Society*. Brooklyn: Verso.

Darian-Smith, Eve, and Philip C. McCarty. 2017. *The Global Turn: Theories, Research Designs, and Methods for Global Studies*. Oakland: University of California Press.

Dávila, Arlene. 2016. *El Mall: The Spatial and Class Politics of Shopping Malls in Latin America*. Oakland: University of California Press.

de los Reyes, Ignacio. 2014. "El exprisionero de Guantánamo fascinado por el mate uruguayo." *BBC Mundo*. December 8, 2014. Accessed January 29, 2016. http://www.bbc.com/mundo/noticias/2014/12/141208_uruguay_guantanamo_prisioneros_refugiados_guantanamo_mate_irm.

de Ramón, Armando. 2010. *Historia de Chile: Desde la invasión incaica hasta nuestros días (1500–2000)*. Santiago de Chile: Editorial Catalonia.

DeShazo, Peter, and Johanna Mendelson Forman. 2010. "Latin America and the Middle East: The Dynamic of an Evolving Relationship." Preliminary report, FIU-SOUTHCOM Academic Partnership.

DeYoung, Karen. 2019. "Pompeo Focuses on Iran and Hezbollah at Latin America Counterterrorism Conference." *Washington Post*, July 19, 2019. Accessed January 10, 2022. https://www.washingtonpost.com/national-security/pompeo-focuses-on-iran-and-hezbollah-at-latin-america-counterterrorism-conference/2019/07/19/2c14c36a-aa65-11e9-9214-246e594de5d5_story.html.

Dirlik, Arif. 2000. *Postmodernity's Histories: The Past as Legacy and Project*. Lanham, MD: Rowman & Littlefield.

Dominguez, Francisco, Geraldine Lievesley, and Steve Ludlam, eds. 2011. *Right-Wing Politics in the New Latin America*. New York: Zed Books.

Dorfman, Ariel, and Armand Mattelart. 1991. *How to Read Donald Duck: Imperialist Ideology in the Disney Comic*. New York: I.G. Editions.

dos Santos Guimarães, Joel. 2012. "Arabs and Agribusiness." *Brazil-Arab News Agency*. February 7, 2012. Accessed May 31, 2014. http://www2.anba.com.br/noticia_fronteira.kmf?cod=13061802.

Downie, James. 2013. "Pope Francis's Stinging Critique of Capitalism." *Washington Post*, November 26, 2013. Accessed January 30, 2016. https://www.washingtonpost.com/blogs/post-partisan/wp/2013/11/26/pope-franciss-stinging-critique-of-capitalism/.

Drew, Christopher, and Nicola Clark. 2012. "In Appeal, W.T.O. Upholds a Decision Against Boeing." *New York Times*, March 12, 2012. Accessed January 30, 2016. http://www.nytimes.com/2012/03/13/business/global/trade-group-upholds-ruling-on-boeing-subsidies.html?_r=0.

du Gay, Paul, and Michael Pryke, eds. 2002. *Cultural Economy*. London: Sage.

The Economist. 2012. "Shell Companies: Launderers Anonymous." September 22, 2012. Accessed January 30, 2016. http://www.economist.com/node/21563286.

———. 2014. "The Tragedy of Argentina: A Century of Decline." February 15, 2014. Accessed January 30, 2016. http://www.economist.com/news/briefing/21596582-one-hundred-years-ago-argentina-was-future-what-went-wrong-century-decline.

Eggert, David. 2015. "Bill Clinton: 'Make Something Good Happen' After Attacks." Associated Press. November 18, 2015. Accessed January 29, 2016. http://bigstory.ap.org/article/f7ebd75133be426ca6e67bb8768c802d/bill-clinton-make-something-good-happen-after-attacks.

Elkin, Judith Laikin. 2014. *The Jews of Latin America*. 3rd ed. Boulder, CO: Lynne Rienner.

Elliott, Larry. 2016. "Richest 62 People as Wealthy as Half of World's Population, Says Oxfam." *The Guardian*, January 18, 2016. Accessed January 29, 2016. http://www.theguardian.com/business/2016/jan/18/richest-62-billionaires-wealthy-half-world-population-combined.

El Mercurio (Santiago de Chile). 2015. "Pdte. del Banco de Palestina viene a abrir oficina: Será el primer banco árabe en Latinoamérica." October 25, 2015. Accessed February 1, 2016. http://diario.elmercurio.com/detalle/index.asp?id={26d3e357-4310-4624-894b-a862e4b0eefd}.

Elsey, Brenda. 2011. *Citizens and Sportsmen: Fútbol and Politics in Twentieth-Century Chile*. Austin: University of Texas Press.

Emerson, Robert M., Rachel I. Fretz, and Linda L. Shaw. 1995. *Writing Ethnographic Fieldnotes*. Chicago: University of Chicago Press.

Erkmen, T. Deniz. 2015. "Houses on Wheels: National Attachment, Belonging, and Cosmopolitanism in Narratives of Transnational Professionals." *Studies in Ethnicity and Nationalism* 15, no. 1: 26–47.

Evans, Peter. 2008. "Is an Alternative Globalization Possible?" *Politics & Society* 36, no. 2: 271–305.

Ewalt, David M. 2005. "C. Montgomery Burns." *Forbes*. December 6, 2005. Accessed January 29, 2016. http://www.forbes.com/2005/12/06/montomery-burns-wealt_cx_de_05fict15_1206burnsprofile.html.

Fanon, Frantz. 2005. *The Wretched of the Earth*. New York: Grove Press.

Farrell, Sean. 2011. "Gulliver Moves HSBC Away from 'World's Local Bank' Tag in Review." *The Independent* (London), May 11, 2011. Accessed January 30, 2016. http://www.independent.co.uk/news/business/news/gulliver-moves-hsbc-away-from-worlds-local-bank-tag-in-review-2282646.html.

Fattah, Hassan M. 2005. "Syrian Troops Leave Lebanon After 29-Year Occupation." *New York Times*, April 26, 2005. Accessed December 1, 2015. http://www.nytimes.com/2005/04/26/international/middleeast/26cnd-lebanon.html?_r=0.

Ferabolli, Silvia. 2017. "Regions that Matter: The Arab–South American Interregional Space." *Third World Quarterly* 38, no. 8: 1767–1781.

———. 2021. "Space Making in the Global South: Lessons from the GCC-Mercosur Agreement." *Contexto Internacional* 43, no. 1: 9–31.

Field, Les W. 2017. "The Colombia-Israel Nexus: Toward Historical and Analytic Contexts." *Latin American Research Review* 52, no. 4: 639–653.

Figge, Lukas, and Pim Martens. 2014. "Globalisation Continues: The Maastricht Globalisation Index Revisited and Updated." *Globalizations* 11, no. 6: 875–893.

Fisher, William F., and Thomas Ponniah, eds. 2019. *Another World Is Possible: World Social Forum Proposals for an Alternative Globalization*. London: Zed Books.

Fitch, Melissa A. 2015. *Global Tangos: Travels in the Transnational Imaginary*. Lanham, MD: Bucknell University Press.

Florida, Richard. 2011. "A Floating Silicon Valley for Techies Without Green Cards." *CityLab*. December 2, 2011. Accessed January 29, 2016. http://www.citylab.com/tech/2011/12/floating-city-inventors-without-green-cards/624/.

Foote, Nicola, and Michael Goebel, eds. 2014. *Immigration and National Identities in Latin America*. Gainesville: University Press of Florida.

Forero, Juan, and Janine Zacharia. 2011. "Palestinians Seek Global Recognition through South America." *Washington Post*, February 17, 2011. Accessed May 31, 2014. http://www.washingtonpost.com/wp-dyn/content/article/2011/02/16/AR2011021602232.html.

Fraser, Nancy. 2019. *The Old Is Dying and the New Cannot Be Born: From Progressive Neoliberalism to Trump and Beyond*. Brooklyn: Verso.

Freedman, Jonathan. 2005. "'The Ethics of Identity': A Rooted Cosmopolitan." *New York Times*, June 12, 2005. Accessed January 30, 2016. http://www.nytimes.com/2005/06/12/books/review/the-ethics-of-identity-a-rooted-cosmopolitan.html?_r=1.

Friedman, Thomas L. 2005. *The World Is Flat: A Brief History of the Twenty-first Century*. New York: Farrar, Straus and Giroux.

———. 2012. *The Lexus and the Olive Tree: Understanding Globalization*. New York: Picador.

Fujii, Lee Ann. 2017. *Interviewing in Social Science Research: A Relational Approach*. New York: Routledge.

Fukuyama, Francis. 1992. *The End of History and the Last Man*. New York: Free Press.

Fulcher, James. 2004. *Capitalism: A Very Short Introduction*. New York: Oxford University Press.

FUNAG (Fundação Alexandre de Gusmão). 2001. *Relações entre o Brasil e o Mundo Árabe: construção e perspectivas*. Brasília: FUNAG.

Funk, Kevin. 2012. "'Today There Are No Indigenous People' in Chile?: Connecting the Mapuche Struggle to Anti-Neoliberal Mobilizations in South America." *Journal of Politics in Latin America* 4, no. 2: 125–140.

———. 2013. "The Political Economy of South America's Global South Relations: States, Transnational Capital, and Social Movements." *The Latin Americanist* 57, no. 1: 3–20.

———. 2015a. "The Global South Is Dead, Long Live the Global South! The Intersectionality of Social and Geographic Hierarchies in Global Capitalism." *New Political Science* 37, no. 4: 582–603.

———. 2015b. "U.S.–Latin American Relations after September 11, 2001: Between Change and Continuity." In *The Palgrave Encyclopedia of Imperialism and Anti-Imperialism*, edited by Immanuel Ness and Zak Cope, 454–462. New York: Palgrave Macmillan.

———. 2016. "A Not-So-Fateful Triangle? Latin America, China, and the United States." *International Studies Review* 18, no. 4: 725–727.

———. 2018. "Between Freedom and Futility: On the Political Uses of Corporate Globalizing Discourses." *Journal of Cultural Economy* 11, no. 6: 565–590.

———. 2019. "Making Interpretivism Visible: Reflections after a Decade of the Methods Café." *PS: Political Science & Politics* 52, no. 3: 465–469.

———. 2020. "Constructing 'Progressive Neoliberal' Citizens: The Political Economy of Corporate Global Imaginaries." In *The Global Citizenship Nexus: Critical Studies*, edited by Debra Chapman, Tania Ruiz-Chapman, and Peter Eglin, 211–240. New York: Routledge.

Funk, Kevin, and Sebastián Sclofsky. 2021. "The Liberal Ideology: On Intellectual Pluralism and the Marginalization of Marxism in US Political Science." *PS: Political Science & Politics* 54, no. 3: 593–597.

García Canclini, Néstor. 2014. *Imagined Globalization*. Durham, NC: Duke University Press.

Garcia Fonseca, Bruna. 2020. "Grupo Parlamentar Brasil Países-Árabes é lançado em webinar." *ANBA (Agência de Notícias Brasil-Árabe)*. April 24, 2020. Accessed June 4, 2021. https://anba.com.br/grupo-parlamentar-brasil-paises-arabes-e-lancado-em-webinar/.

García Márquez, Gabriel. 1967. *Cien años de soledad*. Buenos Aires: Editorial Sudamericana.

———. 1981. *Crónica de una muerte anunciada*. Bogotá: Oveja Negra.

———. 1986. *La aventura de Miguel Littín clandestino en Chile*. Bogotá: Oveja Negra.

Gardini, Gian Luca. 2011. "Latin American Foreign Policies between Ideology and Pragmatism: A Framework for Analysis." In *Latin American Foreign Policies: Between Ideology and Pragmatism*, edited by Gian Luca Gardini and Peter Lambert, 13–34. New York: Palgrave Macmillan.

———. 2012. *Latin America in the 21st Century: Nations, Regionalism, Globalization*. London: Zed Books.

Garsd, Jasmine. 2015. "Saudade: An Untranslatable, Undeniably Potent Word." NPR Music. January 8, 2015. Accessed January 30, 2016. http://www.npr.org/sections/altlatino/2014/02/28/282552613/saudade-an-untranslatable-undeniably-potent-word.

Gelles, David, and Dan Horch. 2015. "Two Deals Bring Attention to Banking's Safra Family." *New York Times*, February 18, 2015. Accessed January 29, 2016. http://dealbook.nytimes.com/2015/02/18/two-deals-bring-attention-to-bankings-safra-family/?_r=1.

George, Susan. 2005. "If You Want to Be Relevant: Advice to the Academic from a Scholar-Activist." In *Critical Globalization Studies*, edited by Richard P. Appelbaum and William I. Robinson, 3–10. New York: Routledge

Gilbert, Dennis. 2016. "The Middle Class: Political, Economic, and Social Perspectives." *Latin American Research Review* 51, no. 1: 255–265.

Gilpin, Robert. 2001. *Global Political Economy: Understanding the International Economic Order*. Princeton, NJ: Princeton University Press.

Glade, William. 1983. "The Levantines in Latin America." *The American Economic Review* 73, no. 2: 118–22.

Glick, Edward B. 1959. "Latin America and the Palestine Partition Resolution." *Journal of Inter-American Studies* 1, no. 2: 211–222.

Glick Schiller, Nina, Linda Basch, and Cristina Blanc-Szanton. 1992. "Transnationalism: A New Analytic Framework for Understanding Migration." *Annals of the New York Academy of Sciences* 645: 1–24.

Goldman, Emma. 1917. *Anarchism and Other Essays*. 3rd ed. New York: Mother Earth Publishing Association.

Gomes, Fabiola. 2014. "Brazil Can Fill U.S. Chicken Exports to Russia—Industry." Reuters. August 7, 2014. Accessed January 30, 2016. http://in.reuters.com/article/ukraine-crisis-brazil-chicken-idINL2N0QC28I20140806.

Gomez, Edward M. 2005. "World Views: U.S. Snubbed at First South American-Arab Summit." *SFGate*. May 17, 2005. Accessed May 31, 2014. http://www.sfgate.com/politics/article/WORLD-VIEWS-U-S-snubbed-at-first-South-2670152.php.

González, Nancie L. 1993. *Dollar, Dove, and Eagle: One Hundred Years of Palestinian Migration to Honduras*. Ann Arbor: University of Michigan Press.

Goodson, Scott. 2016. "Emirates Hello Tomorrow—Why It Helped Build the World's Favorite Airline." *HuffPost*. June 1, 2016. Accessed April 10, 2018. https://www.huffpost.com/entry/emirates-hello-tomorrow-w_b_10220336.

Gramsci, Antonio. 1971. *Selections from the Prison Notebooks*. New York: International Publishers.
Grandin, Greg. 2015. "The TPP Will Finish What Chile's Dictatorship Started." *The Nation*. September 11, 2015. Accessed January 29, 2016. http://www.thenation.com/article/the-tpp-will-finish-what-chiles-dictatorship-started/.
Grayson, Kyle, Matt Davies, and Simon Philpott. 2009. "Pop Goes IR? Researching the Popular Culture–World Politics Continuum." *Politics* 29, no. 3: 155–163.
Grimley, Naomi. 2016. "Identity 2016: 'Global Citizenship' Rising, Poll Suggests." *BBC News*. April 28, 2016. Accessed April 26, 2017. http://www.bbc.com/news/world-36139904.
Grondona, Mariano. 2003. "Kirchner, entre Lula, Chávez, Powell y Lagos." *La Nación* (Buenos Aires). June 15, 2003. Accessed January 30, 2016. http://www.lanacion.com.ar/503898-kirchner-entre-lula-chavez-powell-y-lagos.
Gruffydd Jones, Branwen, ed. 2006. *Decolonizing International Relations*. Lanham, MD: Rowman & Littlefield.
Guardiola Rivera, Oscar. 2011. *What If Latin America Ruled the World?: How the South Will Take the North Through the 21st Century*. London: Bloomsbury.
Gustafson, Per. 2009. "More Cosmopolitan, No Less Local: The Orientations of International Travelers." *European Societies* 11, no. 1: 25–47.
Gutiérrez Rivera, Lirio. 2014. "Assimilation or Cultural Difference? Palestinian Immigrants in Honduras." *Revista de Estudios Sociales* (Bogotá) 48: 57–68.
Haass, Richard. 2017. *A World in Disarray: American Foreign Policy and the Crisis of the Old Order*. New York: Penguin.
Haffner, Jacqueline A. H., and Carla A. R. Holand. 2012. "Relações econômicas entre o Brasil e o Oriente Médio no governo Lula." *Ciências & Letras* (Porto Alegre) 51: 135–156.
Hall, Peter A. 2003. "Aligning Ontology and Methodology in Comparative Research." In *Comparative Historical Analysis in the Social Sciences*, edited by James Mahoney and Dietrich Rueschemeyer, 373–406. New York: Cambridge University Press.
Hardt, Michael, and Antonio Negri. 2000. *Empire*. Cambridge, MA: Harvard University Press.
Harold, Christine. 2004. "Pranking Rhetoric: 'Culture Jamming' as Media Activism." *Critical Studies in Media Communication* 21, no. 3: 189–211.
Harrington, Brooke. 2016. *Capital without Borders: Wealth Managers and the One Percent*. Cambridge, MA: Harvard University Press.
———. 2019. "'Aristocrats Are Anarchists': Why the Wealthy Back Trump and Brexit." *The Guardian*, February 7, 2019. Accessed June 16, 2021. https://www.theguardian.com/us-news/2019/feb/07/why-the-wealthy-back-trump-and-brexit.
Harris, Jerry. 2016. *Global Capitalism and the Crisis of Democracy*. Atlanta: Clarity.
Harvey, David. 1990. *The Condition of Postmodernity: An Enquiry into the Origins of Cultural Change*. Malden, MA: Blackwell.
———. 2006. *Spaces of Global Capitalism: A Theory of Uneven Geographical Development*. New York: Verso.
———. 2007. *A Brief History of Neoliberalism*. New York: Oxford University Press.
———. 2010. *The Enigma of Capital and the Crises of Capitalism*. New York: Oxford University Press.
———. 2018. *Marx, Capital, and the Madness of Economic Reason*. New York: Oxford University Press.
Haughney, Diane. 2006. *Neoliberal Economics, Democratic Transition, and Mapuche Demands for Rights in Chile*. Gainesville: University Press of Florida.

Heemskerk, Eelke M., and Frank W. Takes. 2016. "The Corporate Elite Community Structure of Global Capitalism." *New Political Economy* 21, no. 1: 90–118.

Hellinger, Daniel. 2015. *Comparative Politics of Latin America: Democracy at Last?* 2nd ed. New York: Routledge.

Henríquez, Andrea. 2008. "Chile recibirá a refugiados palestinos." *BBC Mundo*. March 19, 2008. Accessed January 29, 2016. http://news.bbc.co.uk/hi/spanish/international/newsid_7305000/7305722.stm.

Herrera Navarro, Ramón. 2008. *Chávez y el mundo árabe*. Caracas: El Perro y la Rana.

Hickel, Jason. 2018. *The Divide: Global Inequality from Conquest to Free Markets*. New York: W. W. Norton.

Hilu da Rocha Pinto, Paulo Gabriel. 2010. *Árabes no Rio de Janeiro: Uma Identidade Plural*. Rio de Janeiro: Cidade Viva.

Hirst, Paul, Grahame Thompson, and Simon Bromley. 2009. *Globalization in Question*. 3rd ed. Malden, MA: Polity.

Ho, Karen. 2005. "Situating Global Capitalisms: A View from Wall Street Investment Banks." *Cultural Anthropology* 20, no. 1: 68–96.

———. 2009. *Liquidated: An Ethnography of Wall Street*. Durham, NC: Duke University Press.

Hoffman, Stanley. 1977. "An American Social Science: International Relations." *Daedalus* 106, no. 3: 41–60.

Holder, Alex. 2017. "Sex Doesn't Sell Any More, Activism Does. And Don't the Big Brands Know It." *The Guardian*, February 3, 2017. Accessed March 7, 2017. https://www.theguardian.com/commentisfree/2017/feb/03/activism-sells-brands-social-conscience-advertising.

Howe, Marvine. 1974. "Arabs Weigh Investment of Oil Revenue in Brazil." *New York Times*, February 26, 1974, 49, 57.

Hozić, Aida A. 2006. "The Balkan Merchants: Changing Borders and Informal Transnationalization." *Ethnopolitics* 5, no. 3: 243–256.

———. 2014. "Between 'National' and 'Transnational': Film Diffusion as World Politics." *International Studies Review* 16, no. 2: 229–239.

Hu-DeHart, Evelyn. 2009. "Multiculturalism in Latin American Studies: Locating the 'Asian' Immigrant; or, Where Are the *Chinos* and *Turcos*?" *Latin American Research Review* 44, no. 2: 235–242.

Huntington, Samuel P. 1993. "The Clash of Civilizations?" *Foreign Affairs* 72, no. 3: 22–23, 25–32, 39–41, 49.

———. 2004. "Dead Souls: The Denationalization of the American Elite." *The National Interest*. March 1, 2004. Accessed January 13, 2014. http://nationalinterest.org/article/dead-souls-the-denationalization-of-the-american-elite-620?page=show.

Hyland, Jr., Steven. 2011. "'Arisen from Deep Slumber': Transnational Politics and Competing Nationalisms among Syrian Immigrants in Argentina, 1900–1922." *Journal of Latin American Studies* 43, no. 3: 547–574.

———. 2017. *More Argentine Than You: Arabic-Speaking Immigrants in Argentina*. Albuquerque: University of New Mexico Press.

Itamaraty (Ministry of External Relations of Brazil). 2008. "Tratado Constitutivo da União de Nações Sul-Americanas—Brasília." May 23, 2008. Accessed May 17, 2013. http://www.itamaraty.gov.br/sala-deimprensa/notas-a-imprensa/2008/05/23/tratado-constitutivo-dauniao-de-nacoes-sul.

Itzigsohn, José, and Julián Rebón. 2015. "The Recuperation of Enterprises: Defending Workers' Lifeworld, Creating New Tools of Contention." *Latin American Research Review* 50, no. 4: 178–196.

Jackson, Patrick Thaddeus. 2015. "Must International Studies Be a Science?" *Millennium* 43, no. 3: 942–65.

Jansen, Bart. 2017. "Airline Group Urges Trump to Keep Borders Open." *USA Today*, March 2, 2017. Accessed March 17, 2017. http://www.usatoday.com/story/travel/flights/todayinthesky/2017/03/02/airline-group-urges-trump-keep-borders-open/98644448/.

Jardina, Ashley. 2019. *White Identity Politics*. Cambridge, UK: Cambridge University Press.

Johnson, Chalmers. 1997. "Preconception vs. Observation, or the Contributions of Rational Choice Theory and Area Studies to Contemporary Political Science." *PS: Political Science and Politics* 30, no. 2: 170–174.

Jones, Reece. 2016. *Violent Borders: Refugees and the Right to Move*. Brooklyn: Verso.

Jordan, Miriam. 2014. "Investor Visas Soaked Up by Chinese." *Wall Street Journal*, August 27, 2014. Accessed January 29, 2016. http://www.wsj.com/articles/investor-visas-soaked-up-by-chinese-1409095982.

Juris, Jeffrey S. 2008. *Networking Futures: The Movements against Corporate Globalization*. Durham, NC: Duke University Press.

Justo, Marcelo. 2014. "Las tretas que usan las empresas para evadir impuestos." *BBC Mundo*. October 15, 2014. Accessed January 29, 2016. http://www.bbc.com/mundo/noticias/2014/10/141015_paraisos_fiscales_tretas_evasion_fiscal_aw.

Kahn, Hilary, ed. 2014. *Framing the Global: Entry Points for Research*. Bloomington: Indiana University Press.

Kamola, Isaac. 2013. "Why Global? Diagnosing the Globalization Literature Within a Political Economy of Higher Education." *International Political Sociology* 7, no. 1: 41–58.

———. 2019. *Making the World Global: U.S. Universities and the Production of the Global Imaginary*. Durham, NC: Duke University Press.

Kanna, Ahmed. 2011. *Dubai, the City as Corporation*. Minneapolis: University of Minnesota Press.

Kapoor, Nisha. 2018. *Deport, Deprive, Extradite: 21st Century State Extremism*. Brooklyn: Verso.

Karam, John Tofik. 2007. *Another Arabesque: Syrian-Lebanese Ethnicity in Neoliberal Brazil*. Philadelphia: Temple University Press.

———. 2011. "Crossing the Americas: The U.S. War on Terror and Arab Cross-Border Mobilizations in a South American Frontier Region." *Comparative Studies of South Asia, Africa and the Middle East* 31, no. 2: 251–266.

———. 2012. "Beside Bandung: Historicizing Brazil in the *América do Sul-Países Árabes* Summit." Conference paper presented at the colloquium, "Relations Between the Middle East and Latin America: A Decade of South-South Revival," The Holy Spirit University of Kaslik, Lebanon. November 28–29, 2012.

———. 2013a. "On the Trail and Trial of a Palestinian Diaspora: Mapping South America in the Arab–Israeli Conflict, 1967–1972." *Journal of Latin American Studies* 45, no. 4: 751–777.

———. 2013b. "The Lebanese Diaspora at the Tri-Border and the Redrawing of South American Geopolitics, 1950–1992." *Mashriq & Mahjar: Journal of Middle East Migration Studies* 1, no. 1: 55–84.

———. 2020. *Manifold Destiny: Arabs at an American Crossroads of Exceptional Rule.* Nashville: Vanderbilt University Press.
Kearney, M. 1995. "The Local and the Global: The Anthropology of Globalization and Transnationalism." *Annual Review of Anthropology* 24: 547–565.
Keck, Margaret E., and Kathryn Sikkink. 1998. *Activists beyond Borders: Advocacy Networks in International Politics.* Ithaca, NY: Cornell University Press.
Khalili, Laleh. 2020. *Sinews of War and Trade: Shipping and Capitalism in the Arabian Peninsula.* New York: Verso.
Khan, Aisha, ed. 2015. *Islam and the Americas.* Gainesville: University Press of Florida.
Khanna, Parag. 2016. "The New World Order Is Ruled by Global Corporations and Megacities—Not Countries." April 20, 2016. Accessed April 25, 2017. https://www.fastcompany.com/3059005/the-new-world-order-is-ruled-by-global-corporations-and-megacities-not-countries.
Kiersey, Nicholas J., and Iver B. Neumann, eds. 2013. *Battlestar Galactica and International Relations.* New York: Routledge.
Kiersey, Nicholas, and William Sokoloff. 2019. "The Question of Tactics in an Age of Authoritarian Neoliberalism." *New Political Science* 41, no. 4: 505–513.
King, Gary, Robert O. Keohane, and Sidney Verba. 1994. *Designing Social Inquiry: Scientific Inference in Qualitative Research.* Princeton, NJ: Princeton University Press.
Klein, Herbert S., and Francisco Vidal Luna. 2019. *Feeding the World: Brazil's Transformation into a Modern Agricultural Economy.* New York: Cambridge University Press.
Klein, Naomi. 2003. "Iraq Is Not America's to Sell." *The Guardian*, November 6, 2003. Accessed January 30, 2016. http://www.theguardian.com/world/2003/nov/07/usa.iraq1.
———. 2008. *The Shock Doctrine: The Rise of Disaster Capitalism.* New York: Picador.
Klich, Ignacio, and Jeffrey Lesser, eds. 1998. *Arab and Jewish Immigrants in Latin America: Images and Realities.* Portland, OR: Frank Cass.
Koller, Veronika. 2007. "'The World's Local Bank': Glocalisation as a Strategy in Corporate Branding Discourse." *Social Semiotics* 17, no. 1: 111–131.
Konings, Martijn. 2015. *The Emotional Logic of Capitalism: What Progressives Have Missed.* Stanford, CA: Stanford University Press.
Koo, Hagen. 2016. "The Global Middle Class: How Is It Made, What Does It Represent?" *Globalizations* 13, no. 4: 440–453.
Kowalczyk, Anna. 2020. "Transnational Capitalist Classes and the State in Chile." *New Political Economy* 25, no. 6: 897–912.
Krasner, Stephen D. 1985. *Structural Conflict: The Third World against Global Liberalism.* Berkeley: University of California Press.
Kremerman, Marco. 2013. "El futuro del Plan Laboral de la dictadura." *El Mostrador* (Santiago de Chile). October 18, 2013. Accessed January 30, 2016. http://www.elmostrador.cl/noticias/opinion/2013/10/18/el-futuro-del-plan-laboral-de-la-dictadura/.
Krisher, Tom. 2017. "Auto Workers Union Preparing 'Buy American' Ad Campaign." Boston.com. February 17, 2017. Accessed March 7, 2017. https://www.boston.com/cars/2017-presidents-day-auto-sales/2017/02/17/auto-workers-union-preparing-buy-american-ad-campaign.
Krishnaswamy, Revathi, and John C. Hawley, eds. 2007. *The Postcolonial and the Global.* Minneapolis: University of Minnesota Press.

Kristensen, Peter Marcus. 2015. "Revisiting the 'American Social Science'—Mapping the Geography of International Relations." *International Studies Perspectives* 16, no. 3: 246–269.
Kuttner, Robert. 2018. *Can Democracy Survive Global Capitalism?* New York: W. W. Norton.
Kymlicka, Will, and Kathryn Walker. 2013. *Rooted Cosmopolitanism: Canada and the World*. Vancouver: University of British Columbia Press.
La Nación (Buenos Aires). 2015. "Bachelet marca diferencias: 'Chile es un país serio.'" June 10, 2015. Accessed February 1, 2016. http://www.lanacion.com.ar/1800315-bachelet-marca-diferencias-chile-es-un-pais-serio.
Lapavitsas, Costas. 2019. *The Left Case against the EU*. Medford, MA: Polity.
Lash, Scott, and John Urry. 1994. *Economies of Signs & Space*. London: Sage.
Law, John, and Evelyn Ruppert. 2013. "The Social Life of Methods: Devices." *Journal of Cultural Economy* 6, no. 3: 229–240.
Legg, Benjamin. 2015. "The Bicultural Sex Symbol: Sônia Braga in Brazilian and North American Popular Culture." In *Performing Brazil: Essays on Culture, Identity, and the Performing Arts*, edited by Severino J. Albuquerque and Kathryn Bishop-Sanchez, 202–223. Madison: University of Wisconsin Press.
Lesser, Jeffrey. 2013. *Immigration, Ethnicity, and National Identity in Brazil, 1808 to the Present*. New York: Cambridge University Press.
Levine, Daniel H. 2012. *Politics, Religion & Society in Latin America*. Boulder, CO: Lynne Rienner.
Levitt, Peggy. 2001. *The Transnational Villagers*. Berkeley: University of California Press.
Levy, Dan. 2010. "Banking on Airports: Q&A with HSBC's Global Advertising Head." *Sparksheet*. January 29, 2010. Accessed April 11, 2018. http://sparksheet.com/banking-on-airports-qa-with-hsbcs-global-advertising-head/.
Lipschutz, Ronnie D. 2000. *After Authority: War, Peace, and Global Politics in the 21st Century*. Albany: State University of New York Press.
Lisle, Debbie. 2006. *The Global Politics of Contemporary Travel Writing*. New York: Cambridge University Press.
Lissardy, Gerardo. 2015. "Como o Brasil virou o principal refúgio de sírios na América Latina." *BBC Brasil*. January 14, 2015. Accessed January 29, 2016. http://www.bbc.com/portuguese/noticias/2015/01/150113_sirios_refugiados_brasil_pai.
Logroño Narbona, María del Mar, Paulo G. Pinto, and John Tofik Karam, eds. 2015. *Crescent over Another Horizon: Islam in Latin America, the Caribbean, and Latino USA*. Austin: University of Texas Press.
Long, David, and Brian C. Schmidt, eds. 2005. *Imperialism and Internationalism in the Discipline of International Relations*. Albany: State University of New York Press.
Loofbourow, Lili. 2013. "'No to Profit': Fighting Privatization in Chile." *Boston Review*. May 16, 2013. Accessed January 30, 2016. http://www.bostonreview.net/world/%E2%80%9Cno-profit%E2%80%9D.
Lukács, Georg. 1972. *History and Class Consciousness: Studies in Marxist Dialectics*. Cambridge, MA: The MIT Press.
Luxner, Larry. 2001. "The Arabs of Honduras." *Saudi Aramco World* (July/August). Accessed May 28, 2014. http://www.saudiaramcoworld.com/issue/200104/the.arabs.of.honduras.htm.
———. 2005. "The Arabs of Brazil." *Saudi Aramco World* (September/October). Accessed May 28, 2014. http://www.saudiaramcoworld.com/issue/200505/the.arabs.of.brazil.htm.

MacLean, Nancy. 2017. *Democracy in Chains: The Deep History of the Radical Right's Stealth Plan for America.* New York: Viking.
Magee, Christine. 2015. "With $10M From High Profile Angels, Globality Will Aim to Restructure Global Trade." *TechCrunch.* September 22, 2015. Accessed January 29, 2016. http://techcrunch.com/2015/09/22/with-10m-from-high-profile-angels-globality-will-aim-to-restructure-global-trade/.
Marcuse, Herbert. 1964. *One-Dimensional Man: Studies in the Ideology of Advanced Industrial Society.* Boston: Beacon.
Marston, Rebecca. 2012. "How Globe-trotting Executives Manage Travel Demands." *BBC News.* January 16, 2012. Accessed January 29, 2016. http://www.bbc.com/news/business-16487813.
Martín, Félix E. 2009. "Economic Interdependence, Trade, and Peace in South America." *The Whitehead Journal of Diplomacy and International Relations* 10, no. 1: 143–165.
Marx, Karl. (1978) 1843a. "For a Ruthless Criticism of Everything Existing." In *The Marx-Engels Reader*, 2nd ed., edited by Robert C. Tucker, 12–15. New York: W. W. Norton.
———. (1978) 1843b. "On the Jewish Question." In *The Marx-Engels Reader*, 2nd ed., edited by Robert C. Tucker, 26–52. New York: W. W. Norton.
———. (1978) 1844. *Economic and Philosophic Manuscripts of 1844.* In *The Marx-Engels Reader*, 2nd ed., edited by Robert C. Tucker, 66–125. New York: W. W. Norton.
———. (1978) 1845. "Theses on Feuerbach." In *The Marx-Engels Reader*, 2nd ed., edited by Robert C. Tucker, 143–145. New York: W. W. Norton.
———. (1978) 1846. *The German Ideology: Part I.* In *The Marx-Engels Reader*, 2nd ed., edited by Robert C. Tucker, 146–200. New York: W. W. Norton.
———. (1978) 1852. "The Eighteenth Brumaire of Louis Bonaparte." In *The Marx-Engels Reader*, 2nd ed., edited by Robert C. Tucker, 594–617. New York: W. W. Norton.
———. (1978) 1867. *Capital, Volume One.* In *The Marx-Engels Reader*, 2nd ed., edited by Robert C. Tucker, 294–438. New York: W. W. Norton.
Marx, Karl, and Friedrich Engels. (1978) 1888. *Manifesto of the Communist Party.* In *The Marx-Engels Reader*, 2nd ed., edited by Robert C. Tucker, 469–500. New York: W. W. Norton.
Maurer, Bill. 2000. "A Fish Story: Rethinking Globalization on Virgin Gorda, British Virgin Islands." *American Ethnologist* 27, no. 3: 670–701.
McCann, Bryan. 2006. "The Political Evolution of Rio de Janeiro's Favelas: Recent Works." *Latin American Research Review* 41, no. 3: 149–163.
McCrum, Robert. 2011. *Globish: How English Became the World's Language.* New York: W. W. Norton.
McFall, Liz. 2004. *Advertising: A Cultural Economy.* London: Sage.
Meena, Krishnendra. 2016. "Border Theory and Globalization: Perspectives from the South." *International Studies* 50, no. 1–2: 1–15.
Mendes, Jaqueline. 2018. "Brasil lidera mercado de carne para muçulmanos, entenda por quê." *Estado de Minas* (Belo Horizonte). April 24, 2018. Accessed November 22, 2019. https://www.em.com.br/app/noticia/economia/2018/04/24/internas_economia,953748/brasil-lidera-mercado-de-carne-para-muculmanos.shtml.
MercoPress (Montevideo). 2011a. "Embraer Has Dominant Position in the Middle East 60/120 Pax Jet Segment." November 15, 2011. Accessed November 9, 2014. http://en.mercopress.com/2011/11/15/embraer-has-dominant-position-in-the-middle-east-60-120-pax-jet-segment.

———. 2011b. "US Condemns South American/Arab Leaders Summits, Say Wikileaks Cables." February 7, 2011. Accessed May 31, 2014. http://en.mercopress.com/2011/02/07/us-condemns-south-american-arab-leaders-summits-say-wikileaks-cables.

———. 2012. "Brazil/Arab World Trade Soared More Than 28% in 2011, Reaching 25.13bn Dollars." January 31, 2012. Accessed May 31, 2014. http://en.mercopress.com/2012/01/31/brazil-arab-world-trade-soared-more-than-28-in-2011-reaching-25.13bn-dollars.

Mignolo, Walter D. 2005. *The Idea of Latin America*. Malden, MA: Blackwell.

Mignolo, Walter D., and Arturo Escobar, eds. 2013. *Globalization and the Decolonial Option*. New York: Routledge.

Miles, Tom. 2014. "EU Widens Trade Row with New Boeing Subsidy Claim." Reuters. December 19, 2014. Accessed January 30, 2016. http://www.reuters.com/article/us-eu-usa-boeing-idUSKBN0JX1T120141219.

Mills, C. Wright. 1956. *The Power Elite*. New York: Oxford University Press.

Milner, Andrew. 2019. "Class and Class Consciousness in Marxist Theory." *International Critical Thought* 9, no. 2: 161–176.

Mittelman, James H. 2017. *Implausible Dream: The World-Class University and Repurposing Higher Education*. Princeton, NJ: Princeton University Press.

Molloy, Parker. 2017. "15 Companies that Took Bold Stands against Trump's Immigration Ban." Upworthy. February 3, 2017. Accessed June 29, 2019. https://www.upworthy.com/15-companies-that-took-bold-stands-against-trumps-immigration-ban.

Moore, Jr., Barrington. 2007. "The Critical Spirit and Comparative Historical Analysis." In *Passion, Craft, and Method in Comparative Politics*, edited by Gerardo L. Munck and Richard Snyder, 86–112. Baltimore: Johns Hopkins University Press.

Moore, Jen, and Manuel Pérez-Rocha. 2019. *Extraction Casino: Mining Companies Gambling with Latin American Lives and Sovereignty Through International Arbitration*. Institute for Policy Studies. Accessed January 15, 2022. https://ips-dc.org/report-extraction-casino/.

Morales, Constanza. 2015. "Bank of Palestine inicia el proceso para ser el primer banco árabe en la región." *La Tercera* (Santiago de Chile). October 31, 2015. Accessed January 30, 2016. http://www.latercera.com/noticia/negocios/2015/10/655-653787-9-bank-of-palestine-inicia-el-proceso-para-ser-el-primer-banco-arabe-en-la-region.shtml.

Morrison, Scott. 2005. "'*Os Turcos*': The Syrian-Lebanese Community of São Paulo, Brazil." *Journal of Muslim Minority Affairs* 25, no. 3: 423–438.

Moulián, Tomás. 2014. "The Credit-Card Citizen." In *The Chile Reader: Culture, Politics, History*, edited by Elizabeth Quay Hutchison, Thomas Miller Klubock, Nara B. Milanich, and Peter Winn, 547–552. Durham, NC: Duke University Press.

Moya Mena, Sergio I. 2011. "Relaciones con Medio Oriente: ¿nuevo eje estratégico de la política internacional latinoamericana?" *Revista Relaciones Internacionales* 80, no. 1: 1–19.

Munck, Ronaldo, and Pablo Pozzi. 2019. "Israel, Palestine, and Latin America: Conflictual Relationships." *Latin American Perspectives* 46, no. 3: 4–12.

Murshed, Syed Mansoob, Pedro Goulart, and Leandro A. Serino, eds. 2013. *South-South Globalization: Challenges and Opportunities for Development*. New York: Routledge.

Nagle, Angela. 2018. "The Left Case against Open Borders." *American Affairs* 2, no. 4: 17–30.

Needell, Jeffrey D., ed. 2015. *Emergent Brazil: Key Perspectives on a New Global Power*. Gainesville: University Press of Florida.

Ness, Immanuel. 2016. *Southern Insurgency: The Coming of the Global Working Class*. London: Pluto.

Neumann, Iver B. 2008. "Discourse Analysis." In *Qualitative Methods in International Relations: A Pluralist Guide*, edited by Audie Klotz and Deepa Prakash, 61–77. New York: Palgrave Macmillan.

Nexon, Daniel H., and Iver B. Neumann, eds. 2006. *Harry Potter and International Relations*. Lanham, MD: Rowman & Littlefield.

North, Liisa L., and Timothy D. Clark, eds. 2018. *Dominant Elites in Latin America: From Neo-Liberalism to the "Pink Tide."* New York: Palgrave Macmillan.

O'Mara, Margaret. 2019. *The Code: Silicon Valley and the Remaking of America*. New York: Penguin.

Ong, Aihwa. 1999. *Flexible Citizenship: The Cultural Logics of Transnationality*. Durham, NC: Duke University Press.

Oren, Ido. 2003. *Our Enemies and US: America's Rivalries and the Making of Political Science*. Ithaca, NY: Cornell University Press.

———. 2009. "The Unrealism of Contemporary Realism: The Tension between Realist Theory and Realists' Practice." *Perspectives on Politics* 7, no. 2: 283–301.

———. 2016. "A Sociological Analysis of the Decline of American IR Theory." *International Studies Review* 18, no. 4: 571–596.

Palieraki, E. 2018. "Broadening the Field of Perception and Struggle: Chilean Political Exiles in Algeria and Third World Cosmopolitanism." *African Identities* 16, no. 2: 205–218.

Panitch, Leo, and Sam Gindin. 2012. *The Making of Global Capitalism: The Political Economy of American Empire*. Brooklyn: Verso.

Pastor, Camila. 2017. *The Mexican Mahjar: Transnational Maronites, Jews, and Arabs under the French Mandate*. Austin: University of Texas Press.

Patterson, Rubin. 2013. "Transnational Capitalist Class: What's Race Got to Do With It? Everything!" *Globalizations* 10, no. 5: 673–690.

Paul, Kari. 2019. "'Breathtaking Arrogance': Senators Grill Facebook in Combative Hearing over Libra Currency." *The Guardian*, July 16, 2019. Accessed July 19, 2019. https://www.theguardian.com/technology/2019/jul/15/big-tech-behemoths-face-grilling-from-us-lawmakers-as-hearings-kick-off.

Pearl Balloffet, Lily. 2020. *Argentina in the Global Middle East*. Stanford, CA: Stanford University Press.

Pearlstein, Steven. 2011. "Dani Rodrik's 'The Globalization Paradox.'" *Washington Post*. March 13, 2011. Accessed January 30, 2016. http://www.washingtonpost.com/wp-dyn/content/article/2011/03/11/AR2011031106730.html.

Phillips, Peter. 2018. *Giants: The Global Power Elite*. New York: Seven Stories Press.

Piketty, Thomas. 2017. *Capital in the Twenty-First Century*. Cambridge, MA: Harvard University Press.

Polanyi, Karl. 2001. *The Great Transformation: The Political and Economic Origins of Our Time*. 2nd ed. Boston: Beacon.

Prashad, Vijay. 2007. *The Darker Nations: A People's History of the Third World*. New York: The New Press.

———. 2013. *The Poorer Nations: A Possible History of the Global South*. New York: Verso.

Quijano, Aníbal. 2000. "Coloniality of Power, Eurocentrism, and Latin America." *Nepantla: Views from South* 1, no. 3: 533–580.

Raheb, Viola, ed. 2012. *Latin Americans with Palestinian Roots*. Bethlehem, Palestine: Diyar Publisher.

Rebolledo Hernández, Antonia. 1994. "La 'turcofobia': Discriminación antiárabe en Chile, 1900–1950." *Historia* (Santiago de Chile) 28, no. 1: 249–272.

Rein, Raanan, and Ariel Noyjovich. 2018. *Los muchachos peronistas árabes: Los argentinos árabes y el apoyo al Justicialismo.* Buenos Aires: Sudamericana.
Reis da Silva, André, and José O. Pérez. 2019. "Lula, Dilma, and Temer: The Rise and Fall of Brazilian Foreign Policy." *Latin American Perspectives* 46, no. 4: 169–185.
Ribeiro, Darcy. 2000. *The Brazilian People: The Formation and Meaning of Brazil.* Gainesville: University Press of Florida.
Richards, Patricia. 2014. "Decolonizing Globalization Studies." *The Global South* 8, no. 2: 139–154.
Rivas, Zelideth María, and Debbie Lee-DiStefano, eds. 2016. *Imagining Asia in the Americas.* New Brunswick, NJ: Rutgers University Press.
Robertson, Justin. 2015. *Localizing Global Finance: The Rise of Western-Style Private Equity in China.* New York: Palgrave Macmillan.
Robin, Corey. 2013. "The Hayek-Pinochet Connection: A Second Reply to My Critics." Coreyrobin.com. June 25, 2013. Accessed January 29, 2016. http://coreyrobin.com/2013/06/25/the-hayek-pinochet-connection-a-second-reply-to-my-critics/.
———. 2017. *The Reactionary Mind: Conservatism from Edmund Burke to Donald Trump.* 2nd ed. New York: Oxford University Press.
Robinson, Edward. 2014. "For Libertarian Utopia, Float Away on 'Startup' Nation." *Bloomberg Business.* May 30, 2014. Accessed January 29, 2016. http://www.bloomberg.com/news/articles/2014-05-30/for-libertarian-utopia-float-away-on-startup-nation.
Robinson, William I. 2004. *A Theory of Global Capitalism: Production, Class and State in a Transnational World.* Baltimore: Johns Hopkins University Press.
———. 2008. *Latin America and Global Capitalism: A Critical Globalization Perspective.* Baltimore: Johns Hopkins University Press.
———. 2014. *Global Capitalism and the Crisis of Humanity.* New York: Cambridge University Press.
Robson, David. 2015. "The Countries that Don't Exist." *BBC Future.* November 4, 2015. Accessed January 29, 2016. http://www.bbc.com/future/story/20151103-the-countries-that-dont-exist.
Rocha, Alexandre. 2019a. "Brazil's Nods to Israel May Displease Arab Consumer." *Brazil-Arab News Agency.* April 16, 2019. Accessed May 29, 2019. https://anba.com.br/en/brazils-nods-to-israel-may-displease-arab-consumer/.
———. 2019b. "Office in Jerusalem Points to an Imbalance." *Brazil-Arab News Agency.* April 1, 2019. Accessed May 29, 2019. https://anba.com.br/en/office-in-jerusalem-creates-an-imbalance/.
Rodrik, Dani. 2012. *The Globalization Paradox: Democracy and the Future of the World Economy.* New York: W. W. Norton.
Rogers, Charlotte, and Molly Fleming. 2019. "'Together We Thrive': Has HSBC Nailed It or Not Gone Far Enough?" *MarketingWeek.* January 9, 2019. Accessed October 17, 2019. https://www.marketingweek.com/together-we-thrive-hsbc-nailed-it-not-gone-far-enough/.
Rose, Gillian. 2001. *Visual Methodologies: An Introduction to the Interpretation of Visual Materials.* London: Sage.
———. 2014. "On the Relation between 'Visual Research Methods' and Contemporary Visual Culture." *The Sociological Review* 62, no. 1: 24–46.
Rosenberg, Justin. 2000. *The Follies of Globalisation Theory.* New York: Verso.
———. 2005. "Globalization Theory: A Post Mortem." *International Politics* 42, no. 1: 2–74.
———. 2007. "And the Definition of Globalization Is . . . ? A Reply to 'In at the Death?' by Barrie Axford." *Globalizations* 4, no. 3: 417–421.

Rossi, Ugo. 2017. *Cities in Global Capitalism*. Cambridge, UK: Polity.
Rothkopf, David. 2008. *Superclass: The Global Power Elite and the World They Are Making*. New York: Farrar, Straus and Giroux.
Rouse, Joseph. 2005. "Power/Knowledge." In *The Cambridge Companion to Foucault*, 2nd ed., edited by Gary Gutting, 95–122. New York: Cambridge University Press.
Rupert, Mark, and M. Scott Solomon. 2006. *Globalization & International Political Economy: The Politics of Alternative Futures*. Lanham, MD: Rowman & Littlefield.
Saddy, Fehmy, ed. 1983. *Arab-Latin American Relations: Energy, Trade, and Investment*. New Brunswick, NJ: Transaction Books.
———, ed. 2016. *The Arab World and Latin America: Economic and Political Relations in the Twenty-First Century*. London: I. B. Tauris.
Santiso, Javier. 2013. *The Decade of the Multilatinas*. New York: Cambridge University Press.
Sassen, Saskia. 1991. *The Global City: New York, London, Tokyo*. Princeton, NJ: Princeton University Press.
———. 2007. *A Sociology of Globalization*. New York: W. W. Norton.
———. 2011. "Saskia Sassen on Sociology, Globalization, and the Re-shaping of the National." *Theory Talks*. September 6, 2011. Accessed March 6, 2014. http://www.theory-talks.org/2011/09/theory-talk-43.html.
Schaffer, Frederic Charles. 2006. "Ordinary Language Interviewing." In *Interpretation and Method: Empirical Research Methods and the Interpretive Turn*, edited by Dvora Yanow and Peregrine Schwartz-Shea, 150–160. Armonk, NY: M. E. Sharpe.
———. 2016. *Elucidating Social Science Concepts: An Interpretivist Guide*. New York: Routledge.
Schneider, Ben Ross. 2013. *Hierarchical Capitalism in Latin America: Business, Labor, and the Challenges of Equitable Development*. New York: Cambridge University Press.
Scholte, Jan Aart. 2005. *Globalization: A Critical Introduction*. 2nd ed. New York: Palgrave Macmillan.
Schwartz, Joseph M. 2014. "Resisting the Exploitation of Contingent Faculty Labor in the Neoliberal University: The Challenge of Building Solidarity between Tenured and Non-Tenured Faculty." *New Political Science* 36, no. 4: 504–522.
Sclofsky, Sebastián, and Kevin Funk. 2018. "The Specter That Haunts Political Science: The Neglect and Misreading of Marx in International Relations and Comparative Politics." *International Studies Perspectives* 19, no. 1: 83–101.
Scott, James. 1985. *Weapons of the Weak: Everyday Forms of Peasant Resistance*. New Haven, CT: Yale University Press.
———. 2007. "Peasants, Power, and the Art of Resistance." In *Passion, Craft, and Method in Comparative Politics*, edited by Gerardo L. Munck and Richard Snyder, 351–391. Baltimore: Johns Hopkins University Press.
SELA (Sistema Económico Latinoamericano y del Caribe). 2012. "Las relaciones de América Latina y el Caribe con el Medio Oriente: Situación actual y áreas de oportunidad" (June). Caracas.
Sharif, Regina. 1977. "Latin America and the Arab-Israeli Conflict." *Journal of Palestine Studies* 7, no. 1: 98–122.
Shepherd, Laura J. 2013. *Gender, Violence and Popular Culture: Telling Stories*. New York: Routledge.
Sherman, Rachel. 2019. *Uneasy Street: The Anxieties of Affluence*. Princeton, NJ: Princeton University Press.
Shim, David. 2014. *Visual Politics and North Korea: Seeing Is Believing*. New York: Routledge.

Sims, Calvin. 1998. "The World; Formerly Arrogant, Utterly Argentine." *New York Times*, May 24, 1998. Accessed January 30, 2016. http://www.nytimes.com/1998/05/24/weekinreview/the-world-formerly-arrogant-utterly-argentine.html.

Sklair, Leslie. 2001. *The Transnational Capitalist Class*. Malden, MA: Blackwell.

———. 2006. "Iconic Architecture and Capitalist Globalization." *City* 10, no. 1: 21–47.

———. 2013. *Globalization: Capitalism and Its Alternatives*. 3rd ed. New York: Oxford University Press.

———. 2016. "The Transnational Capitalist Class, Social Movements, and Alternatives to Capitalist Globalization." *International Critical Thought* 6, no. 3: 329–341.

———. 2017. *The Icon Project: Architecture, Cities, and Capitalist Globalization*. New York: Oxford University Press.

Slobodian, Quinn. 2018. *Globalists: The End of Empire and the Birth of Neoliberalism*. Cambridge, MA: Harvard University Press.

Smith, Adam. 2008. *An Inquiry into the Nature and Causes of the Wealth of Nations: A Selected Edition*. New York: Oxford University Press.

Smith, Neil. 2005. "Neo-Critical Geography, Or, The Flat Pluralist World of Business Class." *Antipode* 37, no. 5: 887–99.

Smith, Steve, Ken Booth, and Marysia Zalewski, eds. 1996. *International Theory: Positivism and Beyond*. New York: Cambridge University Press.

Solimano, Andrés. 2012. *Chile and the Neoliberal Trap: The Post-Pinochet Era*. New York: Cambridge University Press.

Soss, Joe. 2006. "Talking Our Way to Meaningful Explanations: A Practice-Centered View of Interviewing for Interpretive Research." In *Interpretation and Method: Empirical Research Methods and the Interpretive Turn*, edited by Dvora Yanow and Peregrine Schwartz-Shea, 127–149. Armonk, NY: M. E. Sharpe.

Sparke, Matthew. 2007. "Everywhere but Always Somewhere: Critical Geographies of the Global South." *The Global South* 1, no. 1–2: 117–126.

Spence, Lester K. 2015. *Knocking the Hustle: Against the Neoliberal Turn in Black Politics*. New York: Punctum Books.

Spiegel, Steven L., Elizabeth G. Matthews, Jennifer M. Taw, and Kristen P. Williams. 2012. *World Politics in a New Era*. 5th ed. New York: Oxford University Press.

Sprague, Jeb, ed. 2016. *Globalization and Transnational Capitalism in Asia and Oceania*. New York: Routledge.

———. 2019. *Globalizing the Caribbean: Political Economy, Social Change, and the Transnational Capitalist Class*. Philadelphia: Temple University Press.

Stanford, Jim. 2011. "The North American Free Trade Agreement: Context, Structure and Performance." In *The Handbook of Globalisation*, 2nd ed., edited by Jonathan Michie, 324–355. Cheltenham, UK: Edward Elgar.

Starrs, Sean Kenji. 2017. "The Global Capitalism School Tested in Asia: Transnational Capitalist Class vs Taking the State Seriously." *Journal of Contemporary Asia* 47, no. 4: 641–658.

Steger, Manfred B. 2008. *The Rise of the Global Imaginary: Political Ideologies from the French Revolution to the Global War on Terror*. New York: Oxford University Press.

Steger, Manfred B., and Amentahru Wahlrab. 2016. *What Is Global Studies? Theory & Practice*. New York: Routledge.

Stein, Samuel. 2019. *Capital City: Gentrification and the Real Estate State*: Brooklyn: Verso.

Steinberg, Philip E., Elizabeth Nyman, and Mauro J. Caraccioli. 2012. "Atlas Swam: Freedom, Capital, and Floating Sovereignties in the Seasteading Vision." *Antipode* 44, no. 4: 1532–1550.

Stevens, Jacqueline. 2015. "Forensic Intelligence and the Deportation Research Clinic: Toward a New Paradigm." *Perspectives on Politics* 13, no. 3: 722–738.
Stiglitz, Joseph. 2017. *Globalization and Its Discontents Revisited: Anti-Globalization in the Era of Trump*. New York: W. W. Norton.
Stocking, Jr., George W., ed. 1993. *Colonial Situations: Essays on the Contextualization of Ethnographic Knowledge*. Madison: University of Wisconsin Press.
Struna, J. 2013. "Global Capitalism and Transnational Class Formation." *Globalizations* 10, no. 5: 651–657.
Sum, Ngai-Ling, and Bob Jessop. 2013. *Towards a Cultural Political Economy: Putting Culture in Its Place in Political Economy*. Cheltenham, UK: Edward Elgar Publishing.
Summers, Lawrence. 2008. "America Needs to Make a New Case for Trade." *Financial Times*. April 28, 2008. Accessed January 14, 2014. http://blogs.ft.com/economistsforum/2008/04/america-needs-to-make-a-new-case-for-trade/.
Tarrow, Sidney. 2005. *The New Transnational Activism*. New York: Cambridge University Press.
Tawil, Marta. 2013. "México ante Medio Oriente durante el gobierno de Felipe Calderón." *Foro Internacional* (Ciudad de México) LIII, no. 3–4: 667–706.
Tawil Kuri, Marta, ed. 2016. *Latin American Foreign Policies towards the Middle East: Actors, Contexts, and Trends*. New York: Palgrave Macmillan.
Taylor, Charles. 1971. "Interpretation and the Sciences of Man." *The Review of Metaphysics* 25, no. 1: 3–51.
Taylor, Ian. 2017a. *Global Governance and Transnationalizing Capitalist Hegemony: The Myth of the 'Emerging Powers.'* New York: Routledge.
———. 2017b. "Transnationalizing Capitalist Hegemony: A Poulantzian Reading." *Alternatives: Global, Local, Political* 42, no. 1: 26–40.
Taylor, Yvette, ed. 2010. *Classed Intersections: Spaces, Selves, Knowledges*. New York: Routledge.
Thomas, Zoe. 2016. "Is it Time to Stop Thinking of Cars in Terms of Nationality?" *BBC News*. January 27, 2016. Accessed January 29, 2016. http://www.bbc.com/news/business-35330292.
Thompson, E. P. 1966. *The Making of the English Working Class*. New York: Vintage Books.
Tickner, Arlene. 2003. "Seeing IR Differently: Notes from the Third World." *Millennium: Journal of International Studies* 32, no. 2: 295–324.
———. 2008. "Latin American IR and the Primacy of *lo práctico*." *International Studies Review* 10, no. 4: 735–748.
Tickner, Arlene B., and David L. Blaney. 2012a. "Introduction: Thinking Difference." In *Thinking International Relations Differently*, edited by Arlene B. Tickner and David L. Blaney, 1–24. New York: Routledge.
Tickner, Arlene B., and David L. Blaney, eds. 2012b. *Thinking International Relations Differently*. New York: Routledge.
Tooze, Adam. 2021. *Shutdown: How COVID Shook the World's Economy*. New York: Viking.
Truzzi, Oswaldo. 2018. *Syrian and Lebanese Patrícios in São Paulo: From the Levant to Brazil*. Champaign: University of Illinois Press.
Tsing, Anna. 2000. "The Global Situation." *Cultural Anthropology* 15, no. 3: 327–360.
Tucker, Robert C., ed. 1978. *The Marx-Engels Reader*. 2nd ed. New York: W. W. Norton.
Twine, Francine Winddance. 1997. *Racism in a Racial Democracy: The Maintenance of White Supremacy in Brazil*. New Brunswick, NJ: Rutgers University Press.
Ustan, Mustafa. 2012. *La Inmigración árabe en América: Los árabes otomanos en Chile—identidad y adaptación (1839–1922)*. Clifton, NJ: Editorial La Fuente.

Valdés, Juan Gabriel. 2008. *Pinochet's Economists: The Chicago School of Economics in Chile*. Cambridge, UK: Cambridge University Press.
van Apeldoorn, Bastiaan, and Naná de Graaff. 2016. *American Grand Strategy and Corporate Elite Networks*. New York: Routledge.
van der Pijl, Kees. 1984. *The Making of an Atlantic Ruling Class*. London: Verso.
———. 1998. *Transnational Classes and International Relations*. New York: Routledge.
van Fossen, Anthony. 2016. "Flags of Convenience and Global Capitalism." *International Critical Thought* 6, no. 3: 359–377.
Varadarajan, Latha. 2014. "The Transnationalism of the Embattled State." *New Political Science* 36, no. 3: 366–386.
Vargas, Pilar, and Luz Marina Suaza. 2007. *Los árabes en Colombia: Del rechazo a la integración*. Bogotá: Planeta.
Varinsky, Dana. 2017. "Trump's 'Buy American' Policy Directly Conflicts with How His Own Hotels Operate." *Business Insider*. January 28, 2017. Accessed January 28, 2017. http://www.businessinsider.com/trump-hotel-imports-2017-1.
Varoufakis, Yanis. 2018. "Our New International Movement Will Fight Rising Fascism and Globalists." *The Guardian*, September 13, 2018. Accessed July 28, 2019. https://www.theguardian.com/commentisfree/ng-interactive/2018/sep/13/our-new-international-movement-will-fight-rising-fascism-and-globalists.
Vasconcelos, Álvaro, Arlene Clemesha, and Feliciano de Sá Guimarães, eds. 2018. *Brasil e Oriente Médio: O Poder da Sociedade Civil*. São Paulo: Universidade de São Paulo, Instituto de Relações Internacionais.
Vasconcelos, José. 1997. *The Cosmic Race: A Bilingual Edition*. Baltimore: Johns Hopkins University Press.
Vélez, Federico. 2015. *Latin American Revolutionaries and the Arab World: From the Suez Canal to the Arab Spring*. Farnham, UK: Ashgate.
Walker, Andrew. 2010. "Tenacity and Risk—the Lebanese in West Africa." *BBC News*. January 25, 2010. Accessed January 30, 2016. http://news.bbc.co.uk/2/hi/africa/8479134.stm.
Wallis, Victor. 2015. "Intersectionality's Binding Agent: The Political Primacy of Class." *New Political Science* 37, no. 4: 604–619.
Waltz, Kenneth N. 1979. *Theory of International Politics*. Reading, MA: Addison-Wesley.
WAM (Emirates News Agency). 2011. "Dubai Exports Sees More Companies Exporting to Brazil in Coming Years." August 3, 2011. Accessed February 27, 2014. http://www.wam.org.ae/servlet/Satellite?c=WamLocEnews&cid=1289994553178&pagename=WAM%2FWAM_E_PrintVersion.
Washington Times. 2005. "Arab Roots Grow Deep in Brazil's Rich Melting Pot." July 11, 2005. Accessed May 28, 2014. http://www.washingtontimes.com/news/2005/jul/11/20050711-092503-1255r/?page=all.
Watson, Imogen. 2019. "HSBC Continues Its 'Together We Thrive' Pledge with 'We Are Not an Island' Campaign." *The Drum*. January 3, 2019. Accessed October 17, 2019. https://www.thedrum.com/news/2019/01/03/hsbc-continues-its-together-we-thrive-pledge-with-we-are-not-island-campaign.
Weber, Max. 2004. "The 'Objectivity' of Knowledge in Social Science and Social Policy." In *The Essential Weber: A Reader*, edited by Sam Whimster, 359–404. London: Routledge.
———. 2011. *The Protestant Ethic and the Spirit of Capitalism*. New York: Oxford University Press.

Weeks, John. 2016. "Trump's Victory Represents the Fulfilment of Neoliberalism, Not Its Failure." *OpenDemocracy*. November 13, 2016. Accessed January 24, 2017. https://www.opendemocracy.net/john-weeks/trumps-victory-is-fulfilment-of-neoliberalism-not-its-failure.

Weinstein, Barbara. 2015. *The Color of Modernity: São Paulo and the Making of Race and Nation in Brazil*. Durham, NC: Duke University Press.

Weldes, Jutta. 2015. "High Politics and Low Data: Globalization Discourses and Popular Culture." In *Interpretation and Method: Empirical Research Methods and the Interpretive Turn*, 2nd ed., edited by Dvora Yanow and Peregrine Schwartz-Shea, 228–238. New York: Routledge.

Wellbaum, Andrea. 2007. "Brasil acoge refugiados palestinos." *BBC Mundo*. September 20, 2007. Accessed January 29, 2016. http://news.bbc.co.uk/hi/spanish/misc/newsid_7002000/7002800.stm.

Wimmer, Andreas, and Nina Glick Schiller. 2002. "Methodological Nationalism and beyond: Nation-State Building, Migration and the Social Sciences." *Global Networks: A Journal of Transnational Affairs* 2, no. 4: 301–334.

Wintour, Patrick. 2018. "Clinton, Blair, Renzi: Why We Lost, and How to Fight Back." *The Guardian*, November 22, 2018. Accessed July 25, 2019. https://www.theguardian.com/world/2018/nov/22/clinton-blair-renzi-why-we-lost-populists-how-fight-back-rightwing-populism-centrist.

The World Bank. 2013. "Universal Healthcare on the Rise in Latin America." February 14, 2013. Accessed February 1, 2016. http://www.worldbank.org/en/news/feature/2013/02/14/universal-healthcare-latin-america.

Worstall, Tim. 2014. "This Is What Adam Smith Meant by Invisible Hand." *Forbes*. April 25, 2014. Accessed April 24, 2017. https://www.forbes.com/sites/timworstall/2014/04/25/this-is-what-adam-smith-meant-by-invisible-hand/#422baea46694.

Wright, Erik Olin. 2015. "Why Class Matters." *Jacobin*. December 23, 2015. Accessed February 7, 2016. https://www.jacobinmag.com/2015/12/socialism-marxism-democracy-inequality-erik-olin-wright/.

Yanow, Dvora. 2006. "Thinking Interpretively: Philosophical Presuppositions and the Human Sciences." In *Interpretation and Method: Empirical Research Methods and the Interpretive Turn*, edited by Dvora Yanow and Peregrine Schwartz-Shea, 5–26. Armonk, NY: M. E. Sharpe.

Yanow, Dvora, and Peregrine Schwartz-Shea, eds. 2006. *Interpretation and Method: Empirical Research Methods and the Interpretive Turn*. Armonk, NY: M. E. Sharpe.

Yanow, Dvora, and Peregrine Schwartz-Shea, eds. 2015. *Interpretation and Method: Empirical Research Methods and the Interpretive Turn*. 2nd ed. New York: Routledge.

Young, Cristobal. 2018. *The Myth of Millionaire Tax Flight: How Place Still Matters for the Rich*. Stanford, CA: Stanford University Press.

Zapatista Army of National Liberation. 2005. "Sixth Declaration of the Selva Lacandona." In *Contemporary Latin American Social and Political Thought* (2008), edited by Iván Márquez, 282–300. Lanham, MD: Rowman & Littlefield.

Zukin, Sharon, Philip Kasinitz, and Xiangming Chen. 2015. *Global Cities, Local Streets: Everyday Diversity from New York to Shanghai*. New York: Routledge.

Zurcher, Anthony. 2014. "Burger King Abdicates US Citizenship." *BBC News*. August 26, 2014. Accessed January 29, 2016. http://www.bbc.com/news/blogs-echochambers-28943400.

INDEX

Page locators in italics refer to figures

Abugattas, Juan, 99
accumulation, 9; chains, 7, 23, 27, 40, 42, 47, 141, 150, 158; "international space of," 66; territorial-based, 70, 144–45
advertisements, 3, 16, 175–217; audience understanding of, 183–84, 198, 208–10, 216, 230–31; "common sense" imaginaries in, 185, 189, 206; corporate case studies, 186–206; counter discourses to, 213, 215–16, 220, 223–31; creators of, 187–88, 209; Emirates Airline, 3, 12, 99, 176, *177–82*, 187–88, 190–95, *192*; and formation of global subjectivity, 184–86, 189–90; Global South as target of, 177–81, 188, 191–92, 194, 196, *205*; HSBC, 1, 184, 186, 187, 188, 195–200, *197*, *200*; humanistic, 177–79, 183, 208; Itaú, 184, 186, 187, 188, 200–204, *202*, *203*; to "middling groups," 185, 192, 194; North challenged in, 203–5, *205*, 207; political uses of "banal cosmopolitanism" in, 176–84, 209, 216n1; and popular culture, 183–85, 201–4, *202*, *203*, 207, 230; regional cultural icons used in, 176–77, 184, 187, 200–207, 211; South-South relations in, 194, 196, 204–6, *205*; "subversive" messages in, 177–78, 191–92, 198, 205, 207; "tomorrow" focus of, 12, 176, *177*, *178*, *182*, 184, 187–88, 190–95, *192*, 198, 209; triumphalist sentiments in, 204–5. *See also* neoliberal rhetoric; popular culture
Adweek, 195
agency, 5–8, 15–16, 72; Global South said to lack, 22, 76, 79–83, 162, 204
agricultural exports, 93, 98–99, 116, 126; halal certification, 117, 119, 122, 131–32, 136, 139, 140, 162
air travel, 99, 147, 192–94. *See also* Emirates Airline
Algeria, 77, 98

Allende, Salvador, 3–4, 39, 77, 115, 161
alternatives to global capitalism, 5, 7–8, 12, 17, 35, 213–16
altruism, and profit motive, 134–36, 139
Amado, Jorge, 86–87
Amar, Paul, 82, 85
Amorim, Celso, 58, 76, 96, 106
Anderson, Benedict, 7, 53, 70, 71
Anheuser-Busch InBev, 1
Anievas, Alexander, 50
Aniston, Jennifer, 190, *191*
"antiglobalism," neoliberal, 225–26
Appadurai, Arjun, 36
Appel, Hannah, 207
Arab and South American Library and Research Center, 81, 131
Arab-Argentine Chamber of Commerce, 131
Arab-Brazilian Chamber of Commerce, 58–59, 81, 98
Arab-Brazilians, 66, 89, 93–95
Arab-Chilean business elites, 115, 118–19
Arab-Latin American relations: Arab-Argentine trade association, 140; Arab-Brazilian trade association, 24, 117, 146, 151–59; Arab-Chilean trade association, 111, 113–26; Arab-descendent elites, 85–95, 110–11; Buenos Aires-based financial firm, 146; and cultural capital, 10, 24, 62, 94, 110, 150, 158, 165–67; foreign policy and commercial relations, 95–101; and free trade agreements, 4, 116, 160–61; Iraqi-Brazilian trade association, 113, 130–37, 139; Muslim world, trade with, 95, 97, 117, 119, 154; political economy of, 101–7; recovering history of, 76–77, 88; São Paulo-based organization, 146; state-centric literature on, 77–78, 103–4; US terrorism allegations, 83–84, 95, 103. *See also* immigration; Latin America; religion; South-South relations

Arab world, 6, 10, 20, 24; Brazil's economic relations with, 58–59; food security, 116, 163–64; Gulf region, 116, 147–51; Lula's relations with, 95–96, 98, 154; pan-Arab cultural capital, 158; sovereign wealth funds, 116, 147. *See also specific countries*
Araújo, Ernesto, 32
Argentina, 20, 98; Arab-descendant population, 87, 126–30; boom years of 2010s, 126; capitalist critiques of, 128, 148–50; Falklands/Malvinas War, 148; nationalism, 127–30; Pope Francis from, 129–30
Argentine Israelite Mutual Association, 84
Asian and Pacific Rim economies, 75n1, 118, 122, 125, 142n6, 159
Atlantium, 32
Aufstehen (Get, Stand, or Rise Up), 227
authoritarianism: Chile, 116, 128, 161; in employment regimes, 17; neoliberal, 9–10, 40, 226; right-wing, 25, 103, 224–26
La aventura de Miguel Littín clandestino en Chile (*Clandestine in Chile: The Adventures of Miguel Littín*) (García Márquez), 86
Ayoade, Richard, 199

Ba'athist regime (Iraq), 132–33
Bachelet, Michelle, 117, 122, 161
Baghdad (Iraq), 133
Bannon, Steve, 9, 225
Bari, Gustavo, 140
BBB bloc, 109
BBC Mundo, 101
BBC Two, 2
Beck, Ulrich, 176
Beder, Sharon, 180
Bessner, Daniel, 210
Best, Jacqueline, 15, 16, 198
Bey, Yasiin, 32
Biden, Joe, 103
Biradavolu, Monica R., 45
Bishara, Rafael, 113, 126–30, 148; national framework of, 126–27, 130
Bloomberg Businessweek, 190–93, *191*, 193
Blyth, Mark, 210
Boeing, 149

Bogaert, Koenraad, 6, 9
Bohland, Jon, 190
Bolsa Família (Family Allowance) program (Brazil), 136
Bolsonaro, Jair, 100, 128, 154; Israel, support for, 97–98, 101, 154; religious support for, 109, 110
Bolton, John, 103
Bonin, Hubert, 195
borders, 3–4; cross-border solidarity, 63, 230; exceptions to "borderless world," 192–93, 228; left case against, 227; operation across in Sklair's theory, 41–42, 46–48, 54; real-world, 213–14; threats of cross-border capital flight, 29, 39; "Tomorrow thinks borders are so yesterday" ad campaign, 12, 184, 187, 190–195
Boric, Gabriel, 160
bourgeoisie, 4, 5, 34–36, 46, 54, 55; fully globalized, imaginary of, 185
Braga, Alice, 201, *202*
Branscome, Eva, 216
Brazil, 20; agribusiness lobby, 97; agricultural exports to Arab world, 93, 98–99; Arab-Brazilian Chamber of Commerce, 58–59, 81, 98; Arab-descendant population, 87, 89, 93–95; Arab world, economic relations with, 58–59, 66, 93–100; BBB bloc, 109; Bolsa Família (Family Allowance) program, 136; center-left government, 102; foreign policy, 153; Iraqi-Brazilian trade association, 113, 130–37; Itaú (bank), 184, 186, 187, 188, 200–204, *202*, *203*. *See also* Bolsonaro, Jair; Lula da Silva, Luiz Inácio
Brazil-Arab Countries Economic Forum, 78, 106
Brazilian Trade and Investment Promotion Agency, Apex-Brasil, 58
Brazilian Workers' Party, 133
Bremer, Paul, 132
Bresser-Pereira, Luiz Carlos, 51
Brexit, 8, 194, 199–200, *200*, 210, 211
BRICS (Brazil, Russia, India, China, and South Africa), 151, 204
bridging role of globalizing elites, 114–15, 123, 147, 150, 151, 187

Britain: Brexit, 8, 194, 199–200, *200*, 210, 211; "War on Terror," 229
Brown, Wendy, 1, 3, 45, 223–24
Buchanan, James M., 39
Budd, Adrian, 10, 48, 170
Buenos Aires (Argentina), 84; *porteños*, 127, 129; Recoleta neighborhood, 146–47
Bukele, Nayib, 86
bureaucrats, globalizing, 56, 59
Burger King, 30–31

Callao (Peru), 118
Campbell, Matthew, 25, 190
capital: as "dead labor," 60–61; international vs. global, 54; as sovereign, 45, 73; structural and social power of, 5–6; threats of cross-border flight, 29, 39; types of, 56. *See also* capitalism; capitalists; global capitalism; global capitalist class; neoliberalism
Capital (Marx), 60–61
capitalism: class relations as focus of, 5; as concept, 103; emotional logic of, 177; human action determined by, 59–60; intra-capitalist competition, 40; Keynesian, 38; neoliberalism as policy vehicle for, 39; as structural power, 59–60; suppression by, 38–39; transnational, 36–44; varieties of, 50–51; world, 37, 46. *See also* global capitalism; neoliberalism; profit motive
capitalists: as alienated, 60; intra-capitalist subjective differences, 62, 67; Marxist definition of, 55–56; place-based, global identity formation of, 10, 11, 18, 22, 71–72, 172, 208, 220; real-world, studying, 5–6, 218; reflexivity, lack of, 157. *See also* denational identity; global capitalist class; transnational capitalist class
Cardoso, Fernando Henrique, 112
Carroll, William K., 7, 8, 15, 21–22, 48, 71
Castañeda, Jorge, 102
Castells, Manuel, 8, 27, 163, 185
Catrani, Luz, 169
Cattani, Antonio David, 218, 219
Chalabi, Ahmed, 132, 143n13

chambers of commerce, 119, 125; Arab-Argentine, 131; Arab-Brazilian, 58–59, 81, 98; Dubai, 106; United States, 193
Chang, Ha-Joon, 49, 207, 211
Chapman, Debra D., 228, 231
Chapman-Ruiz, Tania, 228, 231
Chávez, Hugo, 102, 106
Chesky, Brian, 212
Chibber, Vivek, 51
Chicago Boys (Chile), 9–10, 40, 116, 143n11
Chicago School, 39
Chile, 20, 98, 140; agricultural products, 116, 162; Arab-Chilean business elites, 115, 118–19; Arab-Chilean trade group, 111, 113–26; Arab-descendant population, 87, 120; Asia-Pacific focus, 118, 122, 125, 142n6; center-left government, 102; Chicago Boys, 9–10, 40, 116, 143n11; free trade agreements, 116, 160–61, 163; inequality, 128–29, 140, 162, 164; international development apparatus, 111, 113–14; international trade bureaucracy, 117, 146, 159–60, 164; *mestizaje*, 91; military coup, 1973, 115; Ministry of Foreign Affairs, 114, 123, 161; neoliberalism in, 115–16, 128, 143n11; October 2020 plebiscite, 128; Palestinian bank in, 122–23; Palestinian diaspora in, 88–89, 114, 125; Pinochet regime, 115, 128, 160; as source of inspiration for elites, 128; as start of global neoliberal restructuring, 39–40; state disinterest in Arab world, 117–18; union movement suppressed in, 160; US-backed coup, 3–4
Cien años de soledad (*One Hundred Years of Solitude*) (García Márquez), 86
cities: as base for global capitalist system, 57; global/megacities, 36, 50–51. *See also* Buenos Aires; Dubai; Santiago de Chile; São Paulo
citizenship, global: defining, 208; flexible, 10, 12, 46, 73, 180; as identity for respondents from South, 178–79; North privileged in, 228
citizenship, renounced by global capitalists, 30–31
Clark, Tim, 194

class consciousness, 110–13; attributed to global capitalist class, 7, 27–28, 44, 49; place-based variations on, 50; state role in, 65
classed intersections, 110–13, 135–36
Clinton, Hillary, 226
O Clone (The Clone) (soap opera), 87, 90
Club Deportivo Palestino (Palestinian Sports Club), 125
Coalition Provisional Authority (Iraq), 132
Colombia, Israel's military ties with, 100
colonialism, 50, 80, 88, 107n1, 108, 195
commerce, 22, 30, 54, 57–59, 77
"common sense" imaginaries, 185, 189, 206
Comprehensive and Progressive Agreement for Trans-Pacific Partnership, 159
Condé Nast Traveler's, 206
The Condition of Postmodernity (Harvey), 189
consciousness, 62–63; assumed depth of, 156–57. *See also* class consciousness
Copa América regional soccer tournament, 124–25
corporate imaginaries, 223–31; and formation of global subjects, 184–86, 189–90
Correa, Rafael, 102
cosmopolitanism: "banal," political uses of, 176–84, 209, 216n1; conflated with profit seeking, 53–55; as mindset, 8, 27–28, 35, 51, 57, 64; rooted, 174n8
Costa Rica, 124
Council of Arab Ambassadors, 154
counter-imaginaries, 29, 38, 72, 182, 190; alternatives to global capitalism, 5, 7–8, 12, 17, 35, 213–16; continued state regulatory role, 213–14, 222–23; corporate imaginaries, countering of, 220–21, 228–31. *See also* global imaginaries; social movements
COVID-19 pandemic, 2, 210, 226
Cox, Robert, 42, 44
critique, ethos of, 16
Cuadros, Alex, 9
Cuba, 103
cultural capital, 10, 24, 62, 94, 110; of denationalizing and globalizing capitalists, 150, 158, 165–67; fostering of, 119–20, 153; pan-Arab, 158
cultural political economy (CPE), 15–17, 19, 177, 206; corporate imaginaries and formation of global subjects, 184–86, 189–90

Dardot, Pierre, 64, 67
Darian-Smith, Eve, 8, 13, 76
Dávila, Arlene, 21, 185
"Davos Man," 2, 8, 29–30, 33–34, 46, 56–57
"Dead Souls: The Denationalization of the American Elite" (Huntington), 29
democracy, neoliberal attack on, 4, 66, 223, 225–26
denational, as term, 43, 144
denational identity, 43–44, 48, 71, 113, 157–59, 167; place-based imaginaries within, 141–42, 150–51, 165–66; as real phenomenon, 169; trend toward, 170–72
Dependency and Development in Latin America (Cardoso and Faletto), 112
dependency theory, 82–83, 112
A Descoberta da América pelos Turcos (The Discovery of America by the Turks) (Amado), 86–87
diaspora, South-South, 20–24, 120; immigration and making of political elite, 85–95; Palestinian, 88–89, 100, 114, 125
Diogenes of Sinope, 70
diplomats, 118
Doha (Qatar), 117
Dow Chemical Company, 54–55
Downie, James, 130
DP World, 118
Dubai (United Arab Emirates), 55, 116; airports, 193–94; Chamber of Commerce and Industry, 106; and Emirates Airline, 190; Gulfood food and beverage exhibition, 119–20; as logistics hub, 58
du Gay, Paul, 16
Dunn, John, 18

"economic constitution," 41, 65
The Economist, 127, 132, 188, 201
Eglin, Peter, 228, 231
Egypt, 98, 150, 155

Elsey, Brenda, 90–91
Embraer (Brazilian firm), 99
Emirates Airline, 3, 99, 176, 209; *Bloomberg Businessweek* cover, 190–93, *191*; "Hello Tomorrow" campaign, *177*, *178*, *182*, 187–88, 191–92, *192*; "Tomorrow thinks borders are so yesterday" campaign, 12, 184, 187, 190–95
Empire, 2–3
Engels, Friedrich, 4, 34–36, 63, 109, 132, 141, 214, 230
ethnic identity, 23–24, 50–51, 88, 90–95, 110–11
ethnography, 11, 18, 19–20, 34, 79, 111
Etihad Airways, 99
Europe, 80
European Union, 149, 227
Evangelical Christianity, 109–10
exports, 20, 59, 132–34, 155–56; agricultural, 93, 98–99, 116, 117, 119, 122, 126, 131–32, 136, 139, 140, 162

Facebook, 30, 214, 222
Faletto, Enzo, 112
Falklands/Malvinas War, 148
Fanon, Frantz, 229
"fascist solution," 224
Fayad, Julieta, 140, 168–69
Federation of Arab-South American Chambers of Commerce, 77–78
Flexible Citizenship (Ong), 10
food security, 116, 163–64
food supply chain, 119–20, 126
foreign policy, 78, 83, 85; Brazil, 153; Chile, 161; criticism of United States, 100–101; and economic interests, 104–5; Latin American, 95–101; pragmatic-ideological bifurcation, 101–5
Foreign Policy Group, 2
Foucault, Michel, 229
Francis, Pope, 129–30, 139
Fraser, Nancy, 226
free market, 4, 142n6, 211, 223
free trade, as concept, 103
free trade agreements, 4, 116, 160–61
Friedman, Milton, 31, 115–16
Friedman, Patri, 31

Friedman, Thomas, 5, 36, 70, 72, 169
Fujii, Lee Ann, 19
future: alternatives to global capitalism, 5, 7–8, 12, 17, 213–16; imaginaries of, 218–31

García Márquez, Gabriel, 86
Gardini, Luca, 102
Garsd, Jasmine, 133
Geertz, Clifford, 18, 68
Geneva School, 39, 41, 65, 67
gente bien, 129, 139
George, Susan, 6
The German Ideology (Marx), 63, 157
Gill, Stephen, 44
Gilpin, Robert, 37
Gindin, Sam, 2, 6, 9, 48–49, 61–62, 64, 66–67
Glick Schiller, Nina, 43, 45–46, 171
global, as term, 19, 41, 43–44
Global Business Forum on Latin America, 106
global capitalism: bridging role of, 114–15, 123, 147, 150, 151, 187; continuing role of state in, 64–66, 222–23; fissures in, 17; "flat world," 5, 29, 41, 145, 173, 175, 193, 196, 214; structure and agency in, 5–8, 16, 221; as system, 5–7, 41, 43, 55, 57, 70, 72–74, 107, 161, 183, 196, 204; as universalizing force, 21, 29, 35, 51, 174n8, 177, 193, 199, 206, 209, 228, 231. *See also* capitalism; global capitalist class; rooted globalism
Global Capitalism and the Crisis of Humanity (Robinson), 33–34
global capitalism school, 8, 11, 27–29, 70, 196; influences on, 33–36; strong globalisation thesis, 72, 75n1, 170, 175; transnationalism, focus on, 36–44. *See also* Marxist theory; Robinson, William I; Sklair, Leslie
global capitalist class: billionaires, 62 richest, 1–2; citizenship, renunciation of, 30–31; class consciousness attributed to, 7, 27–28, 44, 49; as class for itself, 7, 25, 28, 44, 47, 49, 53, 62–64, 70–71, 74, 141, 145, 170, 173, 175, 183, 186, 198, 207; as class in itself, 7, 44, 47, 49, 53, 63, 65, 207, 215; genesis of concept, 29–36; imagined community of, 44–55, 70, 220; language choices of elites, 20, 113, 118–19, 127, 129, 138, 147–48,

global capitalist class (*Cont.*)
    156, 161, 167–68, 202; lifestyle similarities within, 52–53; lifeworlds of, 6, 14–16, 19, 21, 25, 61–62, 137, 141, 146, 159, 218, 220; Marxist theory contradicted by idea of, 73; members of defined, 55–59; nostalgia, 123–25, 129, 133–34, 139; objective vs. subjective evidence for, 7, 28, 46–47, 50–53, 59, 63, 65; race, ethnicity, or national origin within, 50–51; as rhetorical strategy, 212–13; as ruling class, 46–47; state, interaction with, 65, 105–6; unease with globality, 123, 138–39; weak evidence for, 27–28. *See also* capitalists; denational identity; global capitalism; global identity; transnational capitalist class
global economy, world economy contrasted with, 40–41, 44
"global futurist" narratives, 209
global identity, 10, 11, 18, 22, 71–72, 113, 172, 208, 220; place-based imaginaries within, 165–66; as real phenomenon, 169
global imaginaries, 11–12, 18, 71–72; corporate, 184–86, 189–90, 223–31; people-first, 183–84; "sunny," 25, 192, 206, 209, 213, 221–22. *See also* advertisements; counter-imaginaries
globalism, rooted, 8–12, 28, 74, 170–73, 174n8, 220, 229
"globalist" ideology, 31, 181
globality, 8, 11–12, 183; as political project, 7, 25, 183
Globality (start-up), 1
globalization, 1; bourgeois world-making, 34–35; elite understandings of, 19; ideological commitment to, 43–44; as master concept, 13; reification of, 6, 65, 72–73, 125; as term, 36–37
Globalization in Question (Hirst, et al.), 75n1
Global North: academic focus on, 21–22, 76, 79–85, 170, 196, 218; challenges to in advertisements, 203–5, 205, 207
Global South, 22–23, 75n1; advertising targeted to populations of, 177–81, 188, 191–92, 194, 196, 205; colonialist legacies, 50, 80, 88, 107n1, 108, 195; lack of agency attributed to, 22, 76, 79–83, 162, 204. *See also* Arab world; Latin America; South-South diaspora; South-South relations
global studies, 12–17, 32–33; critical, 15–17, 19, 33, 223; decolonization of, 76–77; Global North privileged in, 21–22, 76, 79–85, 170, 196, 218. *See also* political science
Global Studies Association, 33
global subjectivity, 43–44, 71; formation of, 184–86, 189–90
The Global Turn: Theories, Research Designs, and Methods for Global Studies (Darian-Smith and McCarty), 14
glocalisation, 199, 202–4
Goldman, Emma, 60
Goodson, Scott, 187
Gore, Al, 1
governance: global, 80, 211, 215, 220–21; national, 73, 182, 222
government officials, 57, 58, 59, 119, 147
Gramsci, Antonio, 224
"Green New Deal," 214
Green Zone (Baghdad), 133
Grimley, Naomi, 178, 208
Grondona, Mariano, 116
Gulf Cooperation Council (GCC), 125, 142n6
Gulf-Latin American exchange, 116, 147–51
Gulfood food and beverage exhibition, 119–20

halal certification, 117, 119, 122, 131–32, 136, 139, 140, 162
Hardt, Michael, 2–3, 37, 45, 66
Hartsfield-Jackson Atlanta International Airport, 195
Harvey, David, 40, 49, 54, 189, 193
Al-Hassani, Kadim, 113, 130–37, 139
Hayek, Friedrich, 9, 39, 73
Hayek, Salma, 86
Hezbollah, 83, 84
Ho, Karen, 215–16, 221
Holder, Alex, 212
homo economicus, 60
Honduras: Arab-descendant population, 87, 88–89
Hozić, Aida, 53
HSBC (Hongkong and Shanghai Banking Corporation), 1, 184, 186, 187, 188, 195–200,

197; "Global Citizen" campaign, 199–200, *200*; "Together We Thrive" campaign, 199
Hu-DeHart, Evelyn, 82, 86
human emancipation, 14, 60
Huntington, Samuel, 27, 32, 192, 209; Davos Man, 8, 29–30, 33–34, 46, 56; definition of transnational elites, 56–57
Hussein, Saddam, 132–33, 143n13
Hymer, Stephen, 44
hyper-globalization, 141, 208

"I Am a Global Latin American" campaign (Itaú), 184, 187–88, 200–204, *202*, *203*
Iberian Peninsula, 88
"ideal types," 41, 44, 71–72, 75n1, 173, 180–81, 220
identities: and clothing, 121, 125–26; combination of national/transnational and global identities, 161–65, 168, 170, 172–73; ethnic, 23–24, 50–51, 88, 90–95, 110–11; flexible, 8, 46; Marx's insistence on class-based, 70–71; national, 29–30, 43, 78, 91–92, 130, 137, 212; nonterritorial, 32, 43; as palimpsests, 170, 172, 220; transnational, 11, 28–29, 46. *See also* denational identity; global identity
imaginaries: "common sense," 185, 189, 206; corporate, and formation of global subjects, 184–86; future of, 218–31; national, 25, 43, 70–71, 74, 91, 94, 228–30; nation-based, and left, 228–30; people-first, 183–84; "sunny," 25, 192, 206, 209, 213, 221–22; transnational, 43. *See also* counter-imaginaries; global imaginaries; place-based imaginaries
imagined communities, 7, 10, 70, 183–84; of global capitalists, 44–55, 70, 220; private sector as, 166–67
Imagined Communities (Anderson), 53, 71
The Immigrants (soap opera), 92
immigration, 43, 75n1, 76, 99–101; and capitalist labor exploitation, 75n1, 227; Japanese, 91, 92; Lebanese in Argentina, 126–30; lighter-skinned immigrants valorized, 92; and making of political elite, 85–95; merchants, 89; and Orientalism, 88, 90–95; in popular and haute culture, 86–87; restrictions on, 192–93, 212, 226–28, 230; Syrian-Lebanese ancestry, 87–88, 107n2, 126; in US context, 92; US "Muslim ban," 192, 212. *See also* diaspora, South-South

Indian Entrepreneurs in Silicon Valley: The Making of a Transnational Techno-Capitalist Class (Biradavolu), 45
inequality, 1–2, 14–15, 17, 36, 75n1, 107n1, 208, 214, 221; Chile, 128–29, 140, 162, 164; neoliberal rhetoric appears to challenge, 178–79
inevitability, rhetoric of, 12, 29, 179–81, 186, 193–94, 196–97, 205–7, 215
An Inquiry into the Nature and Causes of the Wealth of Nations (Smith), 34
International Air Transport Association, 193
International Relations, 32, 37, 79, 80, 82, 102
interpretivism, 14–20, 186, 189, 213, 219, 221–22; and classed intersections, 110–13, 135–37, 221; interpretive turn, 18, 68; need for, 28, 67–74; and relational interviews, 17–20; and study of place-based identities, 108, 111–12
intersectional approaches, 108–11, 171; classed intersections, 111–13, 135–36
interviews, 43–44; interpretivist/relational, 17–20, 24–25, 68–70. *See also specific interviewees*
"investor visas," 31, 211, 223
Iran, 83, 84, 196
Iraq: Ba'athist regime, 132–33; Iraqi-Brazilian trade association, 113, 130–37, 139; privatization in, 132, 136, 137; trade equals reconstruction ideology, 134–35; US invasion of, 132–33, 143n13
Israeli-Palestinian conflict, 95, 99–101, 161
Itamaraty (Brazilian Ministry of Foreign Affairs), 135
Itaú (Brazilian bank): "I Am a Global Latin American" campaign, 184, 187–88, 200–204, *202*, *203*; "World powers" advertisement, 204–5, *205*
Itaú Unibanco Holding, 200

Jansen, Bart, 193
Japanese immigrants, 91, 92

Jessop, Bob, 16
Jewish populations in Latin America, 100
Journal of Critical Globalisation Studies, 33
Juniac, Alexandre de, 193

Kahn, Hilary E., 13–14, 19
Kapoor, Nisha, 229
Karam, John Tofik, 20, 59, 76, 84, 93, 94, 132, 158
Kast, José Antonio, 224
Keohane, Robert, 79, 162
Khanna, Parag, 36
Khoury, Jaime, 146–51, 166–67, 193, 196; bridging role of, 147, 150, 151; language choices of, 147–48, 168; on state role, 148–49
Kirchner, Cristina Fernández de, 128, 148, 169
Klein, Naomi, 38, 132
Koller, Veronika, 198–99
Konings, Martijn, 177
Krugman, Paul, 213

labor: authoritarian employment regimes, 17; flexibilization of, 39, 60; as global class, 42; migrant, 75n1; surplus value extracted from, 60–61, 140
labor movements, suppression of, 60, 160
La Moneda presidential palace (Santiago, Chile), 115
languages: Arabic loanwords in Latin American, 88; choices of, and place-based or placeless imaginaries, 167–68; corporate choices of, 201–2; English spoken in business world, 118, 122, 138, 147–48, 167–68, 202; spoken by global capitalist class, 20, 113, 118–19, 127, 129, 138, 147–48, 156, 161, 167–68, 202
Las Condes (Santiago, Chile), 114
Lash, Scott, 189
Latin America: economic deceleration, 2010s, 96–98; external-peace-and-internal-violence paradox, 79; foreign policy and commercial relations, 95–101; intellectuals, 78, 81–85; and Israeli-Palestinian conflict, 95, 99–101; left-identified governments, 95–97, 100; "left turn"/"pink tide," 95–97, 102, 205; Moorish presence among Iberian immigrants, 88; neoliberalism, critical stances toward, 102–3; Orientalism in, 88, 90–95, 119; presidents of Arab ancestry, 86; pro-Palestinian posture, 100–101; Triple Frontier area, 83–85; turn toward Arab world, 96; universities, 81–82; US hegemony, decline of, 100–101; whiteness, in context of, 92–93, 201. *See also* Arab-Latin American relations; *specific countries*
Latin America Mid-East Investors Forums, 106
Latin American Studies Association, 82
LatinFinance, 106
Laval, Christian, 64, 67, 140
Lavalle, Ricardo, 122
Law, John, 16
Lebanon, 126–30, 142–43n8
Lebanon-focused Argentine commercial group, 113, 126–30, 146
left, 25–27; academic elite, 57; centrist and center-left circles, 29–30; "left turn"/"pink tide," 95–97, 102, 205; "modern" vs. "close-minded," 102; and nation-based imaginaries, 228–30; retreat from globalism, 226–27; sense of global community, 230. *See also* counter-imaginaries; social movements
"The Left Case against Open Borders" (Nagle), 227
Legg, Benjamin, 201
Le Pen, Marine, 29–30, 225
Lesser, Jeffrey, 92
libertarians, 31
Libra (global digital currency), 222
Lipschutz, Ronnie, 36
Liquidated: An Ethnography of Wall Street (Ho), 221
Littín, Miguel, 86
local-global connections, 8, 10, 13–14, 27, 72, 168, 202
Los 80 (*The '80s*) (drama), 87
Lula da Silva, Luiz Inácio, 58, 66, 100, 106, 117, 152–53; Arab world, relations with, 95–96, 98, 154; capitalist support for, 136;

on "reencounter" between civilizations, 76, 88

Macedo, Edir, 109
Macri, Mauricio, 128, 136, 224
Magee, Christine, 1
Makhoul, Diego, 113–26, 147, 202; Arab CEOs, relationships with, 120–21; bridging, expertise in, 114–15, 123; "interesting opportunities" rhetoric of, 117, 119–22, 138–39; language choices of, 113, 118–19, 138, 168; Naddaf as role model for, 123, 151–52, 167; national and transnational framework of, 124–26, 199; on nature of life, 123–24
The Making of an Atlantic Ruling Class (van de Pijl), 21
The Making of Global Capitalism (Panitch and Gindin), 2
Maluf, Paulo, 93
Manifesto of the Communist Party (Marx and Engels), 5, 34–36, 63, 214, 230
manufactured goods, 99
markets: backed by state, 64; competitive, 59–60, 73, 149; domestic bias, 34; free market, 4, 142n6, 211, 223; open, as concept, 103; state mutually co-constitutive with, 65, 211, 215
Marx, Karl, 4, 109, 132, 140–41, 220; bourgeoisie's role in world system of capitalism, 34–37, 47, 54; class in itself and class for itself, 7, 47, 53; on consciousness, 62–63; "critical thinking," view of, 16; insistence on class-based identities, 70–71; "Mr. Moneybags" illustration, 60–61, 144–45, 166; on surplus-value, 60–61, 140, 166; Works: *Capital*, 60–61; *The German Ideology*, 63, 157; *Manifesto of the Communist Party* (with Engels), 5, 34–36, 63, 214, 230
Marxist theory, 15, 27, 32, 59–67; contradicted by idea of global capitalist class, 73; nationalism as anomaly for, 70–71. *See also* global capitalism school
Massú, Nicolás, 86
material-ideational relationships, 23–24, 28, 52–53, 62–65, 164–65, 190, 220
McCann, Bryan, 218–19

McCarty, Philip, 8, 13, 76
McFall, Liz, 189
meaning-making, 18, 68–69, 72, 189, 198
Mearsheimer, John, 33
medical profession, 164
merchant capitalist groups, 22, 54, 56–59, 77–78, 86, 89, 161, 163, 169; Phoenician legacy, 126–27
Mercosur, 142n6, 148
Mexico: Arab-descendant population, 87; Zapatistas, 4
middle class, 45, 125, 185, 218
The Middle East and Brazil: Perspectives on the New Global South (Amar), 85
Mignolo, Walter, 88
Milanovic, Branko, 2
Mills, C. Wright, 30
Mises, Ludwig von, 39, 60, 73
Morales, Constanza, 123
Morales, Evo, 102
Morocco, 98
multipolar global order, logic of, 95–96, 101, 104–5
Muniz, Vik, 201, 203, *203*
Muslims and Muslim world, trade with, 95, 97, 117, 119, 154

Naddaf, Georges, 123, 146, 151–59; denational identity framework of, 157–58, 167; language choices of, 168; as role model for Makhoul, 123, 151–52, 167; state outreach efforts by, 153–55
Nagle, Angela, 227, 230
Napoleon, 34
Nasr, Helmi, 89
national, as term, 43
national identity, 29–30, 43, 78, 91–92, 130, 137, 212
national imaginaries, 25, 43, 70–71, 74, 91, 94; and left, 228–30
national interests, 9, 41–42, 53–54, 102
nationalism, 32, 127–30, 141; as alternative future, 216; as anomaly for Marxist theory, 70–71; eradication of, 41; methodological, 45–46; neonationalism, 210; and newspapers, 53; we-means-the-homeland framework, 162, 172

nation-state, 36, 40, 74; continued existence of, 64, 80, 171, 219; "real or imagined," 46, 47, 53, 145. *See also* state
Negri, Antonio, 2–3, 37, 45, 66
neoliberalism: anthropomorphization of, 6; as anti-statist, 9, 65; authoritarianism, support for, 9–10, 40, 226; in Chile, 115–16, 128, 143n11; and contingent historical processes, 67, 74; democracy, attack on, 4, 66, 223, 225–26; "Frankenstein monster" variety of, 210, 225; governing rationality of, 39; institutional enforcers of, 65; as political project, 6–7, 39, 66, 74, 145, 181, 183, 193–94, 215; "progressive," 25, 199, 226, 229; right-wing extremism as response to, 223–27; utopian rhetoric, 4, 27, 31–32, 41, 54–55, 215, 221; visual discourses of, 177, 189; "world order," 3, 4, 12, 36, 40–41. *See also* capitalism; neoliberal rhetoric
neoliberal rhetoric, 173, 175–76; aimed at undermining regulation, 3, 12, 29, 38–39, 66–67, 73–74, 180–84, 207, 213; "globalist" ideology, 31, 181; globalization as inevitable, 12, 29, 179–81, 186, 193–94, 196–97, 205–7, 215; humanizing side of, 177–79; as self-interested, 179–80. *See also* advertisements; neoliberalism
Netanyahu, Benjamin, 154
Network for Critical Studies of Global Capitalism, 33
network ties, 2, 10, 27, 30, 48, 56, 163
neutral ground, 54–55, 190; "seasteading," 27, 31
newspapers, 53
New York Times, 127
Nicaragua, 103
nonterritorial identity, 32, 43
North, as term, 107n1
North American Free Trade Agreement (NAFTA), 4
nostalgia, 123–25, 129, 133–34, 139; *saudade*, 133

Oman, 147
Ong, Aihwa, 10, 12, 73, 180, 207
Orbán, Viktor, 225

Order 39 (Coalition Provisional Authority), 132
Orientalism, Latin American, 88, 90–95, 119
Orthodox Christian immigrants, 89
Ottoman Empire, 87, 88

Pacific Alliance, 125, 142n6
Palestine, 155; bank in Chile, 122–23
Palestinian diaspora, 88–89, 100, 114, 125
Panitch, Leo, 2, 6, 9, 48–49, 61–62, 64, 66–67
Partnership for Open and Fair Skies, 193
Paterson, Matthew, 15, 16, 198
patriotism, 34, 57, 129–30
people-first global imaginaries, 183–84
Perry, Rick, 83
Peru, 118
petrodollars, 76–77, 116
Phillips, Peter, 30
Phoenicians, 126–27
Piñera, Sebastián, 113, 115, 161, 224
Pinochet, Augusto, 9, 39–40, 115, 128
place, politics of, 216
place-based imaginaries, 14, 22–23, 137; "dead generations," tradition of, 141, 165; within denational identity, 141–42, 150–51, 165–66; as dominant for majority of population, 27; and nostalgia, 123–25, 129, 133–34, 139; simultaneity of place-based and placeless identity markers, 161–65, 168, 173; stickiness/resilience of, 8–12, 25, 28, 64, 70–71, 74, 139–41, 171, 175, 177, 206, 216, 220; transnational, 43, 46; and workers, 47. *See also* denational identity; global identity; national identity; transnationalism
placelessness, 8, 14, 22–23, 43, 50, 168, 169, 171, 214, 220; politics of, 216
Polanyi, Karl, 211, 224
political economy, 78, 80, 85; of Arab-Latin American relations, 101–7; cultural (CPE), 15–17, 19, 177, 184–86, 189–90, 206; global, 5, 15, 41, 45, 46, 107
political leaders, 106, 214
Pompeo, Mike, 84
popular culture, 91, 183–85, 207, 230; elites from in advertising, 201–4, *202*, *203*. *See also* advertisements
populism, 29–30, 102

positivism, 13, 15, 17–18, 69, 112, 158, 221–22
The Power Elite (Mills), 30
pragmatic-ideological bifurcation, 101–5
Prashad, Vijay, 178
private interests, 41–42, 208
privatization, 132, 136, 137, 211
production: bourgeois mode of, 4, 35; globalization of, 1, 40, 42, 46; of ideas, 63; means of, 47, 55–57, 60; scholarly, 77–78, 81; transnationalization of, 47, 75n1
profit motive, 35, 59–62, 68, 135–38, 145; and altruism, 134–36, 139; cosmopolitanism conflated with, 53–55; denationalized, 166; in humanistic advertising, 178–79, 183, 208; place-based, 137–38. *See also* capitalism
"progressive" neoliberalism, 25, 199, 226, 229
Pryke, Michael, 16
public-private networks, 78, 94

Qasim, Aqil, 113, 130–37, 139
Qatar, 117, 118, 119
Qatar Airways, 99

race, and global capitalist class, 50–51; whiteness, in Latin American context, 92–93, 201
Rebón, Julián, 6
regulation: capitalist avoidance of, 31, 55; continued state role in, 213–14, 222–23; difficulty of, 182, 215; in *Manifesto*, 214; neoliberal rhetoric aimed at undermining, 3, 12, 29, 38–39, 66–67, 73–74, 180–84, 207, 213; reregulation, 211; supportive of elite interests, 9, 66
religion, 3, 108–10, 136; Catholicism, 17, 88, 89, 93, 109, 128; Evangelical churches, 109–10
Republican Party, 83
Ribeiro, Darcy, 93–94, 95, 108
right-wing extremism, 4, 27, 29–30, 32–34, 57, 184, 199, 216; "antiglobalist" stance, 225–26; authoritarianism of, 25, 103, 224–26; far-right governments, 97, 154, 210; and religion, 110; as response to neoliberalism, 223–27

Robinson, William I., 7, 8, 17, 21, 27–28, 55, 72–74, 75n1, 158, 224; agency, view of, 72; anecdotal evidence used by, 50, 52–53; on class consciousness, 49, 52; definition of transnational bourgeoisie, 55; on identity in global system above local/territorial level, 7, 42, 46, 145, 168, 173; "objective class existence," 46–47; on role of state, 58, 64, 74; theory of global capitalism, 33, 37–40, 42; *Works: Global Capitalism and the Crisis of Humanity*, 33–34; *A Theory of Global Capitalism*, 33
Rodrik, Dani, 207–8
Romney, Mitt, 83
rooted cosmopolitanism, 174n8
rooted globalism, 8–12, 25, 28, 74, 174n8, 220, 229; toward understanding of, 170–73. *See also* global capitalism
Rosenberg, Justin, 37
Rothkopf, David, 2, 30, 41, 52, 64
Rousseff, Dilma, 58, 97, 136
Royal Air Maroc, 99
Ruiz-Chapman, Tania, 228
Rupert, Mark, 216
Ruppert, Evelyn, 16

Saddy, Fehmy, 101
Safra, Joseph, 22
Sanhattan financial district (Santiago, Chile), 114, 121
Santiago (Chile), 90, 114–15, 121–22, 125; Sanhattan financial district, 114, 121
Santiso, Javier, 23
Santorum, Rick, 84
Santos, Juan Manuel, 100
São Paulo (Brazil), 89, 131, 146
Sassen, Saskia, 6–7, 10, 19, 42, 43, 55, 175; denationalized classes, view of, 48, 57, 71, 74, 171; on "free-floating cosmopolitan classes," 51, 180; global classes as embedded locally, 48, 51; on interview techniques, 68; "partial dependence" of capitalists on state, 73
saudade (cultural marker), 133
Saudi Arabia, 98
Saverin, Eduardo, 30
Schaffer, Frederic, 20

scholarship: advertisements, analysis of, 185–86; class-based disparity in knowledge production, 218–19; empirical approaches, 6, 28, 45, 50, 68, 78, 95, 112–13, 170–73, 174n8, 184; on globality, 27, 32, 48, 51; International Relations, 32, 37, 79, 80, 82, 102; lack of focus on economic elites, 5–7, 218; by Latin American intellectuals, 78, 81–85; positivist approaches, 13, 15, 17–18, 69, 112, 158, 221–22; production of, 77–78, 81; social movements disempowered by Marxist-inspired analysis, 29, 72–73, 181, 231; subaltern actors as preferred focus of, 218–19; on transnationalism, 45–49. *See also* critical global studies; cultural political economy (CPE); global capitalism school; global studies; interpretivism

Scholte, Jan Aart, 36
Schwartz-Shea, Peregrine, 16, 17, 68, 186, 215
Scott, James, 18, 68, 80
"seasteading," 27, 31
Shakira, 86
The Shock Doctrine (Klein), 38
Silicon Valley, 31, 50, 223
The Simpsons (television show), 109
Sims, Calvin, 127
Six-Day War (1967), 100
Sklair, Leslie, 8, 21–22, 27–28, 59, 68, 71, 73, 176; cosmopolitanism conflated with profit seeking, 53–55; four "fractions" of capitalist class, 56; and Global Studies Association, 33; interview techniques, 51–52; operation across state borders in theory of, 41–42, 46–48, 54; theorization of "transnational capitalist class," 46, 47, 48, 53, 145; *The Transnational Capitalist Class*, 33

Slim, Carlos, 22, 86, 117
Slobodian, Quinn, 40, 65–67
Smith, Adam, 27, 34, 54, 61
Smith, Neil, 214
soccer, politics of, 90–91, 124–25, 142n5, 150, 153, 204
social movements, 5, 38, 218, 221; disempowered by Marxist-inspired analysis, 29, 72–73, 181, 231. *See also* counter-imaginaries

solidarity: cross-border, 57, 60, 63, 230; global, 26, 164, 166, 208; undermining of, 4, 227
Solimano, Andrés, 4
Solomon, M. Scott, 216
Soros, George, 225
South, as term, 107n1
South-South relations, 58, 76–77; in advertisements, 194, 196, 204–6, 205; as danger to North-centric imaginary, 79–85, 196; multipolar global order, logic of, 95–96, 101, 104–5. *See also* Arab-Latin American relations; Global South
sovereign, capital as, 45, 73
sovereignty: local, 216; popular, 222–23, 231; waning of, 1–3, 41, 222–23
sovereign wealth funds, 116, 147
space and time, 13, 141
space of flows, 27, 185
Sparke, Matthew, 178, 210
Spiegel, Steven L., 80
state: capture of by capitalist interests, 105, 182, 208; continuing regulatory role of, 213–14, 222–23; continuing role in global capitalism, 48–49, 64–66, 222; interplay with elites, 105–6; market backed by, 64–65, 149–50; markets co-constitutive with, 65, 211, 215; protectionism, 210–11; reconfiguration of, 9, 58; role in making of global capitalism, 9, 64, 210–11; two roles of, 149. *See also* nation-state
state action, 6, 9, 64, 211
state-centrism, 32, 37, 77–78, 103–4
stateless global capitalists, 27, 30–31, 145
Steger, Manfred, 13, 16, 17, 71–72
Streeck, Wolfgang, 227
structure, 5–8, 16, 221
Sum, Ngai-Ling, 16
Summers, Lawrence, 30
Summit of South American and Arab Countries (ASPA), 95, 96, 106, 117, 122
Summits of South American-Arab Countries, 20–21
"superclass," 30, 34
"The Super-Rich and Us" (*BBC Two*), 2
surplus value, 60–61, 140, 166
Syria, 126, 142–43n8

Syrian-Lebanese ancestry, 87–88, 107n2, 126, 135, 158
Syrian refugees, 89

Taylor, Yvette, 110
Temer, Michel, 97
A Theory of Global Capitalism: Production, Class and State in a Transnational World (Robinson), 33
Terence, 207
terrorism, US allegations of, 83–84, 95, 103
Thatcher, Margaret, 5, 39, 214
Thiel, Peter, 31
Thompson, E. P., 11
Tickner, Arlene, 82
Timerman, Héctor, 100
transdisciplinary approaches, 13–16, 82
transnational, as term, 43
transnational capitalist class, 21, 30, 44, 71–72; anecdotal arguments for, 48, 52; distinct from global capitalist class, 42–43; distinct from national or local capitalists, 46, 49; four "fractions" of, 56; national interests not prioritized, 53–54; as new ruling class, 46–47. *See also* global capitalist class; transnationalism
The Transnational Capitalist Class (Sklair), 33
Transnational Classes and International Relations (van der Pijl), 33
transnational corporations (TNCs), 48, 55–56, 58
transnationalism, 10–11, 21–22, 28–29, 36–44, 137–41; as attachment to multiple places, 43, 46; global contrasted with, 41; as product of world capitalism, 46; scholarship on, 45–49; "transnational managerial class," 42, 44. *See also* place-based imaginaries; transnational capitalist class
Transnationality Index, 48
Triple Frontier area (Brazil, Paraguay, and Argentina), 83–85
triumphalist discourse, 204–5, 215–16
Trotsky, Leon, 51
Trump, Donald, 9, 40, 210, 212, 223, 225
Truzzi, Oswaldo, 89

Tsing, Anna, 209–10
"turco," as term, 90, 93

UNASUR Constitutive Treaty, 101
UN Conference on Trade and Development (UNCTAD), 48
Union of South American Nations (UNASUR), 96, 101
United Arab Emirates (UAE), 98. *See also* Dubai (United Arab Emirates)
United States: Iraq, invasion of, 132–33, 143n13; Latin American criticism of, 100; as leader in post-World War II economic order, 9, 64; nationalism, 210–11; and pragmatic-ideological bifurcation, 102–3; right-wing military regimes backed by, 99–100; "War on Terror," 83–84, 95, 229
universalizing force, global capitalism as, 21, 29, 35, 51, 174n8, 177, 193, 199, 206, 209, 228, 231
universities, Arab and Latin American, 81–82
Urry, John, 189
Uruguay, 102
utopian visions, capitalist, 4, 31–32, 41, 215, 221; neutral ground, 54–55; "seasteading," 27, 31

Vale (Brazilian mining giant), 147
Valenzuela, Julio, 146, 159–65, 204; denational identity framework of, 157–59; and international trade bureaucracy, 159–60, 164; language choices of, 167–68; as medical doctor, 159, 163; national/transnational and global identity frameworks of, 161–65, 168, 170, 172–73; solidarity-based belief system, 164, 166
van der Pijl, Kees, 21, 33
Varadarajan, Latha, 219
Vargas, Getúlio, 89
Varoufakis, Yanis, 229–30, 231
Vasconcelos, José, 91
Venezuela, 100, 102, 103
Virginia School, 39
visual discourses, 177, 189
voting blocs, 109–10

Wahlrab, Amentahru, 13, 16, 17
Walled States, Waning Sovereignty (Brown), 3
Walt, Stephen, 33
Waltz, Kenneth, 79–80
"War on Terror," 83–84, 95, 229
Weapons of the Weak (Scott), 80
Weber, Max, 18, 68, 71
Weeks, John, 210
Weldes, Jutta, 185, 189
whiteness, in Latin American context, 92–93, 201
Wimmer, Andreas, 45–46
working class, 38, 45, 50, 63, 230
world capitalism, 37, 46

World Cup (2014), 124–25
World Economic Forum, 2
world economy, 40–41, 44, 196, 210
"world order," 3, 4, 12, 36, 40–41
"world passport," 32
World Trade Organization (WTO), 65, 149
The Wretched of the Earth (Fanon), 229
Wright, Erik Olin, 62

xenophobia, rise of, 198, 214, 224–25

Yanow, Dvora, 16, 17, 68, 69, 186

Zapatistas, 4
Žižek, Slavoj, 227

KEVIN FUNK is a Fellow in Global Thought with the Committee on Global Thought at Columbia University, where he is also a Lecturer in the Department of Political Science and an affiliated faculty member of the Institute of Latin American Studies.